CINDERELLA ATE MY DAUGHTER

ALSO BY PEGGY ORENSTEIN

Waiting for Daisy: A Tale of Two Continents, Three Religions, Five Infertility Doctors, an Oscar, an Atomic Bomb, a Romantic Night, and One Woman's Quest to Become a Mother

Flux: Women on Sex, Work, Love, Kids, and Life in a Half-Changed World

Schoolgirls: Young Women, Self-Esteem, and the Confidence Gap

CINDERELLA ATE MY DAUGHTER

DISPATCHES FROM THE FRONT LINES OF THE NEW GIRLIE-GIRL CULTURE

PEGGY ORENSTEIN

HARPER

An Imprint of HarperCollins*Publishers*
www.harpercollins.com

Names and identifying details of some individuals have been changed to protect their privacy.

HarperCollins books may be purchased for educational, business, or sales promotional use. For information, please write: Special Markets Department, HarperCollins Publishers, 10 East 53rd Street, New York, NY 10022.

Portions of this book appeared in altered form in *The New York Times Magazine*.

FIRST EDITION

Designed by William Ruoto

Library of Congress Cataloging-in-Publication Data

Orenstein, Peggy.
  Cinderella ate my daughter : dispatches from the front lines of the new girlie-girl culture / Peggy Orenstein. — 1st ed.
    p. cm.
  Includes bibliographical references and index.
  ISBN 978-0-06-171152-7
  1. Girls—Psychology. 2. Femininity. 3. Mothers and daughters.
I. Title.
  HQ777.O74 2011
  305.23082—dc22

                                          2010028724

11 12 13 14 15   ID/RRD   10 9 8 7 6 5 4 3 2 1

For Daisy

Contents

Contents

CINDERELLA ATE MY DAUGHTER

Chapter One

Why I Hoped for a Boy

*h*ere is my dirty little secret: as a journalist, I have spent nearly two decades writing about girls, thinking about girls, talking about how girls should be raised. Yet, when I finally got pregnant myself, I was terrified at the thought of having a daughter. While my friends, especially those who'd already had sons, braced themselves against disappointment should the delivery room doc announce, "It's a boy," I felt like the perpetual backseat driver who freezes when handed the wheel. I was supposed to be an *expert* on girls' behavior. I had spouted off about it everywhere from *The New York Times* to the *Los Angeles Times*, from the *Today* show to FOX TV. I had been on NPR *repeatedly*. And that was the problem: What if, after all that, I was not up to the challenge myself? What if I couldn't raise the ideal daughter? With a boy, I figured, I would be off the hook.

And truly, I thought having a son was a done deal. A few years before my daughter was born, I had read about some British guy who'd discovered that two-thirds of couples in which the husband was five or more years older than the wife had a boy as their first child. Bingo. My husband, Steven, is nearly a decade older than I am. So clearly I was covered.

Then I saw the incontrovertible proof on the sonogram (or what they said was incontrovertible proof; to me, it looked indistinguishable from, say, a nose) and I suddenly realized I had wanted a girl—desperately, passionately—all along. I had just been afraid to admit it. But I still fretted over how I would raise her, what kind of role model I would be, whether I would take my own smugly written advice on the complexities surrounding girls' beauty, body image, education, achievement. Would I embrace frilly dresses or ban Barbies? Push soccer cleats or tutus? Shopping for her layette, I grumbled over the relentless color coding of babies. Who cared whether the crib sheets were pink or glen plaid? During those months, I must have started a million sentences with "*My* daughter will never . . ."

And then I became a mother.

Daisy was, of course, the most beautiful baby ever (if you don't believe me, ask my husband). I was committed to raising her without a sense of limits: I wanted her to believe neither that some behavior or toy or profession was *not* for her sex nor that it was *mandatory* for her sex. I wanted her to be able to pick and choose the pieces of her identity freely—that was supposed to be the prerogative, the privilege, of her generation. For a while, it looked as if I were succeeding. On her first day of preschool,

at age two, she wore her favorite outfit—her "engineers" (a pair
of pin-striped overalls)—and proudly toted her Thomas the
Tank Engine lunchbox. I complained to anyone who would listen about the shortsightedness of the Learning Curve company,
which pictured only boys on its Thomas packaging and had made
"Lady," its shiny mauve girl engine, smaller than the rest. (The
other females among Sodor's rolling stock were passenger cars—
passenger cars—named Annie, Clarabel, Henrietta, and, yes, Daisy.
The nerve!) Really, though, my bitching was a form of bragging.
My daughter had transcended typecasting.

Oh, how the mighty fall. All it took was one boy who, while
whizzing past her on the playground, yelled, *"Girls* don't like
trains!" and Thomas was shoved to the bottom of the toy chest.
Within a month, Daisy threw a tantrum when I tried to wrestle
her into pants. As if by osmosis she had learned the names and
gown colors of every Disney Princess—I didn't even know what
a Disney Princess was. She gazed longingly into the tulle-draped
windows of the local toy stores and for her third birthday begged
for a "real princess dress" with matching plastic high heels. Meanwhile, one of her classmates, the one with Two Mommies, showed
up to school every single day dressed in a Cinderella gown. With
a bridal veil.

What was going on here? My fellow mothers, women who
once swore they would never be dependent on a man, smiled indulgently at daughters who warbled "So This Is Love" or insisted
on being addressed as Snow White. The supermarket checkout
clerk invariably greeted Daisy with "Hi, Princess." The waitress
at our local breakfast joint, a hipster with a pierced tongue and a
skull tattooed on her neck, called Daisy's "funny-face pancakes"
her "princess meal"; the nice lady at Longs Drugs offered us a
free balloon, then said, "I bet I know your favorite color!" and

handed Daisy a pink one rather than letting her choose for herself. Then, shortly after Daisy's third birthday, our high-priced pediatric dentist—the one whose practice was tricked out with comic books, DVDs, and arcade games—pointed to the exam chair and asked, "Would you like to sit in my special princess throne so I can sparkle your teeth?"

"Oh, for God's sake," I snapped. "Do you have a princess drill, too?"

She looked at me as if I were the wicked stepmother.

But honestly: since when did every little girl become a princess? It wasn't like this when I was a kid, and I was born back when feminism was still a mere twinkle in our mothers' eyes. We did not dress head to toe in pink. We did not have our own miniature high heels. What's more, I live in Berkeley, California: if princesses had infiltrated our little retro-hippie hamlet, imagine what was going on in places where women actually shaved their legs? As my little girl made her daily beeline for the dress-up corner of her preschool classroom, I fretted over what playing Little Mermaid, a character who actually gives up her *voice* to get a man, was teaching her.

On the other hand, I thought, maybe I should see princess mania as a sign of progress, an indication that girls could celebrate their predilection for pink without compromising strength or ambition; that at long last they could "have it all": be feminist *and* feminine, pretty *and* powerful; earn independence *and* male approval. Then again, maybe I should just lighten up and not read so much into it—to mangle Freud, maybe sometimes a princess is just a princess.

I ended up publishing my musings as an article called "What's Wrong with Cinderella?" which ran on Christmas Eve in *The New York Times Magazine*. I was entirely unprepared for the response. The piece immediately shot to the top of the site's "Most E-mailed" list, where it hovered for days, along with an article about the latest conflict in the Middle East. Hundreds of readers wrote in—or e-mailed me directly—to express relief, gratitude, and, nearly as often, outright contempt: "I have been waiting for a story like yours." "I pity Peggy Orenstein's daughter." "As a mother of three-year-old twin boys, I wonder what the land of princesses is doing to my sons." "I would hate to have a mother like Orenstein." "I honestly don't know how I survived all those hyped-up images of women that were all around *me* as a girl." "The genes are *so* powerful."

Apparently, I had tapped into something larger than a few dime-store tiaras. Princesses are just a phase, after all. It's not as though girls are still swanning about in their Sleeping Beauty gowns when they leave for college (at least most are not). But they did mark my daughter's first foray into the mainstream culture, the first time the influences on her extended beyond the family. And what was the first thing that culture told her about being a girl? Not that she was competent, strong, creative, or smart but that every little girl wants—or should want—to be the Fairest of Them All.

It was confusing: images of girls' successes abounded—they were flooding the playing field, excelling in school, outnumbering boys in college. At the same time, the push to make their appearance the epicenter of their identities did not seem to have abated one whit. If anything, it had intensified, extending younger (and, as the unnaturally smooth brows of midlife women attest, stretching far later). I had read stacks of books devoted to girls' adolescence, but where was I to turn to understand the new culture of *little* girls, from toddler to "tween," to help decipher the potential impact—if any—of the images and ideas they were absorbing about who they should be, what they should buy, what made them *girls*? Did playing Cinderella shield them from early sexualization or prime them for it? Was walking around town dressed as Jasmine harmless fun, or did it instill an unhealthy fixation on appearance? Was there a direct line from Prince Charming to *Twilight*'s Edward Cullen to distorted expectations of intimate relationships?

It is tempting, as a parent, to give the new pink-and-pretty a pass. There is already so much to be vigilant about, and the limits of our tolerance, along with our energy, slip a little with each child we have. So if a spa birthday party would make your six-year-old happy (and get her to leave you alone), really, what is the big deal? After all, girls will be girls, right? I agree, they will—and that is exactly why we need to pay more, rather than less, attention to what is happening in their world. According to the American Psychological Association, the girlie-girl culture's emphasis on beauty and play-sexiness can increase girls' vulnerability to the pitfalls that most concern parents: depression, eating disorders, distorted body image, risky sexual behavior. In one study of eighth-grade girls, for instance, self-objectification—judging your body by how you think it looks to others—accounted for half the differential in girls' reports of depression and more than two-thirds of the variance in their self-esteem. Another linked the focus on appearance among girls that age to heightened shame and anxiety about their bodies. Even brief exposure to the typical, idealized images of women that we all see every day has been shown to lower girls' opinion of themselves, both physically and academically. Nor, as they get older, does the new sexiness lead to greater sexual entitlement. According to Deborah Tolman, a professor at Hunter College who studies teenage girls' desire, "They respond to questions about how their bodies feel—questions about sexuality or arousal—by describing how they think they look. I have to remind them that looking good is *not* a feeling."

All of that does not suddenly kick in when a girl blows out the candles on her thirteenth birthday cake. From the time she is born—in truth, well before—parents are bombarded with zillions of little decisions, made consciously or not, that will shape their daughter's ideas and understanding of her femininity, her sexuality, her self. How do you instill pride and resilience in her? Do you shower her with pink heart-strewn onesies? Reject the Disney Princess Pull-Ups for Lightning McQueen? Should you let your three-year-old wear her child-friendly nail polish to preschool? What's your policy on the latest Disney Channel "it" girl? Old Dora versus New Dora? Does a pink soccer ball celebrate girlhood? Do pink TinkerToys expand or contract its definition? And even if you think the message telegraphed by a pink Scrabble set with tiles on the box top that spell "F-A-S-H-I-O-N" is a tad retrograde, what are you supposed to do about it? Lock your daughter in a tower? Rely on the tedious "teachable moment" in which Mom natters on about how if Barbie were life-sized she'd pitch forward smack onto her bowling ball boobs (cue the eye rolling, please)?

Answering such questions has, surprisingly, become *more* complicated since the mid-1990s, when the war whoop of "Girl Power" celebrated ability over body. Somewhere along the line, that message became its own opposite. The pursuit of physical perfection was recast as a source—often *the* source—of young women's "empowerment." Rather than freedom *from* traditional constraints, then, girls were now free *to* "choose" them. Yet the line between "get to" and "have to" blurs awfully fast. Even as new educational and professional opportunities unfurl before my daughter and her peers, so does the path that encourages them to equate identity with image, self-expression with appearance, femininity with performance, pleasure with pleasing, and sexuality with sexualization. It feels both easier and harder to raise a girl in that new reality—and easier and harder to be one.

I didn't know whether Disney Princesses would be the first salvo in a Hundred Years' War of dieting, plucking, and painting (and perpetual dissatisfaction with the results). But for me they became a trigger for the larger question of how to help our daughters with the contradictions they will inevitably face as girls, the dissonance that is as endemic as ever to growing up female. It seemed, then, that I was not done, not only with the princesses but with the whole culture of little girlhood: what it had become, how it had changed in the decades since I was a child, what those changes meant, and how to navigate them as a parent.

I'm the first to admit that I do not have all the answers. Who could? But as a mother who also happens to be a journalist (or perhaps vice versa), I believed it was important to lay out the context—the marketing, science, history, culture—in which we make our choices, to provide information that would help parents to approach their decisions more wisely.

So I returned to the land of Disney, but I also traveled to American Girl Place and the American International Toy Fair (the industry's largest trade show, where all the hot new products are introduced). I trolled Pottery Barn Kids and Toys "R" Us. I talked to historians, marketers, psychologists, neuroscientists, parents, and children themselves. I considered the value of the original fairy tales; pondered the meaning of child beauty pageants; went online as a "virtual" girl; even attended a Miley Cyrus concert (so you know I was dedicated). And I faced down my own confusion as a mother, as a woman, about the issues that raising a girl raises in me about my own femininity.

As with all of us, what I want for my daughter seems so simple: for her to grow up healthy, happy, and confident, with a clear sense of her own potential and the opportunity to fulfill it. Yet she lives in a world that tells her, whether she is three or thirty-three, that the surest way to get there is to look, well, like Cinderella.

But I'm getting ahead of myself. Let's go back and begin where all good stories start.

Once upon a time.

Chapter Two

What's Wrong with Cinderella?

When Daisy was three, I lost her. Or, more precisely, I allowed her to get lost. She dashed off into the crowd at a reception after my niece's bat mitzvah, and I did not stop her. How much trouble could she get into, I reasoned: there were at least fifty Jewish mothers in the room. On the other hand, there was also a steep flight of marble stairs, doors that opened onto a dark parking lot leading to a reedy swamp, and a kitchen full of unattended chefs' knives. So when twenty minutes passed and she hadn't checked in, I began to get a little edgy. Okay, I panicked.

I pushed through the crowd shouting her name, leaving riled-up grandmothers in my wake. Then one of my niece's friends tugged at my sleeve. "She's over there," the girl said, pointing to a knot of ten or so teenagers.

I still did not see my child. So I stepped closer and peered over a boy's shoulder. There was Daisy, lying on the ground, her arms folded corpselike across her chest, her lips pursed, her expression somber.

"What about Isaac?" asked a girl, pushing forward a skinny six-year-old boy.

Without opening her eyes, Daisy shook her head.

"Michael?" a second girl tried. Another terse shake.

"Jeff?" Again the wordless dismissal.

I asked the boy in front of me what was going on.

"She's Snow White," he explained. "She ate the poison apple, and now we're trying to find the right prince to wake her."

I had never told Daisy the story of Snow White. I had purposely kept it from her because, even setting aside the obvious sexism, Snow herself is such an incredible pill. Her sole virtue, as far as I can tell, is tidiness—she is forever scrubbing, dusting, nagging the dwarves to wash their filthy mitts. (Okay, the girl has an ear for a catchy melody, I'll give you that. But that's where it ends.) She is everything I imagined my daughter would reject, would not, in fact, ever encounter or even understand if she did, let alone embrace: the passive, personality-free princess swept off by a prince (who is enchanted solely by her beauty) to live in a happily-ever-after that he ultimately controls. Yet here was my girl, somehow having learned the plotline anyway, blissfully lying in wait for Love's First Kiss.

Daisy lifted a hand. *"Harry!"* she announced. *"Harry* has to be the prince." Two girls instantly peeled off to search for her eleven-year-old cousin, while everyone else remained standing there, gazing at my princess, enthralled.

She was so confident of their presence that she still hadn't opened her eyes.

∽∭∾

God knows, I was a Disney kid. I still have my bona fide mouse ears from 1970, monogrammed with an embroidered, loopy yellow PEGGY. I wore out my Close 'n Play on my Magic Mirror storybook records of *Peter Pan, Alice in Wonderland,* and even *Cinderella.* But until I had a daughter, I had never heard of the Disney Princesses. As a concept, I mean. It turns out there was a reason for that. They did not exist until 2000. That's when a former Nike executive named Andy Mooney rode into Disney on a metaphoric white horse to rescue its ailing consumer products division.

I spoke with Mooney one day in his fittingly palatial office in Burbank, California. In a rolling Scottish burr that was pretty darned Charming, he told me the now-legendary story: how, about a month into his tenure, he had flown to Phoenix to check out a "Disney on Ice" show and found himself surrounded by little girls in princess costumes. Princess costumes that were— horrors!—*homemade.* How had such a massive branding opportunity been overlooked? The very next day he called together his team and they began working on what would become known in-house as "Princess." It was a risky move: Disney had never marketed its characters separately from a film's release, and old-timers like Roy Disney considered it heresy to lump together those from different stories. That is why, these days, when the ladies appear on the same item, they never make eye contact. Each stares off in a slightly different direction, as if unaware of the others' presence. Now that I have told you, you'll always notice it. And let me tell you, it's freaky.

It is also worth noting that not all of the eight DPs are of royal extraction. Part of the genius of "Princess," Mooney admitted, is that its meaning is so broadly constructed that it actually has no meaning. Even Tinker Bell was originally a Princess, though her reign did not last. Meanwhile, although Mulan (the protofeminist young woman who poses as a boy to save China) and Pocahontas (an Indian chief's daughter) are officially part of the club, I defy you to find them in the stores. They were, until late 2009, the brownest-skinned princesses, as well as the ones with the least bling potential. You can gussy up Pocahontas's eagle feathers only so much. As for Mulan, when she does show up, it's in a kimono-like *hanfu*, the one that makes her miserable in the movie, rather than in her warrior's gear. Really, when you're talking Princess, you're talking Cinderella, Sleeping Beauty, Ariel, and Belle (the "modern" Princess, whose story shows that the right woman can turn a beast into a prince). Snow White and Jasmine are in the pantheon, too, though slightly less popular.

The first Princess items, released with no marketing plan, no focus groups, no advertising, sold as if blessed by a fairy godmother. Within a year, sales had soared to $300 million. By 2009, they were at $4 billion. Four *billion* dollars! There are more than twenty-six thousand Disney Princess items on the market, a number which, particularly when you exclude cigarettes, liquor, cars, and antidepressants, is staggering. "Princess" has not only become the fastest-growing brand the company has ever created, it is the largest franchise on the planet for girls ages two to six.

To this day, Disney conducts little market research on the Princess line, relying instead on the power of its legacy among mothers as well as the instant-read sales barometer of the theme parks and Disney Stores (Tiana, the much-ballyhooed "first African-American Princess," was somewhat of an exception, but we will get to her in a later chapter). "We simply gave girls what they wanted," Mooney said of the line's success, "although I don't think any of us grasped how much they wanted this. I wish I could sit here and take credit for having some grand scheme to develop this, but all we did was envision a little girl's room and think about how she could live out the princess fantasy. The counsel we gave to licensees was: What type of bedding would a princess want to sleep in? What kind of alarm clock would a princess want to wake up to? What type of television would a princess like to see? It's a rare case where you find a girl who has every aspect of her room bedecked in Princess, but if she ends up with three or four of these items, well, then, you have a very healthy business." Healthy, indeed. It has become nearly impossible for girls of a certain age *not* to own a few Princess trinkets. Even in our home, where neither Steven nor I have personally purchased a Princess item, several coloring books, a set of pencils, a Snow White doll, and a blow-up mattress have managed to infiltrate.

Meanwhile, by 2001, Mattel had brought out its own "world of girl" line of princess Barbie dolls, DVDs, toys, clothing, home decor, and myriad other products. At a time when Barbie sales were declining domestically, they became instant best sellers. Even Dora the Explorer, the intrepid, dirty-kneed adventurer, ascended to the throne: in 2004, after a two-part episode in which she turns into a "true princess," the Nickelodeon and Viacom consumer products division released a satin-gowned Magic Hair Fairytale Dora with hair that grows or shortens when her crown is touched. Among other phrases the bilingual doll utters: "Vámonos! Let's go to fairy-tale land!" and "Will you brush my hair?"

I do not question that little girls like to play princess: as a child, I certainly availed myself of my mom's cast-off rhinestone tiara from time to time. But when you're talking about 26,000 items (and that's just Disney), it's a little hard to say where "want" ends and "coercion" begins. Mooney was prepared for that concern and for my overall discomfort with the Princesses, who, particularly in his consumer products versions, are all about clothes, jewelry, makeup, and snaring a handsome husband.

"Look," he said, "I have friends whose son went through the Power Rangers phase who castigated themselves over what they must've done wrong. Then they talked to other parents whose kids had gone through it. The boy passes through. The girl passes through. I see girls expanding their imagination through visualizing themselves as princesses, and then they pass through that phase and end up becoming lawyers, doctors, mothers, or princesses, whatever the case may be."

He had a point. I have never seen a study proving that playing princess *specifically* damages girls' self-esteem or dampens other aspirations. And trust me, I've looked. There is, however, ample evidence that the more mainstream media girls consume, the more importance they place on being pretty and sexy. And a ream of studies shows that teenage girls and college students who hold conventional beliefs about femininity—especially those that emphasize beauty and pleasing behavior—are less ambitious and more likely to be depressed than their peers. They are also less likely to report that they enjoy sex or insist that their partners use condoms. None of that bodes well for Snow White's long-term mental health.

Perhaps you are now picturing poor, hapless girls who are submissive, low-achieving, easily influenced: the kind whose hair hangs in front of their faces as they recede into the background.

I know I have a hard time connecting such passivity to my own vibrant, vital daughter. Yet even can-do girls can be derailed—and surprisingly quickly—by exposure to stereotypes. Take the female college students, all good at math, all enrolled in advanced calculus, who were asked to view a series of television commercials: four neutral ads (showing, say, cell phones or animals) were interspersed with two depicting clichés (a girl in raptures over acne medicine; a woman drooling over a brownie mix). Afterward they completed a survey and—*bing!*—the group who'd seen the stereotyped ads expressed less interest in math- and science-related careers than classmates who had seen only the neutral ones. Let me repeat: the effect was demonstrable after watching *two ads*. And guess who performed better on a math test, coeds who took it after being asked to try on a bathing suit or those who had been asked to try on a sweater? (Hint: the latter group; interestingly, male students showed no such disparity.)

Meanwhile, according to a 2006 survey of more than two thousand school-aged children, girls repeatedly described a paralyzing pressure to be "perfect": not only to get straight As and be the student body president, editor of the newspaper, and captain of the swim team but also to be "kind and caring," "please everyone, be very thin, and dress right." Rather than living the dream, then, those girls were straddling a contradiction: struggling to fulfill all the new expectations we have for them without letting go of the old ones. Instead of feeling greater latitude and choice in how to be female—which is what one would hope—they now feel they must not only "have it all" but *be* it all: Cinderella *and* Supergirl. Aggressive *and* agreeable. Smart *and* stunning. Does that make them the beneficiaries of new opportunities or victims of a massive con job?

The answer is yes. That is, both are true, and that is what's so insidious. It would be one thing if the goal were more realistic or if girls were stoked about creating a new femininity, but it's not and they aren't. The number of girls who fretted excessively about their looks and weight actually *rose* between 2000 and 2006 (topping their concern over schoolwork), as did their reported stress levels and their rates of depression and suicide. It is as if the more girls achieve the more obsessed they become with appearance—not dissimilar to the way the ideal of the "good mother" was ratcheted up just as adult women flooded the workforce. In her brilliant book *Enlightened Sexism*, Susan Douglas refers to this as the bargain girls and women strike, the price of success, the way they unconsciously defuse the threat their progress poses to male dominance. "We can excel in school, play sports, go to college, aspire to—and get—jobs previously reserved for men, be working mothers, and so forth. But in exchange we must obsess about our faces, weight, breast size, clothing brands, decorating, perfectly calibrated child-rearing, about pleasing men and being envied by other women."

⟨⟩

A new banner unfurled over the entrance of Daisy's preschool when I dropped by one fall morning: a little girl, adorned with a glittering plastic-and-rhinestone tiara and matching earrings, grinned down from it. WELCOME TO OUR CAMPUS, the banner read. The image might have irritated me in any case—even my kid's *school* had bought into the idea that all girls should aspire to the throne—but what was really cringe-making was the fact that this was part of a Jewish temple. When I was growing up, the last thing you wanted to be called was a "princess": it conjured up images of a spoiled, self-centered brat with a freshly bobbed nose who runs to "Daddy" at the least provocation. The Jewish American Princess was the repository for my community's self-hatred, its ambivalence over assimilation—it was Jews turning against their girls as a way to turn against themselves. Was this photograph a sign we had so transcended the *Goodbye, Columbus* stereotype that we could now embrace it?

"What about Queen Esther?" asked Julie, the mother of one of Daisy's classmates, when I questioned the picture's subtext. "She saved the Jewish people. Shouldn't girls try to be like her?"

Julie, a forty-five-year-old owner of a Web consulting company, was among several mothers I had asked to join me after drop-off for a chat about princess culture. Each one had a preschool-aged daughter obsessed with Disney royalty. They also knew I had my qualms about the subject, which they did not necessarily share. I wanted to know, from a mother's perspective, why they allowed—in some cases even encouraged—their girls to play princess. Did they think it was innocuous? Beneficial? Worrisome? Healthy?

"I think feminism erred in the 1960s by negating femininity," announced Mara, a thirty-six-year-old education consultant who was currently home with her kids. Her voice sounded tight, almost defiant. "That was a mistake. I want my daughter to have a strong identity as a girl, as a woman, as a *female*. And being pretty in our culture is very important. I don't want her to ever doubt that she's pretty. So if she wants to wear a princess dress and explore that side of herself, I don't want to stand in the way."

She folded her arms and collapsed back on her chair, as if she had said her piece. But before I could respond, she cocked her head and added, "On the other hand, I also have a son, and we really encourage his intelligence. I worry about that. A reward for her is 'You look so pretty, you look so beautiful.' People tell her that all the time, and we do, too. We tell *him*, 'You're so smart.'"

Dana, a thirty-eight-year-old stay-at-home mom, who had been watching Mara with a slightly awestruck expression, spoke up. "For me it's a matter of practicality," she said. "Having those Disney Princess outfits around the house is really helpful for the endless playdates. And Eleanor loves to swim, so she identifies with Ariel."

I began to ask Dana how she felt about the rest of the *Little Mermaid* story, but she cut me off. "Oh, I don't let the actual *story* in the house," she said. "Just the *costumes*. Eleanor doesn't know the stories."

That turned out to be Mara's policy, too. The issue to her was not princesses, it was plotlines. "Those stories are horrible," she said, making a face. "Every single one is the same: it's about romance, love, and being rescued by the prince. I *will* protect my daughter from that."

Thinking back on my own girl's inexplicable acquaintance with the Snow White story, I had to wonder whether that was possible. I'd believed I could keep out the tales *and* the toys but had failed on both counts. What were the odds, then, that you could permit one without the other? I had spent a lot of time with Dana's daughter and already knew she could give a full recitation of Ariel's story. Dana shrugged. "Well, yeah, she hears it from her friends," she admitted. "But at least not at home."

What gave those mothers pause, then, was the fantasy the stories promoted that a man would take care of you. Yet the tales also provide the characters with some context, a narrative arc. Cinderella may ride off with the prince, but before that, she spends much of her time dressed in tatters, offering children object lessons about kindness, forbearance, and humility. Without that backstory, what was left? What did they imagine a storyless "princess" represented to the girls?

That's when Julie piped up. "I think it's all about being looked at," she said, "being admired. And about special treatment." She rolled her eyes. "Receiving it, not giving it."

"And it's *fun*," Dana pointed out.

Hell, yeah, it's fun. Who doesn't love nail polish with flower appliqués? Who doesn't like to play dress-up now and again, swoosh about in silk and velvet? Daisy once whispered conspiratorially to me, "Mom, did you know that girls can choose all kinds of things to wear, but boys can only wear pants?" There it was: dressing up fancy, at least for now, was something she felt she *got* to do, not something she *had* to do. It was a source of power and privilege, much like her game of Snow White in which the action revolved around and was controlled by her.

Whereas boys . . . even here in Berkeley, a friend's seven-year-old son was teased so ruthlessly about his new, beloved pink bike that within a week he refused to ride it. It is quite possible that boys, too, would wear sequins if only they could. Isabelle Cherney, a professor of psychology at Creighton University, found that nearly half of boys aged five to thirteen, when ushered alone into a room and told they could play with anything, chose "girls'" toys as frequently as "boys'"—provided they believed nobody would find out. Particularly, their fathers: boys as young as four said their daddies would think it was "bad" if they played with "girls'" toys, even something as innocuous as miniature dishes. Boys were also more likely to sort playthings based on how they perceived gender roles (such as "Dad uses tools, so hammers are for boys"), whereas girls figured that if they themselves enjoyed a toy—*any* toy—it was, ipso facto, for girls. So it seems that, even as they have loosened up on their daughters, dads continue to vigorously police masculinity in their sons. I believe it: consider the progressive pal of mine who proudly showed off the Hot Wheels set he had bought for his girl but balked when his boy begged for a tutu. Who's to say, then, which sex has greater freedom?

I am almost willing to buy that argument: that boys are the ones who are more limited; that little girls *need* to feel beautiful; that being on display, being admired for how they look, is critical to their developing femininity and fragile self-esteem; that princess sets their imaginations soaring; that its popularity is evidence that we've moved past 1970s feminist rigidity. Except that, before meeting with the preschool moms, I had flipped through a stack of drawings each child in Daisy's class had made to complete the sentence "If I were a [blank], I'd [blank] to the store." (One might say, for instance, "If I were a ball, I'd bounce to the store.") The boys had chosen to be a whole host of things: firemen, spiders, superheroes, puppies, tigers, birds, athletes, raisins. The girls fell into exactly four camps: princess, fairy, butterfly, and ballerina (one especially enthusiastic girl claimed them all: a "princess, butterfly, fairy ballerina"). How, precisely, does that, as Disney's Andy Mooney suggested, expand their horizons? The boys seemed to be exploring the world; the girls were exploring femininity. What they "got" to do may have been uniquely theirs, but it was awfully circumscribed. "Yeah, I was surprised," the teacher admitted when I asked about it. "The girls had so little range in their ideas. We tried to encourage them to choose other things, but they wouldn't."

Of course, girls are not buying the 24/7 princess culture all on their own. So the question is not only why *they* like it (which is fairly obvious) but what it offers their parents. Julie may have been onto something on that front: princesses are, by definition, special, elevated creatures. And don't we all feel our girls are extraordinary, unique, and beautiful? Don't we want them to share that belief for as long as possible, to think that—just by their existence, by birthright—they are the chosen ones? Wouldn't we like their lives to be forever charmed, infused with magic and sparkle? I know I want that for my daughter.

Or do I? Among other things, princesses tend to be rather isolated in their singularity. Navigating the new world of friendships is what preschool is all about, yet the DPs, you will recall, won't even *look* at one another. Daisy had only one fight with her best friend during their three years of preschool—a conflict so devastating that, at pickup time, I found the other girl sobbing in the hallway, barely able to breathe. The source of their disagreement? My darling daughter had insisted that there could be only *one* Cinderella in their games—only *one* girl who reigned supreme—and it was she. Several hours and a small tantrum later, she apologized to the girl, saying that from now on there could be *two* Cinderellas. But the truth was, Daisy had gotten it right the first time: there *is* only one princess in the Disney tales, one girl who gets to be exalted. Princesses may confide in a sympathetic mouse or teacup, but, at least among the best-known stories, they do not have girlfriends. God forbid Snow White should give Sleeping Beauty a little support.

Let's review: princesses avoid female bonding. Their goals are to be saved by a prince, get married (among the DP picture books at Barnes & Noble: *My Perfect Wedding* and *Happily Ever After Stories*) and be taken care of for the rest of their lives. Their value derives largely from their appearance. They are rabid materialists. They *might* affect your daughter's interest in math. And yet . . . parents cannot resist them. Princesses seem to have tapped into our unspoken, nonrational wishes. They may also assuage our fears: Cinderella and Sleeping Beauty may be sources of comfort, of stability in a rapidly changing world. Our daughters will shortly be tweeting and Facebooking and doing things that have yet to be invented, things that are beyond our ken. Princesses are uncomplicated, classic, something solid that we can understand and share with them, even if they are a bit problematic. They provide a way to play with our girls that is similar to how we played, a common language of childhood fun. That certainly fits into what Disney found in a survey of preschool girls' mothers: rather than "beautiful," the women more strongly associate princesses with "creating fantasy," "inspiring," "compassionate."

And "safe." That one piqued my interest. By "safe," I would wager that they mean that being a Princess fends off premature sexualization, or what parents often refer to as the pressure "to grow up too soon." There is that undeniable sweetness, that poignancy of seeing girls clomp off to the "ball" in their incongruous heels and gowns. They are so gleeful, so guileless, so delightfully delighted. The historian Gary Cross, who writes extensively on childhood and consumption, calls such parental response "wondrous innocence." Children's wide-eyed excitement over the products we buy them pierces through our own boredom as consumers and as adults, reconnecting us to our childhoods: it makes us *feel* again. The problem is that our very dependence on our children's joy erodes it: over time, they become as jaded as we are by new purchases—perhaps more so. They rebel against the "cuteness" in which we've indulged them—and, if we're honest, imposed upon them—by taking on the studied irony and indifferent affect of "cool."

Though both boys and girls engage in that cute-to-cool trajectory, for girls specifically, being "cool" means looking hot. Given that, then, there may indeed be, or at least *could* be, a link between princess diadems and Lindsay Lohan's panties (or lack thereof). But in the short term, when you're watching your pre-schooler earnestly waving her wand, it sure doesn't feel that way. To the contrary: princess play feels like proof of our daughters' innocence, protection against the sexualization it may actually be courting. It reassures us that, despite the pressure to be preco-cious, little girls are still—and ever will be—little girls. And that knowledge restores our faith not only in wonder but, quite pos-sibly, in goodness itself. Recall that the current princess craze took off right around the terrorist attacks of September 11, 2001, and continued its rise through the recession: maybe, as another cultural historian suggested to me, the desire to encourage our girls' imperial fantasies is, at least in part, a reaction to a newly unstable world. We *need* their innocence not only for consumerist but for *spiritual* redemption.

Sound far-fetched? This is not the first time princess obsession has cropped up during a time of societal crisis. The original Euro-pean fairy tales rose from a medieval culture that faced all manner of economic and social upheaval. Frances Hodgson Burnett's book *A Little Princess* was published in 1905, a time of rapid urbanization, immigration, and spiraling poverty; Shirley Temple's film version was a hit during the Great Depression. Little Shirley may actually be the ultimate example of girlish innocence conferring adult sal-vation (with the comic pages' *Little Orphan Annie* a close second). A mere six years old when she starred in her first film, with her irrepressible, childlike optimism she gave Americans hope during a desperate era: President Franklin Roosevelt even reportedly pro-claimed, "As long as our country has Shirley Temple, we will be all right." Imagine! Her cinematic formula—which typically included at least one dead parent so adults in the audience could project them-selves into that vacant role—put her at the top of the box office for three years running, beating out Clark Gable, Joan Crawford, and Gary Cooper. She remains the most popular child star of all time. She also became the first celebrity aggressively marketed to little girls. During the height of her fame, there were Shirley Temple songbooks, handkerchiefs, jewelry, handbags, sewing cards, coloring books, soap, mugs, dresses, hair bows, records—anything that could carry her image did, and the appetite for her seemed endless. Like the Disney Princesses, the first Shirley Temple doll was released independently of a movie—in time for Christmas 1934. Within a year, it accounted for a third of all doll sales. Another doll, released to coincide with both a film and Shirley's eighth birthday, was, according to the company that manufactured it, "the biggest non-Christmas toy event in history." Though I doubt parents in that era were (consciously or not) trying to prolong girls' innocence through those dolls, they were surely celebrating it—perhaps, after a fashion, even feeding off it: if Shirley herself gave the country's morale a boost during hard times, perhaps her likeness, cradled in the arms of a beaming daughter, gave heart to individual families.

Unlike animated royalty, however, Shirley Temple was a flesh-and-blood girl, whose reign could not go on indefinitely—she had no choice but to relinquish the crown once she entered puberty. What's more, unlike much of today's princess schlock, Shirley Temple dolls were synonymous with quality: they ran a whopping $4.49, which was almost quadruple the price of competing dolls. In that way, they were less like the Disney Princesses and closer to what seems—at least at first glance—like the princess antidote: the upscale, down-to-earth American Girl collection.

oৎৎৎ৩

Ten-year-old Sophie is no longer into American Girl. That's what her mother, my friend Karen, reported apologetically when I invited them to join me for a jaunt to American Girl Place, the brand's Mecca-like store in Manhattan. Eventually Sophie agreed to go, if reluctantly. For research. Because, as I said, she was no longer into American Girl. She was no longer into it—until she got there.

American Girl Place, which sits on the corner of Fifth Avenue and 49th Street, across from Saks, contains three stories of dolls, dresses, books, and the most cunning miniature furniture you have ever seen. It houses a doll hospital (where, after "treatment," repaired dolls are returned with a hospital gown, an identification bracelet, a "Get Well Soon" balloon, and a certificate of good health) and a hair salon (where stylists strap dolls into tiny barber's chairs for facials and new 'dos). There is also a café, where I had cadged a coveted reservation for the three of us plus Sophie's doll Kaya.

There was no line around the block when we arrived, as there routinely had been several years before when the store first opened, but, on a dreary winter afternoon, there were still throngs of little girls streaming in, most of them already clutching dolls or toting them in specially designed backpacks.

"Mama, *look*!" Sophie cried, pointing to a blue wrought-iron daybed with butterfly-themed linen and its own trundle.

"Sophie, *look*!" Karen replied half jokingly, pointing at a book with a pink-and-turquoise cover titled *Clutter Control*.

Sophie ignored her, looking eagerly around. "Can I get *two* things?" she asked.

"Let's see what you choose," Karen said firmly. But Sophie was already running toward the escalator to check out the second floor.

American Girl was born in 1986, started by a former teacher, TV reporter, and textbook editor named—I kid you not—Pleasant Rowland. Pleasant conceived of her dolls one holiday season while shopping for presents for her nieces. Every doll she saw seemed to be either cheaply made, unattractive, or fashion-obsessed. And nothing, she felt, communicated "anything about what it meant to be a girl growing up in America." Rather than a bucket of Barbies, Rowland dreamed of offering girls a doll they would treasure, that would forge a bond between mothers and daughters, that could even become an heirloom, passed from generation to generation. She wanted her dolls to offer an alternative, morally inspiring vision of girlhood, one that would, in the process, express her own passion for history. The American Girl dolls in the historical line, then, represented different eras in the country's past: among them were Kirsten, "a pioneer girl of strength and spirit"; Felicity, "a spunky Colonial girl"; Addy, a "courageous girl" who escapes slavery (who is still the *only* black girl in the historical line); and Kaya, Sophie's doll, a Nez Percé Indian from the mid–eighteenth century. The dolls are eighteen inches high with notably realistic, childlike proportions—no Barbie bosoms here, though at a hefty $110 per doll, they are also up to twenty times as expensive. Six books (purchased separately) tell each doll's story. Their worlds can be re-created with astonishingly detailed period clothing, furniture, and other paraphernalia. The kit for Kit, a Depression-era girl who dreams of being a journalist, includes a miniature "reporter's set" with an authentic-looking leather-bound notebook, tiny pencil, and eraser; a period camera (complete with box of Kodak film and five preshot photos); and a stack of newspapers, tied with twine, showing her byline splashed across the front page.

Be still, my heart! I thought, leaning in to get a closer look.

Eavesdropping as we strolled through the store, I noticed that, like me, the mothers were captivated by the tiny jars of canned peaches, the realistic 1930s cookstove, the wee 1940s-style chifforobe with its faux cut-glass mirrors and hanging quilted dress bag.

The girls, on the other hand, were into the clothes.

"I want the pink dress!" a blond four-year-old screeched twenty-four times in the space of thirty seconds. Her mother finally grabbed it off the rack.

The formula was brilliant: moms were hooked by the patina of homespun values and the *Antique Road Show* aesthetic of the accessories; then the girls angled for fashions. Most walked out laden with some of each.

By 1998, the Pleasant Company was pulling down more than $300 million in annual sales. That year brought two changes: the first American Girl Place opened (the dolls had previously been sold exclusively through mail order), and Pleasant sold her empire to Mattel—the maker of the same disposable doll she had been trying to combat. You can't really blame the woman, though: who wouldn't compromise an ideal or two for a $700 million payday? Mattel has since added the Just Like You line, which jettisons the historical format, letting girls customize dolls with hair, eye color, and skin tone that matches their own (outfits and furnishings to bring the dolls' "stories" alive sold separately). They also partnered with Bath & Body Works to produce a Real Beauty product line, though that did not last: maybe even Mattel recognized the contradiction in telling an eight-year-old that a perfume called "Truly Me" would help her feel good about "just being yourself."

Before my visit, I was familiar with American Girl only through the books, which I had flipped through at the public library. The titles in each series are identical: *Meet* [doll's name];

[doll's name] *Learns a Lesson*; [doll's name]*'s Surprise*; *Happy Birthday*, [doll's name]; [doll's name] *Saves the Day*; and *Changes for* [doll's name]. In one typical story, Molly, a "loveable, patriotic girl growing up on the home front during World War II" whose father is fighting in Europe, plays a series of pranks on her pesky brother. Eventually the stakes escalate, and she learns that peace can be harder than war. Our heroines may confront a smidgen of sexism, racism, or even, on occasion, tragedy, but nothing a little pluck and ingenuity can't conquer. Which is fine with me: it's not as though I would want my seven-year-old exposed to the details of the Triangle Shirtwaist Factory fire. Reading the books, though, I was struck by their presentation of the past as a time not only in which girls were improbably independent, feisty, and apparently without constraint but, in a certain way, in which they were *more* free than they are today: a time when their character mattered more than their clothing, when a girl's actions were more important than how she looked or what she owned—a time before girlhood was consumed and defined by consumerism. I found myself comparing Kit, the courageous, impoverished Depression-era girl who is committed to becoming a muckraking reporter, to Yasmin, a character from Bratz.com, which competes for the same six- to eleven-year-old demographic: Yasmin has "got a lot of strong opinions and loves to share them," "enjoys curling up with a cool autobiography about celebs she admires," and blogs about "staying involved with your community while still doing fun things like getting makeovers."

Suddenly American Girl's price tag didn't look so bad.

And maybe it wouldn't be, if the doll and books were the end of it. But that little cookstove would set you back $68 and the chifforobe another $175. For *doll* furniture. Therein lies the paradox of American Girl: the books preach against materialism, but you could blow the college fund on the gear. In fact, Kit, Addy, Molly, and their friends could never afford the dolls that represent them—an irony that became particularly piquant in fall 2009 with the introduction of Gwen, a $95 limited-edition doll who was supposed to be *homeless*. The truth is, I asked Sophie and Karen to join me on this outing because Daisy had not yet heard about American Girl, and I was not eager to hasten her discovery. It's not that I object to the dolls, exactly, and I surely understand supporting a girl's interest in the line, but I would prefer to stave it off, if not avoid it entirely: there has to be a less expensive way to encourage old-fashioned values.

We headed up the escalator to the café, a black-and-white-striped confection iced with pink daisies and whimsical mirrors. Inside, dolls were seated in clip-on "treat seats" and given their own striped cups and saucers. *Everything* was for sale: the doll seat ($24), the tea set ($16), the pot that held the daisies ($8). All around us mothers were smiling, nibbling their quiche, reveling in this New York reprieve from the pressures of Paris (Hilton, that is). While my gaze was elsewhere, Sophie took a bite of a cucumber slice and slipped it onto Kaya's plate, then pretended the doll had eaten it. She was ten years old but, swept away by the moment, was willing to believe in the kind of magic she already knew was not real. They might as well have put up a sign: check your cynicism at the door. I was happy to comply.

Almost. It turned out that Kaya, like Disney's Pocahontas, did not inspire a lot in the way of outfits or accessories. Not fun. Sophie asked if she could buy a new doll using money she had been saving from her birthday and allowance. Karen hesitated—this was the child who wasn't "into" American Girl anymore—but then agreed. She even sprang for matching girl-doll outfits ($107) as well as a $20 salon appointment for Kaya. Then she bought the daybed and trundle ($68) because, well . . . even Karen didn't know why. "I can't believe I'm succumbing!" she moaned. When we got to the cash register, she was told the butterfly bedding was sold separately—for another $26. Karen sighed in disgust. "Are you writing this down?" she said to me. She turned to the salesclerk. "Okay, I'll get the bedding."

She slapped down her AmEx. "My husband is going to think I've lost my mind," she muttered.

I glanced across the street to the window display at Saks Fifth Avenue. It held a hypnotically spinning red-and-white-striped disc with two words in the center in tall black letters: WANT IT. The same phrase ran endlessly around the window's edge. At least, I thought, that store was up front about its agenda.

Pleasant Rowland herself has called the dolls something mothers can "do" for their girls. But as Sophie, Karen, and I trudged eastward on 49th Street, our arms weighted down by giant shopping bags, it occurred to me that you don't "do" $500 worth of merchandise. You buy it. It is a peculiar inversion: the simplicity of American Girl is expensive, while the finery of Princess comes cheap. In the end, though, the appeal to parents is the same: both lines tacitly promise to keep girls young and "safe" from sexualization. Yet they also introduce them to a consumer culture that will ultimately encourage the opposite—one in which Mattel and Disney (the parent companies, respectively, of the two brands) play a major role. Both Princess and American Girl promote shopping as the path to intimacy between mothers and daughters; as an expression, even for five-year-olds, of female identity. Both, above all, are selling innocence. And nothing illustrates the gold mine it has become—or the contradictions it represents—better than the color pink.

Chapter Three

Pinked!

*t*he annual Toy Fair at New York's Javits Center is the industry's largest trade show, with 100,000 products spread over 350,000 feet of exhibition space. And I swear, at *least* 75,000 of those items were pink. I lost count of the myriad pink wands and crowns (feathered, sequined, and otherwise bedazzled) and infinite permutations of pink poodles in purses (with names like Pucci Pups, Fancy Schmancy, Sassy Pets, Pawparazzi . . .). The Disney Princesses reigned over a new pink Royal Interactive Kitchen with accompanying pink Royal Appliances and pink Royal Pots and Pans set (though I would have thought one of the perks of monarchy would be that someone else did the cooking). There were pink dinnerware sets emblazoned with the word PRINCESS; pink fun fur stoles and boas; pink princess beds; pink diaries (embossed with PRINCESS, BALLERINA, or butterflies); pink jewelry boxes; pink vanity mirrors, pink brushes, and toy pink blow-dryers; pink telephones; pink bunny ears; pink gowns; pink height charts; a pink Princess and the Pea board game (one square instructed, "Wave like a princess, pretty as you can be"); My Little Pink Book Board Game ("a cool game for girls in which they secretly choose a dream date from their Little Pink Book of guys and then try to be the first to guess who everyone else is dating"); and a pink toy washing machine. All of those, however, were perhaps to be expected. Less explicable were the pink spy kits; pink roll-aboard suitcases; pink cameras; a giant pink plush squid (which, from behind, looked exactly like a giant penis); a pink plush boa constrictor; a pink plush beanstalk (or really *any* plush beanstalk); pink rocking horses; pink cowgirl hats ("There's something wrong here," I heard one toy store buyer comment, "it needs rhinestones or glitter or something to sell"); pink gardening gloves; pink electric pianos; pink punching balls; pink gumball machines (with pink gumballs); pink kites; pink pool toys; pink golf clubs, sleds, tricycles, bicycles, scooters, and motorcycles, and even a pink tractor. Oh, and one pink neon bar sign flashing LIVE NUDES.

It's not that pink is intrinsically bad, but it is such a tiny slice of the rainbow, and, though it may celebrate girlhood in one way, it also repeatedly and firmly fuses girls' identity to appearance. Then it presents that connection, even among two-year-olds, not only as innocent but as *evidence* of innocence. Looking around, I despaired at the singular lack of imagination about girls' lives and interests, at the rows and rows of make-your-own jewelry/lip gloss/nail polish/fashion show craft kits at the drumbeat of the consumer feminine.

"Is all this pink really necessary?" I asked a bored-looking sales rep hawking something called Cast and Paint Princess Party.

"Only if you want to make money," he said, chuckling. Then he shrugged. "I guess girls are born loving pink."

Are they? Judging by today's girls, that would seem to be true—the color draws them like heat-seeking missiles. Yet adult women I have asked do not remember being so obsessed with pink as children, nor do they recall it being so pervasively pimped to them. I remember thinking my fuchsia-and-white-striped Danskin shirt with its matching stirrup pants was totally bitchin', but I also loved the same outfit in purple, navy, green, and red (yes, I had them all—there must have been a sale at Sears). My toys spanned the color spectrum, as did my hair ribbons, school notebooks, and lunchboxes. The original Easy-Bake oven, which I begged for (and, dang it, never got), was turquoise, and the Suzy Homemaker line—I had the iron, which really worked!—was teal. I can't imagine you would see that today. What happened? Why has girlhood become so monochromatic?

Girls' attraction to pink may seem unavoidable, somehow encoded in their DNA, but according to Jo Paoletti, an associate professor of American studies at the University of Maryland, it's not. Children weren't color-coded at all until the early twentieth century: in the era before Maytag, all babies wore white as a practical matter, since the only way of getting clothes clean was to boil them. What's more, both boys and girls wore what were thought of as gender-neutral dresses. When nursery colors were introduced, pink was actually considered the more masculine hue, a pastel version of red, which was associated with strength. Blue, with its intimations of the Virgin Mary, constancy, and faithfulness, symbolized femininity. (That may explain a portrait that has always befuddled me, of my father as an infant in 1926 wearing a pink dress.) Why or when that switched is not clear, but as late as the 1930s, in a poll of its customers conducted by the New York City department store Lord & Taylor, a solid quarter of adults still held to that split. I doubt anyone would get it "wrong" today. Perhaps that is why so many of the early Disney heroines—Cinderella, Sleeping Beauty, Wendy, Alice in Wonderland, *Mary Poppins*'s Jane Banks—were dressed in various shades of azure. (When the company introduced the Princess line, it deliberately changed Sleeping Beauty's gown to pink, supposedly to distinguish her from Cinderella.) It was not until the mid-1980s, when amplifying age and sex differences became a dominant children's marketing strategy, that pink fully came into its own, when it began to seem innately attractive to girls, part of what defined them as female, at least for the first few critical years.

I hadn't realized how profoundly marketing trends dictated our perception of what is natural to kids, including our core beliefs about their psychological development. Take the toddler. I assumed that phase was something experts—people with PhDs at the very least—developed after years of research into children's behavior: wrong-o. Turns out, according to Daniel Cook, a historian of childhood consumerism, it was popularized as a marketing gimmick by clothing manufacturers in the 1930s. Trade publications counseled department stores that, in order to increase sales, they should create a "third stepping-stone" between infant wear and older kids' clothes. They also advised segregating girls' and boys' clothing no later than age two: parents whose sons were "treated like a little man" were thought to be looser with their purse strings. It was only *after* "toddler" became common shoppers' parlance that it evolved into a broadly accepted developmental stage. If that seems impossible to believe, consider the trajectory of "tween," which was also coined, in the mid-1980s, as a marketing contrivance (originally describing children aged eight to fifteen). Within ten years, it was considered a full-blown psychological, physical, and emotional phase, abetted, in no small part, by the classic marketing bible *What Kids Buy and Why*. Its author confidently embedded "tween" in biology and evolution, marked by a child's "shift from right brain focus to left brain focus" and ending with a "neural 'housecleaning'" in which "millions of unmyelinated neurons are literally swept out of existence." Whatever *that* means. Scientifically proven or not, as phases go, "tween" is a conveniently elastic one: depending on who is talking, it now stretches from children as young as seven (when, according to the cosmetic company Bonne Bell, girls become "adept at using a lip gloss wand") to as old as twelve. That is hardly a span that has much common ground—nor, I would argue as a parent, *should* it have.

Splitting kids, or adults, or for that matter penguins, into ever-tinier categories has proved a surefire way to boost profits. So, where there was once a big group that was simply called "kids," we now have toddlers, preschoolers, tweens, young adolescents, and older adolescents, each with their own developmental/ marketing profile. For instance, because of their new "perceptual filters," *What Kids Buy and Why* counsels, thirteen- to fifteen-year-olds may still appreciate the wisecracks of Bugs Bunny, but a new passion for "realism" draws them to sports figures such as Michael Jordan; no accident, then, that those two were teamed up to shill for Nike in the mid-1990s. Even children one year old and under are being hailed as "a more informed, influential and compelling audience than ever before." *Informed?* An article published by the Advertising Educational Foundation stated, "Computer interaction and television viewing make this kid segment very savvy, and has led to dramatic changes in today's American families." Children as young as twelve to eighteen months can recognize brands, it went on, and are "strongly influenced" by advertising and marketing. *Yikes!* Meanwhile, I have seen the improbable term "pre-tween" ("pre"-between *what*, exactly?) floated to describe—and target—the five-year-old girl who has a discerning fashion sense and her own Lip Smackers collection.

One of the easiest ways to segment a market is to magnify gender differences—or invent them where they did not previously exist. That explained the token pink or lavender building sets, skateboards, tool belts, and science kits scattered throughout the Toy Fair. (The exception was Tonka, which had given up on girls altogether with its slogan "Boys: They're Just Built Different.") That pinkification could, I suppose, be read as a good-faith attempt at progress. The advent of pink TinkerToys, "designed especially for girls" (who can construct "a flower garden, a butterfly, a microphone and more"), might encourage preschool girls to use mechanical and spatial skills that might otherwise lie fallow. Or it might reinforce the idea that the "real" toy is for boys while that one measly pink Lego kit *in the whole darned store* is girls' consolation prize. It could even remind girls to shun anything that *isn't* pink and pretty as not for them, a mind-set that could eventually prove limiting. And what about the girl who chooses something else? I recalled taking Daisy to the park one day with a friend who had a pink Hello Kitty scooter and matching helmet. Daisy's scooter was silver; her helmet sported a green fire-breathing dragon.

"How come your helmet's not pink?" her friend asked. "It's not a girls' one."

Daisy furrowed her brow, considering, then said, "It's for girls *or* boys." Her friend looked skeptical. Even though I was relieved by Daisy's answer, I found the question itself disturbing. Would other girls view her with suspicion—even exclude her—if she did not display the proper colors? I hoped her friend would get the message and broaden her repertoire. I hoped Daisy would resist the pressure to narrow hers.

⟊

I took a break from the Toy Fair and strolled uptown to Times Square, home of the international flagship Toys "R" Us store. Part emporium, part amusement park, the post–FAO Schwarz monolith (Toys "R" Us swallowed up that venerable vendor in 2009) features a three-story neon-lit Ferris wheel at the entrance. Each car has a different theme: *Toy Story*, Mr. and Mrs. Potato Head, Monopoly, a fire truck. There are also a five-ton animatronics T. rex (which scared the bejeezus out of several toddlers during my brief visit), the New York skyline constructed entirely from Legos, and a two-story "Barbie Mansion" painted the iconic Pantone 219, often referred to as "Barbie Pink."

I paused in front of a display of plush Abby Cadabby dolls: throughout the store, I had noted Abby bath sets, costumes, books, party packs, sing-along CDs, backpacks—the typical array of licensed gimcracks. A resident of *Sesame Street*, Abby is a three-year-old "fairy in training" with cotton-candy-colored skin, a button nose, sparkly purple pigtails, pink wings, and a wand. She was launched in 2006; her presence in the neighborhood brought the grand total of female Muppets, after thirty-seven seasons, to five (Miss Piggy was on *The Muppet Show*, not *Sesame Street*, and, by the way, was voiced by Frank Oz, a man).

That in itself is astonishing—*Sesame Street*, which has skillfully tackled differences involving race, language, disability, and culture, can't figure out gender?

Not that it hasn't tried. The show has introduced a new female Muppet nearly every year, only to see them fizzle. Just as with real women, audiences seem to judge them by different standards than the males. "If Cookie Monster was a female character, she'd be accused of being anorexic or bulimic," the show's executive producer, Carol-Lynn Parente, has quipped. And, she added, were he a girl, Elmo's "whimsy" might be misread as "ditziness." But the real fur ceiling has to do with appearance. Lulu, a shy, scruffy-looking monster introduced in 2000, was a flat-out flop—mainly because "she wasn't that attractive" (unlike that dreamboat Grover?). The most successful female Muppet has been Zoe, who was the first character entirely conceived of by Sesame Workshop executives rather than the creative team, as well as the first one intentionally designed to be good-looking. Apparently, though, they did not go far enough. While Zoe is cute, in a radioactive orange kind of way, her release fell short of expectations, the—*ka-ching!*—hope of creating a female Elmo. Even slapping a tutu on her did not help. Perhaps, one of her creators later mused, the problem was that she wasn't pink. The Workshop was not going to make that mistake again. With Abby, every detail was researched, scrutinized, and tested. Designers labored over the size of her nose (large may be funny, but it's not *pretty*) as well as its shape (too snoutlike in one version). Her eyelids were an issue, too—how much should show? In the end, they cover only the outermost part of her exaggerated, circular whites, giving the character a vulnerable, slightly cross-eyed appearance. Her lashes are long and dreamy. Her voice is sibilant, babyish in its pitch, and her catchphrase is "That's so magic!" She practically begs to be hugged.

Workshop executives have denied they created Abby with a licensing bonanza in mind; the fact that she is so infinitely marketable, that she dovetailed precisely with the pink-fairy-princess megatrend among girls, was apparently a mere happy coincidence. Besides, as Liz Nealon, the executive vice president and creative director of Sesame Workshop, has explained, the company was simply following the logic of dramatic convention. "If you think about *The Mary Tyler Moore Show*," she said. "Some girls relate to Rhoda, who's our Zoe, and some girls really relate to Mary, who's a girly girl." I don't know which reruns she's been watching, but the last I checked, that description fit not Mary but the airheaded Georgette—and who wants their daughters "relating" to *her*? No matter. Workshop execs claimed that Abby's character was ideal for exploring the challenges children face when they are new at school or different from other kids. That makes all kinds of sense—because everyone knows it's easy to fit in when you are snaggle-toothed and fat and have bad fur. What is really, really hard for a girl is being cute, sparkly, and magical.

I hate to sound like Peggy the Grouch, but it seemed disingenuous to spin the same old sweet-and-cute, pink-and-sparkly version of girlhood as an attempt at diversity or redress for some perceived historical slight. I was annoyed that the show I admired—and had loved as a child—for celebrating differences and stomping stereotypes so blithely upheld, even defended, this one. Yet it wasn't the first time I had heard that argument. At every geographic outpost from Disneyland to Sesame Street, executives described the same "taboo-breaking" vision, with an identical self-righteous justification about "honoring the range of play patterns girls have." All this pink-and-pretty, they claimed, was about giving girls *more* choices, not fewer. Like Disney's Andy Mooney, marketers would tell me, "We're only giving girls what they want," as if magnifying kids' desires is less coercive than instigating them. Even Dora the Explorer, who, according to Brown Johnson, the president of animation for Nickelodeon, was consciously developed as an alternative to the "Barbie image of girlhood," morphs into something else in the toy store. During a phone conversation, Johnson told me that Dora was drawn to resemble a real child, "not tall or elongated." She was envisioned as powerful, brave, indifferent to beauty. Her clothes were loose and functional, her hair cut in a simple bob. "Part of the DNA of Nickelodeon when it comes to gender portrayal," Johnson said, "is to not have everyone be perfect-looking."

But how did that square with what fans find on the shelves of Target and Claire's: the Dora Star Catcher Lip Gloss Bracelets; Dora's Let's Get Ready Vanity; Dora hair care kit; Dora Style Your Own Cellphone; Dress and Style Dora? The "adorable" boogie board? Wow! Way to counteract Barbie! I could almost hear Johnson purse her lips through the phone as she prepped the corporate damage control. "There's a delicate tension between the consumer products group and the production group," she said crisply. Followed by the familiar phrase "One of the important aspects of Dora's success is to not deny certain play patterns kids have."

In 2009, Nick introduced a "new" Dora aimed at five- to eight-year-olds, whom the company referred to as tweens. This Dora was, um, tall and elongated with long, luscious hair and round doe eyes. Her backpack and map had disappeared. Rather than shorts and sneaks, she sported a fashionable pink baby-doll tunic with purple leggings and ballet flats. The character's makeover set the Momosphere angrily abuzz: was Dora becoming a "Whora"? That was not, I imagine, the response Nick and Mattel were hoping for. But to my mind, sluttiness was not the issue. New Dora wasn't sexy, not at all—she was *pretty*, and that prettiness was now inextricable from her other traits. No longer did she turn "gender portrayal" on its head by "not looking perfect." New Dora stands as a reminder to her rugged little sister that she better get with the program, apparently by age five.

There's no question that new Dora is appealing. Of course she is, just as Abby Cadabby is the quintessence of adorable. Girls love them. In a vacuum, I might love them, too. And perhaps the problem is not so much that *they* exist as what still does *not*. Abby would trouble me far less if there could be a female Muppet as surly as Oscar or as id-driven as Cookie or as goofy as Grover: if there were more "play patterns" to "honor" than just this one.

I get why manufacturers play to pink—it makes good business sense. A marketing executive I spoke with at LeapFrog, which is based in Emeryville, California, told me that her company even had a name for it: "the pink factor." "If you make a pink baseball bat, parents will buy one for their daughter," she explained. "Then, if they subsequently have a son, they'll have to buy a second bat in a different color. Or, if they have a boy first and then a daughter, they'll want to buy a pink one for their precious little girl. Either way, you double your sales." But as a parent, I wonder what all that pinkness—the color, the dominance of the play pattern it signals—is teaching girls about who they are, what they should value, what it means to be female?

⚬⚬⚬

A family portrait hangs near the front door of the home of a friend of mine. It is a bright, playful, almost cartoonlike painting in which they are surrounded by their worldly belongings. There is my friend, dressed in jeans and a T-shirt, pressing a cell phone to her ear with one hand, her computer perched on a table close by. She and her husband are both writers; their books stand at their feet like additional family members. Their younger daughter sits cross-legged on a couch wearing a frothy tutu; their older daughter carries their son piggyback-style. The windows implausibly reflect the facade of their two-story home, as well as the kids' wooden play structure in the backyard. You have never met them, you don't know who they are, but those clues are enough for you to deduce their class, education, lifestyle. You can imagine them now, put them into context, can't you?

I thought about that portrait as I wandered back to the Javits Center. It's so tempting to say these are just toys. Some scholars would indeed argue that I'm projecting my own adult apprehension onto Fashion Angels or My Bling Bling Barbie that has nothing to do with a child's experience of the dolls or how she plays with them. And to a point I agree: just because little girls wear the tulle does not mean they've drunk the Kool-Aid. Plenty of them shoot baskets in ball gowns or cast themselves as the powerful evil stepsister bossing around the sniveling Cinderella. Yet even if girls stray from the prescribed script, doesn't it exert its influence? Don't our possessions reflect who we are; shape, even define, our experience? The belongings surrounding my friends in their portrait form a shorthand statement about their identities—and, I might add, a pretty accurate one. So what do the toys we give our girls, the pinkness in which they are steeped, tell us about what we are telling *them*? What do they say about who *we* think they are and ought to be?

At one time, playthings were expressly intended to communicate parental values and expectations, to train children for their future adult roles. Because of that, they can serve as a Rorschach for cultural anxieties. Take baby dolls. In the late nineteenth century, industrialization shifted the source of the family income outside the home. Without the need for free labor, middle-class couples no longer felt compelled to have more than one child. Nor were girls of the era particularly enamored with dolls: less than 25 percent in an 1898 survey cited them as their favorite toy. A few years later, however, President Theodore Roosevelt, who was obsessed with the waning birth rates among white Anglo-Saxon women, began waging a campaign against "race suicide." When women "feared motherhood," he warned, our country "trembled on the brink of doom." Baby dolls were seen as a way to revive the flagging maternal instinct of white girls, to remind them of their patriotic duty to conceive; within a few years dolls were ubiquitous, synonymous with girlhood itself. Miniature brooms, dustpans, and stoves tutored those same young ladies in the skills of homemaking, while "companion" dolls—including the decidedly straight-bodied Patsy, who came with a wardrobe of little dresses—provided lessons in the feminine arts of grooming, intimacy, and caretaking. Boys, by contrast, were plied with Tinker-Toys and blocks, Erector sets and model trains, preparing them to step into a new world of science and industry.

That division continued, more or less, until the cultural upheavals of the 1960s. Suddenly sex roles were thrown into flux. Expectations for girls were less clear, the paths to both manhood and womanhood muddled. To what, exactly, were girls now supposed to aspire? With what should they play? What would supplant washing machines and irons as preparation for their futures?

Enter Barbie.

It's hard to imagine now, but when she was introduced in 1959, the bombshell with the high-heeled feet was considered a rebel: single and childless, she lived a glamorous life replete with boyfriends (hinting at the possibility of recreational sex). She had a beach house in Malibu (which she had apparently paid for herself), a host of exciting careers (Fashion Editor! Tennis Pro! Stewardess!), and no evidence of parents (Barbie Millicent Roberts was initially supposed to be a teenager, though her age has become nonspecific). Sure, she had a wedding gown (which was to die for), but she was not about to be trapped in a soapbox of domestic drudgery like the baby-boomer girls' dissatisfied mothers. There is, it's worth noting, no "Mom-with-three-ungrateful-children Barbie." In that sense, the doll represented a new, independent vision of womanhood, an escape from "the problem that had no name." She was a feminist icon! The hitch, of course, was that her liberation was predicated on near-constant attention to her appearance. Long before Elle Woods or Carrie Bradshaw, Barbie was the first "I am woman, see me shop" feminist, with all the inconsistencies that implied.

Whether you love or loathe Barbie, you cannot have grown up in the last half century untouched by her influence. Movies have been made about her (check out the bootlegs of Todd Haynes's banned film *Superstar: The Karen Carpenter Story* on YouTube); books have been penned (*Forever Barbie* is a must). What other toy can make such claims? In one 11.5-inch polyvinyl chloride package, she embodies fifty years of cultural ambivalence over standards of beauty and appropriate role models for girls. My own relationship with the doll has evolved from desperately wanting one as a kid (my mom, an instinctive anticonsumerist, forbade any plaything that you had to add to, ruling out not only Barbie but Lego, Hot Wheels, and nearly everything else fun) to, in the apotheosis of my "wymyn's studies" phase, condemning the doll as a tool of the patriarchy to, these days, finding her kind of quaint.

Maybe "quaint" is the wrong word. What Barbie has become is "cute," in the way I described earlier: in which the toys we buy for our kids jump-start our own moribund sense of wonder. It is an interesting twist—when Barbie was introduced, moms disapproved of her, looking askance at her pinup proportions. That was precisely her appeal to girls: she helped them to stake out their turf in the land of "cool." Fifty years later, baby boomers and Gen Xers who had treasured the doll were so eager to share her with their own daughters that they didn't wait until the girls were eight to twelve (Barbie's original demographic); they presented her to their three-year-olds. That instantaneously made her anathema to her intended market. A headline-grabbing 2005 British study revealed that girls aged six to twelve enjoyed torturing, mutilating, and microwaving their Barbies nearly as much as they liked dressing them up for the prom. What interested me about the report, though, was the reason the researchers offered for that behavior: girls "saw her as representing their younger childhood out of which they felt they had now grown." Rather than sexuality or sophistication, then, Barbie was now associated with baby stuff.

As her audience dipped younger, Barbie herself began to change. Today's pleasantly open-faced dolls barely resemble the original. Yes, the vintage version was based on a German sex toy, but the effect was urbane rather than tawdry. Early Barbie exuded a self-knowing poise; her eyes cut to the side as if she harbored a secret. She was not even especially beautiful: the effect was more of a Grace Kelly–like elegance. I *still* wouldn't mind having one of those. Twenty-first-century Barbie's eyes are rounder and wider and point directly forward; the fire engine red pout has transformed into a friendly pink smile; the curves of her face have softened; her hair is shinier and blonder. All of this has made the doll look warmer, younger, *prettier.* Even her breasts have shrunk (at least a little) while her waist has been broadened. The astronauts, surgeons, and presidents of her glory days have been largely replaced by fairies, butterflies, ballerinas, mermaids, and princesses whose wardrobes are almost exclusively pink and lavender (with the occasional foray into turquoise). Original Barbie would be appalled: her palette was never so narrow—even her tutu was silver lamé. Yet the "cuter" Barbie became, the lower her sales fell: in the fourth quarter of 2008 alone, they sank by 21 percent. Some of that was a by-product of the tanked economy, but the exodus had begun long before. Following the cute-begets-cool formula (with "cool" carrying increasingly "hot" connotations), girls as young as six were rejecting the watered-down, mom-approved doll for something edgier, something called, appropriately enough, Bratz.

Bratz dolls were released in 2001 by a small, privately owned company called MGA—just months, as it happened, after the debut of the Disney Princesses—and they aimed to catch girls just as they aged out of that line, to seamlessly usher them into a new, more mature fantasy. With their sultry expressions, thickly shadowed eyes, and collagen-puffed moues, Bratz were tailor-made for the girl itching to distance herself from all things rose petal pink, Princess-y, or Barbie-ish. Their hottie-pink "passion for fashion" conveyed "attitude" and "sassiness," which, anyone will tell you, is little-girl marketing-speak for "sexy." Rather than donning a Cinderella gown and tripping off to the ball themselves, which would be woefully juvenile, seven-year-olds could send their Bratz Princess doll—rocking a tiara, purple fitted corset, and black net skirt—off in her limo to party in a Vegas Bratz pal's hot tub. How awesome was that? Bratz brilliantly distilled Barbie's acquisitiveness while casting off the rest: why be a role model when you can be simply a model?

Bratz, in short, were cool.

Even if moms didn't like the dolls—and generally, they did not—they bought them anyway, much as their own mothers had once bought Barbies: perhaps they succumbed to what marketers call the "nag factor," or they were afraid of the "forbidden fruit" effect in which the denied toy becomes all the more alluring. Or maybe they couldn't resist the Tokyo-A-Go-Go! Sushi Lounge, which, I have to say, was pretty special. At any rate, for seven years, Bratz gave Barbie a run for her money, gobbling up a full 40 percent of the fashion doll market. Then, in 2008, Mattel struck back, suing MGA for copyright infringement: Bratz's creator, it seemed, had been in Mattel's employ when he had designed the dolls. Mattel initially won the case and, within a year, had all but stripped the shelves of its competitor.

Bratz's downfall, then, had nothing to do with a drop in popularity or parental objections. Nor did it mark the end of the grade school diva. Consider the "girls' editions" of classic board games, each of which appears to have been dipped in Pepto-Bismol. The sparkly pink Ouija board includes a deck of seventy-two cards that "Ask the questions that girls want to know." ("Who will text me next?" "Will I be a famous actress someday?") Pink Yahtzee includes a fuzzy shaker and dice that boast, rather than numbers, hearts, butterflies, flowers, cell phones, flip-flops, and dresses. Monopoly Pink Boutique Edition claims to be "All about the things girls love! Buy boutiques and malls, go on a shopping spree, pay your cell phone bill, and get text and instant messages." The raspberry-tinted fantasy these products peddle assumes, like Disney Princess, that all girls long to be the fairest of them all (and the best dressed and the most popular), but something, somewhere, has shifted. The innocence that pink signaled during the Princess years, which seemed so benign, even protective, has receded, leaving behind narcissism and materialism as the hallmarks of feminine identity. The customization of these toys verges on parody; it also discourages the possibility of cross-sex friendship. Could you share your Pink Glam Magic 8 Ball with a pal who happened to be a boy? My sources say no.

With Bratz on ice, the similar My Scene and Fashionista Barbie sales soared, and the doll's earnings rebounded. Meanwhile, in 2009 MGA rolled out Moxie Girlz, which it positioned as a toned-down Bratz for a more economically somber era. And it's true, the clothing, though garish, is less revealing; the accessories are somewhat less excessive. But the dolls still wear the same provocative expression as their predecessors: they have similar shadow-rimmed eyes, and their lips are still freakishly full and lacquered to a high gloss. Their tagline may be "Be true * Be you," but, like pink products all along the age span that urge girls to "be yourself," "celebrate you," "express yourself," they define individuality entirely through appearance and consumption. I suspect that if Bratz had never existed, Moxies would create similar controversy, but the aesthetic of the former permanently pushed the frontiers of propriety; it effectively desensitized parents, dulled our shockability, so that now anything less bootylicious, even by just a smidgen, seems reasonable. The bigger surprise was that Mattel has skewed so hard in the other direction. In 2010, the company launched Monster High—a line of dolls, apparel, Halloween costumes, Webisodes, and eventually a television show and feature film, all aimed at girls ages six and up. Made up of the "children of legendary monsters," the school's student bodies resemble undead streetwalkers, only less demure. Take Clawdeen Wolf, "a fierce fashionista with a confident no-nonsense attitude" whose favorite activities are "shopping and flirting with the boys." Her least favorite school subject is gym, because "they won't let me participate in my platform heels." The company's timing was fortuitous: that summer, a federal appeals court overturned the $100 million verdict against MGA, paving the runway for the comeback of Bratz. The doll wars are *on*. Honestly, it is enough to make a mom beg for the days of little dustpans and baby bottles.

⚓

On the Toy Fair's last day, I visited the Fisher-Price showroom, for which I needed a special pass: not just anyone can sneak a peek at next year's Talking Elmo. The preschool girls' section was decorated with a banner on which the words BEAUTIFUL, PRETTY, COLORFUL were repeated over and over (and over) in pink script. The display included a pink DVD player, a pink camera, stick-on jewelry that could be colored with pink or orange pens (and stored in a pink purse or pink jewelry box), a Cuddle and Care Baby Abby Cadabby, and a Dora the Explorer "styling head." In the next room, a banner over the boys' section, scripted in blue, exclaimed, ENERGY, HEROES, POWER. Among the multicolored toys were "planet heroes" action figures, a robotic dinosaur, a jungle adventure set, and a Diego Animal Rescue Railway. Outside, on the streets of Manhattan, it was the twenty-first century, but the scene here in toy land was straight out of *Mad Men*, as if the feminist movement had never happened.

I'm not saying that Fisher-Price (or Mattel or Disney or even MGA) is engaged in some nefarious scheme to brainwash our daughters—or, for that matter, our sons. They wouldn't make those products or spin those sales pitches if they didn't work, and it's not as though little girls themselves are laying down the cash. So again I found myself mulling over why we parents want to—

even need to—amplify the differences between boys and girls. If the baby doll propaganda of the early twentieth century reflected adult fears that white girls would reject maternity, what anxieties account for the contemporary surge of pink-and-pretty? The desire to prolong innocence, to avoid early sexualization, may be part of it, but that does not explain the spike in cosmetics sales for preschoolers, press-on nails for six-year-olds, or R-rated fashion dolls. There is some evidence that the more freedom women have, the more polarized a culture's ideas about the sexes become: an annual survey administered to students at the University of Akron since the 1970s, for instance, found *greater* differences in perceived gender-related traits over time, especially when it came to femininity. The conviction that women are more "sympathetic," "talkative," and "friendly" rose significantly among both male and female respondents. And although women no longer saw "athleticism" or "decisiveness" as inherently masculine, men still did. Men also felt that women had become both more domineering *and* more timid, while associating masculinity more strongly than ever with the adjectives "adventurous," "aggressive," "competitive," and "self-confident."

How is one to interpret that trend? Does it indicate a need to keep the sexes distinct, one we eagerly reinforce in our youngest children? A deep-seated fear that equality between men and women will create an unappealing sameness? Or could it be that, with other factors stripped away, so many barriers broken down, we can finally admit to difference without defensiveness? Maybe even if girls aren't born loving pink, precisely, their behaviors, tastes, and responses are nonetheless hardwired, at least to a degree, and today's parents are able to accept that without judgment, even savor it. Perhaps the segregation of girl and boy cultures is inevitable. Biologically driven.

Clearly, before going any further, I needed to understand, once and for all, how much of children's gender behavior was truly inborn and how much was learned. Yet, as I left the Fisher-Price showroom, I wondered: even if nature proved dominant, what impact might this new separate-but-equal mentality have on children's perceptions of themselves, one another, and their future choices?

Chapter Four

What Makes Girls Girls?

*W*hen I was in seventh grade, my English teacher assigned our class "X: A Fabulous Child's Story." Originally published in *Ms.* magazine and later as a stand-alone picture book, it was a kind of sci-fi fable about a child, code-named X, whose sex would not be revealed until it announced itself at puberty. The scientists conducting this "Very Important Xperiment" provided X's parents with a manual containing tens of thousands of pages of instructions (there were "246½ pages on the first day of school alone!"). Mom and Dad cared for X equally; both parents played dolls and trucks with the child, shot marbles, and jumped rope. And guess what? It turned out that X "Xcelled" at everything—spelling, running, baking, football, playing house! Under X's influence, X's classmates threw off the yoke of gender tyranny: boys ran vacuums and girls ran lawn mowers. Irate parents demanded that X be evaluated by a shrink, who, tears of joy streaming down his (yes, *his*) cheeks, declared that X was "the least mixed-up child I've ever Xamined."

And they all lived neutrally ever after.

The story was supposed to illustrate how gender, really, is all a bunch of socially constructed hooey, which was the prevailing belief of the time. We were, our teacher told us, totally Free to Be You and Me (a play, as it happens, I would be cast in a few years later, performing in shorts, toe socks, and "Mork from Ork" rainbow-striped suspenders). Or were we? Flash forward three decades to 2009, when a real-life story of X caromed across the Internet: a Swedish couple had decided to indefinitely conceal their child's gender. Pop (the pseudonym they gave the child in interviews to protect the family's privacy) was two years old when the story broke. According to the newspaper *Svenska Dagbladet*, Pop's wardrobe included dresses and trousers; Pop's parents changed the child's hairstyle regularly. Pop was free to play with whatever Pop wished. "It's cruel to bring a child into this world with a blue or pink stamp on its forehead," Pop's mother proclaimed.

My sister journalists disagreed. Strongly, and not just because of the challenge posed by avoiding a definite pronoun in writing. Attitudes had shifted profoundly. Not only were there no second-wave feminist huzzahs for Pop's parents' courage in attempting to buck the new pressures of hypergendered childhood (less than a century ago—when, if you recall, all children wore frilly white dresses and unshorn hair until at least age three—Pop's androgyny would have been no biggie), but one writer decried the "violence committed on the child's sense of self" in denying Pop overt knowledge of Pop's sex, calling what the parents were doing tantamount to "child abuse." Another grimly invoked the example of a "militant feminist friend" who let her daughter play only with cars and trucks—until the day she found the girl rocking a blanket-wrapped Tonka while feeding it a bottle through its chassis. Several cited the classic 1967 case of David Reimer, one of a pair of twin boys, who was raised as "Brenda" after a bungled circumcision left him—whoops!—without a penis. When he discovered the truth as a teenager, David underwent reconstructive surgery and received testosterone injections to become a boy again, saying he had felt male all along; at age thirty-eight, he declared the experiment of his life a failure and committed suicide.

Why such rancor? It wasn't as if Pop's parents were physically reassigning their child's sex. Nor were they dictating Pop's choice of toys or clothing. Besides, banning dolls and insisting a girl play solely with trucks is hardly an exercise in equality. Quite the contrary: it disparages the feminine, signals that boys' traditional toys and activities are superior to girls'. Leaving that misconstrual aside, however, this was not the first time I'd heard the cautionary tale of the over-the-top mother forcing trucks on her despairing daughter in the name of feminism. Always attributed to "a friend of a friend," it invariably ended with—triumphant drumroll, please!—the girl swaddling and bottle-feeding her truck "babies" (though if conventionally feminine toys were verboten, how did the girls get the bottles anyhow?). It has always smacked to me of urban legend, like the story about poisonous spiders under airplane toilet seats or cell phones sparking fires in gas stations: something that *seems* as though it ought to be true because it confirms our suspicions about the unnatural consequences that will result from meddling with the natural order of things. Either way, it illustrates how fully biological determinism has come roaring back into fashion.

Doing the math, I realized that the journalists who were most outraged by Pop were the ones who would've been the daughters—metaphorically or literally—of 1970s feminists, girls who had been stuffed into endless pairs of shapeless overalls (which in itself would scar a person for life). Their moms had doubtless been well meaning, but their ideals were misguided. And boring. And they backfired: there was no way all those Carries, Terris, Randis, and Jos were going to inflict that neutered femininity on their daughters. When they had children, then—which coincided with marketers' discovery of the power of microsegmentation by age and sex—they were primed, eager, to embrace the new "postfeminist" girlie-girl. They were beyond the notion of "gender-free" childhood; they no longer needed to squash kids' inborn preferences in the name of equality, they could *vive la différence* as Mama N. intended. Good-bye, X; hello, Cinderella.

It is impossible—or at the very least unwise—to explore the culture of girlhood without confronting the question of "nature or nurture" head-on. There *have* to be innate differences between the sexes, right? How else to explain the Machiavellian manipulations of three-year-old girls or the perpetual motion of preschool boys? How else to understand the male attraction to all things that roll or the female fascination with faces? For most of us, such beliefs are a matter of life experience, grounded in instinct and personal observation rather than a bibliography of double-blind studies. I wanted to know whether there was really something essential and immutable about maleness and femaleness. Are boys and girls destined to be miniature Martians and Venusians? Or are they more like Canadians and Americans: mostly alike except for some weird little quirks, such as how they pronounce the word "about"? And even if the latter turns out to be true and the disparities are minimal, how much—if at all—do we really want to mess with them; how much do we want our children to be products of social engineering? As long as we don't consider the behaviors and interests of one sex as *inferior* to the other's, who cares? Does gender segregation matter, for either the good or the ill? What, I wondered, could science tell me about the stubbornly separate cultures of boys and girls?

༄

To begin to answer those questions, I consulted Lise Eliot, a neuroscientist and the author of *Pink Brain, Blue Brain*, a fascinating book for which she sifted through more than a thousand studies comparing males' and females' brains and behaviors. She was kind enough to offer me a quick remedial lesson in biology. Male fetuses, she explained, are bathed in testosterone in the womb; that signals the reproductive organs to do the guy thing. There is another hormonal spike shortly after birth. Boy babies also tend to be larger (both their brains and bodies) and somewhat fussier than girls and are more vulnerable to illness. For the most part, however, at least in the beginning, the behavior and interests of the two sexes are nearly indistinguishable. Both go gaga over the same toys: until they're about a year old, they are equally attracted to dolls; and until they're around three, they show the same interest in actual babies. In other words, regardless of how we dress them or decorate their rooms, when they are tiny, children do not know from pink and blue.

Then the whole concept of labeling kicks in—sometime between the ages of two and three they realize that there is this thing called "boy" and this thing called "girl" and something important differentiates them. But whatever, they wonder, could that be? There is a legendary story about a four-year-old boy named Jeremy, the son of a psychology professor at Cornell, who wore his favorite barrettes to school one day. "You're a *girl*," one of his classmates said accusingly, but the boy stood firm. No, he explained, he was a boy because he had a penis and testicles. The other child continued to taunt him. Finally, exasperated, Jeremy pulled down his pants to prove his point. His tormentor merely shrugged. "*Everyone* has a penis," he said. "Only girls wear barrettes." (Jeremy, incidentally, is probably well into his forties by now and, I imagine, wishes people would stop repeating this anecdote.)

The point is, the whole penis-vagina thing does not hold quite the same cachet among the wee ones as it does among us. Yet if toting the standard equipment is not what makes you male or female, exactly what does?

Well, *duh*, it's barrettes.

At least that's what kids think: it is your clothing, hairstyle, toy choice, favorite color. Slippery stuff, that. You can see how perilously easy it would be to err: if you wore pink or your mom cut your hair too short, you might inadvertently switch sex. It could happen: until around age five kids don't fully realize that their own identities (not to mention their anatomies) are fixed. Before that, as far as they're concerned, you could grow up to be either a mommy or a daddy. And they don't understand that other people's sex stays the same despite superficial changes— that a man who puts on a dress is still a man—until as late as age seven. "In general, the concept of permanence is hard for children to grasp," Eliot said. "The prefrontal cortex of the brain is what looks to the future, and that's the slowest part to develop. Another example would be death: young children have a very hard time understanding that a pet or a person they love who has died is gone forever. They may listen to what you say and seem to get it, but secretly they believe it can change."

It makes sense, then, that to ensure you will stay the sex you were born you'd adhere rigidly to the rules as you see them and hope for the best. That's why four-year-olds, who are in what is called "the inflexible stage," become the self-appointed chiefs of the gender police. Suddenly the magnetic lure of the Disney Princesses became more clear to me: developmentally speaking, they were genius, dovetailing with the precise moment that girls need to *prove* they are girls, when they will latch onto the most exaggerated images their culture offers in order to stridently shore up their femininity.

Initially, as a parent, I found this came as a bit of a relief. The pod princess that had taken over my daughter's body did not represent a personal failure on my part; it was entirely unrelated to anything I did or did not do, wear, or say. I couldn't even blame it on her preschool classmates. Her extremism, it turns out, was natural, something kids will and, apparently, should go through. At the same time, that left me in a quandary: Did that mean my battle to minimize the pink and the pretty had been misguided? Worse than that, was it actually harmful? I flashed on a trip to the grocery store—the O.K. Corral of our Disney Princess showdowns. Daisy had pointed to a Cinderella sippy cup. "There's that princess you don't like, Mama!" she had shouted.

"Mmm-hmm," I'd said noncommittally.

"Why don't you like her, Mama?" she had asked. "Don't you like her blue dress?"

I'd had to admit I did.

She had thought about that. "Then don't you like her face?"

"Her face is all right," I'd said, though I was not thrilled to have my Japanese-Jewish child in thrall to those Teutonic features. (And what the heck are those blue things covering her ears?) "It's just, honey, Cinderella doesn't really *do* anything."

Over the next forty-five minutes, we would run through that conversation, verbatim, approximately thirty-seven million times, as Daisy pointed out Cinderella Band-Aids, Cinderella paper cups, Cinderella cereal boxes, Cinderella pens, Cinderella crayons, and Cinderella notebooks—all cleverly displayed at the eye level of a three-year-old trapped in a shopping cart—as well as a bouquet of Cinderella Mylar balloons bobbing over the checkout line (any day now, I had muttered to myself, they'll come out with Cinderella tampons). The repetition had been excessive, even for a preschooler. At the time I'd wondered what it was about my answer that confounded her. Now, in retrospect, I fretted: what if, instead of helping her realize "Aha! Cinderella is a symbol of the patriarchal oppression of all women, another example of corporate mind control, and power to the people!" my daughter had been thinking "Mommy doesn't want me to be a girl?" By forbidding her immersion in Princess products, had I unintentionally communicated that being female (to the extent that Daisy was able to understand it) was a bad thing? Wasn't there something else she could cling to, some other way she could assert her femininity, besides dousing herself in Sleeping Beauty perfume? In one kindergarten class I read about, for instance, boys hopped to the front of the room to get their milk at snack time; during art, girls skipped to the shelf where paper was kept. Hopping made you a boy, skipping a girl. Anyone who got it "wrong" was subject to ridicule. That may sound absurd, but really, is it any more random than declaring that only girls can wear skirts?

But the Big Kahuna of sex differences, according to Eliot, is toy choice. Boys push cars, girls push strollers. You even see it in primates. In a 2002 study, researchers gave two stereotypically masculine toys (a police car and a ball), two stereotypically feminine toys (a doll and a cooking pot), and two neutral toys (a picture book and a stuffed animal) to forty-four male and forty-four female vervet monkeys. The vervets had never seen the items before and were (obviously) unaware of their connotations. The results? Though males and females were similarly drawn to the neutral items, the males gravitated toward the boy toys, while the females went for the doll and—grrr!—the cooking pot. A fluke? Maybe, but six years later, that finding was replicated by a second group of researchers studying rhesus monkeys. Meanwhile, among us humans, girls who are born with a genetic disorder that causes them to produce high levels of male hormones are more physically active than other girls and favor traditional "boy" toys.

Listening to Eliot, I began to think that the toy makers might be right in gender coding their wares. This was not just business, it was not just marketers' manipulation. I mean, if boys will be boys and girls will be girls—even among *monkeys*, for heaven's sake—there is no point in further discussion, is there? Pop will reveal Popself any day now by becoming obsessed with either Bob the Builder or Barbie (or their Swedish equivalents). And X is fated to remain in the realm of fiction.

That may be where most parents intuitively land, if less ambivalently than I, but it is not the whole story. Toy choice turns out to be one of the largest differences between the sexes over the entire life span, bigger than anything except the preference (among most of us) for the other sex as romantic partners. But its timing and intensity shore up every assumption and stereotype we adults hold: little boys naturally like backhoes, ergo men won't ask for directions. That blinds us to the larger truth of how deeply those inborn biases are reinforced by a child's environment.

Eliot's own research is in something called "neuroplasticity," the idea that our inborn tendencies and traits, gender-based or otherwise, are shaped by our experience. A child's brain, she explained, changes on a molecular level when she learns to walk, learns to talk, stores a memory, laughs, cries. Every interaction, every activity, strengthens some neural circuits at the expense of others—and the younger the child, the greater the effect. So though kids may be the most rigid about gender during the princess years, their brains are also at their most malleable, the most open to long-term influence on the abilities and roles that go with their sex. In other words, Eliot said, nurture *becomes* nature. "Think about language. Babies are born ready to absorb the sounds and grammar and intonation of *any* language, but then the brain wires itself up to only perceive and produce a *specific* language. After puberty, it's possible to learn another language, but it's far more difficult. I think of gender differences similarly: the ones that exist become amplified by the two different cultures that boys and girls are immersed in from birth. That contributes to the way their emotional and cognitive circuits get wired."

The environment in which children are raised affects their behaviors as well as their aptitudes. Boys from more egalitarian homes, for example, are more nurturing toward babies than other boys are and more flexible about toy choice. Meanwhile, in a study of more than five thousand three-year-olds, girls with older brothers had stronger spatial skills than both other girls *and* boys with older sisters; boys with older sisters were also less rough in their play than their peers. (The sibling effect worked only one way, incidentally—the younger sibling had no impact whatsoever on the older's gendered behavior, nor, interestingly, did opposite-sex twins exert such influence on each other.) Similarly—and notably for parents—in 2005, researchers found that mathematically inclined girls whose fathers believed females aren't "wired" for the subject were less interested in pursuing it. Even the tragic case of David/Brenda—the boy with the botched circumcision who killed himself after being raised as a girl—is no proof that biology trumps culture. David was nearly two when his sex was surgically reassigned as female, old enough, according to Eliot, for his brain to have absorbed a great deal about his gender; he also had an identical twin who remained male, a constant reminder of what might have been. What's more, a 2005 review of similar cases found that only seventeen of seventy-seven boys whose sex was reassigned chose to revert to male. The other sixty lived out their lives contentedly as women.

Hormones, genes, and chromosomes, then, aren't quite as powerful as we tend to believe. And that has implications for how we raise and educate our children. "If you believe it's all immutable, then what is the harm in plunking girls in a pink ghetto or letting boys get by without doing art or singing or all the things they used to like to do before they got associated with girls?" Eliot asked. "But if you believe these disparities in adults are shaped by development and experience . . ." She paused a moment. "Of course, this assumes you see a value in bringing out the full spectrum of emotional and cognitive abilities in any individual."

ᏻᎥᎥᎥᎥᏬ

On a blisteringly hot morning in Phoenix, Arizona, I stood behind a one-way mirror, the kind cops on TV use when they're watching an interrogation. But the "suspects" on the other side of the glass were not criminals: they were just a passel of preschoolers getting ready for "outside time." A little boy with freckles and a sandy Dennis the Menace cowlick came right up to his reflection, pressed his face against it, and stuck out his tongue. The woman I was with laughed. "They're used to us coming and watching," she explained, "so they figure someone is probably back here."

Released onto the playground, the children dashed around the spongy surface, splitting off from one another like amoebas, forming and re-forming their groups. The pattern in their chaos eventually became clear—girls and boys might alight next to each other but soon whirled away, back to their own kind.

And that's nothing special, right? Girls play with girls; boys play with boys. You would see it at any preschool anywhere. It was nothing special: yet to the woman I had come here to meet, Carol Martin, a professor of child development at Arizona State University and one of the country's foremost experts on gender development, it meant everything. Martin and her colleague Richard Fabes co-direct the Sanford Harmony Program, a multimillion-dollar privately funded research initiative, aimed (for now) at preschoolers, kindergarteners, and middle schoolers. Its goal, over time, is to improve how boys and girls think of and treat the other sex in the classroom, on the playground, and beyond: to keep their small behavioral and cognitive differences from turning into unbreachable gaps.

Martin, who has a shock of white hair and preternaturally blue eyes, has spent three decades looking at how kids develop ideas about masculinity and femininity, as well as the long-term implications of those beliefs. In addition to the Sanford program, she has been conducting research on "tomboys." Among her findings: a third of girls aged seven to eleven that she surveyed identified themselves with the term. Yet in previous studies up to three-quarters of adult women claimed that they had been "tomboys" as kids. That interested me: presumably, most of them were mis-remembering their past, but why? Why would recalling them-selves as less conventionally feminine be so appealing? Maybe because tomboys are resisters; they're thought of as independent, adventurous, brave—characteristics that women may prize more as adults than they did as girls. Perhaps in hindsight they feel more trapped by the trappings of girlhood than they did at the time, more conflicted about its costs. Or maybe, like me, they're merely comparing their experience with what they see around them today —the explosion of pink froth—and thinking "Well, I was never like *that*."

Martin and I left the preschool, which was on the Arizona State campus, and strolled over to the social science building to join Fabes, several other faculty members, and a group of graduate students in a conference room. This team had spent hours watch-ing preschoolers in action, painstakingly tagging their behaviors: solo play, parallel play, same-sex play, cross-sex play (that is, one boy and one girl), mixed-sex play. Fabes flipped open a laptop and, as an example, began projecting a video clip against the wall. The classroom I had just left came into view, but with different kids. A group of boys huddled around a table talking and playing (it was unclear exactly with what), while a gaggle of girls worked together to build a fort of blocks. Fade to black. In a second clip, a boy and a girl stood next to each other, watering plants.

"That's a missed opportunity," Fabes commented, pointing at the screen. "I don't understand why teachers don't see this."

I looked at him blankly. It seemed like a good thing to me: a boy and a girl playing happily together. What was the problem? "They're not playing together," he corrected. "They're playing *next* to each other. That's not the same thing. People see girls and boys playing side by side and consider that interaction, but it's not."

Typically, it is girls who initiate the church-and-state separation of childhood, pulling away at around age two and a half from boys who are too rough or rowdy. Shortly after that, the boys reciprocate, avoiding girls even more scrupulously than the girls did them. By the end of the first year of preschool, children spend most of their time, when they can choose, playing with others of their sex. When they do have cross-sex friendships, they tend not to cop to them in public—the relationships go underground. As much as the story of X would like us to think otherwise, that self-segregation, like toy choice, is universal, crossing all cultures—it appears, Martin said, to be innate. The threat of cooties continues, with boys and girls inhabiting their own worlds, through elementary school until middle school, when children realize there might be something to this opposite-sex business after all.

Every cliché I have staunchly refuted plays out in childhood single-sex groups: girls cluster in pairs or trios, chat with one another more than boys do, are more intimate and cooperative in their play, and are more likely to promote group harmony. They play closer to teachers and are more likely than boys to choose toys and activities structured by adults. Boys, on the other hand, play in packs. Their games are more active, rougher, more competitive, and more hierarchical than girls'. They try to play as far as possible from adults' peering eyes.

Martin and Fabes make clear that they are not pushing for 1970s X-style neutrality. They do not want to discourage or even necessarily diminish segregated play. "We just want to offset its limitations," Martin explained. "A little girl who only plays with girls and learns the gender behavior and interaction of little girls . . . well, what they do together is limited. Same with little boys." Single-sex peer groups reinforce kids' biases, and over time, as Lise Eliot pointed out, that changes their brains, potentially defining both their abilities and possibilities. By age four, girls—who have a small inherent advantage in verbal and social skills—have outstripped boys in those areas. Around the same time, boys, who have a slight natural edge in spatial skills, begin pulling ahead on that front.

This separation of cultures, as anyone who was ever a child will recall, also contributes to an us-versus-them mentality between males and females. That not only provides endless material for third-rate stand-up comics but, Fabes and Martin believe, undermines our intimate relationships. Years of same-sex play leave kids less able to relate to the other sex—and can set the stage for hostile attitudes and interactions in adolescence and adulthood. "This is a public health issue," Fabes proclaimed. "It becomes detrimental to relationships, to psychological health and well-being, when boys and girls don't learn how to talk to one another. That divergence of behavior and communication skills in childhood becomes the building blocks for later issues. Part of the reason we have the divorce rates we do, domestic violence, dating violence, stalking behaviors, sexual harassment, is lack of ability to communicate between men and women."

Eliminating divorce or domestic violence may be an ambitious mandate for a preschool curriculum, but it's not without basis: young children who have friends of the other sex have a more positive transition into dating as teenagers and sustain their romantic relationships better. But how does one go about changing behavior that is not merely entrenched but, apparently, inborn? Sometimes, Martin explained, it is easier than one might imagine. Take the case of the boy and girl watering the plants: an alert teacher just needs to mention how the kids are helping each other. "When teachers comment on mixed-sex or crossed-sex play, the likelihood it will happen increases. When they stop commenting, it stops happening. So they need to reinforce it." Although the curriculum is still in its earliest phases of development, Martin said, it will focus on creating "a higher sense of unity" as a classroom rather than as girls and boys—by choosing a group mascot together, for example. Teachers will be advised not to divide children by gender when lining them up to go outside; there might be "buddy days" or other cooperative learning opportunities during which boys and girls work together. Teachers can integrate discussions of similarities into classroom activities ("Lots of kids like pizza: some are girls and some are boys"). There will also be a series of lessons about exclusion and inclusion involving "Z," a genderless cartoon alien who is trying to figure out our world. Kids may still largely stick with their own sex, Martin acknowledged, and that's fine, but maybe they will play more together as well.

Consciously encouraging cross-sex play clearly runs counter to toy marketers' goals. It also defies a hot trend in education reform: using brain research to justify single-sex classrooms in public schools. Proponents such as Leonard Sax, the author of *Why Gender Matters* and president of the National Association for Single Sex Public Education, claim that the differences between boys and girls are so profound, so determinative, so immutable that coeducation actually does kids a disservice. Among the assertions: boys hear less well than girls (and thus need louder teachers), see action better, and are most alert when taught while standing up in a chilly room. Girls, by contrast, like it hot—their classrooms should be around 75 degrees and decorated in warm hues—prefer sitting in a circle, and excel at seeing colors and nuances. Even if all that were true (a dubious assumption: multiple studies have, for instance, shown that sex-based hearing and vision differences are so negligible as to be irrelevant), presumably, segregation would only deepen those divides, increasing the distance between boys and girls and making them strangers to each other.

At any rate, gender is a pretty weak predictor of a child's potential gifts or challenges; the differences within each sex in any given realm (including math and verbal skills) tend to be far greater than the ones between them. Jay Giedd, the chief of brain imaging at the Child Psychiatry Branch of the National Institute of Mental Health, told *The New York Times* that assigning kids to classrooms based on gender differences would be like assigning them to locker rooms based on height: since males tend to be bigger, you'd send the tallest 50 percent of kids to the boys' side and the shortest 50 percent to the girls'. You might end up with a better-than-random outcome, but not by much: there are simply too many exceptions to the rule. Nonetheless, the number of single-sex public schools and classrooms has skyrocketed since the mid-1990s, due largely to the influence of Sax and his colleagues. That made me rethink Lise Eliot's comment about her work: the presumption that we, as a society, want to bring out the full potential in all of our children. What parent would disagree with that? Yet we are often reluctant to examine assumptions and actions that amplify gender differences—even if that means we create a self-fulfilling prophecy.

I am not against single-sex schools in the private sphere (as long as they don't justify their existence through half-baked "brain research"), but I would much rather have Daisy and her classmates, male and female, take part in something like the Sanford program. I hope Martin and Fabes are right and their work can, down the line, improve relationships between the sexes, both in the workplace and in the home (at least, as Fabes joked, "we can guarantee none of our research subjects will divorce in the next five years"). I hope it encourages kids to work together more effectively regardless of differences within or between the sexes— teaching them to appreciate the bumps in the playing field rather than trying to level it entirely. But it will be years before they know for sure, before the curriculum is fully in place, before they figure out how to evaluate its long-term efficacy.

I left Phoenix feeling less concerned that Daisy had suddenly gone femme on me—that now seemed both unavoidable and healthy. At the same time, if early experiences with mixed-sex play have a lifelong positive impact on kids' behavior, aptitudes, and relationships, the segmentation of every possible childhood item by sex was more troubling than I had initially imagined—and for a whole new slew of reasons. I felt better educated as I headed home, better grounded in theory, but no closer to understanding how to put it into practice while raising a daughter: where was the point that exploration of femininity turned to exploitation of it, the line between frivolous fun and JonBenét? Maybe to stake out that middle ground, I needed to check out the extreme.

Chapter Five

Sparkle, Sweetie!

At six in the morning on a summer Saturday in Austin, Texas, Taralyn Eschberger was getting ready to sparkle. She was perched on a chair in the Hill Country Ballroom of a Radisson hotel, her blue eyes still bleary with sleep as a makeup artist fussed around her, plucking sponge rollers from her hair, teasing and combing out the curls, preparing to augment them with a cascading hairpiece whose strawberry blond shade precisely matched Taralyn's own. Next, to bring out her features, came blush, candy pink lipstick, cerulean eye shadow, black liner and mascara; then press-on nails that simulated a French manicure. The makeup artist held up a hand mirror, and Taralyn nodded, satisfied. A little bronzer on her legs to even out her spray tan (which keeps her from looking washed out under harsh stage lights), and she would be ready to compete for the $2,000 Ultimate Supreme prize at the Universal Royalty Texas State Beauty Pageant.

Did I mention that Taralyn was five years old?

Taralyn's mom, Traci, a former dancer turned medical sales rep, watched from a few feet away, smiling. She could well have been a beauty queen herself: tall and slim, with highlighted blond hair, enviably perky breasts, gleaming white teeth, and, even at this hour of the morning, her own makeup meticulously in place. She showed me the dress Taralyn would wear in the pageant, a two-piece off-the-shoulder turquoise number with a crystallized Swarovski rhinestone-encrusted bodice, a frothy, multitiered tutu skirt, and a detachable choker necklace. Serious contenders like the Eschbergers can pay up to $3,000 a pop for these hand-sewn "cupcake dresses," though since the seamstress who made this one "just *loves* Taralyn" and uses the girl as a model, Traci got it at cost. Even so, the $16,000 Taralyn had won so far during her year in competition wouldn't nearly cover her expenses: the dance coach, the makeup artist, the home tanning equipment, the head shots, the extravagant frocks and swimwear, not to mention the entry fees—which can run as high as $1,000—as well as travel, accommodations, and meals for the thirty pageants she'd attended in Florida, Tennessee, Kentucky, and Texas. With that level of investment, Traci said, you had better bring your best game: you had better be prepared. You had better pay attention to every detail, and every detail had better be perfect. In addition to hair and makeup, girls in the tooth-losing phase famously wear "flippers"—custom-made dental prosthetics that cover any gaps to create a flawless smile. Taralyn had one but rarely used it. "When the judges are sitting further away from the stage, it does make their smile look bigger," Traci said. "But it doesn't look natural. It doesn't look like her. I like her cute little smile."

Taralyn hopped off the chair, presented herself for Traci's approval. "You look just like a princess!" the older woman exclaimed, and her daughter grinned. I recalled museum portraits I had seen of eighteenth-century European princesses—little girls in low-cut gowns, their hair piled high, their cheeks and lips rouged red—that were used to attract potential husbands, typically middle-aged men, who could strengthen the girls' families' political or financial positions. So, yes, I thought, I suppose she does look like a princess.

Any sane mother would find the pageant world appalling, right? They would feel queasy, as I did, at overhearing a woman advise her six-year-old that "one of the judges is a man, so be sure you wink at him!" or a father telling a TV reporter that he enjoys getting a sneak peek at what his four-year-old will look like when she's sixteen. It would be easy pickin's for me to attack parents who tart up their daughters in hopes of winning a few hundred bucks and a gilded plastic trophy; who train them to shake their tail feathers on command, to blow kisses at the judges and coyly twirl their index fingers into their dimpled cheeks.

But really, what would be the point? That story has been told, to great success and profit. *Toddlers & Tiaras*, which each week follows families through a different pageant, has been a megahit for TLC, and the more evil and clueless the "momsters" it covers, the better. Traci herself was once featured on the show, grabbing Taralyn's arm and reprimanding her for flubbing a routine. ("They filmed two days of positive footage," Traci told me, "then that was what they chose to air. We were stupid to fall for it. We were dumb.") MTV, HBO, *The Tyra Banks Show*, *Good Morning America*, *Nightline*, and even England's august BBC have all featured the "controversy" over baby beauty queens. The formula each of those followed was as clever as it was foolproof: a parade of preschoolers tricked out like Las Vegas showgirls was followed by commentary from psychologists who (with good reason) link self-objectification and sexualization to the host of ills previously mentioned—eating disorders, depression, low self-esteem, impaired academic performance. The moms defend their actions, the psychologists rebut, the moms get the last word, the girls take the stage again, and the piece is over. The shows purport to be exposés, but in truth they expose nothing, change nothing, challenge nothing. What they do is give viewers license, under the pretext of disapproval, to be titillated by the spectacle, to indulge in guilty-pleasure voyeurism. They also reassure parents of their own comparative superiority by smugly ignoring the harder questions: even if you agree that pageant moms are over the line in their sexualization of little girls—*way* over the line—where, exactly, is that line, and who draws it and how? What might those little princesses reveal about how the rest of us, we supposedly more enlightened parents, raise our own daughters?

A spangled blue curtain hung behind the stage of the Radisson's ballroom. A row of glittering tiaras and banner-draped trophies—some up to five feet high—stood in front of it. A table off to one side was laden with smaller trophies, giant teddy bears, and "goodie bags" stuffed with candy and toys. Every contestant at a Universal pageant walks away with a prize; for that privilege, they pay a mandatory $295 general entry fee (which includes the

Formal Wear competition), a $125 DVD fee, a $15-per-person admission fee, plus optional fees of $50 to $100 each for additional events such as the swimsuit competition, facial beauty, "Mini Supremes" (which carries a $200 cash prize), talent, and hair/makeup. It was easy to see how child pageants, which are the fastest-growing segment of the pageant market, have become a reported multibillion-dollar industry.

Universal Royalty had already been featured three times on *Toddlers & Tiaras*. It is the country's largest "high-glitz" child pageant system, according to its owner, Annette Hill, a former child beauty queen herself, whose two grown daughters were also pageant vets. A tall African-American woman dressed simply in a black sheath, her hair swept into a French twist, Miss Annette, as she is known, was also the pageant's mistress of ceremonies: she stood behind a lectern introducing contestants in each category, from infants on up. Her nonstop stage patter included the children's names, their favorite foods (pizza for the older kids; "a big plate of mashed bananas" for the babies), TV shows (*"Hannah Montana*, of course"), hobbies ("swimming, talking on the phone, and shopping and shopping and shopping!"), as well as a detailed description of each outfit. The girls strutted across the stage in turn, pausing to wave at the judges or to pose with their chin on folded hands, jiggling their heads like baby dolls newly come to life. Surprisingly, few were classically pretty and several were on the chunky side—stripped of their glitz, I would never have pegged them for pageant queens. But beauty was not exactly what they were being judged on. It was more about how well they performed pageant conventions—the walk, the stage presence, the nonstop smile, the nymphet moves—and, of course, the flashy outfits and gaudy makeup. Judges and parents referred to this as "the total package."

Taralyn was one of the front-runners in the pageant's sweet spot, the four- to six-year-old division, in which competition was fiercest. Her chief rival, Eden Wood, was a chubby-cheeked, tow-headed four-year-old from Taylor, Arkansas (population 566), who had been on the pageant circuit since age one. Eden's mother, Mickie (who, like many of the moms, was once a contestant herself), was notorious for her on-the-spot, uninhibited coaching. Most of the girls' mothers used hand signals, similar to the kind you would see at high-end dog shows, to remind their daughters of where they were supposed to walk, when to stop, when to spin. But Mickie planted herself a few yards behind the judges, out of their sight lines but well within her daughter's, and performed Eden's routine exuberantly right along with the girl. Mickie was a big, busty woman, but she could still shake it. It was a mesmerizing sight—together mother and daughter bent their arms at the elbow, turned up their palms, and twirled. Together they blew kisses over their shoulders at the judges, together they vamped and waved, together they leaned forward and shimmied. Their movements were so synchronized that it seemed as if they were attached by an invisible string, marionette and puppeteer. Periodically Mickie punctuated their dance with encouraging shouts of "E. E.!" and "Go, baby!" and "Get it, girl!" Miss Annette, meanwhile, noted that Eden's ambition was "to rule the world."

Pageant parents are surely not the only ones who could be accused of living through their children. Think about gymnastics, ice skating, ballet, competitive cheerleading, acting, soccer, spelling bees, concerto contests, math meets. A number of those, while requiring more specialized skills, can be as potentially objectifying of girls as pageants. And for each, I suspect, you'd hear the same justifications as the ones I heard from every single pageant mom I spoke with, almost as if they had memorized a script:

Pageants build a child's confidence, give her a kind of poise that will someday be useful in job interviews and professional presentations. Their daughters do plenty of things that have nothing to do with beauty or body (Eden Wood drives a miniature pink 4×4 all-terrain vehicle back in Arkansas). Pageants are about old-fashioned Hollywood-style glamour, not sexualization—if you think a five-year-old looks sexy, then *you* are the sick one. What's more, their girls *choose* to compete: "If she didn't want to do this, there's no way I could make her," I was repeatedly assured, and "The second she says she doesn't want to do it, we'll stop." Hearing that reminded me of the classic marketers' defense: "We just gave the girls what they wanted." But once again the questions arose: Where does desire end and coercion begin? When does "get to" become "have to"? I'm not sure parents who are that deeply invested in their children's success are able to tell. And if love, however subtly, seems conditional on performance—whether on the playing field, in the classroom, or onstage—how can a child truly say no?

"Did you see how she watched her mother?" Traci Eschberger asked when Eden's routine was over.

I nodded. "It was amazing," I replied, still in awe of the display.

Traci smiled tightly—that was not the response she was going for. "Eden has been doing this for years," she explained, "and she *still* has to watch her mother for every move? Taralyn never had to do that."

Case in point: when Taralyn hit the stage, Traci offered her no direction, though she did stand where her daughter could see her and occasionally called out, "Sparkle, sweetie!" which, as it happens, is precisely what Shirley Temple's mother used to say before the cameras rolled. Taralyn sauntered across the stage, threw the requisite kisses, then, in a move all her own, skipped along the front edge, pointing to each judge in turn and winking. She was so light on her feet, she almost floated. It was clear she had inherited her mother's grace and athleticism. I mentioned this to Traci, who nodded, pleased, then added, "You can't force that. She loves to perform. She *wants* to be onstage."

After a break, the swimsuit competition began. Taralyn's father, Todd, an affable redhead in a maroon polo shirt, entered the ballroom with their nine-year-old son, Tallon, also a strawberry blond and, like Taralyn, a handsome kid. Or he would have been, if circumstances had been different. Tallon was born with severe mental and physical disabilities: his brain, for reasons that were never determined, had not developed past infancy, leaving him unable to hear, talk, walk, or even sit up on his own. He was gripping an electronic plastic Simon game, its lights flashing in random patterns that users are supposed to memorize and replicate. Although he couldn't play, he seemed fascinated by the blinking colors. Todd parked Tallon's wheelchair on an aisle and took a seat next to him, stroking the boy's arm as he watched the girls onstage. Occasionally, Tallon banged his toy too loudly against his wheelchair tray; Todd gently extracted it, then handed it back a few minutes later. His patience never wavered, nor did Traci's. Their devotion to their son was both rock-solid and devoid of self-pity. I might question what they were doing to their daughter, but I admired how they cared for their son.

After Tallon was born, his doctors had advised the Eschbergers against having any more children. They didn't listen. "I said, 'You know what?'" Traci recalled. "'We have to have faith that we'll have a normal, happy child.' And now I think God is blessing us on the other end of the spectrum because Taralyn's very bright and talented. So we have both ends. We have one child who will not, unfortunately, be able to do a whole lot. But we're just thankful he's still with us."

I glanced from Tallon to Taralyn, with her wide smile and supple body. Her brother's health crises had been hard on her. That's part of why the family had been so gung ho about the pageants. "I feel guilty because she lost the first two years of her life because of Tallon," Traci told me. "At that point, we couldn't leave the house. It was that debilitating." Pageants became a way for Taralyn to escape, a "special time" when the focus was solely on her. Often, she and her mother would go to competitions alone and enjoy a bit of girl bonding. "We cherish these weekends," Traci said. "We really do. We get to stay at the hotel, and Taralyn gets to go swimming and jump on the bed."

Of course, that "special time" did not have to involve dressing up like Pretty Baby. Still, I could sympathize with the pride—the relief—the Eschbergers must feel whenever Taralyn is crowned, when she is publicly celebrated not only for her normalcy but for her miraculous perfection. I could only imagine how difficult the family's path has been, the lifelong burden Taralyn will carry: the mixture of resentment and protectiveness, love and guilt. She did deserve something of her own, a place to be free, to be a child—maybe even, for a moment, to feel that she, or at least her life, is perfect. And isn't that, at its core, what the princess fantasy is about for all of us? "Princess" is how we tell little girls that they are special, precious. "Princess" is how we express our aspirations, hopes, and dreams for them. "Princess" is the wish that we could protect them from pain, that they would never know sorrow, that they will live happily ever after ensconced in lace and innocence.

I had seen several television shows featuring the Eschbergers, but none had mentioned Tallon. I suspect that would have complicated the story, elicited sympathy from the disapproving audience, humanized the parents—thrown shades of gray into a narrative that is best seen in black and white. I'm not letting the Eschbergers (or parents like them) off the hook, but it is so easy to portray the freak-show aspects of these families. No question, they have taken the obsession with girls' looks to an appalling extreme; but, one could argue, the difference between them and the rest of us may be more one of degree than of kind. "Ordinary" parents might balk at the $3,000 dress or the spray tan, but guess what? In 2007, we spent a whopping $11.5 billion on clothing for our seven- to fourteen-year-olds, up from $10.5 billion in 2004. Close to half of six- to nine-year-old girls regularly use lipstick or gloss, presumably with parental approval; the percentage of eight- to twelve-year-olds who regularly use mascara and eyeliner doubled between 2008 and 2010, to 18 and 15 percent, respectively. "Tween" girls now spend more than $40 million a *month* on beauty products. No wonder Nair, the depilatory maker, in 2007 released Nair Pretty, a fruit-scented line designed to make ten-year-olds conscious of their "unwanted" body hair. And who, according to the industry tracking group NPD, most inspires girls' purchases? Their moms. As a headline on the cheeky feminist Web site Jezebel.com asked, "How Many 8-Year-Olds Have to Get Bikini Waxes Before We Can All Agree the Terrorists Have Won?"

◦━━◦

Watching the pageant contestants promenade onstage, I thought about a suburban shopping mall I had visited some months earlier to check out a store called Club Libby Lu. Aimed at the VIP (Very Important Princess) ages four to twelve—again, a span whose extremes, it seems, should have little in common—it was conceived of by Mary Drolet, a Chicago-area mother and former executive at Claire's (she later sold out to Saks for $12 million). Walking into a link of the chain, I had to tip my tiara to her: Libby Lu's design was flawless, from the logo (a crown-topped heart) to the colors (pink, pink, pink, purple, and more pink) to the display shelves scaled to the size of a ten-year-old (though most of the shoppers I saw were closer to six). The decals on the walls and dressing rooms—I LOVE YOUR HAIR, HIP CHICK, SPOILED—were written in what they called "girlfriend language." The young salesclerks at this "special secret club for superfabulous girls" were called "club counselors." The malls themselves were chosen based on a secret formula called the GPI, or "Girl Power Index," which, in an Orwellian bit of doublespeak, predicts potential profitability.

Inside, I browsed through midriff-baring tops with ROCK STAR scrawled across them in sequins, cheerleader outfits, feather-covered princess phones, pillows emblazoned with the word BLING in rhinestones. I moseyed over to the "Style Studio," where a seven-year-old girl was being transformed into a "Priceless Princess" through a "Libby Du" makeover. Her hair was teased into an elaborate updo, crowned with a tiara, and liberally sprayed with glitter. Blue eye shadow was stroked across her lids, followed by a dusting of blush and watermelon pink lip gloss. *Hello, Taralyn!* Libby Lu also offered birthday parties at which, after their makeovers, girls could ramp up the tunes and strut a catwalk pretending to be Pussycat Dolls or supermodels. So, okay, they weren't competing for money (however, the makeovers *cost* as much as $35 per child), and they probably were not doing it every weekend—though kids do go to an awful lot of birthday parties, and they are often all the same—but still, how different was the message?

When Libby Lu started, the typical customer was about ten, but over the next few years that age gradually drifted downward, so that the girls I saw making their own cosmetics at the Sparkle Spa station were closer to Taralyn's age. Marketers call that KGOY—Kids Getting Older Younger. The idea, similar to the rejection of Barbie for Bratz by six-year-olds, is that toys and trends start with older children, but younger ones, trying to be like their big brothers and sisters, quickly adopt them. That immediately taints them for the original audience. And so the cycle goes. That's why the cherry-flavored Bonne Bell Lip Smackers that I got as my first "real" makeup at age twelve are now targeted at four- to six-year-olds (who collect flavors by the dozens). I have often idly wondered, since those same KGOY theorists claim that adults stay *younger* older—fifty is the new thirty!—whether our children will eventually surpass us in age. Or perhaps we will all meet at a mutually agreed upon ideal, a forever twenty-one.

But I don't want my daughter to be twenty-one when she is twelve. I don't think *she* will want to be twenty-one when she is twelve, not really. As it is, girls are going through puberty progressively earlier. The age of onset of menstruation has dropped from seventeen at the beginning of the twentieth century to barely twelve today; pediatricians no longer consider it exceptional for an eight-year-old to develop breasts. That means ten-year-old girls frequently resemble sexually mature women—sexually mature women who have been encouraged, in an unprecedented way, to play at being hot since early childhood. Yet, although they are physically more advanced, the pace of girls' psychological and emotional development has remained unchanged; they only look, and act, older on the outside. In his thoughtful book *The Triple Bind*, Stephen Hinshaw, the chair of the Department of Psychol-

ogy at the University of California, Berkeley, warns that imposing any developmental task on children before they are ready can
cause irreparable, long-term harm. Consider the trend toward
academically accelerated preschool: at best, young children who
are drilled on letters and numbers show no later advantage compared with those in play-based programs. In some cases, by high
school their outcomes are *worse*. That inappropriately early pressure seems to destroy the interest and joy in learning that would
naturally develop a few years later. Girls pushed to be sexy too
soon can't really understand what they're doing. And that, Hinshaw argues, is the point: they do not—and may never—learn to
connect their performance to erotic feelings or intimacy. They
learn how to act desirable but not how to desire, undermining
rather than promoting healthy sexuality.

It would seem, then, that parents should be working harder
than ever to protect their daughters' childhoods, to prevent them
from playing Sesame Street Walker. And most parents you would
talk to, whatever their policy on child-friendly eye shadow for
three-year-olds, would say that is exactly what they are trying to
do. But I can't help recalling an article describing the ways pageant moms rationalize their behavior. Two strategies particularly
caught my eye. The first was "denial of injury"—the idea that the
children are not harmed by the experience and may actually benefit. The second was "denial of responsibility": they may personally disapprove of pageants, but their four-year-olds *so* wanted
to compete that they had no choice but to comply. Rejigger that
wording a bit, substitute "Disney Princess 21-piece play makeup
set" or "mani-pedi birthday party" or "Rock & Republic Jeans,"
and it sounds like a conversation you would hear on any suburban
playground.

I don't mean to imply that shielding one's daughter from

sexually charged toys, clothing, music, and images is easy. They are, after all, standard fare in the aisles of the big-box stores. Even Walmart's size 4–6X Sassy Vampiress Halloween getup with its tight pink-and-black bustier top (for what bust, I ask you?) hardly raises an eyebrow. One exception: in 2010, a video went viral featuring a group of eight- and nine-year-old competitors in a national contest—dressed in outfits that would make a stripper blush—bumping and pumping to Beyoncé's "Single Ladies (Put a Ring on It)." The routine sparked public outcry, was berated on CNN and FOX News, and truly, it was a gift to the world's wired pedos. But I sympathized (sort of) with the girls' parents, who went on *Good Morning America* to defend them: the choreography had been lifted from a scene in *Alvin and the Chipmunks 2*, in which gratuitously tarted-up "Chipettes" shook their furry booties to the same tune while Al and his bros leered. No one had objected to *that*. The girls were only mimicking what they had seen in a family film (which, by the by, has raked in more than $440 million worldwide).

I am hardly one to judge other mothers' choices: my own behavior has been hypocritical, inconsistent, even reactionary. There was the time when Daisy was four and we were walking through the Los Angeles airport on the way to visit her paternal grandma. Daisy's eye fell on a display of Ty Girlz dolls, made by the same company that brought you Beanie Babies, best known for the faux pas of creating dolls based on Malia and Sasha Obama without permission (which the company was forced to rename). Ty Girlz are like a plush version of Bratz, for the fashion-forward preschooler. They have names such as "Oo-LaLa Olivia," "Classy Carla," and "Sizzlin' Sue." But they're cuddly. And apparently they exude some invisible gamma ray that hypnotizes small girls. "Mama!" Daisy cried, dashing over to the wire rack of dolls that had been placed in front of a newsstand. "Can I have one of those?" I took in the Angelina Jolie lips, the heavily shadowed eyelids, the microscopic skirts, the huge hair—and I kept right on walking.

"No," I said.

"But maybe for my birthday?" she tried.

Something in me snapped. "No!" I said, more firmly than was strictly necessary. "Not for your birthday, not for Chanukah, not for anything. You will never, *ever* get one of those dolls!"

"But *why not?*" she pressed.

I wanted to yell, *"BECAUSE THEY'RE SLUTTY, THAT'S WHY!"* But I didn't, because Lord knows I did not want to have to explain what "slutty" meant. Instead I relied on the default parenting phrase, a prim "Because they're inappropriate."

"But *why* are they unappropriate?"

Suddenly I was furious. Why should I even have been put into a position where I had to have this conversation with my four-year-old? I felt as though Ty Girlz had me over a barrel, a barrel to whose slats I would have to become increasingly accustomed. I didn't want to tell her why I objected to the dolls, because the explanation itself was as "unappropriate" as the product. And, yes, it could have been an opportunity for yet another lesson, but I was sick and tired of being confronted by these endless "teachable moments." It was beginning to dawn on me that I had been caught in a cunningly laid trap: I was attempting to offer Daisy more choices—a broader view of her possibilities, of her femininity—by repeatedly saying no to her every request. What were the odds *that* was going to work? Even the forbidden-fruit argument I so often hear seemed a scam: it still forced me to buy something I did not even want her to know about in the hope that it would quench her desire rather than stoke it, that she would, as Disney's

Andy Mooney had said, "pass through the phase" rather than internalize it (earning his company a tidy profit in the meanwhile).

So I found myself ping-ponging through girl land. I gave in on Polly Pocket with her endless itty-bitty rubber clothes, but not to the Pollywheels Race to the Mall racetrack set ("The first car to reach the boutique captures a shopping bag!"). Yes to Groovy Girls (which, like Pollys, have gotten markedly skinnier and more fashion-conscious since they were introduced), but absolutely no way to Ty Girlz. And Barbie? Oh, Barbie, Barbie, Barbie. The fifty-year-old vector of all body-image complaints. She, too, has been the catalyst of many a toy store meltdown—mine, not my daughter's. I am not proud of the incident at Target when, while I was off searching for cleanser, Steven told Daisy she could have a cheesy blue Fairytopia Barbie with crappy plastic wings. I demanded that he take it away from her. She started to cry. So I gave it back.

"You're confusing her," Steven said.

I did the mature thing: I blamed him.

"Look, I'm sorry I started this," he replied. "But you need to decide where you stand on this stuff and stick to it."

He was right, so I took the doll away again. I promised I would get her a *well-made* Barbie instead, perhaps a Cleopatra Barbie I had seen on eBay, which, at the very least, was not white or blond and had something to offer besides high-heeled feet. As if the ankh pendant and peculiar tan made it all okay.

"Never mind, Mama," she sobbed. "I don't need it." Then I started to cry, too, and bought her the damned Barbie.

No wonder my kid is confused. So am I.

By noon, the four- to six-year-old competition was over, and crowning would not begin until eight that evening. Taralyn, still full of energy, continued to perform her routines in a corner, just for her own pleasure, then, obligingly, several more times for the TV crews who descended on her. "I haven't seen this many reporters outside of some kind of presidential press conference," Traci joked.

It was true: there were moments that day when it seemed as though there were more press than contestants. And the cameras all focused on Taralyn and Eden, though they were far from the only girls here. I wandered over to where Jamara Burmeister, age seven, was preparing for her first statewide contest, in the six- to seven-year-old division. Jamara was the only girl under eleven dressed in a floor-length gown: its full, Cinderella-style skirt was rose and white, decorated with bows and accessorized with elbow-length gloves and a strand of pearls. Her hair was swept up, a few tendrils escaping. She looked comparatively dignified, more like a flower girl than a high-glitz competitor. Which meant, essentially, that she was doomed.

"We didn't know," explained Jamara's mother, Tammi. "We'd never done this before."

Their only pageant experience was back home in south Texas, where contestants were more natural and, unlike in Universal pageants, were evaluated in part by how they handled interview questions both onstage and in unrehearsed private meetings with the judges.

It was Jamara's father who had originally pushed to put her into pageants, after seeing an episode of *Toddlers & Tiaras*. "He saw those girls and thought, 'Jamara could do that,'" Tammi said. "Because she's, well . . ." She paused and smiled. "Every parent thinks their child is beautiful. But Jamara has got 'it,' you know?"

Jamara entered her town pageant earlier this year and won handily. "She was so enthusiastic," Tammi said, "we decided to try this. It's her thing, and we're going to run with it."

Pageant families come from all walks of life. There are those, like the parents of JonBenét Ramsey, who are white and affluent, who spend thousands of dollars on dance classes, voice coaches, gowns, wigs, head shots. Eden Wood's mother, Mickie, said she has spent about $70,000 on her daughter's pageant career. Most of the folks competing in Austin, though, were of more modest means. Jamara, who like many contestants was Latina, raised money for her gown and entry fees by going door-to-door among the businesses in her small town asking for sponsorship. As Tammi adjusted the girl's skirt and fussed with her hair, she told me that she and her husband could not afford the competition on their own. They run an answering service and, last year, in addition to their own five children, took in three more, those of an employee with a drug problem, to keep them out of the foster care system. "We prayed about it a lot," she said of that decision. "It was the right thing to do."

Again I found myself looking at a pageant mom through a different, more compassionate lens. As with Traci, there was something else going on here. It seemed that, for a variety of reasons—a disabled child, the hope of upward mobility, an escape route from small-town life—these little girls had become the repository of their family's ambitions. That made a certain kind of sense. Historically, girls' bodies have often embodied families' upwardly mobile dreams: flawless complexions, straight teeth, narrow waists—all have served as symbols of parental aspirations.

A few days ago, I might have been appalled to see a seven-year-old decked out like Jamara, but after six hours of immersion in the world of pageants, my standards had begun to shift. I was starting to see the girls as their parents did—as engaging in a little healthy fun, merely playing an elaborate version of dress-up. Yet even pageants had not always promoted the Lolita look. Back in the 1960s, when children's competitions began, all a contestant needed to enter was a party frock, a pair of Mary Janes, and a satin hair bow. The rest was introduced over time, as prize money escalated, competition intensified, and both contestants and pageants needed to distinguish themselves. "I thought it was bizarre, too, when we started," Traci Eschberger had told me. "I didn't think I'd ever do it. I do think all that makeup makes them look older. But we wash it off as soon as the pageant ends. As long as she's having fun and it's not hurting her."

Maybe that's what happens to us in the "real" world, too. Our tolerance for hypersexualization rises without our realizing it. Moxie Girlz seem subdued after our exposure to Bratz. We get used to seeing twelve-year-olds in lip gloss, low-slung jeans, and crop tops that say BAD GIRL, and soon the same outfit seems unremarkable on an eight-year-old. A woman who did not get her first manicure until she was twenty-five finds herself throwing a "primping" birthday party for her seven-year-old at a nail salon in Brooklyn. Parents in San Francisco send kids whose ages are still in the single digits to a spa summer camp where they "de-stress" by creating their own makeup and moisturizer (as if third-graders are in danger of developing wrinkles?). It is easy to become impervious to shock, to adjust to each new normal. Also, as mentioned earlier, even brief exposure to stereotypes—in advertisements, television shows, and the like—unconsciously increases women's and girls' acceptance of them. At one point, looking around the ballroom, I actually caught myself thinking, Hell, my daughter could do this, too.

By nine that night, an hour into the crowning ceremony, the girls were exhausted. One four-year-old lay splayed across three chairs, arms akimbo, asleep, still wearing her cupcake gown, snoring sweetly, small bubbles of spit gathering at the corner of her mouth. The rest of the girls had become a blur of sequins, fake tans, and big hair. I could hardly tell one from another. According to Miss Annette, Taralyn and Eden were in a dead heat for the top prize. "The judges are looking at personality," she said. "They're looking at facial beauty. They're looking at expressions, the overall appearance of the dress, the modeling ability. So it's a very, very hard competition, very stressful."

When the lesser awards for the four- and five-year-olds were announced, Taralyn cleaned up, winning trophies for most beautiful, most photogenic, best swimsuit, and best personality. But it was Eden who took the division crown. I assumed that was a loss, but Traci's smile as she clapped for her daughter's rival looked too real. She explained that if you win the division, which carries no cash prize, you're done: out of the running for everything else. So this result was actually a good thing, what they wanted.

Jamara, meanwhile, did not win a single trophy in her division. Her parents didn't know that should give them hope for the bigger prizes until I told them. A few minutes later, she took the crown for Little Miss Sweetheart. No cash came with the title, but she and her family seemed pleased. "I don't feel bad that she didn't win something bigger," said her father, Jason, who had dressed in a suit and tie for the occasion. "I don't want her to alter herself like these other girls. I just want her to feel comfortable with her looks and feel good about her natural beauty. That's what's important to us."

"This was definitely out of our league," added Tammi, Jamara's mother. "It's not what we're used to. It wouldn't have occurred to me to buy one of those tutus. But we're just starting out. It was a learning experience. Next time we'll know. And we'll be back."

Across the room, Taralyn sat on the floor near her mother, surrounded by her trophies. She had dumped out the contents of her goodie bag and was busily gobbling up the candy and twisting the Play-Doh into pretend rings and bracelets. She did not much seem to care about what was happening onstage, though when the Grand Talent winner was about to be announced she squeezed her eyes shut and gritted her teeth in anticipation. When the name called was not hers, she relaxed. "Yes!" she said happily, then went back to playing. She was still in it.

Finally, all the sets of "ice crystal rhinestone" crowns, gilt trophies, and monogrammed sashes had been handed out except one, as had all the smaller cash prizes for the "Mini Supremes." Miss Annette milked the final, suspenseful moment like a pro. "And the winner of the Universal Royalty Texas State Pageant Overall Grand Supreme and a two-*thousand*-dollar cash prize is . . ." She waved the money, twenty crisp hundred-dollar bills which, as is typical in pageants, had been spread out and stapled into a double-decker fan. "Miss . . ." Another wave of the cash. *"TARALYN ESCHBERGER!!!"* Taralyn let out a war whoop as Todd hoisted her aloft and Traci leapt to her feet, clapping wildly. The girl ran to the stage, accepted the fan of money, then displayed it to the crowd, remembering first to place her feet in perfect third position and paste her best beauty queen smile on her face. TV cameras rolled and flashbulbs popped: in child pageants, the money shot *is* the money shot.

The evening's other winners joined Taralyn onstage for a

photo session. Partway through, she stifled a yawn—it was nearly ten o'clock, long past her bedtime—but before anyone noticed, she put that trouper smile right back on, pulled back her shoulders, and . . . sparkled.

Maybe someday Taralyn will wash off her pageant mask forever, rebel against it. Maybe she won't. Maybe she will even put her own child into pageants, either because she loved the experience or because she is trying to recapture the attention and adoration she received on nights like this. Maybe the affirmation of her beauty will indeed build her confidence—given how important girls, *all* girls, learn beauty is, why wouldn't it?—or maybe being judged as if she were an object will eventually undermine it. Maybe one day Taralyn will come to believe she is loved only for her beauty, loved only if she can *stay* beautiful—thin and unblemished, with the right breasts and teeth—if she can be perfect, if she does not let her parents down. One prominent former child beauty queen, nineteen-year-old Brooke Breedwell, who at age five was featured in the BBC documentary "Painted Babies," has attributed her poise as an adult to her pageant experience. She has also said that pageants damaged her relationship with her mother and instilled a crippling need to be perfect at anything she tries. Who knows whether the same will be true for Taralyn?

As the stagehands struck the set, they offered bouquets of helium balloons to the children who were straggling out. Taralyn was ecstatic with hers. She was only five, after all. Two thousand dollars meant nothing to her, but twenty balloons—now, *that* was a prize. "I could have just gone down to the party store and saved a lot of money," her father, Todd, said to me, and smiled.

We both watched as Taralyn zoomed across the room with her balloons, laughing. Just like an ordinary five-year-old. Just a little girl having fun.

Chapter Six

Guns and (Briar) Roses

Mama, can I have this for Chanukah?" I was standing in Mr. Mopp's, our charmingly dilapidated neighborhood toy shop, looking for a birthday present for a friend's toddler. Although Daisy was barely five at the time, I could not, for the life of me, remember what bestirred the three-year-old heart. The changes kids go through are so quick, so intense, and you are so bloody exhausted when they're happening. It feels as though you'll never forget, but you always do. All I could recall about three was that it was the age when kids supposedly stop shoving pennies up their noses. So how to celebrate that blessed milestone, the safety of small parts: A Playmobil set, perhaps? Marbles? I admit I felt a certain pressure: the child in question was a princess-loving female, but her mother (and all of the other moms who would be at the party) knew how I felt about that. They would be watching, skeptical and bemused, to see if I could come up with a viable alternative.

While I mulled over the options, Daisy hit the dress-up rack and promptly became mesmerized by a pair of purple plastic mules festooned with faux ostrich feathers accompanied by a string of cheap, glittery beads that wouldn't hold together for five seconds. Tawdry *and* badly made—what a bargain! She pretty much expected the "no" she got when she showed me that one. A few minutes later, though, she was back, brandishing something else: a die-cast silver cap gun with a shiny pink grip and matching vinyl holster cunningly embellished with a cowgirl on a horse.

How many ways could that toy blow the modern mommy's mind? But rather than being appalled, I found myself sinking into reverie. I have two older brothers, and as a girl I had loved playing with their hand-me-down pistols: the feel of the grip in my hand, the shiny muzzle, the satisfying snap when the hammer released, the acrid sulfur smell rising from a roll of red caps, the thrilling possibility of burning a finger (did that ever really happen?). I was not a violent kid. Nor am I a violent adult: I road-tripped from rural Ohio to New York City in the 1980s to march against nuclear proliferation. I took to the streets in San Francisco during the first invasion of Iraq. (At the time of the second, Daisy's nap time conflicted with the protests. Priorities change . . .) In fact, I am already against the *next* war. In other words, playing with guns did not make me a sociopath. On the other hand, there was no industry trying to convince me that violence was the cornerstone of my femininity, no pressure to define myself by my bullets.

Daisy already owned a cowgirl hat, woven of straw and trimmed in red. I had bought it when she was around four years old, because I thought it was adorable—and because I hoped it might offset the princess stuff.

"But what do cowgirls *do*, Mama?" she asked when I placed it on her head.

I was at a bit of a loss. Among my peers, cowboy play had ridden off into the sunset when we realized that the Indians were not necessarily the bad guys. So what was left? Judging by TV shows about the Wild West, such as David Milch's *Deadwood*, the answer was cussing, whoring, and getting stinking drunk.

"Um," I said, reaching for another option, "I guess they keep track of all the cows?"

So much for the romance of the Old West. She never wore the hat again.

But a gun. Should I let her have a *gun*?

Thinking quickly, I told her we were not there to buy a present for *her*, but if she wanted, she could put the gun on her birthday list. Then, when we got home, I asked Steven what he thought. He shook his head. "I don't see any reason to have war toys in the house," he said.

But, I pressed, didn't you love your guns as a child?

"Sure," he admitted. "But that was a different time."

I also polled my friends. "No way," said the one with five children. Then she paused. "Well, if one of the girls wanted one it would be okay, that would be defying stereotypes. But not the boys. *Never* the boys." This from a woman whose house was awash with light sabers, Transformers, and swords.

"Do you also refuse the girls makeup and Barbies but let the boys have them?" I asked.

At this point she began to get annoyed, so I let the subject drop.

And honestly, let's be realistic. Playing with a toy gun—even yelling "Bang! Bang! You're dead"—was not going to turn my kid (or hers) into Hannibal Lecter. In addition to my beloved pistols, I watched stupefying amounts of Tom and Jerry and Road Runner cartoons (probably while hopped up on Froot Loops followed by a Pixy Stix chaser), though, admittedly, I found them as excruciating as I do the recent craze for Larry David–style "cringe humor."

The truth is, there is virtually no research on the impact of violent images or play on girls. For whatever reason—biological, environmental, developmental—girls are not as drawn to bashing one another as boys are. Their aggression tends to be more interpersonal than physical. It is worth considering, though, that adults tend to ignore behavior that doesn't fit our beliefs about gender and seize upon that which does. So when boys point their fingers like pistols, we chalk it up to nature; when girls do it (and I have seen Daisy draw her "hand guns" on friends a number of times), it goes unnoticed. Either way, violent play is not by definition bad or harmful for kids. Any child shrink worth her sand table will tell you it can help them learn about impulse control, work out the difference between fantasy and reality, cope with fear. But there is a catch: according to Diane Levin, a professor of education and coauthor of *The War Play Dilemma*, violent play is useful only if it *is* truly play, if kids control the narratives, if they are using their imaginations to create the story lines, props, outcomes. That is what has changed since my own cap gun days, she explained. Beginning in the 1980s, children's television advertising was deregulated; the number of commercials instantly doubled—you could run the same cereal ad three times in a row if you wanted. Programs themselves essentially became vehicles to sell toys. My Little Pony. Rainbow Brite. Care Bears. Girls were flooded with a resurgence of sweet and pretty. Boys were deluged with action figures: Masters of the Universe, Teenage

Mutant Ninja Turtles, Power Rangers. In surveys of parents and teachers across the country, Levin found that, rather than engaging in creative play, children began imitating what they saw on-screen, reenacting rote scripts with licensed products. Whether in Portland, Maine, or Portland, Oregon, their play became homogenized. Nor was there evidence that their stories were evolving, that they were making the kind of inner meaning out of their dramas that would provide psychological resolution, as they once had.

So to an extent, then, my husband was right: times had indeed changed. As for guns that are not "really" guns, Levin told me, "We're fooling ourselves if we think those are better. When you give kids a light saber, you know exactly what they are going to do with it, and every kid who has one will do the exact same thing. There is no creativity there." Like princess play, then, boys' gunplay may resonate with parents' own childhood memories, but, given the marketing culture in which they are immersed, their relationship to those toys and images, as well as the impact on them, may be different.

I will leave the world of boys for someone else to explore, but it is clear that children of both sexes crave larger-than-life heroes. They need fantasy. They also, it seems, need a certain amount of violent play. I'm not talking Resident Evil 4, where within minutes gamers confront a female corpse pinned to a wall with a pitchfork through her face, but something that allows them to triumph in their own way over this thing we call death, to work out their day-to-day frustrations; to feel large, powerful, and safe. Because as much as we want to believe that children are innocent, by the time they enter the dog-eat-dog jungle of preschool, they have realized that everyone is capable of senseless cruelty and spite. Even their parents. Even themselves. The Big Bad Wolf is out there, baby, and Mom and Dad may not be able to stop him.

Which brings me back to fairy tales. After World War II, Allied commanders banned publication of the Grimm brothers' stories in Germany, believing that their bloodlust had contributed to the Nazi atrocities. For the same reason, they fell out of favor among American parents. Take the brothers' "Snow White": at the end the wicked queen is invited to her stepdaughter's wedding, where—surprise!—she is forced into a pair of red-hot iron shoes and made to dance until she dies. Like I need my five-year-old to have that image in her head?

The thing is, though, if you believe the psychologist Bruno Bettelheim, we avoid the Grimms' grimness at our peril. His classic book *The Uses of Enchantment* argues that the brothers' gore is not only central to the tales' appeal, it's crucial to kids' emotional development. (An earlier intellectual rock star, John Locke, disagreed; he deemed the fairy tales too gruesome for little ears, but then again, he also thought the offspring of the poor should be put to work at age three.) According to Bettelheim, fairy tales and *only* fairy tales—as opposed to myths or legends—tap into children's unconscious preoccupations with such knotty issues as sibling rivalry or the fear of an omnivorous mother. In their tiny minds, a fearsome giant may be transformed into the school bully, a menacing wolf into a neighbor's pit bull. Fairy tales demonstrate that hardship may be inevitable, but those who stand fast emerge victorious. What's more, he wrote, the solutions to life's struggles that fairy tales suggest are subtle, impressionistic, and therefore more useful than either the spoon-fed pap that passes for kiddie "literature" these days or the overly concrete images of television (and now the Internet). He goes so far as to say that without exposure to fairy tales a child will be emotionally stunted, unable to create a meaningful life.

I guess *Knuffle Bunny Too* won't do.

Nor, apparently, will the stacks of revisionist, modern-day princess books I had checked out of the library. Anyway, most of them seem to equate "pro-girl" with "anti-boy," which does not strike me as an improvement. Take *The Paper Bag Princess*, a staple of kindergarten classrooms everywhere. The heroine outwits a dragon that has kidnapped her prince, but not before the beast's fiery breath frizzles her hair and destroys her dress, forcing her to don a paper bag. The ungrateful prince then rejects her, telling her to come back when she is "dressed like a real princess." She summarily dumps him and skips off into the sunset happily ever after, alone.

To me, that is *Thelma & Louise* all over again. Step out of line, and you end up solo or, worse, sailing crazily over a cliff to your doom. I may want my girl to do and be whatever she dreams of as an adult, but I also hope she will find her Prince (or Princess) Charming and make me a grandma. I do not want her to be a fish without a bicycle; I want her to be a fish with another fish. Preferably, a fish who loves and respects her and also does the dishes, his share of the laundry, and half the child care. Yet the typical "feminist alternative" to the marry-the-prince ending either portrays men as simpletons or implies that the roles traditionally ascribed to women are worthless. Thus you get *Princess Smartypants*, in which our heroine, uninterested in marriage, bestows a chaste smooch on the prince who has won her hand in a contest sponsored by her father, the king; the prince promptly turns into a frog, and she is freed to live contentedly with her pets. To me, that's not progress; it's payback.

Unquestionably, the Grimms routinely bumped off mothers, equated beauty with virtue, and pitted women against one another in a battle over husbands. Understandably, parents' first impulse is to keep the stories' grisliness far, far away from their children. But what if Bettelheim was right? What if their horrors do help our kids to explore their fears safely, to answer the Big Questions of existence? Should we deny them that wealth in favor of a $50 "official" Cinderella gown? Maybe I had been hasty in dismissing fairy tales as a bastion of passive heroines and Prince Charming hype. Uncle Walt may have most successfully reinterpreted the tales for our era, but why should he get the final say? Maybe I needed to revisit the traditional stories myself.

What do you know: I began with a (toy) gun to my head and found that when I stared down the barrel, I was once again looking smack into the eyes of Cinderella.

⚬⚬⚬

Calling the Grimms' fairy tales the "originals" is as absurd as conferring that designation on Disney's. The brothers culled their stories from a rich, distinctly adult oral storytelling tradition, then edited, embellished, and heavily sanitized them. Did you seriously think the prince merely *kissed* the comatose Sleeping Beauty? That Rapunzel and her beau whiled away their time in that phallic tower holding hands? Before the Grimms gussied them up for the nursery, both girls were in a family way—each pregnant with *twins!*—well before the Happily Ever After kicked in. Fairy tales have been called the porn of their day: bawdy, raucous, full of premarital shenanigans and double entendre. They were also rife with incest or the threat of it. The Grimms took that out, too. The brothers' delicacy, however, did not extend to violence: on the contrary, they ratcheted up the bloody bits, believing they would scare children out of bad behavior.

As for Cinderella (whom the Grimms called "Aschenputtel," a name which, understandably, did not catch on)? There are at least five hundred versions of that story told around the world. The Chinese Yeh-Shen, whose story was recorded in A.D. 850, gets her mojo from the carcass of a dead fish. The Japanese Hachikazuki spends years with a flowerpot wedged on her head. The Russian Cinderella is saved by a magic cow; in Brazil she is born with an enchanted snake curled around her neck. There are Cinderellas in African tribes and Native American ones. Her slippers are made of glass, fur, or gold, and sometimes there is no footwear at all. But the basic plotline never wavers: a beautiful, kind girl is brought low by a parent's untimely death, then humiliated by her new guardian; she is transformed through some act of bippity-boppity-boo so that her exterior sparkles as brightly as her heart; she loses an item of clothing while fleeing a love-besotted noble-man who relentlessly tracks her down; there is the big reveal of her true identity—bummer for the evil relatives!—and she lives happily ever after with the man of her dreams. Apparently we, like our preschoolers, are suckers for that arc. Even today, Cinderella stories are guaranteed box-office hits: *Pretty Woman*, *Ever After*, *Maid in Manhattan*, *Ella Enchanted*, *Princess Diaries* (I *and* II)—even *Enchanted*, which gently spoofed the genre. Something so enduring, so universal must have—well—*something*, right? Perhaps I had judged this particular princess too harshly.

There is no pumpkin in the Grimms' "Aschenputtel," no foot-men, not even a fairy godmother. Disney cribbed those from "Cendrillon," a seventeenth-century French version by Charles Perrault. Instead, Jacob and Wilhelm's heroine plants a hazel branch on her dead mother's grave, waters it with her tears, and watches it grow into an enchanted tree. Whenever she wishes for something—such as, oh, a gown for the ball—a dove perched among the leaves tosses it down to her. I liked that: her mother's love was so powerful that it transcended death. Admittedly, the story still sucks for stepmoms. If it is any comfort, psychologists say that splitting the mother into two characters—one good and one evil—serves a developmental purpose: it helps kids work through their inevitable resentment against Mom without directly copping to it. To which my stepmother friends respond: "Whatever."

That aside, making the mother the source of the magic interested me. One of the things I had found most disturbing about the Disney Princesses was that somehow the wand had been transferred to the girl. The heroines of the stories had never before been magic—not even in the studio's own movies. It was not enough that the writers had whacked all the mothers and made their surrogates loathsome; now they had given the boot to the fairy godmother as well—the sole remaining symbol of adult female guidance and protection. It was almost sinister, the implication that women had no place in girls' development. And it certainly reflected the current marketing mentality—cut out the middleman (or, in this case, woman), and sell directly to the child. I often wonder what the long-term results of that change will be: rather than raising a generation of Cinderellas, we may actually be cultivating a legion of stepsisters—spoiled, self-centered materialists, superficially charming but without the depth or means for authentic transformation.

I say: let's bring back that tree!

But the biggest surprise of "Aschenputtel" is that it's not about landing the prince. It is about the girl herself: her strength, her perseverance, her cleverness. It is a story, really, about her evolution from child to woman. It is Cinderella herself who plants the magic tree and requests the finery for the ball (which is celebrated over the course of three days). She walks to the party each night rather than traveling by enchanted coach. She leaves not because she has some arbitrarily imposed curfew but because she has danced enough. Then she escapes both the pursuing prince and her own father by hiding in a dovecote or nimbly scaling a tree. When the prince finally comes a-calling, shoe in hand, Cinderella greets him dressed in her sooty rags. He may be looking for the beauty with the dainty foot, but, as Joan Gould, the author of *Spinning Straw into Gold*, notes, she demands that he witness the woman she has been, dirt and all, not just the one she will become. So while he provides the occasion for her transformation, he is not the one responsible for it—she can only do that herself.

Not bad for a pair of medieval chauvinists. Except for this: as usual, the stepsisters try on the tiny golden slipper before Cinderella does; in order to jam their big fat clodhoppers into it, one slices off her heel and the other her toe. Some fancy academic might see that as a metaphor, a warning to girls against contorting themselves to fit unattainable standards of beauty, but, truly, it is just gross. And the Grimms seem to relish it, describing how the sisters grit their teeth, how the blood "spurts" from the shoe, staining their white stockings. Even Cinderella, seemingly so gracious, proves distressingly vengeful in the end. She invites the stepsisters to join her wedding party, but as they enter the church, one on either side of her, doves (again, perhaps, representing her mother) perched on the bride's shoulders peck out their eyes. That's right: Peck. Out. Their. Eyes. Imagine *those* wedding photos.

Still, I thought, remembering Bettelheim, I would not want to permanently scar my kid by denying her the blinding of the stepsisters. Maybe I could work up to it, start with something easier, like, I don't know, "Rumpelstiltskin." My memory of that story was a little vague, something about a gnome spinning a roomful of straw into gold and flying away on a spoon. How bad could that be?

A few days after the gun incident, I decided to give it a try. I hauled out my annotated Grimms, a 462-page tome with a navy-and-gold filigree cover. Daisy was, well, enchanted. We flipped through, examining its nineteenth- and early-twentieth-century illustrations (Bettelheim, who believed that pictures corrupt the power of the text, would have disapproved). Then I started reading.

"Once upon a time . . ." I began.

At the sound of those ageless words, Daisy snuggled close. I kept going: "there lived a miller who was very poor, but had a beautiful daughter." Okay, I thought, as the story moved forward, maybe the girl is treated like chattel by her dad and is supposed to be delighted to marry the greedy king who initially imprisoned and threatened to kill her if she did not make him rich, but at least there's no gushing blood. And the girl is resourceful, tricking the gnome and saving her baby. She even has a vaudevillian's sense of dramatic timing, stringing her tormentor along, pretending she does not know who he is until . . .

"Could your name possibly be, *Rumpelstiltskin?*"

Daisy's eyes shone as I continued. "The little man screamed and in his rage he stamped his right foot so hard that it went into the ground right up to his waist. Then in his fury he seized his left foot with both hands . . ."

My eye skipped ahead but it was too late: " . . . and tore himself asunder," I finished lamely.

Yikes! What happened to the spoon?

"He did what, Mommy?" Daisy asked, confused.

"Well," I said, "he was so mad, he ripped himself in half."

"Oh," she said, nodding.

Then: "Read another!" she commanded.

What to do? I considered ditching the Grimms for Hans Christian Andersen, maybe trying the original "The Little Mermaid." I have already grumbled about Disney's Ariel, who gives up her *voice* to get a guy. What kind of message is that? I ask you. I suddenly recalled, though, that Ariel got off easy compared with her precursor. In the Andersen version, the sea witch does not painlessly extract the mermaid's voice. Oh, no. She grabs a big old knife and hacks out the poor creature's tongue. Once the girl has her land legs, every step feels like "walking on knife blades so sharp the blood must flow," yet she dances for the prince on command, never hinting at the agony it causes her. As in the Disney film, the prince seems to return her love but then heaves her over for someone else, a princess he wrongly believes has saved his life. In this version, however, he never discovers the truth; he marries the other woman, explaining to the mermaid that he knows she would want him to be happy. Then the lout asks her to hold up the train of his bride's gown during the shipboard ceremony—and *she does it*, knowing all along that his marriage to another means her demise. Late that night, the mermaid's sisters appear; they have shorn their hair and traded it to the sea witch for a magic dagger. All the little mermaid has to do is stab the prince in his heartless heart; his blood on her legs will fuse them back into a fish tail and she will survive. But she can't do it. Instead, she flings herself overboard and disintegrates into sea foam. The only nod to happily-ever-after is that she eventually becomes a "daughter of the air" who, after three hundred years of good deeds, *might* earn an immortal soul. There may be valuable lessons in all of this—don't change for a guy; don't let him treat you like dirt; you deserve to be loved for what is special, magical, unique about you. But jeez, what a buzz kill.

So "The Little Mermaid" was out. But Daisy was still sitting next to me, looking expectant. Okay, Bruno, I thought. It's now or never. I took a deep breath and turned to "Cinderella."

Daisy listened intently for a while, then rolled onto her back and began kicking her legs in the air.

"Do you want me to stop, honey?" I said hopefully.

"No," she said firmly.

So I read it, the whole thing, without censorship, explanation, or any inflection to influence her reaction. Just as Bettelheim said I should. Then I asked what she thought.

"Eh," she said, waggling her hand.

"You didn't like it?"

"It was creepy," she said, wrinkling her nose. "The eye part. Yuck."

"Would you ever want to hear it again?"

She thought about that for a moment. "No," she said, then jumped off the couch and skipped away, chanting "Roo coo coo! Roo coo coo! Blood is dripping from the shoe!" and laughing.

Later, I would search out lesser-known traditional fairy tales about spunky, ingenious girls. I was surprised to find how many there were—at least as many as stories that celebrated the bravery of boys or men, perhaps more. Yet none was problem-free: In "The Robber Bridegroom," the heroine shrewdly foiled her fiancé's plot to murder her—after she secretly watched him tear off another young woman's clothes, hack her body into pieces, and salt it. In "Fitcher's Bird" a feisty girl saved her sisters from an evil wizard who had kidnapped them—by reassembling their limbs, which he had severed so that their "blood ran down all over the floor." In "Furrypelts," a Cinderella variant, a princess fearlessly took control of her destiny, fleeing her castle upon discovering she would be forced into marriage—to her father. "The Six Swans," in which a princess took a seven-year vow of silence to save her cursed brothers, became a favorite with Daisy even though the evil mother-in-law took advantage of the heroine's muteness by stealing each of her three babies upon their births, smearing chicken's blood on the princess's unspeaking mouth, then telling her son that the girl had eaten them (Mom-in-Law also tries to convince the castle cook to make the infants into a stew and feed them to their father). I loved Diane Wolkstein's adaptation of "The Glass Mountain," which amped up the princess's role in her own fate, but Daisy rejected it (as would Dr. Bruno, I reckon). She was partial to an Algonquin Indian legend—admittedly not an official fairy tale—about a young bride who saved herself and her husband from cannibal demons, but . . . cannibals? I put the kibosh on that. No matter how macabre the stories got, though, Daisy did not flinch. None gave her the kind of nightmares that the movie version of *Chitty Chitty Bang Bang* had.

Score one for Bettelheim.

Compared with Stephenie Meyer, the Grimms come off like Andrea Dworkin. Meyer, a Mormon homemaker turned novelist, is the author of the most successful fairy tale in recent memory: the *Twilight* saga. Initially imagined in a "vivid dream," the four-book series had, at this writing, sold more than 100 million copies worldwide, while films based on the first two had grossed more than a billion dollars. No wonder it has been compared to crack for teenage girls.

Twilight follows the ethereally named Bella Swan, who, at age sixteen, moves in with her father in the Pacific Northwest so

Mom can tag behind her new hubby on the minor-league baseball circuit. On the first day of school, Bella meets the prince of her new hometown's royalty: the hypnotically handsome, brilliant, mysterious, wealthy—did I say handsome?—Edward, who at first seems repelled by her. But no, she has merely confused uncontrollable attraction with open disgust: Edward, it turns out, is a "vegetarian" vampire (that is, he does not feed on humans) who finds the scent of Bella's blood intoxicating. Being near him puts her in mortal danger, yet she is powerless to resist. As is he. The two fall in love, and for some 2,444 pages (or about 483 minutes of film) pursue their chaste, star-crossed romance, which is further complicated by Jacob Black, a hunky werewolf, also in love with Bella, whose pack members despise vampires.

But it is Bella, not the supernaturals she falls in with, who is the true horror show here, at least as a female role model. She lives solely for her man; when he leaves her in *New Moon*, the series' second installment—something about needing to protect her from him, which sounds like the vamp version of "It's not you, babe, it's *me*"—she is willing to die for him as well. Realizing that she conjures Edward's image at times of extreme danger, Bella flings herself off a cliff into a stormy sea and nearly drowns: "I thought briefly of the clichés, about how you're supposed to see your life flash before your eyes. I was so much luckier. Who wanted to see a rerun, anyway? I saw *him*, and I had no will to fight. . . . Why would I fight when I was so happy where I was?"

Oh yeah, I want my daughter to be *that* girl.

Even before the self-destructiveness kicks in, Bella has little to recommend her. Scratch that: absolutely *nothing* to recommend her. She is neither smart, interesting, kind, graceful, nor even pretty—more Ugly Duckling than Bella Swan. She is in perpetual need of rescue. She pines for an emotionally unavailable guy who simultaneously vows to protect her and warns that his love for her might make him kill her. She repeatedly reminds him that he is too good for her, and, except for the little business about his being undead, it is hard to disagree. Edward's (and Jacob's) attraction to Bella—at least in the books—is inexplicable.

There has been much hand-wringing over why today's girls would go for such claptrap. Colette Dowling, whose best seller *The Cinderella Complex* explored women's unconscious resistance to independence, has suggested that perhaps girls still feel "some fear they can't really take care of themselves." The social critic Laura Miller mused on *Salon* that "some things, it seems, are even harder to kill than vampires"—specifically, the dream of being rescued by a dreamy-looking, powerful man who instantly perceives how special you are: who will support you, adore you, and cushion you from life's hardships. Yet why should that fantasy be dead or even surprising? We have drilled our daughters in it from the time they wore diapers—diapers decorated with Disney Princesses.

Bella may be a Cinderella; however, she is no Aschenputtel. Her story comes squarely from the Disney tradition, in which the plotline has shifted from the heroine's transformation to the prince's courageous battle to possess her; she, rather than he, is reduced to a narrative device. And that—Bella's overweening blandness—as much as the guilty-pleasure rescue fantasy, may explain the series' appeal: *Twilight*'s heroine is so insipid, so ordinary, so clumsy, so Not Hot.

Isn't that great?

Think about it: what a relief that must be for girls who feel constant pressure to be physically, socially, and academically perfect! Bella does not spend two hours with a flatiron, ace her calculus test, score the winning goal in her lacrosse match, then record a hit song. Bella does not spout acidly witty dialogue. Bella does not wear $200 jeans on her effortlessly slim hips. Even in the Hollywood incarnation, as played by Kristen Stewart, she is relatively plain, modestly attired, and excruciatingly awkward. Yet Edward, the most desirable dude in the room, loves her— now, *that* is a fairy tale. The fact that he refuses to consummate their relationship may make him all the more attractive to post-pubescent girls weary of the mandate to be sexy and please boys. (The couple does consummate their relationship once in book four, on their wedding night, but readers are not privy to the moment.) So, yes, Edward, the dangerous, emotionally withhold-ing male, is a parent's worst nightmare. Yes, Bella's perspective on intimacy is warped. Yes, the series glamorizes dating abuse. Yes, reading the books makes me grind my teeth until my jaw pops. And yet . . . *Twilight* may have given girls something they needed: a way to explore their nascent sexuality on their own terms, to feel desire rather than perform it. Sure, I prefer *Buffy the Vampire Slayer*, whose tough-but-vulnerable heroine meets the challenges of romance and sex head-on, but I understand the im-pulse. *Twilight* lets a girl feel heat without needing to look hot. In that way, its popularity seems less problematic than what girls see every day in magazines and on screens big and small: the example set by real-life, flesh-and-blood celebrity "princesses" as they attempt to transform from girl to woman.

Chapter Seven

Wholesome to Whoresome:
The Other *Disney Princesses*

*t*he photograph captures its subject in that liminal space between girlhood and womanhood. She sits naked, seemingly perched on an unseen bed, a satin sheet clasped to her chest as if caught by surprise. Her hair is tousled, her lipstick slightly mussed. Has she just woken up? If so, was she alone? She gazes at the viewer over one shoulder, her languorous eyes just a touch defiant.

In many ways, it is an artful portrait: the contrast between pale skin and dark hair; the sculptural folds of the sheet; the vulnerability of her emerging sexuality; the shock of her scarlet lips. Maybe if the girl had been older—say, eighteen rather than fifteen—or if she hadn't spent the previous two years positioning herself as the world's most responsible role model for eight-year-olds (a Faustian, if lucrative, bargain), it might all have been perceived differently. But she wasn't. And she had. The girl, of course, was Miley Cyrus, also known as Hannah Montana. Until the publication of that photo in the June 2008 issue of *Vanity Fair*, she had represented all that was good and pure and squeaky clean about Disney's intentions toward our daughters: the promise, begun in the Princess years, that if parents stuck with the brand—letting girls progress naturally from Cinderella to the Disney Channel divas with their TV shows, movie spin-offs, and music downloads—our daughters could enjoy pop culture without becoming pop tarts. Remember the in-house survey at Disney in which moms associated Princess with the word "safe"? That is how we're meant to perceive the entire brand, from toddler to tween. Safe. Innocent. Protective. Sheltering. So when that image blazed across the Internet, parents felt not only furious but betrayed. "Miley Cyrus is younger than my daughter!" railed one daddy blogger. A second wrote, "Holy Hell! What on earth were her parents thinking?" A mom fumed, "She is a *child* for God's sake," and another, referring to the Everest of available Hannah Montana gear, wryly quipped, "Bonfire anyone?"

Poor little rich girl! Miley was quoted in the accompanying article as saying she thought her seminudity was "really artsy. It wasn't in a skanky way," then later had to backpedal hard, releasing a formal mea culpa to her fans. "I took part in a photo shoot that was supposed to be 'artistic' and now, seeing the photographs and reading the story, I feel so embarrassed. I never intended for any of this to happen." Still there was speculation: how premeditated was this "slip"? Was she apologizing all the way to the bank? Were Miley and her master-"minder" father, the country singer Billy Ray Cyrus, consciously trying to nudge the singer's image, to prepare her for the next step of her career? In the *VF* profile, the writer Bruce Handy asked, "How do you grow up in public, both as a person and as a commodity?"

I reread that sentence several times as I scrutinized the notorious photo. Handy might more specifically have wondered how you grow up in public as a *woman* and a commodity, what Miley's attempts and missteps would mean not only for her but for her millions of worshipful fans. By the time girls are five, after all, the human Disney Princess du jour is meant to supplant the animated ones in their hearts. Miley. Lindsay. Hilary. Even, once upon a time, Britney (who launched her career in 1993 as a Mouseketeer on *The All-New Mickey Mouse Club*). All were products of the Disney machine. Each girl's rise became fodder for another media fairy tale, another magical rags-to-riches transformation to which ordinary girls could aspire. But some two hundred years after the Grimm brothers first published their stories, had that trajectory become any more liberating? The nineteenth-century Cinderella, Sleeping Beauty, and Snow White served as metaphors, symbols of girls' coming-of-age, awakening to womanhood. The contemporary princesses do as well, and though the end point may be different—marrying the handsome prince has been replaced by cutting a hit single—the narrative arc is equally predictable. In their own way their dilemmas, too, illuminate the ones all girls of their era face, whether publicly or privately, as they grow up to be women—and commodities.

The year 2000 was a banner year for monarchy. At least at Disney. Because, just as Andy Mooney was having his "could've had a V8" moment at the Phoenix ice show, realizing that the hundreds of girls who were using their *imaginations* to dress as Cinderella could instead be buying *official licensed products*, Anne Sweeney, then president of the Disney Channel Worldwide, was preparing a coronation of her own. Up until that point, the network broadcast mainly classic cartoons for the toddler set as well as films like *Pollyanna* that harkened back to the golden age before Walt himself was (supposedly) cryopreserved. Like Mooney, Sweeney, who had a ten-year-old son, saw a marketing vacuum that begged to be filled: the "underserved" 29 million or so kids who were hovering between Mickey Mouse and MTV. The trick was to find shows that appealed both to tweens and to the parents who still monitored their viewing habits. Nickelodeon had hit the mark a few years earlier with the charming *Clarissa Explains It All*, proving in the process that a female lead could play to both sexes (previous conventional television wisdom had held that while girls would watch a male protagonist without complaint, the reverse was untrue, so hanging a show on a female star would instantly halve your market share). Sweeney, too, saw potential in a perky, semiempowered female character, though—again like Mooney—I'm not sure she realized how monumental that decision would come to be. At any rate, she gave the green light to *Lizzie McGuire*, a sitcom starring the then-twelve-year-old Hilary Duff, which portrayed the frothy fun and foibles of a just-like-you-but-cuter middle school girl.

Lizzie premiered as a weekly show on the Disney Channel in January 2002; it was an instant smash and overnight launched Duff as Disney's first multiplatform "mogurl." Within a year, *Lizzie* was airing daily. There were a series of spin-off *Lizzie* books, a *Lizzie* clothing line, and a *Lizzie* sound track (which went platinum). Duff's face graced Happy Meals, dolls, games, room decor, jewelry. *The Lizzie McGuire Movie*, released in 2003, debuted at number two its opening weekend and grossed nearly $50 million in the United States. Its sound track also went platinum. Duff quit the franchise soon after the film's release, when Disney refused to meet her price on a new contract. She has subsequently attempted, with mixed success, to re-create that empire on her own. For its part, Disney simply replicated *Lizzie*'s formula with a new "property," former Cosby kid Raven-Symoné: filming sixty-five episodes of her equally inoffensive show, *That's So Raven*, in rapid succession—before the star could age—then airing them at leisure (not to mention ad nauseam). There was the now-familiar tsunami of merchandise. The hit movies included *The Cheetah Girls*, based on a series of books about four high schoolers who start a band (Raven starred as the lead singer, Galleria, a word that, as it happens, means "shopping mall"). As Disney Channel's first original musical, *The Cheetah Girls* not only launched its own ginormous juggernaut but laid the groundwork for the eventual monolith *High School Musical*.

Then came Hannah. For those of you who may have spent the last decade on planet Romulus, *Hannah Montana* is a sitcom about a girl with a secret: Miley Stewart (played by Miley Cyrus, who took on the role at age thirteen) is an ordinary teen by day, but by night she becomes—a POP STAR! Only her best friends know the truth; everyone else is miraculously fooled by the Barbie-blond wig she wears onstage. Apparently, in Miley Stewart's world—unlike Miley Cyrus's—there are no paparazzi with telephoto lenses camped outside celebrities' homes, no journalists asking annoying questions, no Internet gossips analyzing their every move or circulating incriminating cell phone pics (one nosey parker reporter does catch up to her in the Hannah Montana movie, only to be won over by her cornpone charm). Miley Stewart's father and minder/manager is played by Billy Ray Cyrus, who—wait for it—is Miley *Cyrus's* real-life father and minder/manager! (He's also the mullet-haired impresario behind the song "Achy Breaky Heart.") *Hannah Montana* debuted in March 2006; as of this writing, it boasted a reported 200 million viewers globally. The album *Hannah Montana 2/Meet Miley Cyrus* spent twelve consecutive weeks in *Billboard*'s top five, the first double album to do so since Stevie Wonder's *Songs in the Key of Life* in 1977. Tickets for Miley/Hannah's 2007 seventy-city Best of Both Worlds Tour sold out within minutes; some were later scalped for thousands of dollars. The limited-release 3-D film of the event earned the highest per screen box-office average *ever* and went on to gross $70 million; a year later, *Hannah Montana: The Movie* pulled in more than $155 million worldwide. The amount of stuff with Hannah/Miley's face on it rivals that of all the animated princesses combined. Toys "R" Us even sells Hannah Montana hand sanitizer. According to *Portfolio* magazine, Cyrus is on track to be worth $1 billion by her eighteenth birthday (eat her dust, Duff).

Hannah's appeal is obvious: she is the fresh-faced girl next door with just enough gumption to make her interesting to kids but not so much as to be threatening to parents. Fans love her wardrobe and bouncy girl-power-lite lyrics; and, for the most part, the songs don't make adults' ears bleed. Hannah is by no means perfect: the show filters its sunny lessons (usually some version of "be yourself") through the lens of celebrity, subtly suggesting that famousness itself is the greatest possible achievement—even as it denies that is the case. Clarissa and Lizzie were comparatively real—or at least real-esque—teens, closer to the ones that graced the small screen back in the day when you had to stand up to change the channel. In that bygone era, Marcia Brady was ashamed to have her boyfriend see her in braces. These days, Hannah Montana, hired as the face of an international campaign for acne cream, is horrified to discover a zit has been Photoshopped onto her billboard-sized forehead. Both characters eventually learn that "looks aren't everything," yet the package that lesson is wrapped in could not be more different (and, for the record, Hannah/Miley, who has her own clothing line at Walmart, notably hedges on that moral, telling her best friend, "Looks are *important*, but they're not everything").

But maybe in a celebrity-saturated world, that is mere quibbling. Better Hannah Montana than the Pussycat Dolls, aimed at the same demographic, who gyrate to lyrics such as "Don't cha wish your girlfriend was a freak like me." Hannah, like the animated princesses, is, more or less, blandly unobjectionable. Her chirpy, if insipid, wholesomeness acts as an assurance to parents—just like playing princess—that our little girls are still little girls. Until, that is, they are not.

⌇⌇⌇

The thing is, as Maurice Chevalier once chortled, little girls grow bigger every day. Child stars have always been pesky that way, and how to handle their inevitable maturation has been a perpetual challenge for the entertainment industry. Even Shirley Temple had to grow up: by the time she had reached age eleven, Fox had terminated her studio contract, effectively putting her out to pasture. Although she subsequently made a few small films, she never reclaimed her childhood success and, to her credit, gracefully exited the business by age twenty-one. Around the same time, MGM forced the sixteen-year-old Judy Garland to bind her breasts for her role as little Dorothy Gale in *The Wizard of Oz* (the blue gingham pattern on her dress was also chosen to obscure her womanly figure). In the early 1960s, Annette Funicello, who famously "blossomed" during her stint as an original Disney Mouseketeer, defied Mr. Disney by donning a navel-baring swimsuit in the "Beach Party" movies; though she was twenty-one at the time, her rebellion sparked a scandal.

It may be all well and good for today's pop princesses to play the G-rated role model at fourteen or fifteen, but by sixteen it no longer feels so sweet: adulthood looms. How can those self-proclaimed paragons prove to the world that they are grown? How can they leave their Snow White reputations behind? What guidance can they offer to their carefully cultivated legions of idolizing prepubescent fans? The answer has become so familiar that it seems almost written into the script. They cast off their values by casting off their clothes. Hilary Duff appeared almost in the buff on the cover of *Maxim* magazine (as did *Clarissa*'s Melissa Joan Hart—who, by then better known for *Sabrina*, was touted by the lad mag as "your favorite witch without a stitch"). So many photos of the scantily clad Vanessa Hudgens, *High School Musical*'s "good girl," have circulated on the Internet that she has been accused of posting them herself to earn some adult street cred. In the video for her breakout hit, "Dirrty," Christina Aguilera, another former Mouseketeer, stepped into a boxing ring clad in a bra, red thong, and ass-baring chaps: "Shake a little somethin' (on the floor) I need that, uh, to get me off," she sang to a roaring crowd, feigning (I hope) masturbation and, later, simulating intercourse with half-naked greased-up men. *I Know Who Killed Me*, a film starring the postadolescent Lindsay Lohan, whom the critic Roger Ebert had once compared to Jodie

Foster, was declared by the *New York Post* to be "a sleazy, inept and worthless piece of torture porn." Lohan, who admitted to drug use in *Vanity Fair* (note to child stars: do not let yourself be profiled by that magazine), has also taken several spins through the revolving door of rehab and cannot seem to keep track of either her panties or her court-mandated alcohol-monitoring bracelet. In the summer of 2010, she was sentenced to a brief, highly publicized jail term after violating probation for a DUI.

But the winner for most spectacular slide from squeaky to skanky has got to be Britney Spears. It is hard to believe now, but the singer's original audience was as young as—maybe younger than—Miley Cyrus's. Six-year-olds adored the singer the way they would a favorite babysitter, the one who lets you brush her hair. Britney was a relatively mature seventeen when she shimmied onto the scene in 1998, and her success was arguably the template for all the contradictory, mixed, or bait-and-switch messages that have since defined mainstream girls' culture: flaunt your sexuality but don't feel it, use it for power but not for pleasure. From the start, Britney tried to have it both ways, selling sex *and* candy. In her breakthrough video, " . . . Baby One More Time" (the ellipses a stand-in for the words "Hit Me"), she wore a short Catholic schoolgirl's skirt, knee socks, and a white blouse tied to reveal her midriff and unbuttoned to show a black bra. A year later, she confessed, "Oops! . . . I did it again!" while writhing on her back under the video camera's leering eye. It is tempting to say that Britney in her prime was just another iteration of Madonna, challenging expectations, messing with assumptions, self-consciously exploiting herself before the culture could do it for her: *commenting on* rather than *participating in* girls' sexualization. She encouraged that connection by infamously tongue-wrestling the older performer onstage—Britney dressed as a bride, Madonna as a groom—while performing "Like a Virgin," at the 2003 MTV Video Awards. But in the end, the comparison fails. I have to admit that I am not a huge Madonna fan. Although I'm happy to hit the dance floor for "Lucky Star," I was never convinced that she was so revolutionary, that she ever really "empowered" anyone but herself. A lot of women who spent their teen years wearing their bras on the outside of their shirts may disagree, but whether you got into her groove or not, Madonna never denied what she was doing—quite the opposite. From the start, with her BOY TOY belt and dangling crucifix, it was she who called the shots: she was self-created, explicit both about her intent and about the contradictions of women's sexuality that she explored. She was also an actual adult—age twenty-five when her first album was released—and she was not aggressively courting second-graders as fans. When she skipped through Venice singing "Like a Virgin," it was darned clear she was not one.

Britney, on the other hand, publicly insisted on her chastity (at least for a while). She was not only a loud-and-proud virgin, urging other girls to follow her example, but acted willfully clueless about the disconnect between her words and deeds. So although in 1999, while still seventeen, she appeared on the cover of *Rolling Stone* in short shorts and a black push-up bra, clutching a stuffed Teletubby, inside the magazine she declared in all earnestness, "I don't want to be part of someone's Lolita thing. It kind of freaks me out." People are so pervy, she would sigh, it wasn't *her* fault if they got the wrong idea. Later, in an *Esquire* interview illustrated by a photo in which she posed naked save for microscopic undies and several artfully placed strands of pearls, she commented, "Look, if you want me to be some kind of sex thing, that's not me." She did it again! How can she be blamed—she just can't help herself! She has no idea what she's doing! She may radiate sex, but how, at her tender age, could she be responsible for that? It was her stubborn disingenuousness—her winking detachment from her actions and impact—that eroticized Britney's (not so) innocence and, unintentionally or not, that of the millions of elementary school–aged girls who slavishly followed her. When they bared their midriffs—or performed sexually charged dance moves or wore "sassy" costumes—they were not in on the joke.

Eventually, though, Britney got older and needed to evolve; when she dropped the act and became consciously rather than "accidentally" sexy, the public turned on her, and the knowing naïf was branded a slut. How were fans supposed to understand that? Suddenly Britney's fairy tale was transformed into a cautionary tale: woe to girls who step over the ever-shifting invisible line between virgin and whore (or as one group of middle school ex-fans referred to Britney, "slore," an elision of "slut" and "whore"). Over the course of five years, the singer married and divorced, shacked up with a guy whose previous girlfriend was eight months pregnant with his child, bounced through rehab, shaved her head, stopped wearing panties in public (what is *with* that?), had two sons, lost them in a custody battle, and finally was hauled from her house on a gurney and diagnosed with bipolar disorder. Given the schizoid comments she had been spewing since high school, was that such a shock? I'm not saying that every girl who teeters on the tightrope between child and woman risks ending up institutionalized, but, again like Cinderella in her time, Britney embodies the predicament of ordinary girls writ large. They, too, struggle with the expectation to look sexy but not feel sexual, to provoke desire in others without experiencing it themselves. Our daughters may not be faced with the decision of whether to strip for *Maxim*, but they will have to figure out how to become sexual beings without being objectified or stigmatized. That is not easy when self-respect has become a marketing gimmick, a way for female pop stars to bide their time before serving up their sexuality as a product for public consumption.

Miley Cyrus grinned down from giant banners flanking the entrance to the Oracle Arena in Oakland, California. MILEY CYRUS: ONLY AT WALMART! they announced. Beneath them, fans lined up five-deep hoping to catch a glimpse of their idol live as she strode from her tour bus in the parking lot to her backstage dressing room. It was the fall of 2009, and this was the second stop on Miley's forty-five-city Wonder World Tour, her first since her spate of miniscandals. The crowd—mostly in the six- to nine-year-old range with a smattering of ten- to twelve-year-olds and a few stray teens—seemed unfazed by her media spankings. They waved homemade cardboard signs with Miley's or Hannah's picture pasted on them, surrounded by hand-drawn flowers, puff-painted hearts, or feathers. MILEY, YOU ROCK THE HOUSE! one read. HANNAH MONTANA SONGS ARE THE BEST! claimed another.

A year ago, my own daughter had come here for a "Disney on Ice" show, invited by a friend who was celebrating her birthday. The party guests had dressed as Cinderella, Belle, Ariel (though Daisy, perhaps due to months of maternal propaganda, chose Pocahontas, the only child to do so in a crowd of thousands). The mob of girls here tonight, including the ones just a year or two older than the ice show crowd, were also dressed up as Disney Princesses, though the nature of the costumes had changed: they wore miniskirts bare-legged with high-heeled boots, topped off by pink-and-black buffalo-checked fedoras; zebra-print shirts with sparkling bodices that would have highlighted their cleavages had they had any. Several little girls swung by in white furry boots and low-rise black pleather "jeggings" (a combo of jeans and leggings). A stretch Hummer pulled up to disgorge a group of what I am guessing were second-graders in black minis with chains slung low across the hips and pink fingerless gloves.

I doubt that the six-year-old with the crimped hair and fuchsia mini would describe what she was wearing as sexy. To her it was just fun, attention-getting; she is the real-life, genuine version of the Britney Spears *Rolling Stone* cover. Disney's Andy Mooney had told me that Princess (and so, presumably, by extension, Hannah & Co.) was "aspirational"; I was not so sure I would want my daughter aspiring to this. Pink-and-pretty had been marketed to parents of preschoolers as evidence of their innocence, a harmless, even natural, way to identify as a girl. Now, for their older sisters, the pitch was changing: looking hot or at least hot-esque—at concerts, on Halloween, after school, in your dance routines—was the way to express femininity, to "be true, be you." Two slightly older girls walked by, gum cracking, hips swaying, eyelids darkened with thick liner. They wore identical skintight microminis, black camisoles, and boots, again with bare legs. One had flung a pink neon feather boa around her neck, the other a chartreuse one. They seemed about twelve, so I figured they were old enough for the look. Then I recalled the beauty pageant I had attended, how quickly I had become accustomed to five-year-olds with spray tans, teased hair, and lipstick, and I reconsidered: when, exactly, had a twelve-year-old Stripperella ceased to shock?

When Miley finally appeared, the crowd crushed forward, screaming at a frequency attainable only by young girls and

Wagnerian sopranos. Next to me, a little girl in a Hello Kitty T-shirt and pink cowboy boots jumped up and down, nearly out of control. "I can't see, I can't see!" she hollered. Miley, dressed in her preshow outfit of black cargo pants with a tank top and oversized shades, crinkled her nose endearingly and waved at the crowd. Her smile seemed genuine as she stopped to pose for photos and sign a few hurried autographs. Even after she was well out of sight the fans continued to shriek, just for the joy of it. A ten-year-old with a SECRET STAR shirt and multicolored barrettes stared in disbelief at the picture of Miley she'd snapped on her cell phone. "I'm sending this to everyone on my contact list *right now*!!" she announced. It was, admittedly, sort of heartening to see girls swoon for a female star rather than for the latest Backstreet/Hanson/Jonas pretty boy.

Inside, real-time text messages sent by the audience scrolled by on screens surrounding the stage. "WE LOVE YOU MILEY!" "I LOVE YOU!" "MY 5-YEAR-OLD'S FIRST CONCERT. SHE LOVES YOU!" When the lights finally dimmed, the crowd hollered again, frantically waving light sticks. Smoke-machine fog rolled across the stage, clearing to reveal what appeared to be a giant chrysalis, surrounded by whirling dancers. A figure stepped out, head covered by a drab shawl. Suddenly flames exploded, lasers bounced across the stage, the figure threw off the shawl, and . . . it was Miley, her brown hair flowing, her cargo pants and tank top replaced by black leather hot pants and a low-cut leather vest. She burst into a song titled "Breakout." "It feels so good to let go-o-o!" she sang.

This was a very different girl from the one who, some two years earlier, on the eve of her fifteenth birthday, had confided to Oprah Winfrey that "I look way young, and that's the way it's more comfortable to me"; the one who had said that she chooses clothing that "will get a thumbs-up from girls and their parents";

the one whom, only a year before, Barbara Walters had introduced as "any parent's antidote to the common crop of teen train
wrecks." Back then, Miley had earnestly told Walters why she
was different from Britney, Jamie Lynn (Britney's sister, the star
of Nickelodeon's *Zoey 101*, who became pregnant out of wedlock
at age sixteen), Lindsay, and the Olsen twins: "Some people don't
have a family to fall back on and faith." She, by implication, was
a girl whom parents could trust not to treat clean values as a
stepping-stone to something else—she was *sincere.*

The *Vanity Fair* photos hit the Web less than three months
later.

Even those who were inclined to cut Miley some slack, to
chalk that incident up to a momentary lapse in judgment, began
to wonder in the summer of 2009, when she debuted her new
single, "Party in the U.S.A.," on the Teen Choice Awards (whose
audience is made up largely of preteen girls). She strutted out of
a trailer in booty shorts and a sparkly tank slit up the sides to expose her bra. As she sang, she stepped offstage, onto an ice cream
cart topped with a pole, the kind that would typically be used as
an umbrella stand; then, hanging on with one hand, she dropped
into a squat, her knees splayed, her back arched. The move was,
to say the least, at odds with the image of the family-friendly pop
star she portrayed on TV.

Once again, controversy broke out: What kind of sticky-sweet
treat was this flavor of the moment selling? Miley claimed the
crouch was insignificant, not to mention personally approved by
her father. Bloggers called the umbrella stand "a stripper pole with
training wheels" and accused Billy Ray of pimping his sixteen-
year-old child rather than doing his paternal duty by protecting
her. Around that time, Miley was also photographed in *Elle* magazine lying on a table wearing a short skirt and thigh-high black

boots. In both cases, she once again apologized to her fans, though she was beginning to come off as the child-star version of Richard Nixon. More and more, the "mistakes" were seen as part of the plan. It was Miley's turn to cast off the role model mantle, along with the worshipful audience who had believed it was real.

By the time I saw Miley in concert, she had agreed, after some tense negotiation, to stay at the Disney Channel for a final season of *Hannah Montana*. But the Mouse House was already moving her out. There is always a new girl in the wings, someone who promises never to disappoint by shucking her principles along with her clothes. For the moment, both Selena Gomez and Demi Lovato—show business veterans who met on the set of *Barney and Friends* in 2002—were being promoted as the Anti-Mileys (Bridgit Mendler, the star of the show *Good Luck Charlie*, is another contender). Selena, who also appeared on *Hannah Montana*, had since 2007 played a girl with magical powers on the Disney Channel's *Sabrina* knockoff, *Wizards of Waverly Place*. Demi's more recent "zit-com," *Sonny with a Chance*, is a more overt *Hannah Montana* rip-off: she plays a small-town girl who lands a role on a TV show and has to adjust to her newfound stardom. As of this writing, Selena seems to be breaking bigger: her first solo album, *Kiss & Tell*, debuted at number nine on the charts. In addition to a *Wizards* made-for-TV movie, she co-starred in the 2010 release *Ramona and Beezus*, and her likeness has been plastered on some 30 million packages of Sara Lee baked goods.

Wizards is, all things considered, a pretty entertaining show. Gomez has the best comic timing of any Disney girl to date: at the very least, her repertoire of reactions extends beyond eye-bugging. The character she plays is strong, smart, and, aside from the hocus-pocus, surprisingly real: she does not seem to be all about being pretty, nor does she always make the right choices.

It goes without saying that Gomez herself comes off as down to earth and adorable. That is her job. A *Wall Street Journal* profile gushed that her every-teen dressing room was decorated "with a bright floral rug, a shag blanket thrown across a sofa and a few scattered bookshelves." A quick Google search of news items generated right around the time of her album's release portrays her as a UNICEF ambassador to Ghana, a dog lover, and someone who "gives back to her community" (bestowing a thousand dollars' worth of supplies on her elementary school alma mater courtesy of OfficeMax). Although she is actually a year older than Miley, she looks younger, and she assured the *Journal* reporter that she is "in no rush to be twenty-five." Sound familiar?

Historical memory for pop culture tends to be short, especially where children's idols are concerned. The parents of today's six-year-olds have only a hazy recall of Hilary Duff's or Britney Spears's or even Lindsay Lohan's stints as "good-girl" icons. So it is easy to convince them that *this* girl is unlike those others, that *this* time it honestly will be different. I want to believe it myself—I like Selena. But I wonder: her virginity has already been made a selling point—like Miley before her, she wears a "true love waits" ring, meaning she has vowed to remain "pure" until marriage, presumably to a Justin Bieber clone on a white horse. I suspect that you cannot commodify a girl's virginity without, eventually, commodifying what comes after. Regardless, how realistic—how *desirable*—is that Disney version of girls' sexuality, either for Selena or for her fans?

Let me be clear here: I object—strenuously—to the sexualization of girls but not necessarily to girls having sex. I expect and want my daughter to have a healthy, joyous erotic life before marriage. Long, long, *long* before marriage. I do, however, want her to understand why she's doing it: not for someone else's enjoyment, not to keep a boyfriend from leaving, not because everyone else is. I want her to do it for herself. I want her to explore and understand her body's responses, her own pleasure, her own desire. I want her to be able to express her needs in relationship, to say no when she needs to, to value reciprocity, and to experience true intimacy. The virgin/whore cycle of the pop princesses, like so much of the girlie-girl culture, pushes in the opposite direction, encouraging girls to view self-objectification as a feminine rite of passage.

The debate over whether Miley's (or Britney's or Vanessa's or someday, mark my words, Selena's) photo spreads are "too seductive" or "too suggestive" for her age is beside the point. Of course they are. They have to be. What other choice do these girls have? What choices are they given? I would like to see the *Hannah Montana* episode in which Miley Stewart confronts the real truth about what it means to be a girl growing up in the privilege and the confines of the spotlight's glare. What would that look like? A lot, I would bet, like Miley Cyrus's actual microscopically dissected life. Ultimately, it was not the *Vanity Fair* shoot or the stripper stunt or the hooker heels that crossed the line: it was the fetishizing of Miley's wholesomeness, the inevitable trajectory from accidentally to accidentally-on-purpose to simply on-purpose sexy. Why isn't it until that final leap, when a girl actively acknowledges and participates in what is happening, that parents of young fans cry foul?

Back at the Oracle Arena, Miley paced the runway; flipped her mane; got jiggy with the boys in the band; lay down on her back, legs tucked under, jamming on an air guitar. She donned a harness and went airborne while performing her hit "Fly on the Wall." She soared again on a candy apple red Harley during a cover of Joan Jett's classic "I Love Rock and Roll." During the entire ninety-minute set, however, she sang only two *Hannah Montana* songs (one of which was conspicuously steamed up), and through multiple costume changes she never went near a blond wig. This was emphatically a *Miley* show, but many of the grade school fans there that night, not to mention their moms, had failed to get that memo—and they were not happy about it. The little girl sitting next to me, who, judging by her missing teeth, was about seven, watched the spectacle, her ponytail bobbing with the rhythm of each song. But eventually she seemed to grow impatient, possibly overwhelmed by the thumping bass.

"Where's Hannah?" she asked her mother. The older woman glanced at the stage where Miley was getting busy, grinding her pelvis against a backup guitarist with lank hair and an untucked plaid shirt. Then she turned back to her child.

"I don't know, honey," she said, shaking her head. "I guess she's not here."

Chapter Eight

It's All About the Cape

One of Daisy's classmates, Ava, is five years old. She is five years old, and she is fat. She was a fat infant. She was a fat toddler. It is pretty clear that she'll stay a fat little girl and she'll likely be a fat teenager. Fat—that is to say, having a body mass index above what is considered medically healthy—is her natural state, the way she is built. She is a big girl with a big appetite. And that, her mother, Holly, knows, could make Ava's life difficult. Holly worries that her daughter will spend her girlhood locked in a losing battle against her size, sinking into self-loathing when she fails. She wonders daily how she can help her daughter to eat healthfully, be more physically active, but also feel good about the body she's got. She and her husband work with Ava's pediatrician on portion control, on how to distract their perpetually hungry daughter from reaching for seconds or thirds. Sometimes, though, Holly admitted, she fights the urge to just snatch the food right out of the child's mouth. The weight would be an issue if Ava were a boy, too, but for a girl, one who is already enamored of Hannah and Selena and all things teenagerly, Holly said she feels as if "there is a train heading straight for us.

"It must be so nice not having to worry about this," she sighed as we sat in her kitchen, our two girls upstairs in Ava's room playing Calico Critters. I shook my head, told Holly she was mistaken: rare is the mother—whether her girl is thin, fat, or somewhere in between—who does not worry about her daughter's body image. The standards of female beauty are so punishing that even should a girl miraculously fit them, she may still believe she falls short. As mothers, we may not want our daughters to feel compelled to conform to that ideal, but what to do with a child who, either physically or temperamentally, cannot—or does not want to? What is the alternative to thin, pretty, and hot (regardless of other qualities) as the source of feminine power and identity?

Holly herself is tall and slim. She has never had to work at that, which is not to say she doesn't have her own issues about weight and food. Growing up, she would walk away from friends when the topic turned to pounds, and she refused to step on a scale. "It was so important to me *not* to think about it," she said, "which means, of course, that it did have a hold on me. But I lived in my head. The truth is, I hardly had a perception of myself as having a body. Ava is a really embodied person."

Ava also happens to be a little ray of sunshine, one of the most delightful, happy, intuitive children I have ever met. But lately, the occasional cloud has skittered across her bright eyes. She is beginning to recognize that there is something about her that is different from other children, and whatever that something is, it matters. Take the boy on the school playground who taunted her for being "fat." Ava marched home and wrote him a note saying she had not appreciated the comment. She presented him with it the next morning. "I was so impressed," Holly said. "I thought, 'Oh, please, hold on to that ability for your whole life. Because you probably *will* need it.'"

There have been other incidents, too, and so far, Ava has stood her ground. I marveled that these kindergartners already knew that being fat was *shameful*, not a characteristic so much as a matter of character. I mean, of course they did, right? I had read the studies that said nearly half of girls in first through third grades want to be thinner; that 81 percent of ten-year-old girls were afraid of getting fat; that half of nine-year-old girls surveyed were already dieting; and that by seven Canadian girls of normal weight believed they were too heavy. I had even heard glimmers of fatphobia from my own daughter, while playing Old Maid (a politically incorrect game in any event): Daisy did not so much as twitch an eyebrow when she picked the twinkling-eyed spinster with the blue sunbonnet—my girl has a poker face that would rival the gambler Annie Duke's—but she groaned whenever she drew the Fat Lady. When I asked her why, she rolled her eyes and whispered, "Mom, she's *fat*."

Where did that come from? I never, *ever* comment on my own body size in front of her and certainly don't mention hers. Did she learn it from her classmates? Absorb it from the movies and books that routinely portray fat people as stupid, greedy, or sinister (when was the last time you saw a chubby Disney Princess, animated or human)? Could revulsion toward overweight people be natural? After all, the Bible warns against gluttony, and the ancient Greeks preached (though did not always follow) a doctrine of moderation. Or, as with the assumption that girls are born loving pink, have we so thoroughly internalized our response to fat that we've forgotten it was not always thus? Plump women may today be portrayed as unattractive and loved only by their cats, but pinups of mid-nineteenth-century stage stars show bosomy ladies with bodacious thighs and ham-hock arms. In that era, it was slender women who were considered suspect—desiccated and asexual—especially once they had hit middle age. Those not blessed with embonpoint would mask their deficiency under layers of bustles and ruffles. Children were considered sickly unless they were stuffed like Thanksgiving turkeys. Ava would have been held up as the model daughter and Holly as the perfect mother.

According to the historian Peter Stearns's book *Fat History*, public sentiment began shifting toward the svelte in the 1890s, when overweight was first linked to chronic disease. Fat did not take on a moral dimension, however, until the cause was taken up by Christian ministers, who railed against the increasing sedentariness of the postindustrial middle class. The timing of that trend was fortuitous: their previous target—rising materialism—was proving unpopular. Weight, Stearns writes, was a perfect substitute, not only replacing conspicuous consumption but legitimizing it: as long as you exercised restraint over eating, you could freely indulge your appetite for luxury. Initially, fat was equally demonized in both sexes, but by the 1920s, the focus had narrowed primarily to women and girls. Since then, one could argue, the more extreme our consumer culture has become, the more hostile we have grown toward even slight overweight in women. Not just concerned, not just disapproving, but *repelled*. And all the while, our own scales tip ever heavier.

"Maybe in ten years, by the time Ava is a teenager, the pendulum will have swung," Holly said, hopefully. "Then again, you have Kate Moss going around saying 'Nothing tastes as good as skinny feels.'"

Now, this is where I should step in to give advice to Holly, to you, to *myself* about how to combat the outrageous expectations foisted onto our daughters, to ensure, whether they are thin, fat, or anywhere in between, that they grow up with a positive and healthy body image: how to insulate them from eating disorders or simply garden-variety hatred of their butts. And believe me, after twenty years of writing and talking about girls, I know what to say: I have delivered the script hundreds of times at colleges and high schools, in churches and temples, to parent groups, teachers, Girl Scout leaders. So, for the record, here is what you are Officially Supposed To Do: stress what your daughter's body can *do* over how it is decorated. Praise her for her accomplishments over her looks. Make sure Dad is on board—a father's loving regard and interest in a girl, as the first man in her life, is crucial. Involve her in team sports: a flotilla of research shows that participation lowers teen pregnancy rates, raises self-esteem, improves grades, probably cures the common cold. Volunteerism can give girls greater perspective and purpose, reducing body obsession. Media literacy can raise consciousness about marketers' manipulations.

I would have rattled off those solutions with the greatest confidence and authority—before I had a daughter of my own. Because the truth is, regardless of what we say, from the get-go everything else, everyone else, in our culture tells girls that their weight and looks matter—a lot. Though appearance *shouldn't* dictate how they are treated by others—let alone their self-worth—it does. Talent? Effort? Intelligence? All are wonderful, yet by middle school, how a girl feels about her appearance—particularly whether she is thin enough, pretty enough, and hot enough—has become the single most important determinant of her self-esteem (which, by the way, makes self-esteem itself a trickier concept than most people realize; it is not an inherent good but must be derived from appropriate sources). If Princesses, Moxies, and Mileys are not responsible for that, exactly, Lord knows they reinforce it. Even as I wish it were otherwise—even as I *fight* for it to be otherwise—I, too, know in my heart that how girls look does make a difference in how the world perceives them, and the more progress they make in other areas, the more that seems to be true.

And true for longer. Take an article I recently saw in *More* magazine: "Stars Who Make over 40 Look Fab." The publication runs pieces like this all the time, and I can never decide whether they make me feel better or worse about my own (I'll just say it) middle age. Though I applaud its rebel yell that women can remain attractive as we get o-l-d-e-r, I also feel a creeping despair—like, dang, now I *have* to be. I was secretly looking forward to letting it all go to hell at a certain point. But more than that, the mag did not even mention that every single one of the women they were holding up as role models had dyed away their gray; most had frozen time with Botox; others had moved on to a full complement of fillers, tucks, and lifts. Is that now so presumed, once princess ascends to queen, that it goes without saying? These were not great-looking older women. They were great-looking women who both can't afford to get old and *can* afford not to. These days postforty women in the spotlight who go au naturel are considered courageous if not downright foolhardy. That perception is gradually trickling down to the rest of us. It is a nasty bind, as psychologists (and former models) Vivian Diller and Jill Muir-Sukenick write in *Face It*, a guide for women on coping with changing appearance: "Should women simply grow old naturally, since their looks don't define them, or should they fight the signs of aging, since beauty and youth are their currency and power?" Whether we like it or not, whichever we choose is a statement, one that earlier generations were not forced to make. What's more, in another twist on KGOY, women are asking that question at ever-younger ages. Most of the 9.3 million women who underwent cosmetic procedures in 2008 were between thirty-five and fifty; nearly another quarter were between nineteen and thirty-four. That trend has created a market for a new picture book, *My Beautiful Mommy*, in which a little girl does everything she can "to help Mommy achieve her beautiful results."

And Mommy had best get ready to return the favor, because just as the imperative to look good has extended further up the age spectrum, it is also creeping further down. Nearly 43,000 children under age eighteen (mostly girls, of course) surgically altered their appearance in 2008—over twice as many as a decade earlier. That does not include the tens of thousands who scheduled chemical peels, dermabrasion, or laser hair removal. Or (and someone please explain *this* to me) the 12,000 injections of Botox administered in 2009 to children ages thirteen to nineteen, presumably to prevent rather than remove wrinkles. So—stick with me here—that means girls are now simultaneously getting older younger *and* staying younger older. It also explains why the identical midriff-baring crop top is sold to eight-year-olds, eighteen-year-olds, and forty-eight-year-olds. The phases of our lives have become strangely blurred, as girls try to look like adult women and adult women primp and preen and work out like crazy in order to look like girls. Once again we are in fairy-tale territory, but instead of the jealous queen, it is the MILF who is gazing in the Magic Mirror, competing with her daughter to be Fairest of Them All.

A century ago, female self-improvement did not presume a

stint under the scalpel, hours at the gym, or even a trip to the cosmetics counter. In her indispensable book *The Body Project*, the historian Joan Jacobs Brumberg wrote that for girls growing up before World War I, becoming a better person meant being *less* self-involved: helping others, focusing on schoolwork, becoming better read, cultivating empathy. To bring home the point, she compared New Year's resolutions of girls at the end of the nineteenth century with those at the end of the twentieth. Here's what a young woman of yore wrote:

"Resolved: to think before speaking. To work seriously. To be self-restrained in conversations and actions. Not to let my thoughts wander. To be dignified. Interest myself more in others."

And the contemporary girl:

"I will try to make myself better in any way I possibly can. . . . I will lose weight, get new lenses, already got new haircut, good makeup, new clothes and accessories."

As in the American Girl books, it seems that though the nineteenth-century girl may have lived in a more repressive era— before women could vote, when girls' sights were set solely on marriage and motherhood—her sense of self-worth was enviably internal, a matter of deed over dress. Whatever other constraints she felt, her femininity was not defined by the pursuit of physical perfection; it was about character. I wonder why we adult women, with all our economic, political, and personal freedoms, have let this happen to our daughters.

When I was reporting *Schoolgirls*, a book for which I followed students at two different middle schools through eighth grade, I noticed my own habit, after a few days' absence, of greeting my young subjects by commenting on some aspect of their appearance: their earrings, a new shirt, their hairstyles. I decided, as an experiment, to stop cold turkey, to find another way to connect:

asking how a play rehearsal was going or what they were reading in English class. Anything. It felt surprisingly forced: physical compliments grease the conversational wheels among women and girls. After the book's publication, I would speak about that experience, encouraging my audience to give it a try themselves for a few days. They would nod their heads; then, after a beat, someone would ask uncomfortably, "You mean we shouldn't say *anything* about their looks?" How about this, I would counter: try not commenting on your *own* looks—on the size of your thighs or the tightness of your jeans. At least not in front of your daughter. Girls receive enough messages every day reducing them to their appearance without women they love delivering them, too.

Like Holly—like all of the women I know—I want to raise a girl who has a reasonable perspective on her body regardless of her shape, who does not plunge into a shame spiral whenever she looks at herself sideways in a mirror. Someone, in other words, who is not like me. My high school memories include hiding laxatives in my school locker, breaking sticks of sugar-free gum in half and calling that lunch. The hopeless feeling that accompanied my self-imposed starvation remains more vivid to me than anything else from that time. Although my body and I have reached if not peace, at least a state of détente, "fat" remains how I experience anger, dissatisfaction, disappointment. I feel "fat" if I can't master a task at work. I feel "fat" if I can't please those I love. "Fat" is how I blame myself for my failures. "Fat" is how I express my anxieties. A psychologist once told me, "Fat is not a feeling." If only it were that simple. As for so many women, the pathology of self-loathing is permanently ingrained in me. I can give in to it, I can modify it, I can react against it with practiced self-acceptance, but I cannot eradicate it. It frustrates me to consider what else I might have done with the years of mental energy I have wasted on this single, senseless issue.

Given all of that, I wonder how I could expect—or even *hope*—to raise a daughter who is both less invested in and more confident about her appearance than I was, even if it is slightly (or wildly) imperfect, as, of course, it will be. Certainly, I do my best, and I follow all the expert advice I have mentioned above, but I don't have an intuitive—a gut, if you will—feeling for whether or not I am on the right track. Not the way I do with ensuring that she is well mannered or values kindness, creativity, intellect. I am hardly the only mother who wrestles with this: I recalled the conversation I'd had about the Disney Princesses with the mothers of Daisy's preschool classmates. One of them felt the answer was to shower her daughter with compliments about her looks as a kind of inoculation: she wanted to impress upon her girl that, regardless of what anyone might say, she was beautiful. Besides, the woman said, if you *never* tell your daughter she is pretty, rather than realizing that appearance is unimportant, she may suspect you think she's ugly. Maybe. Yet *over*-emphasizing a girl's looks is clearly hazardous—and that overemphasis is pervasive. How to find the sweet spot?

I took the quandary to Catherine Steiner-Adair, the director of eating disorders education and prevention at the Klarman Eating Disorders Center at McLean Hospital in Massachusetts. "Well," she said, when I called her, " 'You're beautiful' is not something you want to say over and over to your daughter, because it's not something that you want her to think is so important.

"That said," she continued, "there are times when it *is* important to say it: when she's messy or sweaty, when she's *not* dressed up, so that she gets a sense that there is something naturally beautiful about her as a person. And it's also important to connect beauty and love. To say, 'I love you so much. Everything about you is beautiful to me—*you* are beautiful to me.' That way you're not just objectifying her body."

I appreciated that advice, the way it redefined beauty as something that was both internal and eternal. I passed it along to Holly, who was somewhat less impressed. "I actually think it's fine to reserve 'beautiful' for when she's dressed up or has a new haircut or has done something special," she said. "What's important to me in a day-to-day way is to unhook looks from size, not to link the two for her—or, because of her, for me." Take the challenge of buying Ava's clothes—nix on jeans or those cute little Boden dresses—which will only intensify as she gets older and more aware of Abercrombie and Hot Topic. "Pretty to me is not the point," Holly said. "I think Ava is pretty. I think she's lovely. And I hope she'll think so, too. But she's always going to be a big girl—unless she starts dieting in an unhealthy way."

I ached for Holly and her daughter, for the complicated position they were in. Yet I realized that along with that concern and love I did feel a certain . . . relief. Because, as Holly said, my own daughter *is* thin. True, she may still someday struggle, but I don't have to worry that she will be teased about her size on the first day of summer camp. I wish appearance did not matter so much, that it did not confer so much power. But given that it does, I find that I am grateful for hers. Does that make me a hypocrite?

⚬⚏⚬

Women. Beauty. Power. Body. The ideas and images remain so muddled, so contradictory; how to disentangle them for our girls? By the end of kindergarten, Daisy had, blessedly, exited the Disney Princess phase. "The princesses are just, like"—she struck a "lovely Carol Merrill" pose and simpered—"'I'm so pretty, Handsome Prince, won't you rescue me?'" Later she added, "All Sleeping Beauty ever does is sleep."

I admit to feeling a smidge of guilt (along with pride) at that pronouncement, because it was a reasonable approximation of what I had been drilling into her head for three years—but then again, if Disney could try to brainwash my child, I suppose I could, too. At any rate, I waited anxiously for what might come next: would I be moaning over *Monster High*? Were we bound for Tinker Bell's Pixie Hollow, a realm of moralistic nice girl/mean girl dynamics? Would I have to decide whether to empty my wallet for that full-on American Girl rig (I had been sorely tempted by a newly introduced historical doll, a Russian-Jewish girl from the early twentieth century, whose accessories included a $68 "Sabbath set")? Instead, she surprised me: for her sixth birthday, she asked for a Wonder Woman costume.

Finally, a stage I could get with! I was even willing to up the ante: why stop at Wonder Woman? I trolled eBay for action figures of Hawkgirl and Big Barda (a superheroine from the 1970s who defends her milquetoast husband). I scored a PVC-free Supergirl lunch box. I searched YouTube for snippets of the short-lived animated *Spider-Woman* TV series from 1980. Yes, it gave me pause that the lunch box was pink, that, given her druthers, Big Barda preferred housewifery to crime fighting, and that all of the superheroines have the proportions of Kim Kardashian—more mammary than muscle. It disappointed me, though did not surprise, when Daisy declined a friend's offer of a Wonder Woman from his bobblehead collection: the head was too big for the body, she explained to me later, and the face was, well, kind of butch (my word, not hers). On the other extreme, she was so appalled by Hawkgirl's excessive assets that she never took the toy out of the box. And one day while drawing Supergirl, who wears a

miniskirt and a crop top, she mused, "Sometimes girl superheroes
show their belly buttons. I don't know why." So I hadn't exactly
succeeded in finding a strong feminine image that wasn't idealized or sexualized, but how far was I willing to push it? Maybe
the message that power does not play without the pretty will mess
her up in ten years, but right now, I needed something to say yes
to; like so many moms, I was willing to compromise to find some
mutually acceptable middle ground.

Besides, I figured there were intriguing possibilities in this
new phase. Little girls may have more real-life role models than
they used to, more examples of how to be in the world, but they
have precious few larger-than-life heroes, especially in the all-
important realm of fantasy, where they spend so much of their
free time. It's true, as we've seen, that the research on gender
and play indicates (with the big blinking caveats that there are
vast variations within, as opposed to between, the sexes and that
nature is heavily influenced by nurture) that little boys are more
readily drawn to competitive, rough-and-tumble games, while
little girls (again, big blinking caveat, see above) strive for group
harmony over individual dominance. But all that aside, let's face
it, the options for girls have not exactly been compelling. Who
can even remember Batgirl's secret identity? (She was Barbara
Gordon, the commissioner's daughter—or, in some versions, his
niece.) And, with all due respect, Wonder Woman's invisible airplane is . . . how to put this delicately—*lame* compared with the
gleam of a Batmobile. Still, I think superhero play, when it is not
overdetermined by the *Justice League* script, has something specific to offer girls, something beyond an outlet for aggression or
even the satisfaction (similar to Bettelheim's claims for fairy tales)
of gaining control in an arbitrary world.

I went through a brief Wonder Woman phase myself in the

early 1970s. Even then I could not have told you much about the character's backstory, but I didn't care: all I knew was that I had an excuse to fasten a towel around my neck with a clothespin and climb onto the roof of a friend's garage. The distance to the next building was slightly longer than my leggy child's stride, yet I took a deep breath and leapt—screaming "Wonder Woman! Wonder Woman!"—my towel cape streaming behind me. In that moment of flight, soaring between the two rooftops, I felt—no, I *knew* I was—invincible; the sensation was equal parts exhilarating and frightening. What might I dare to do next? What else was possible?

As a writer, I have revisited that memory in my work more often than any other. It was so different from my typical, earthbound play, and the emotions it elicited were so unfamiliar— feelings of freedom, of power. And isn't that ultimately the superhero's task: coming to grips with the gifts and challenges of power—accepting it, demanding it, wielding it wisely, grappling with moral choices about the nature of might and goodness? Those themes, so rarely explored in the culture of little girls, would seem particularly relevant given the complexities women can still face as leaders. Consider a 2007 survey of 1,231 executives in the United States and Europe, ominously subtitled *Damned if You Do, Doomed if You Don't*. Conducted by Catalyst, a nonprofit organization dedicated to the advancement of women in business, it found that female managers who behave consistently with gender stereotypes—prioritizing "work relationships" and expressing "concern for other people's perspectives"—were liked but considered to be ineffective. Those who were seen as behaving in a more "male" fashion, on the other hand—who "act assertively, focus on work task, display ambition"—were seen as competent but roundly disliked. I was tempted, initially, to dismiss that as a generational issue, something that would take care of itself as old-timers aged out of the workforce. Except that, according to a 2008 J. Walter Thompson report, "Millennial Women Face Gender Issues," 40 percent of men in their *twenties* still say they would prefer a male over a female boss. Nor, when you think about it, have the wildly different connotations of Super*man* and Super*woman* changed over time: the former is mysterious, admirable; the latter is hectic, harried, a woman who does too much and none of it well. That is not something I would want for myself or my girl. Besides, really, how many of us would like to be referred to as the Woman of Steel?

I was mulling over those disparities one sunny Saturday morning as Daisy and I strolled along Berkeley's Fourth Street on our way to our favorite breakfast joint, passing boutiques that sold handcrafted Japanese paper, diaphanous Stevie Nicks–inspired frocks, wooden toys imported from Europe. This was a few weeks before the 2008 Democratic primaries. Daisy spied a bumper sticker plastered on a mailbox: a yellow caricature of Hillary Clinton leering out from a black background. Big block letters proclaimed THE WICKED WITCH OF THE EAST IS ALIVE AND LIVING IN NEW YORK.

"Look, Mama," Daisy said, excitedly. "That's Hillary. What does it say?" What should I have told her? It's not that I thought that Senator Clinton was a victim—she often gave as good as she got. So it was not the attack that disturbed me so much as the form it took, the default position of incessant, even gleeful misogyny toward an unapologetically assertive (even aggressive) high-achieving woman. Contemplating the months of LIFE'S A BITCH, DON'T VOTE FOR ONE T-shirts, the silver-plated thighs of the Hillary nutcrackers (Woman of Steel!), the comparison to the bunny-boiling Alex Forrest of *Fatal Attraction*, I had often wondered whether Clinton was a symbol of how far we'd come as women or how far we had to go. Was she proof to my girl that "you can do anything" or of the hell that will rain down on you if you try? Was she a Wonder Woman or more like the hundred-plus super-heroines listed on the Web site womeninrefrigerators.com—so named because they had all been depowered, raped, driven insane, or chopped up and stuffed in a refrigerator? Damned if you do, doomed if you don't indeed.

Nothing so horrific happened to then-Senator Clinton (though Republican presidential candidate John McCain did respond, "Excellent question!" to someone at a campaign event who asked, "How do we beat the bitch?"); still, analysis of her actual policies was dwarfed by chatter—among both Republicans and Democrats, men as well as women—about the senator's hair, the pitch of her voice, the thickness of her ankles, her "likability," her relative femininity. Rush Limbaugh declared that Americans didn't want to watch a woman grow old in the White House. The journalist Christopher Hitchens called her an "aging and resentful female." Writing in the anthology *Thirty Ways of Looking at Hillary*, the novelist Susanna Moore wished that Clinton were more sensuous. And then there was the *real* debate: over her pantsuits. In a typical swipe, *The Washington Post*'s Robin Givhan wrote, "The mind . . . strays from more pressing concerns to ponder the sartorial: How many pantsuits does Hillary Clinton have in her closet?" There may have been a host of legitimate reasons to support Barack Obama over Clinton, but among them seemed to be that she was not young, pretty, slim, or stylish enough to represent the nation.

That was certainly not the case for the inexperienced-but-babelicious Sarah Palin, whom McCain chose as his running mate. Never mind that as governor of Alaska, she used her position to pursue personal vendettas, hired cronies to fill vacant posts, and fired officials who crossed her. Or that in an interview with CBS news anchor Katie Couric, she was unable to name a single periodical she read regularly to stay informed. Or that, when asked by CNBC, she could not describe the job of the vice president. Palin had been dubbed "America's Hottest Governor," and that propelled her forward. In the weeks after her nomination, top Internet searches involving her name included "Sarah Palin *Vogue*," "Sarah Palin bikini," and "Sarah Palin naked." As with Clinton, the former beauty queen's appearance—her clothing, glasses, and hairstyles (not to mention how much they cost)—seemed as relevant to her leadership potential as her policies. How were girls supposed to interpret that?

I know it is not the 1950s. It's not even the 1970s. Women are university presidents, governors, surgeons, titans of industry—even if not in the numbers one would wish or expect. Yet though we tell little girls "You can be anything you want to be," we know, from life experience, that that is still not quite true. At least not without a price. It's not as if when Daisy was three and announced that she wanted to be a firefighter I chimed in with "Honey, that's great, but last week I read an article about a woman at a firehouse in Austin, Texas, who came to work after a big promotion to find that her male coworkers had smeared her locker with human excrement." Still, as my daughter waited expectantly for me to read that bumper sticker, I did wonder how much to tell her—and when—about the tensions that persist around women and power.

Not surprisingly, friends have given Daisy a library full of "girl-positive" picture books designed to address this very issue. But, as with the "feminist" princess tales, I find I rarely pull them out—not only because they seem a tad spinachy but because they often undermine their own cause. Take *Elenita*, a magic realist tale about a Mexican girl who wants to be a glassblower. Her father says she can't do it: she is too little, and besides, the trade is forbidden to women. The lesson, naturally, is that with a little ingenuity girls can be glassblowers or stevedores or [fill in the blank]. Nice. Still, I found myself hesitating over the "girls can't" section. Daisy had never heard that "girls can't be" or "girls can't do," whether glassblowers, firefighters, or baseball players. Why should I plant the idea in her head only to knock it down? Even my treasured *Free to Be You and Me*, rather than teaching Daisy that William deserves a doll and mommies are people, merely confused her. "What's a sissy?" she asked me as we listened to "Dudley Pippin." And, later, during a sketch in which one newborn baby (voiced by Mel Brooks) is trying to convince another (Marlo Thomas) that *he* is the girl, "Why did that baby just say that girls can't keep secrets?" Overt discrimination and stereotyping may be less pervasive than when I was a child, but how can I explain—and gird her against—the subtler kinds that remain?

Daisy's birthday falls in the middle of summer. So from the end of July all the way through Labor Day, she happily zipped around the backyard swinging her lasso of truth and repelling bullets with her golden bracelets, upholding the forces of justice. Then school started, and within a few weeks I found her Wonder Woman gear balled up behind her dress-up bin. I asked what had happened, and she shrugged.

"None of the other girls want to play superheroes," she said.

They don't? I asked. Really?

"Not for very long, anyway," she hedged. "Mostly they just want to play *princess*." She looked dolefully up at me.

Suddenly I recalled the other part of the superhero story—that the gift of power elevates but also isolates. That's fine if you are a comic book character, not so much if you are a six-year-old girl. Now, I don't know if what she said was entirely true—her female classmates were hardly a bunch of pink-bots—but it didn't matter: that was her perception. This is the kind of thing all the books about raising smart, strong girls fail to mention. Frequently, after I have given a lecture on the topic myself, someone has commented, "My daughter *does* speak up and stand up for herself, and she *doesn't* wear trampy clothes or caked-on makeup. And do you know what she gets called? A bitch." To which I nod sympathetically and say, "If you don't toe the line, whether you are a girl or an adult woman, you do risk being punished. But you have to believe she will ultimately be better off." Now I realized what cold comfort that was. No one wants her child to be the sacrificial lamb to a cause. No one wants her daughter to feel excluded by her peers, to be ostracized for having the wrong clothes, hair, or pop preferences. No one wants her daughter to be caricatured on a bumper sticker. If Holly's daughter, Ava, did not fit the feminine ideal by chance, my daughter seemed to be rejecting it by choice. That was what I had wanted, right? For her to share my values, accept my wisdom? Yet I wondered where it would lead her.

In their insightful book *Packaging Girlhood*, Sharon Lamb and Lyn Mikel Brown write that the culture ultimately offers a girl two models for female identity. She can be "for the boys"—dress for them, perform sexually for them, play the supportive friend or girlfriend. Or she can be "one of the boys," an outspoken, feisty girl who hangs with the guys and doesn't take shit. The latter starts out as the kindergarten girl who is "independent and can think for herself." That would be my daughter. The trouble is, Brown and Lamb say, being "one of the boys" is as restrictive as the other option, in part because it discourages friendship with other girls: a girl who is "one of the boys" separates herself from her female peers, puts them down, is ashamed or scornful of anything associated with conventional femininity.

I was already seeing inklings of that attitude from Daisy. In kindergarten, her best friends were all male; she was sometimes the only girl at a birthday party. That was fine, but she also turned down a playdate with a female classmate, dismissing her as "too pinkie-pink." While looking for sandals online, she rejected pair after pair as too pretty/flowery/pink/girlie. She finally found some flip-flops to her liking in the boys' section (with a supersecret maze embedded in the outsole!). I appreciated the critique of the footwear industry, but her disdain made me uneasy: I thought back to our conversation several years before in the grocery store, when I had tried to explain my aversion to Cinderella. Had my worst fears during that episode come to pass? Rather than becoming more conscious of manipulation, had she instead learned that the things associated with girls—and by extension being a girl itself—were bad? Was the long-term impact of pinkness—all those one-off Scrabble boards and skateboards—to divide girls against themselves? Certainly, I didn't want her to think that all things snips 'n' snails—like, gulp, superheroes?—were *superior*. It was one thing to reject the image of girlhood being sold to her, another to reject girls who might embrace it. All I had wanted was to offer her a sense of worth as a girl that was not contingent on the cut of her clothes, a femininity grounded in something other than the bathroom mirror. Still, I had wanted her to stay allied with other girls. There had to be something like that out there, right?

For a moment, back in the early 1990s—before Britney, before Miley, before Princess and Bratz—it looked as if there might be. It is hard to recall now, but the idea of linking the word "girl" with "power" seemed minimally implausible and to most a contradiction in terms. Yet, launched by the punk-influenced Riot Grrrl movement (which replaced "girl" with a growling *grrrl*), "Girl Power" became a dare, a taunt, a primal scream: it was the word "slut" scrawled across the belly of a fleshy, shaved-headed young woman in a miniskirt and combat boots who was passing out hand-printed copies of her 'zine about incest. Set to a beat by bands like Bikini Kill (whose songs included "Suck My Left One"), the movement went alt-rock mainstream with Hole, whose frontwoman, Courtney Love, pioneered the "kinderwhore" look: ripped baby-doll dresses with fishnets, tiny plastic barrettes in badly dyed hair, overdone smeared makeup. The Riot Grrrls rejected market-driven images of femininity. Their cri de coeur, "Revolution Girl Style Now!" was all about female solidarity, self-reliance, and do-it-yourself media. They were not always pretty. They were not always palatable. They were also not for actual *girls*: although as a thirty-year-old I dug the movement, as a mom—call me old-fashioned—I would not especially want my first-grader "reappropriating" the word "cunt."

Enter the Spice Girls. With one impossibly infectious 1996 hit, "Wannabe" (you remember: "If you wanna be my lover, you gotta get with my friends"), they plucked the rrrrage right out of "Grrrl Power," rendering it apolitically appealing to the tweenybopper set and, more important, to their parents. Their opportunistic philosophy—most of the Pre–Fab Five had never met before auditioning for the band—was "about a positive attitude to life, getting what you want, and sticking by your friends." Who could argue with that? The Spices also offered girls a range of identities that nonetheless let them feel part of the group, a perfect developmental fit with the band's demographic. I recall endless conversations in which my nieces discussed which Spice they were—Sporty, Scary, Baby, Posh, or Ginger—then which Spice I was, then which Spice every female they had ever met might be, including their eighty-year-old grandmother (Old Spice, of course). It was tedious, but if not exactly grrrlishly subversive—where was Chubby Spice? Brainy Spice? Bi-Curious Spice?—it did not seem exactly *offensive*. At least, I figured, they weren't obsessed with the Backstreet Boys. This was a good ten years before *Hannah Montana* debuted, and I appreciated seeing them scream their heads off over other girls, rocking out to music that was made for them and about them. It was actually kind of exciting: the Spices were all about the girlfriends, Girlfriend. At least, that's what they claimed.

Around the time the Spice Girls broke, something called "girlie feminism" was also on the rise: far less threatening than Riot Grrrls, it held that women's traditional roles and skills (whether scrubbing floors, nurturing relationships, or knitting) had intrinsic value; that sexual equality need not require gender neutrality; that painting your nails and wearing a PORN STAR T-shirt were, if not radical acts, at least a woman's right, a viable form of self-expression and personal pleasure. That is, if done by the right people for the right reasons with the right soupçon of irony. The arguments were provocative but difficult to control. Just as they had with Riot Grrrls, Spice Girls skimmed off the easily consumable surface of girlie feminism—cute clothes! makeup!—and tossed its transgressive core. Rather than "empowering," then, the Spice World battle cry, "Strength and courage and a Wonderbra!" became increasingly confusing, especially to fans who weren't old enough to know what a Wonderbra actually was. By 1998, when Ginger Spice ditched her so-called forever friends, "girl power" had devolved into little more than an empty slogan on a shrunken pink T-shirt. The phrase may have started the decade representing one irony, but it ended by expressing quite another. Those extra *r*'s in Riot Grrrl, which had heralded a rejection of consumerized femininity, were replaced by the now-ubiquitous *z* (as in Ty Girlz, Moxie Girlz, Bratz Girlz, Baby Phat Girlz, Glitter Girlz, Clique Girlz, "Disney Girlz Rock"), which embraced it. *Z* did not seek to expand choices, break down barriers, address injustice. *Z* signaled "empowerment" as the power to shop, old-school stereotypes recast as the source of liberation rather than an impediment to it.

Disney Princesses, Miley Cyrus, child-friendly makeup, the proliferation of pink, are all outgrowths of that marketing sleight of hand. And, since the Riot Grrrls dispersed, no homegrown culture has risen up to challenge them. Mothers, meanwhile, want (really, really want, as the Spice Girls might sing) so desperately to guide their daughters to an authentic, unconflicted balance of feminism and femininity, one that will sustain rather than constrain them. Witness, for instance, the success of two "advice manuals" for girls published in 2008: *The Daring Book for Girls* and *The Girls' Book: How to Be the Best at Everything* (as well as their endless sequels, such as *The Double-Daring Book for Girls* and *How to Be the Best at Everything Again*). Both volumes were spin-offs of *The Dangerous Book for Boys*, a gilt-embossed paean to old-school adventure whose tantalizing chapters on building a go-cart and making secret ink from (presumably your own) pee induced nostalgia among fathers—typically the ones purchasing the book—for their own huckleberry childhoods, those halcyon days before cable, Wii, Facebook, and cell phones. The girls' books, however, do something entirely different. Rather than harking back to—heaven forbid!—bygone days, they evoke nostalgia for a time that has yet to be, a girlhood that we mothers may wish we'd had but did not, one that we hope will nourish our daughters and prepare them to be the kind of women we're not sure we were fully able to become.

The Girls' Book, published by Scholastic, is solidly in the *z* camp: that extra X chromosome, it implies, stands for Xcessorize, and "having it all" comes with a hefty credit card debt. The book may advise readers on "how to cross Niagara Falls on a tight-rope," but its more realistic fare includes how to "act like a ce-lebrity," "make your own luxury bubble bath," and "give yourself a perfect manicure." I'm not above seeking a little pick-me-up at the cosmetic counter myself, mind you, but I am not nine years old. Even so, in some ways, I mourn what has been taken from me by the rise of this girlz-with-a-*z* culture—when I was pregnant, I imagined occasionally playing "manicure" with my daughter as my mom had with me; I had a bag of old (probably bacteria-infested) lipsticks and eye shadows that I planned to bequeath to her for dress-up play. But by the time Daisy was three, I had tossed them all and become a hard-liner on all questions of nail polish and makeup. That was for grown-ups, I would tell her, not for little girls. Period. I know my response was extreme, possibly excessively so. But there was so much more out there than when I was a girl that urged her to define herself from the outside in, to believe identity was for sale; adding to all that, even in a small way, felt too much like collusion.

The Daring Book for Girls, by contrast, makes the case for a separate-but-equal girls' culture of play—one that, like its male counterpart, deserves resurrection and preservation. Any for-mer girl (read: current mom) would find its chapters on jacks, hand-clap games, and that staple of Girl Scout campfires, the sit-upon—*the sit-upon!!!!*—pretty much irresistible. I know I did. This might be more of what the 1990s "girlie feminists"—the ones revaluing cooking and crafts—had in mind: a feminism that expects parity with boys and men, yet does not strive to be like them or see their conventional roles and behavior as more desirable. As a nod to the fact that today's girls will not, like their forebears, live their lives in a "separate sphere" from men—as well as acknowledgment that "different" can quickly be tagged as "lesser"—the book also provides tutorials on "How to Negotiate a Salary" and "Finance: Interest, Stocks and Bonds." Useful skills, but ones that will probably appeal primarily to mothers. Girls themselves, I would wager, will see them as the equivalent of a granola bar in the Halloween bag.

Daring Girls was the closest thing I had seen to what I was looking for: a concept of girlhood as a community, a vision that was dynamic and character-building rather than decorative At the same time, most of what was in the book seemed so arbitrary I wondered whether it truly upheld tradition or just created yet another trap. Segmenting play by sex, remember, may be good for sales but not necessarily for kids' development. So you tell me which of these activities (pulled at random from the boys' and girls' books) seems feminine and which masculine: Building a Campfire; Making Cloth Fireproof; Fourteen Games of Tag; Five Pen-and-Paper Games; Snowballs; Cloud Formations (answers: girls, boys, girls, boys, girls, boys). Why can't girls make crystals or juggle (those are in the boys' book)? Why can't boys construct a lemon-powered clock or learn Five Karate Moves (those are in the girls' book)? Perhaps more pointedly: what about the boy who, à la *How to Be the Best at Everything*, wants to "put together the best dance routine"? Now, *that* would be "dangerous."

Maybe the wisest course of action would be to rip off the

covers of all of the books and let children choose for themselves the activities they find feminine or masculine or just plain fun. That could even help with the kind of casual, naturally occurring interaction the Sanford program's Carol Martin and Rick Fabes are trying to foster between boys and girls. I think Daisy would enjoy such a project (once she can read). And I would, too.

As the school year went on, she rebounded from her disappointment and returned to superhero play, albeit mostly when she was by herself. She also added a new character to her repertoire named Wildcat: technically, he was a male superhero; she had feminized him with Batgirl ears and socks on her hands. I was not sure how I felt about that. I know that if I could imbue her with a superpower, it would be the ability to withstand the pressures of the culture around her, to be her own woman despite the potential costs: I would give her the courage of her convictions, the power to be the hero of her own story without ambivalence or fear, to embrace her gifts regardless of her body's size or shape—even if I have not been fully able to embrace mine.

Meanwhile, I did a little digging about Wonder Woman. It turns out her real name was Diana, daughter of Hera, queen of the Amazons. That makes her, of all things . . . a princess.

Chapter Nine

Just Between You, Me, and My 622 BFFs

i think it was the pig snout that put me over the line.

I was trying to meet some girls on the Internet, to chat with them in real time about how they presented themselves on social networking sites and virtual worlds—increasingly popular fantasy landscapes in which users interact with one another through avatars. How did their online selves reflect, reinforce, or differ from who they were offline? What role did this new world have in shaping their identities, their femininity? I had started by hopping onto an award-winning educational site called Whyville, whose 5 million "citizens," largely young teens, could play games, buy "virtual goods," and chat electronically with one her. There is no need to "friend" a person in a virtual world, so it is easy to observe (as well as talk to) complete strangers.

In order to go onto the site, I had to create an avatar—a word that once denoted the human incarnation of a Hindu deity. I put a lot of thought into what she (because I decided to remain a she) should look like. I ended up giving her—or was it myself?—a whimsical, spiky purple 'do, glasses, a goofy grin, and, just for the heck of it, a pig snout for a nose. When I took that bad self "in world," however, I found a land of girls with big hair and chunky highlights; full, glossy pouts; thickly lined doe eyes; and skimpy, fashion-forward outfits. Girls, in other words, who'd styled themselves like a line of hot, trendy dolls. Was that how they saw themselves? How they wished they looked? How they aspired to look? How they thought they should look? A cartoon bubble popped up above the head of a girl named "Sweetiepi," whose avatar was staring directly at me. It said she was "whispering" with another girl, named OMGBrooke. I got the uneasy feeling they were discussing my snout.

Back in the midnineties, the concern among parents and educators was that girls were not going online at the same rate as boys. A digital divide was looming, and it threatened to leave girls stranded on the wrong side of economic opportunity. That notion turned out to be *sooooo* twentieth century. These days, 35 million kids ages three to eighteen—80 percent of kindergartners alone—are online, though by the time you read this those numbers will surely be higher. A solid half of those users are female.

Girls spend the same amount of time as boys on the Internet, but their activities differ. Predictably, more boys are gamers. They are also more likely to produce videos to post on their online profiles or sites such as YouTube. Girls, meanwhile, are out front in communication: more girls than boys blog, instant message, text, create Web pages, and join virtual worlds and social networking sites.

I skimmed that information with mounting disapproval: kids seemed to be going online so young—maybe too young. Then I remembered that Daisy had been on the Internet, tooling around the Nick Jr. site, since she was three years old. I suspect, in fact, that she first associated the word "mouse" not with a rodent but with a piece of computer hardware. I have watched with equal parts curiosity and anxiety as she has navigated with preternatural skill through the site's games. Her obsession with the Dora pages seemed harmless enough, but what would she do next? What would she *see* next?

This was a place in my reporting, I realized, where, to gain deeper insight, I had to leave the littlest girls behind for their older sisters. For one thing, older girls can read, something that instantly expands the online experience. Beyond that, the sites for little girls were all mind-numbingly the same. The virtual worlds of BarbieGirls, Be-Bratz, Ty Girlz, Moxiegirlz were all extensions of their offline counterparts. Each featured similar games girls could play to "earn" points with which to engage in their favorite activity: shopping. They could visit virtual malls to buy stylin' fashions for their avatars or a flat-screen TV for their virtual cribs. They could indulge in makeovers at the spa or purchase pets to pamper. They could also hone their ambitions for the future by playing at rock star or celebrity or . . . rock star or celebrity. On the New Dora's "Dora

Links," for instance, the "mysteries and adventure" in which girls can engage include changing the length of their avatar's hair, eye color, earrings, and necklace and getting "ready for a benefit concert."

The Disney Princesses site could well be crowned the dullest of them all: a user can enter the "enchanting" world of her favorite princess and, in each one, play a version of the *identical game*: Cinderella/Belle/Sleeping Beauty/Ariel is on her way to an important parade/fair/birthday party/tea party but— *Oh no!* She forgot to pick out an outfit and now doesn't have time! Can she count on *you* to do it for her by clicking on one of several predetermined choices? None of this is a surprise, and I am tempted to gloss right over it. Yet more and more of children's time is spent online. Doll sales have declined by nearly 20 percent since 2005. Girls are casting them aside in favor of online play, which offers even fewer opportunities to go off script. It chilled me to read, in the market research group NPD's report on this trend, a quote from a nine-year-old Barbie.com fan who said, "I don't think I'm good at making up imaginary things; I didn't know what to do with dolls." So it is at least worth mentioning that, even more than the original toys, these sites funnel our daughters toward very specific definitions of both girlhood and play.

Sites for the youngest children are protected by the Children's Online Privacy Protection Act (COPPA), which requires "verifiable parental consent" at registration and restricts the amount of personal information—addresses, phone numbers, sex, preferences in music—corporate marketers can collect from children. Chatting is typically limited and inappropriate behavior punished by suspension or expulsion. Once children turn thirteen, however, all bets are off. They are legally considered adults online, free to join any site that is not X-rated (though since the age of users

on those sites is rarely verified, they could join those as well).
You would be hard pressed these days to find an eighth-grader
without a Facebook account. Meanwhile, 3.7 million teens log on
to a virtual world each month. Today's platforms will probably
be obsolete by the time Daisy is a teenager (if not by next year),
but regardless of whatever Web site or matrix or brain implant
arises to take their place, my questions remain the same: How
will the Internet shape my daughter's understanding of herself?
Will its vastness—its infinite nooks and crannies—intensify the
contradictions of girlhood or provide opportunities for refuge?
Will she lose control of her identity or gain new insight into it?
And how can I, as a mom, sort out the legitimate from the sen-
sationalist in the headlines about predators, anonymous bullying
by peers, easy-access porn? (Try Googling "schoolgirls.com" or,
as an eight-year-old daughter of a friend of mine innocently did,
"cute girls.")

I am no Luddite. I am well aware of what an incredible, creative tool the Internet can be, offering split-second access to a
diversity of perspectives and information that previously seemed
unimaginable. But I have heard it said that we adults are immigrants to this land of technology; our kids are natives. They use it
differently than we do. They experience it differently, without our
old-world accents or values. Much as the mall was for a previous
generation, the Internet has become a place where they experiment with identity, friendship, and flirtation. The fact that none
of it is real does not make it any less revealing.

Erin, who is fourteen, has been online since she was in third grade. "I used to love doing the painting pages on the Dragon Tales site," she said, laughing. "I did them until I was much too old."

Erin and three of her friends were sitting in her family's Albany, California, living room. Her mother had set out an array of healthy snacks for us—hummus with carrots, fresh strawberries—but the girls shunned those for a bucket of shamrock-shaped, green frosted sugar cookies bought at the grocery store in celebration of Saint Patrick's Day. Each one here today had been online since she was seven or eight. Each carried her cell phone as if it were a fifth limb. Each owned an iPod touch. Each used computers daily, often in the privacy of her bedroom. Naturally, they all had Facebook accounts, which, judging from my communication with them, they checked numerous times during the school day. They'd had some amazing experiences online: one of the girls, Katie, fourteen, who had been adopted as an infant, told me she had found her birth mother on Facebook. So she'd friended her. "It was an open adoption, so I always knew her name," Katie explained, "but she'd never visited or anything. She was only seventeen when I was born." The two ended up meeting in person some months later, when the woman passed through San Francisco. "It was cool," Katie said, though she had no plans to see the woman again. The casual way she related the story confused me. Finding your birth mother with a few clicks—on Facebook, of all things—would seem momentous, yet Katie was treating it like it was no big deal. Maybe she was just playing it cool, but I wondered whether the unlimited possibility for connection had somehow devalued its worth.

Each of these girls had more than 400 friends on the networking site—one, Felicia, had 622—which was so unremarkable that I almost didn't note it. But really? Six hundred twenty-two friends? There were only about 250 students in her entire grade at school. One of my favorite books as a child was Joan Walsh Anglund's *A Friend Is Someone Who Likes You.* These days, a better title might be *A Friend Is Someone You Have Actually Met in Person.* There is no way Felicia could know all those people offline, though she claimed to have at least *met* each of them. Even so, 622 people can witness everything she writes, every picture she posts. Six hundred twenty-two people can pass that information on to *their* 622 friends. Six hundred twenty-two people are watching her, judging her, at least in theory, every hour of every day. How does that influence a child's development?

Apparently, quite a bit. In short order—a matter of a few years—social networking and virtual worlds have transformed how young people, male as well as female, conceptualize both their selves and their relationships. According to Adriana Manago, a researcher at the Children's Digital Media Center in Los Angeles who studies college students' behavior on MySpace and Facebook, young people's real-life identities are becoming ever more externally driven, sculpted in response to feedback from network "friends." Obviously, teens have always tested out new selves among their peers, but back in the dark ages (say, in the year 2000), any negative response was fleeting and limited to a small group of people they actually knew. Now their thoughts, photos, tastes, and activities are laid out for immediate approval or rejection by hundreds of people, many of whom are relative strangers. The self, Manago said, becomes a brand, something to be marketed to others rather than developed from within. Instead of intimates with whom you interact for the sake of the exchange, friends become your consumers, an audience for whom you perform.

The impact, back in the offline world, appears to be an up-tick in narcissistic tendencies among young adults. In the largest study of its kind, a group of psychologists found that the scores of the 16,475 college students who took the Narcissistic Personality Inventory between 1982 and 2006 have risen by 30 percent. A full two-thirds of today's young adults rank above average; excessive self-involvement is associated with difficulty in maintaining romantic relationships, dishonesty, and lack of empathy. And, it turns out, empathy, too, seems in measurably shorter supply: an analysis of seventy-two studies performed on almost 14,000 college students between 1979 and 2009 showed a drop in that trait, with the sharpest decline occurring since 2000. Social media may not have instigated that trend, but by encouraging self-promotion over self-awareness, they could easily accelerate it.

I don't mean to demonize new technology. I enjoy Facebook myself. Because of it, I am in touch with old friends and relatives who are scattered around the globe. It has also served as a handy vehicle to promote my work, to alert the readers among my "friends" that I have published something new. Yet I am also aware of the ways Facebook and the microblogging site Twitter subtly shifted my self-perception. Online, I carefully consider how any comments or photos I post will shape the persona I have cultivated; offline, I have caught myself processing my experience as it occurs, packaging life as I live it. As I loll in the front yard with Daisy or stand in line at the supermarket or read in bed, part of my consciousness splits off, viewing the scene from the outside and imagining how to distill it into a status update or a Tweet. Apparently, teenagers are not the only ones at risk of turning the self into a performance, though since their identities are less formed, one assumes the potential impact will be more profound.

Girls, especially, are already so accustomed to disconnecting from their inner experience, observing themselves as others might. Unlike earlier generations, though, their imagined audience is all too real: online, every girl becomes a mini-Miley complete with her own adoring fan base that she is bound to maintain. In fact, if you try to choose the screen name "Miley" in a virtual world, you will be told no dice, though you can be Miley1819 or higher, if you would like. According to Manago, girls attract the most positive feedback when they post provocative photos or create hot avatars—as long as they don't go too far. Just as with real celebs, then, girls online engage in perpetual, public negotiation between appearing "beautiful, sexy, yet innocent" (which they reportedly want) and coming off as "a slut" in front of hundreds of people (which they do not). Perhaps that high-wire act, as much as anything, reveals the lie of girls' popular culture: if the sexualization and attention to appearance truly "empowered" girls, they would emerge from childhood with more freedom and control over their sexuality. Instead, they seem to have less: they have learned that sexiness confers power—unless you use it (or are perceived as using it). The fastest way to take a girl down remains, as ever, to attack her looks or sexual behavior: Ugly. Fat. Slut. Whore. Those are the teen girl equivalent of kryptonite.

Erin and her friends have their own ideas about how to strike the right balance. Jessica, fourteen, explained, "I never put up a picture *just* of me. That's slutty."

I asked how merely posting a solo shot of herself could qualify as "slutty." "Well," she responded, "it's self-centered, though, which is kind of the same thing."

She pulled up the profile of one of her classmates to show me what she meant. The other girls crowded around the screen. How strange, I thought; I don't know this girl and never will, but here I was rifling through her photos, reading what other people thought of them. One snapshot showed her leaning forward in a bikini top; in another, she posed with one shoulder thrust coyly toward the viewer. "Look at her," said Felicia, disgusted. "She's dyed her hair *blond*. Badly. And look at that." She pointed to a close-up shot of the girl mugging for the camera with a boy. "He is in her bed! Her *bed*!"

Felicia did not stint on comments about other girls, even though she herself had been branded a slut in eighth grade by classmates who were jealous of the boy she was dating. Also, she has large breasts, which had developed early, and, really, isn't that enough? Her tormentors targeted her both in person and electronically, even creating a Facebook page called "Felicia's a Whore." "I tried to act like it didn't bother me," she said, tersely. "But it was not a lovely situation." Nor an uncommon one. The girls showed me another friend's Formspring page: a free application that allows your Facebook "friends" to ask questions or post comments about you—anonymously. That means that while the person who says "Can I see ur tits live?" or "U r a bitch!" is someone you know (or at least someone you have friended), you can never know exactly *who*. Think of it as the online equivalent of a bathroom stall with all the raunchiness and lord-of-the-flies viciousness that implies. The mind reels at the idea of such technology in the hands of teenage girls, who are already masters of—and suckers for—stealth aggression.

In the early days of the Web, people feared their daughters would be stalked by strangers online, but the far bigger threat has turned out to come from neighbors, friends, peers. In the first high-profile case of cyberbullying, a Missouri girl, Megan Meier, hung herself in her bedroom after a romance with a boy she had met on MySpace—but had never spoken to or seen in person—went sour. "You're the kind of boy a girl would kill herself over,"

Meier wrote in her final post, twenty minutes before her suicide. She was just three weeks shy of her fourteenth birthday. The boy, it was later discovered, did not exist: he had been fabricated by Meier's neighbor, forty-seven-year-old Lori Drew, to punish the girl for spreading rumors about Drew's own daughter. Four years later, in 2010, fifteen-year-old Phoebe Prince put cyberbullying back in the headlines: she hung herself after enduring months of sexual slurs in her South Hadley, Massachusetts, high school hallways, as well as via text message and on Facebook. A few months later, Alexis Pilkington, a popular seventeen-year-old soccer player from Long Island, also took her life after a series of cybertaunts, which persisted on a memorial page created after her death.

Most cases of online harassment do not go that far, but the upsurge of abuse is disturbing. A 2009 poll conducted by the Associated Press and MTV found that half of young people aged fourteen to twenty-four reported experiencing digital abuse, with girls significantly more likely to be victimized than boys. Two-thirds of those who were the target of rumors and hearsay were "very upset" or "extremely upset" by the experience, and they were more than twice as likely as their peers to have considered suicide.

Gossip and nasty notes may be painful staples of middle school and high school girls' lives, but YouTube, Facebook, instant messaging, texting, and voice mail can raise cruelty to exponential heights. Rumors can spread faster and further and, as the case of Phoebe Prince illustrates, there is nowhere to escape their reach—not your bedroom, not the dinner table, not while going out with your friends. The anonymity of the screen may also embolden bullies: the natural inhibitions one might feel face-to-face, along with any sense of accountability, fall away. It is easy, especially among young people, for behavior to spin out of control. Further, this risks exposing them to consequences they did not—or could not—anticipate.

◦◦◦

Portraying girls as victims, particularly of other girls, is distressing, but it is also comfortable, familiar territory. What happens when girls, under the pretext of sexual self-determination, seem to victimize themselves? A 2008 survey by the National Campaign to Prevent Teen and Unplanned Pregnancy found that 39 percent of teens had sent or posted sexually suggestive messages (or "sexts"), and 22 percent of teenage girls had electronically sent or posted nude or seminude photos of themselves. At first I was skeptical of those figures: the teen sexting "epidemic" had the earmarks of media-generated hype, the kind of moral panic that breaks out whenever girls have the audacity to act sexually. Young ladies flashing skin and propositioning boys? Heavens to Betsy, hie them to a nunnery!

Then, mere days after that report was released, a friend of mine found a photo on her fourteen-year-old son's computer of one of his female classmates—a ninth-grader—naked from the waist up. She was not even a girl he knew well. "We're trying to teach our son that women are not playthings," my friend said. "How are we supposed to do that if a girl sends him something like this?"

Good question. How is one to explain such behavior? Part of me, I had to admit, was taken by the girl's bravado: that at age fourteen, she felt confident enough in her body to send a nudie shot to a boy she barely knew. Was it possible that this was a form of progress, a sign that at least some of today's girls were taking charge of their sexuality, transcending the double standard? I wanted to believe it, but the conclusion didn't sit right.

I checked in with Deborah Tolman, a professor of human sexuality studies at Hunter College who for years has been my go-to gal on all matters of girls and desire. As it happened, she had been wrestling with these very questions and had come up with a theory: girls like the one I have described are not connecting more deeply to their own feelings, needs, or desires. Instead, sexual entitlement itself has become objectified; like identity, like femininity, it, too, has become a performance, something to "do" rather than to "experience." Teasing and turning boys on might give girls a certain thrill, even a fleeting sense of power, but it will not help them understand their own pleasure, recognize their own arousal, allow them to assert themselves in intimate (let alone casual) relationships.

Previously, I mentioned that early sexualization can derail girls' healthy development, estrange them from their own erotic feelings. Ninth-graders texting naked photos may be one result. Another might be the annual "slut list" the senior girls at an affluent high school in Millburn, New Jersey, compile of incoming freshmen (which made national news after they posted it on Facebook in 2009); being chosen is at once an honor and a humiliation, marking a girl as "popular" even as it accuses her of lusting after her brother or wanting someone to "bend me over and knock me up." That detached sexuality may also contribute to an emerging phenomenon that Tolman is studying, which she called, bluntly, Anal Is the New Oral. "All girls are now expected to have oral sex in their repertoire," she explained. "Anal sex is becoming the new 'Will she do it or not?' behavior, the new 'Prove you love me.' And still, girls' sexual pleasure is not part of the equation." That is such a fundamental misunderstanding of romantic relationships and sexuality—as a mother, it plunges me into despair. I find myself improbably nostalgic for the late 1970s, when I came of age. Fewer of us competed on the sports field, raised our hands during math class, or graduated from college. No one spoke the word "vagina," whether in a monologue or not. And there was that Farrah flip to contend with. Yet in that oh-so-brief window between the advent of the pill and the fear of AIDS, when abortion was both legal and accessible to teenagers, there was—at least for some of us—a kind of *Our Bodies, Ourselves* optimism about sex. Young women felt an almost solemn, political duty to understand their desire and responses, to explore their own pleasure, to recognize sexuality as something rising from within. And young men—at least some of them—seemed eager to take the journey with us, to rewrite the rules of masculinity so they would prize mutuality over conquest. That notion now seems as quaint as a one-piece swimsuit on a five-year-old. "By the time they are teenagers," Tolman said, "the girls I talk to respond to questions about how their bodies feel—questions about sexuality or desire—by talking about how their bodies look. They will say something like 'I felt like I looked good.'" My fear for my daughter, then, is not that she will someday act in a sexual way; it is that she will learn to act sexually against her own self-interest.

Most young women, thankfully, are not out there making personalized *Playboy* centerfolds. The ones who are may well be the ones engaging in other risky behaviors offline; the statistics on sexting, for instance, are similar, demographically, to those on binge drinking. Megan Meier, the girl who committed suicide in 2006, had a history of depression, as did Alexis Pilkington. Phoebe Prince seems to have been a self-cutter. Does that make them anomalies, or canaries in a coal mine? What about the thirteen-year-old girl "in love" who sends a hot shot to her boyfriend without considering what he will do with it after she dumps him? Or the girl who one time—just one time—does a stupid, thoughtless thing. Which of us hasn't been that girl? In the old days that One Stupid Thing might have sparked ugly rumors, but it could also fade away. The bad judgment you showed when you got drunk at a party and danced topless on a table was ephemeral. But my friend's son, were he so inclined, could forward his classmate's photo to one of his friends, who could forward it to two of his friends and, as in that 1970s shampoo commercial, so on and so on, until all three thousand–plus kids at their high school had a copy—and maybe all the kids in the next town as well. And that, as much as the act itself, is the problem: the indelibility of it, the never-ending potential for replication, the loss of control over your image and identity right when, as a teenager, you need it most.

Electronic media have created a series of funhouse mirrors. They both forge greater intimacy and undermine it—sometimes simultaneously. Determining what, exactly, is going on at any given time is confusing enough for an adult, let alone a child. The ten-year-old daughter of another friend of mine recently invited a pal for a sleepover. Rather than playing in person, the girls wanted to spend the evening using the family's computers—a desktop downstairs, a laptop upstairs—to send each other messages on the virtual world Webkinz.com. Was that just a latter-day version of one of my favorite childhood activities—putting a message in a basket and lowering it down the laundry chute on a string from the second story of my house to the basement, where my best friend awaited? Or was it something else, the beginnings of alienation from living, breathing friends, from the messiness and reciprocity of authentic relationships? Watching the unparalleled social experiment being conducted on our children, it's worth considering—for boys as well as girls—how Internet use enhances their *real* lives, their *real* friendships, their contributions to the *real* world. And if we can't answer all of that in a satisfying way, maybe it is time to give their second lives some second thought.

⚬⚬⚬

So how to prepare our kids for a safe, productive life online? Late one winter afternoon I drove to Black Hawk, a gated community of multimillion-dollar houses in Danville, California. At the top of a long, twisting driveway, a building that could have been a small hotel emerged before me. It was the home of Hilary DeCesare, a former account manager at Oracle and recently divorced mom of three: twelve-year-old twins—a girl and a boy—as well as an eight-year-old girl. DeCesare's home doubled as headquarters of the soon-to-be-launched social networking site she was developing for kids aged eight to thirteen that she hopes will be as revolutionary as Facebook was. To date, there was nothing like it: a COPPA-compliant site that will allow kids to customize their profile pages, create interest groups, play games, write on one another's walls, e-mail, even video chat. A sophisticated software program will scan the site 24/7 for explicit language and the percentage of skin showing on photos and videos. Users will find regular tips posted on their walls to educate them about online safety and etiquette. Anyone caught bullying will be suspended or banished. Parents can monitor their children as closely or loosely as they see fit: approving each friend request and group membership in real time; receiving a weekly or monthly e-mail rundown of their child's activity; or, if they choose, trusting their kids to find their own way. They can restrict their children to preset "canned chat" phrases or allow them to IM one another freely. DeCesare likes to call it "the Internet with training wheels."

DeCesare, a fit blond woman dressed in a powder blue sweater and jeans, met me at the door with a plate of homemade fudge and a surprise. When we had first spoken, some months earlier, her site had been called Girl Ambition (a name that would seem more appealing to mothers than kids) and had been adamantly single-sex. She had focused on girls, she had told me, because they were adopting the social technologies more rapidly than boys. Also because she was a mom as well as an entrepreneur: one who did not like the values promoted by the commercial sites for girls her own daughters frequented. She had hoped to lure them away with a fun alternative that, P.S., would also slip in lessons on goal setting, self-esteem, and healthy body image as well as offer advice on dealing with cyberbullies. In the interim, however, she had realized it didn't make business sense to exclude half the world's kids because of their sex. So she had scaled back the educational component and renamed the company the more neutral (and potentially profitable) Everloop.

We headed into the family library, its shelves stacked with bestselling books by authors such as John Grisham and James Patterson. A volume from the *Gossip Girl* series lay on a table between two computers. A third computer sat on a desk pushed against an adjacent wall. DeCesare had asked her twins to show me around the site, so I could experience it as users would. Her son immediately sat down and began gaming. He did not say much during the rest of my visit. Her daughter Danielle, meanwhile, plopped down in another chair and turned sideways toward me, swinging her feet, her toes tipped with chipped green polish, as she showed off her home page. She had customized the background with a photo of the stars of the *Twilight* series, listed her favorite singer as Taylor Swift and her favorite show as *iCarly*. Her groups included Ro's Soccer Club (started by her little sister), *Star Wars*, and Fashion 101.

DeCesare had told me, as a selling point, that there would be no advertising on Everloop. But watching Danielle, I realized that didn't matter: product promotions are so thoroughly embedded online that ads would be redundant. In addition to groups created by the kids themselves, Everloop will feature corporate-sponsored "supergroups." Imagine an exercise group hosted by Nike, a video group hosted by Flip, a hygiene group hosted by Bonne Bell. Users will also be able to buy "stickers" of favorite products and performers to put on their home pages—a gimmick that basically convinces them to pay for advertising. All of that is in keeping with the larger "advergaming" trend on Internet sites for kids: in the popular virtual world Millsberry (owned by General Mills) users can explore the "Honey Nut Cheerios Greenhouse"; at the not-for-profit Whyville they can drive a Toyota Scion; or work at the McDonald's in Habbo Hotel; or hang out in the Cosmo-Girl lounge at There.com. Parents are often warned that, until children are six, they cannot distinguish between commercials and programming on TV. With the Internet, there is no longer a distinction to make—for them or for us. Frankly, I would prefer traditional advertising to all this embedded stuff; as a parent, I would feel less duped.

When I first met DeCesare, I was jazzed about her site, even though it seemed a little preachy. Now I felt myself beginning to turn. I appreciated the safeguards against sexual deviants, but where was the protection against other sorts of predation? How about some tips on resisting covert marketing along with the ones on combating cyberbullies? A site like Everloop may be fun, even imaginative, but it will also roll back the age at which children will create and present themselves as a brand, one composed of various products and media, most of which portray both girls and boys in stereotypical ways. If that is unhealthy for a college student, I can't see how it would be desirable for an eight-year-old.

DeCesare reminded me that parents had the option to filter any or all of that out. That may be, I said, but realistically, how long could it last? "We're not claiming we're perfect," she responded. "But it is presumed we're going to be creating an environment that's empowering to the kids."

There was that word again: "empowering." She meant that Everloop would allow kids to play online freely yet safely. But really, could any environment be truly empowering if it pushes kids—and girls in particular, since they are more active in social networks—to define themselves by what they buy, how they look, whom they idolize, what they watch? It is telling that girls' embrace of online culture is not translating into their adult ambitions. Even as the percentage of girls using the Internet has soared, the percentage of female college students majoring in computer science has plummeted, dropping by 70 percent between 2000 and 2005. The gender gap in consuming Internet culture may have closed, but the one in creating it has only grown wider.

I would like to ignore the online world of kids—the complications seem endless and overwhelming—but, like any parent today, I can't. I would rather Daisy spend her time honing her identity on an offline playground than an online one, through face-to-face relationships and real-life activities. I do not want the Web to be where she defines her femininity or asserts her independence, any more than my mom wanted me to test mine by hopping on a bus to the mall with her Shoppers Charge in hand. Yet parents also have to be realists, and, as DeCesare reminded me, this is the world in which our children are being raised. "At Everloop, we're trying to give kids unexpected freedom while giving parents like you peace of mind," she assured me. Maybe she is right. Maybe our kids do need those training wheels—and maybe recognizing that will turn DeCesare into the next Tom Anderson, one of the founders of MySpace, who sold out to Rupert Murdoch for $580 million. But for now, she said, "our goal is simple: to get kids ready for the real world, to prepare them for when they go on to other sites. Because," she added, "you know they will."

Chapter Ten

Girl Power—No, Really

i didn't like that princess," Daisy said, wrinkling her nose. "She looked funny."

It was two weeks before Christmas 2009, and that could mean only one thing: the annual release of a new animated Disney film. That year, *The Princess and the Frog* premiered amid a blitz of self-congratulatory hype about the studio's First African-American Princess (though the more impressive event will be the introduction of the *Second* or maybe the *Third* African-American Princess). America's first black president had been elected just weeks before, the news media enthused, and—as if the two were equivalent—now this! About two-thirds of the audience at our local multiplex had been African American—parents with little girls

decked out in gowns and tiaras—which was undeniably striking, even moving. Still, my own response, characteristically, was
mixed: sure, it was about time Disney made up for the racism of
Song of the South, *The Jungle Book*, and *Dumbo* (and *Aladdin* and
Peter Pan), but was peddling a café au lait variation of the same
old rescue fantasy in a thin-and-pretty package the best way to do
that? Was that truly cause for celebration?

"But it's different for black girls," my friend Verna had told
me. Verna, who is African American, is mother to a nine-year-
old daughter. She is also a law professor specializing in the intersection of race, gender, and class in education law and policy.
"There's a saying in our community," she continued, "'We love
our sons but we raise our daughters.' Girls learn that you have to
do. You have to be the worker bee. Princess takes black girls out
of that realm. And you know, discounting the baggage of how
stultifying being placed on a pedestal can be . . . " She laughed. "If
you've never been on it, it looks pretty good."

I took the point, I guess. Certainly, as the mother of a biracial
child myself, I identified with the constant scavenger hunt for toys
and images that in *some* way resembled my kid. Take the wooden
dollhouse I bought for Daisy: its choice of families spanned the
skin tone spectrum, but the manufacturer's progressiveness did
not extend to miscegenation (or, for that matter, to gay parents). I
ended up buying two sets, one white and one Asian, so she could
mix and match. It was, at best, an imperfect solution.

Scarcity breeds scrutiny. Given how few black female leads
there are in G-rated animation (Anyone? Anyone?), Tiana,
fairly or not, was expected to *represent*. *The Princess and the Frog*
was subject to months of speculation before it opened. Outrage
bubbled up when the first pass at Tiana's name was revealed:
"Maddy," which sounded uncomfortably close to "Mammy." Dis-

ney also miscalculated, according to scuttlebutt, by initially making the character a chambermaid for a white woman; in the end, Tiana is a waitress at a restaurant owned by an African-American man. The texture of her hair, the shade of her skin, the fullness of her features, were all debated, as was the suspiciously indeterminate ethnicity of her prince (described as "olive-skinned," he spoke with a Brazilian accent). Disney shrewdly tried to bullet-proof the film by consulting Oprah Winfrey (who also voiced Tiana's mother, Eudora), the NAACP, and an organization called Mocha Moms. Take, *that*, critics! Of course, in the end, Tiana spent most of the film as a (shapely, long-eyelashed) amphibian, which rendered her race more or less moot.

Now here was my daughter, my very own daughter, saying that something about the princess looked off . . . *why?*

"You thought Tiana looked funny?" I asked, trying to keep my voice neutral.

She shook her head impatiently. "No," she said. "Not Tiana. The *princess.*"

"But Tiana *was* the princess," I said.

She shook her head again. "The *princess,*" she repeated, then, after a moment, added, "I liked when she helped the African-American girl, though."

That was when it clicked: Daisy wasn't talking about Tiana; she was talking about Lotte, Tiana's Caucasian friend and foil. *The Princess and the Frog* opened in a flashback: the two of them, as little girls, sitting on the floor of Lotte's icing pink room, while Eudora, a seamstress, read them the story of the princess and the frog. Tiana recoiled as the plot unspooled; Lotte swooned. It was Lotte who had row upon row of pink princess gowns and a pink canopy bed; Lotte was the one who wished on stars; Lotte had the encyclopedic knowledge of fairy tales; Lotte dreamed of marrying the handsome prince and living happily ever after; Lotte, as an ingénue, swept her hair into a Cinderella 'do for the ball. And it was Lotte who, while ultimately good-hearted, was also spoiled, shallow, and ridiculous—oh, and funny-looking; whatever strides Disney has made on race, "ugly" and its stepsibling "fat" still connote stupid or evil in its films. So it was clear—to me, anyway— that the viewer was supposed to dislike, or at least disidentify with, Lotte. But I understood Daisy's confusion: Lotte was also everything that, up until now, Disney has urged our daughters to be and to buy. How was a little girl to interpret that? How were we parents to interpret it? Was Disney mocking itself? Could the studio actually be uneasy with the frenzy of acquisitiveness it had created? Was it signaling that parents should be more on guard against the very culture it had foisted on us?

Yeah, probably not, but Daisy's mix-up gave me the opening I needed to talk with her ("*with*" being the operative word) about the way the film had presented girls and women, to solicit her own ideas about it. That, in the end, is the best weapon we parents have, short of enrolling our daughters in one of those schools where kids knit all day (or moving to Sweden; marketing to children under twelve there is actually *illegal*—can you believe it?). We have only so much control over the images and products to which they are exposed, and even that will diminish over time. It is strategic, then—absolutely vital—to think through our own values and limits early, to consider what we approve or disapprove of and why.

I can't say what others' personal threshold ought to be: that depends on one's child, one's parenting style, one's judgment, one's own personal experience. It would be disingenuous to claim that Disney Princess diapers or Ty Girlz or *Hannah Montana* or *Twilight* or the latest Shakira video or a Facebook account is inherently harmful. Each is, however, a cog in the round-the-clock, all-pervasive media machine aimed at our daughters—and at us—from womb to tomb; one that, again and again, presents femininity as performance, sexuality as performance, identity as performance, and each of those traits as available for a price. It tells girls that how you look is more important than how you feel. More than that, it tells them that how you look *is* how you feel, as well as who you are. Meanwhile, the notion that we parents are sold, that our children are "growing up faster" than previous generations, that they are more mature and sophisticated in their tastes, more savvy in their consumption, and there is nothing we can (or need) do about it is—what is the technical term again?—oh yes: *a load of crap.* Today's three-year-olds are no better than their predecessors at recognizing when their desires are manipulated by grown-ups. Today's six-year-olds don't get the subtext of their sexy pirate costumes. Today's eight-year-olds don't understand that ads are designed to sell them something. And today's fourteen-year-olds are still desperate for approval from their friends—all 622 of them.

⁂

I never expected, when I had a daughter, that one of my most important jobs would be to protect her childhood from becoming a marketers' land grab. I have begun to see myself as that hazel tree in the Grimms' version of Cinderella (minus the Mom-being-dead part): my branches offering her shelter, my roots giving her strength. Instead of stepsisters and stepmother, though, the new "wicked" is an amalgam of images, products, and pitches that, just as surely, threaten to limit and undermine her. I refuse to believe that parents are helpless. We can provide alternatives, especially in the critical early years when children's brains are most malleable: choices that appeal to their desire to *be girls* yet reflect parents' values, worldview, and dreams for them—which I am guessing, unless you are Billy Ray Cyrus, do not include executing squat thrusts in an oversized cage while wearing thigh-high boots and a bird costume. (Billy Ray may want to consider Chris Rock's epiphany after his wife gave birth to a girl: that, as a father, his sole task is to *keep my baby off the pole*.)

I won't lie: it takes work to find other options, and if you are anything like me, your life is already brimful with demands. I know I feel maxed out trying to be a functioning professional, a loving wife, and a fully present mother all at once—and I have only one kid. It would be so much easier to let it slide, to buy whatever it is that will make your daughter happy and keep her occupied for fifteen minutes. You can worry about the rest later, right? If it is any comfort, I have found that I get as much out of making the effort as Daisy does. It's sort of like taking the time to cook myself rather than stopping for fast food (or at *least* driving the extra mile to pick up a healthier form of takeout). In fact, the rising consciousness about kids' nutrition shows the transformative impact parents can have: organic produce is now available at many grocery stores, farmers' markets are thriving, a sweeping federal overhaul of school lunch menus is in the works. Even McDonald's has retooled its menu. If we can force change in the food industry, why not do the same for toys and media?

I wish I could tell you that I had reached my own goals: getting my daughter outside more, taking walks in the woods together, playing sports, making art. Occasionally I have—and I advocate all of that—but mostly, I have just gotten a lot more canny about how we participate in the consumer culture. For the price of one Cinderella gown, for instance, I bought a dozen Papo figurines—tiny knights, princesses, pirates, dragons, unicorns, a stray Maid Marian, a random Joan of Arc—that were not "synergistically" marketed as clothing, home decor, Web sites, DVDs, and breath mints. Perhaps because of that, the play they inspired was less rote, more creative, while still acceptably royal. (I tried slipping a Jane Austen action figure into the mix as well, but, alas, she didn't take.) At bedtime we continue to read legends, mythology, and fairy tales—all of which teem with complex female characters that fire a child's imagination—and have added, among other things, women's stories from biblical literature. Who knew that without Moses' sister Miriam, the Israelites would have died of thirst while wandering the desert?

Speaking of which, if we were stuck on a desert island with a DVD player and could have only one disc, I would want it to be a film by Hayao Miyazaki—gorgeous animation, rich stories, as much a treat for adults as they are for kids. Miyazaki is sometimes called "the Walt Disney of Japan," but that diminishes his brilliance as well as his respect for the youngest members of his audience: he never panders creatively or intellectually. The female protagonists in his films—which include *My Neighbor Totoro*, *Laputa: The Castle in the Sky*, and *Nausicaä of the Valley of Wind*—are refreshingly free of agenda, neither hyperfeminine nor drearily feminist. They simply *happen* to be girls, as organically as, in other directors' films, they *happen* to be boys. In one of my favorites, *Kiki's Delivery Service*, a thirteen-year-old witch must, according to custom, leave her home to find her purpose in the larger world. Her transformation ultimately hinges on self-knowledge rather than a cute makeover or love's first kiss. (Disney distributes the films in the United States and dubs them into

English. Apparently, the studio could not fully keep its paws off: Kiki wears a black witch's dress throughout the film; in this version *only* she says, "I wish it were lilac.")

It turns out, too, that, at least with younger children, "no" is a useful tactic. Your three-year-old has no interest in critical thinking, no ear for subtlety. Your attempt to deconstruct a product or sales pitch, even at its most rudimentary, sounds to her like the squawking of the grown-ups in *Peanuts*. The only thing that penetrates is PRINCESSES and TOOTHPASTE TUBE. Limiting her access to toys or media may inspire some grumbling but will not necessarily create the "forbidden fruit" effect that parents fear. According to a 1999 study, elementary school students who didn't watch violent TV at home were least interested in it in the laboratory. Meanwhile, a 2009 study found that kids that age who were shown violent film clips as part of a media literacy class later reported *more* willingness to use aggression; those taught the curriculum without the clips did not. That said, pointing out inaccurate or unrealistic portrayals of women to younger grade school children—ages five to eight—does seem to be effective, when done judiciously: talking to little girls about body image and dieting, for example, can actually *introduce* them to disordered behavior rather than inoculating them against it. I may be taking a bit of a leap here, but to me all of this indicates that if you are creeped out about the characters from *Monster High*, it is fine to keep them out of your house.

Going all Amish on your middle school or high school daughter, however, is another story. That's when kids chafe against restrictions, become skilled at finding ways around them. It is also when the eye rolling begins in earnest, when girls are exquisitely tuned to the slightest whiff of a lecture. So haranguing your twelve-year-old when she tears it up to "What I wa-wa-want is what you wa-wa-

want. Give it to me baby, like boom boom boom" is not going to reach her. However, open-minded, respectful conversation about the song's underlying message (while acknowledging its catchy beat) very well might. Lyn Mikel Brown and Sharon Lamb, whose *Packaging Girlhood* offers excellent age-appropriate "sample conversations," urge parents to ask girls questions rather than dole out opinions. Though it may sound like a big old *duh*, the best approach is to put reasonable limits on the girlz-with-a-*z* stuff for as long as you can and, over time, engage (without nagging) in regular dialogue with your daughter about what she consumes. Watching TV or listening to music along with your child is also a good idea, *if* you're willing to discuss the content: otherwise, your presence comes off like an endorsement. The point, according to Erica Weintraub Austin, the director of the Edward R. Murrow School of Communication at Washington State University, is not so much to raise children who are cynical about the media as ones who are skeptical.

As it happens, skepticism had marked the beginning of the end of my daughter's interest in the Disney Princesses. And it was sparked—by Disney itself! Specifically, by Daisy's embrace (with my enthusiastic approval) of Mulan, the girl who masqueraded as a male soldier and saved all of China. By rights, Mulan ought not to be in the Princess pantheon; though descended from an "honored" family, she was not herself royal, nor did she marry a prince. Plus, *Mulan II*, a straight-to-DVD sequel, portrays court life for women as little more than sumptuous slavery. In that film, Mulan and her fiancé, Shang, are charged with escorting a trio of princesses across China, where their arranged marriages will secure peace with a rival kingdom. Their showstopping musical number "Like Other Girls" expresses their longing for freedom: "No escorts / No manners / No nursemaids / No worries / No hands folded perfect, like holding a lily . . ."

"Why does she sing that?" Daisy asked one evening when she was around four.

"I suppose because it isn't easy being a princess," I said. "They don't get to decide how to live or what to do. They always have to look and act just so."

"Oh," she said.

The song continued. "I wanna be like other girls. Scrape up my knees like other girls can."

"Pause it," Daisy commanded. Then: "Why does she say *that*?"

"I don't think she really wants to get hurt," I assured her, "but she wishes she could run and jump and play. Real princesses don't have much fun."

"Oh," she said again. We continued on that way, her wanting to pause after each line so I could explain why these princesses were so unhappy being *princesses*.

"Oh," she said every time.

A few days later, as we drove home from preschool, she asked about another song in the movie, "Lesson Number One." It was one of my favorites: in it, Mulan schools a group of little girls on the yin and yang of female warriors.

"Mom?" Daisy asked. "How come in that song Mulan has to be gentle *and* strong but Shang is only strong?"

I looked into the rearview mirror and grinned as my eye caught hers.

⌘

As of summer 2010, several more Princess movies were coming down the pike. Pixar was planning to release *Brave* in 2012—its first *ever* film with a female protagonist. The studio's lack of interest in the XX chromosome has been so entrenched that the original *Toy Story*, made in 1995, didn't have a *single* significant female character, not even the obligatory bookish sidekick (yes, there was the "sweet and loveable porcelain shepherdess" Bo Peep, whom the little boy occasionally uses as his "damsel in distress," but *please!*). Written by Brenda "first-woman-to-direct-an-animated-feature-which-should-be-a-source-of-industry-shame-rather-than-celebration" Chapman (who was subsequently removed from the project), *Brave* tells the story of "impetuous, tangle-haired Merida, [who,] though a daughter of royalty, would prefer to make her mark as a great archer." Sounds promising, though I cannot help but feel, after waiting patiently (and sometimes not so patiently) through twelve genre-busting films about male robots, male superheroes, male cowboys, male rats, male cars, male bugs, male fish, and a small male mailman, that it would have been nice if the movie was *not* about a princess, even a kick-ass one. Honestly, is that too much to ask? Also, my fingers are crossed that her waistline will be several pixels thicker than depicted in the early sketches that were leaked onto the Internet.

Disney, too, was busily readying its next Princess rollout, though the Magic Kingdom had hit some bumps along the royal road: it turned out that, despite the massive hoopla generated over its release, *The Princess and the Frog* was a box-office dud. Relatively speaking, that is: I personally would not sneeze at a $222 million payday. But bear in mind that *Pocahontas* grossed $346 million in 1995, when theater tickets topped out at around $4.50. And *Up*, released six months before *The Princess and the Frog*, was a $731 million jackpot. How to explain the disappointment? Disney blamed it on . . . girls. In an interview with the *Los Angeles Times*, Ed Catmull, the president of Walt Disney and Pixar Animation Studios, surmised that the word "princess" might have scared off half the ticket-buying audience (that is, boys). None of the previous femalecentric movies—not even *Cinderella*—had initially been marketed as a "Princess" film, chiefly because the concept did not yet exist. They were simply *family* movies. (Though "Disney Princess" may have become a liability at the box office, the term remains a merchandising blockbuster—seventeen thousand Tiana dolls sold during the second week of November 2009 alone, even though the film would not open nationally for another month.) Unwilling to take any chances, Disney shelved its plans to plunder Hans Christian Andersen's *The Snow Queen* and retooled its 2010 release, *Rapunzel*, to include a brand-new male character—a "bad-boy" bandit named Flynn Rider—who could be given equal billing with the lady of the locks. The project was retitled *Tangled*, which, as one Internet wag commented, was like renaming *Sleeping Beauty* "Coma."

Maybe *Tangled* will be a spectacular romp. Maybe I will adore it; it could happen. But one thing is for sure: *Tangled* will not be "Rapunzel." And that's too bad, because "Rapunzel" is an especially layered and relevant fairy tale, less about the love between a man and a woman than the misguided attempts of a mother trying to protect her daughter from (what she perceives) as the world's evils. The tale, you may recall, begins with a mother-to-be's yearning for the taste of "rapunzel," a salad green she spies growing in the garden of the sorceress who happens to live next door. The woman's craving becomes so intense, she tells her husband that if he doesn't fetch her some, she and their unborn baby will die. So he steals into the witch's yard, wraps his hand around a plant, and, just as he pulls . . . she appears in a fury. The two eventually strike a bargain: the man's wife can have as much of the plant as she wants—*if* she turns over her baby to the witch upon its birth. "I will care for it like a mother," the sorceress croons (as if that makes it all right). Then again, who would you rather have as a mom: the woman who would do anything for you or the one who would swap you in a New York minute for a bowl of lettuce?

Rapunzel grows up, her hair grows down, and when she is twelve—note that age—Old Mother Gothel, as she calls the witch, leads her into the woods, locking her in a high tower which offers no escape and no entry except by scaling the girl's flowing tresses. One day, a prince passes by and, on overhearing Rapunzel singing, falls immediately in love (that makes Rapunzel the inverse of Ariel—she is loved sight unseen *because* of her voice). He shinnies up her hair to say hello and, depending on which version you read, they have a chaste little chat or get busy conceiving twins.

Either way, when their tryst is discovered, Old Mother Gothel cries, "You wicked child! I thought I had separated you from the world, and yet you deceived me!" There you have it: the Grimms' warning to parents, centuries before psychologists would come along with their studies and measurements, against undue restriction. Interestingly, the prince can't save Rapunzel from her foster mother's wrath. When he sees the witch at the top of the now-severed braids, he jumps back in surprise and is blinded by the bramble that breaks his fall. He wanders the countryside for an unspecified time, living on roots and berries, until he accidentally stumbles upon his Love. She weeps into his sightless eyes, restoring his vision, and—voilà!—they rescue each other. "Rapunzel," then, wins the prize for the most egalitarian romance, but that is not its only distinction: it is the only well-known tale in which the villain is neither maimed nor killed. No red-hot shoes are welded to the witch's feet. Her eyes are not pecked out. Her limbs are not lashed to four horses who speed off in different directions. She is not burned at the stake. Why such leniency? Perhaps because she is not, in the end, *really* evil—she simply loves too much. What mother has not, from time to time, felt the urge to protect her daughter by locking her in a tower? Who among us doesn't have a tiny bit of trouble letting our children go? If the hazel branch is the mother I aspire to be, then Old Mother Gothel is my cautionary tale: she reminds us that our role is not to keep the world at bay but to prepare our daughters so they can thrive within it.

That involves staying close but not crowding them, standing firm in one's values while remaining flexible. The path to womanhood is strewn with enchantment, but it is also rife with thickets and thorns and a Big Bad Culture that threatens to consume them even as they consume it. The good news is, the choices we make for our toddlers can influence how they navigate it as teens. I'm not saying we can, or will, do everything "right," only that there is power—magic—in awareness. If we start with that, with wanting girls to see themselves from the inside out rather than outside in, we will go a long way toward helping them find their true happily-ever-afters.

Acknowledgments

*t*iaras all around to: my agent, Suzanne Gluck, for her fearless navigation of today's publishing industry; Gillian Blake, who set this book ticking, Jennifer Barth, who skillfully saw it through; Ilena Silverman, my enabler; my "mother superiors" and trusted advisers—Sylvia Brownrigg, Ayelet Waldman, Ruth Halpern, Eva Eilenberg, Peg-bo Edersheim Kalb, Elly Eisenberg, Barbara Lee Swaiman, Sara Corbett, Cornelia Lauf, Rachel Silvers, Rinat Fried, Dawn Prestwich, Verna Williams; Pearlee Coty and Lilly Krenn; Teresa Tauchi, the queen of Web design and technology; Fred Stutzman, for saving me from myself; the Orenstein and Okazaki clans; Danny Sager and Brian McCarthy for bed and board (but never bored!); Steven, my own Prince Charming; and Daisy Tomoko, who never ceases to amaze, inspire, and humble me. Thanks, guys: you rule!

Notes

In the case of books, reports, articles in scholarly journals, and chapters of books, full citations will be found in the bibliography.

Chapter 1: Why I Hoped for a Boy

2   I had read about: J. T. Manning et al., "Parental Age Gap Skews Child Sex Ratio," *Nature* 389, no. 6649 (1997): 344.

6   According to the American Psychological Association: American Psychological Association, *Report of the APA Task Force on the Sexualization of Girls*, www.apa.org/pi/wpo/sexualization .html. The report defines sexualization as occurring under *any* of the following conditions: "a person's value comes only from his or her sexual appeal or behavior, to the exclusion of other characteristics; a person is held to a standard that equates physical attractiveness (narrowly defined) with being sexy; a person is sexually objectified—that is, made into a thing for others' sexual use, rather than seen as a person with the capacity for independent action and decision making; and/or sexuality is inappropriately imposed upon a person" (p. 2). According to the report, at least thirty-eight experiments, thirty-two surveys, and two interview studies have

investigated harmful connections between body dissatisfaction and the ideals of sexual attractiveness to which girls are constantly exposed (p. 23).

6   In one study: Deborah L. Tolman, Emily A. Impett, Allison J. Tracy, and Alice Michael, "Looking Good, Sounding Good." See also Emily A. Impett, Deborah Schooler, and Deborah L. Tolman, "To Be Seen and Not Heard."

6   the focus on appearance: Amy Slater and Marika Tiggemann, "A Test of Objectification Theory in Adolescent Girls"; American Psychological Association, *Report of the APA Task Force*, p. 23.

6   Even brief exposure: Duane Hargreaves and Marika Tiggemann, "The Effect of 'Thin Ideal' Television Commercials on Body Dissatisfaction and Schema Activation During Early Adolescence"; Duane Hargreaves and Marika Tiggemann, "The Effect of Television Commercials on Mood and Body Dissatisfaction"; Duane Hargreaves and Marika Tiggemann, "Idealized Media Images and Adolescent Body Image"; Paul G. Davies, Steven J. Spencer, Diane M. Quinn, and Rebecca Gerhardstein, "Consuming Images"; B. L. Fredrickson, T. A. Roberts, S. M. Noll, D. M. Quinn, and J. M. Twenge, "That Swimsuit Becomes You."

Chapter 2: What's Wrong with Cinderella?

13   They did not exist: Andy Mooney, "Remarks by Andy Mooney, Chairman, Disney Consumer Products," New York Licensing Show, New York, June 20, 2006.

13   the now-legendary story: Author's interview with Andy Mooney, Chairman, Disney Consumer Products, July 19, 2006.

13   Disney had never marketed: Author's interview with Mary Beech, Vice President, Girls Franchise Management, Disney Consumer Products, July 19, 2006.

14   It is also worth noting: Author's interview with Andy Mooney, July 19, 2006.

Notes

14   The first Princess items: Ibid.

14   By 2009: Disney Consumer Products, "Disney Consumer Products Poised to Significantly Increase Share of Boys Market," press release, June 3, 2010, www.businesswire.com/news/home/20100603005682/en/Disney-Consumer-Products-Significantly-Increase-Share.

14   more than twenty-six thousand: Author's interview with Andy Mooney, July 19, 2006.

14   "Princess" has not only: Disney Consumer Products, "Disney Consumer Products Poised."

14   To this day: Author's interview with Andy Mooney, July 19, 2006.

15   Meanwhile, by 2001: Author's interview with Sarah Buzby, Director of Barbie Marketing, Mattel, August 9, 2006.

15   Barbie sales were declining: Ibid. See also Nicholas Casey, "Mattel Profits Despite Barbie," *The Wall Street Journal*, February 1, 2008, p. A11

15   in 2004: Author's interview with Brown Johnson, Executive Creative Director, Nickelodeon Preschool Television, August 9, 2006.

16   the more mainstream media: American Psychological Association, *Report of the APA Task Force*, pp. 27–28.

16   teenage girls and college students: Tolman et al., "Looking Good, Sounding Good"; Impett et al., "To Be Seen and Not Heard"; Anna Fels, "Do Women Lack Ambition?" *Harvard Business Review*, April 2004, www.orijen.com.au/resources/1/news-research-docs/HBR%20Do%20women%20lack%20ambition.pdf.

16   They are also less likely: American Psychological Association, *Report of the APA Task Force*, pp. 26–27; Tolman et al., "Looking Good, Sounding Good"; Impett et al., "To Be Seen and Not Heard."

17   Take the female college students: Davies et al., "Consuming Images."

17 who performed better: Fredrickson et al., "That Swimsuit Becomes You."

17 a 2006 survey: Girls Incorporated, *The Supergirl Dilemma*.

18 In her brilliant book: Susan Douglas, *Enlightened Sexism*, p. 16.

21 nearly half of boys: Author's interview with Isabelle Cherney, Department of Psychology, Creighton University, January 25, 2008. See also Isabelle Cherney and J. Dempsey (in press), "Young Children's Classification, Stereotyping, and Play Behavior for Gender Neutral and Ambiguous Toys"; Isabelle Cherney and K. London, "Gender-linked Differences in the Toys, Television Shows, Computer Games, and Outdoor Activities of 5- to 13-Year-Old Children."

21 boys as young as four: Author's interview with Isabelle Cherney, January 25, 2008.

21 Boys were also: Cherney and Dempsey, "Young Children's Classification." Parents of both sexes, even today, are more likely to give children gender-stereotyped toys and encourage them to play with them. What's more, if a new toy is described as being liked by the other sex, it is often avoided, whereas if it is said to be for a child's own sex, it will be embraced. Carol Lynn Martin and Richard Fabes, *Discovering Childhood Development*, pp. 304–305.

24 That certainly fits: Author's interview with Mary Beech, July 19, 2006.

24 Gary Cross: Cross, "Wondrous Innocence"; Cross, "Valves of Adult Desire."

24 They rebel against: Gary Cross, "Valves of Desire"; Cross, "Wondrous Innocence"; Cross, "Valves of Adult Desire"; author's interview with Gary Cross, February 2, 2009.

25 as another cultural historian: Author's interview with Miriam Forman-Brunell, Department of History, University of Missouri–Kansas City, November 15, 2006.

25 Shirley Temple's film version: Ibid.

25 A mere six years old: "Biography of Shirley Temple Black," www

.kennedy-center.org/calendar/index.cfm?fuseaction=show Individual&entity_id=3814&source_type=A; see also Shirley Temple Black, *Child Star.*

25 President Franklin Roosevelt: "Biography of Shirley Temple Black."

26 the top of the box office: Ibid. See also Ken Severson, "Biography for Shirley Temple," www.imdb.com/name/nm0000073/bio.

26 She also became: Gary Cross, *Kids' Stuff*, pp. 117–118.

28 American Girl was born: "A History of Helping Girls Shine," www .americangirl.com/corp/corporate.php?section=about&id=2. See also Gretchen Morgenson, *Forbes Great Minds of Business*, pp. 123–125.

29 Pleasant Company was pulling: "Company News: Mattel Agrees to Buy Maker of American Girl Dolls," *The New York Times*, June 16, 1998, www.nytimes.com/1998/06/16/busi ness/company-news-mattel-agrees-to-buy-maker-of-ameri can-girl-dolls.html.

29 a $700 million payday: Ibid.

31 in fall 2009: Eric Noll, "Meet Gwen Thompson, the 'Homeless' American Girl," *Good Morning America*, September 26, 2009, http://abcnews.go.com/GMA/Weekend/homeless-american -girl-doll-sparks-controversy/story?id=8676579.

Chapter 3: Pinked!

35 Children weren't color-coded: Author's interview with Jo Paoletti, American Studies Department, University of Mary- land, College Park, November 16, 2006.

36 Why or when that switched: Ibid.

36 It was not until the: Ibid.

36 it was popularized: Daniel Thomas Cook, *The Commodification of Childhood*; Cook, "The Rise of 'the Toddler' as Subject and as Merchandising Category in the 1930s."

36 consider the trajectory: Daniel Thomas Cook and Susan B. Kai- ser, "Betwixt and be Tween"; Cook, "The Rise of 'the Toddler.'"

37   classic marketing bible: Daniel Acuff and Robert H. Reiher, *What Kids Buy and Why*, pp. 83–84.

37   girls become "adept": Jayne O'Donnell, "As Kids Get Savvy, Marketers Move down the Age Scale," *USA Today*, April 13, 2007, www .usatoday.com/money/advertising/2007-04-11-tween-usat_N .htm. Some marketers have even stretched "tween" to include six-year-olds. See Alicia de Mesa, "Marketing and Tweens," *Business-Week*, October 12, 2005, www.businessweek.com/innovate/con tent/oct2005/id20051012_606473.htm.

37   we now have toddlers: Acuff and Reiher, *What Kids Buy and Why*; Paul Kurnit, "Kids Getting Older Younger," interview, Advertising Education Foundation, 1999, www.aef.com/on _campus/classroom/speaker_pres/data/35.

37   thirteen- to fifteen-year-olds may still: Acuff and Reiher, *What Kids Buy and Why*, pp. 122–123.

37   children one year old and under: Kurnit, "Kids Getting Older Younger." See also Jennifer Comiteau, "First Impressions; When Does Brand Loyalty Start? Earlier than You Might Think," *Adweek*, March 24, 2003, www.adweek.com/aw/ esearch/article_display.jsp?vnu_content_id=1847851.

38   the improbable term "pre-tween": O'Donnell, "As Kids Get Savvy."

39   her presence: Tanya Barrientos, "A Rude Welcome for Abby, New Girl on *Sesame Street*," *Pittsburgh Post-Gazette*, August 30, 2006, www.post-gazette.com/pg/06242/717302-237.stm.

40   only to see them fizzle: Michael Davis, *Street Gang*, p. 324.

40   "If Cookie Monster was": Susan Dominus, "A Girly-Girl Joins the 'Sesame' Boys," *The New York Times*, August 6, 2006, www .nytimes.com/2006/08/06/arts/television/06domi.html.

40   Lulu, a shy: Ibid.

40   Zoe, who was: Davis, *Street Gang*, pp. 321–323.

40   her release fell short: Ibid., pp. 324–325.

40   With Abby, every detail: Dominus, "A Girly-Girl Joins the 'Sesame' Boys."

41 Workshop executives have denied: Ibid.

41 "If you think about": Ibid.

41 Abby's character was ideal: Ibid.

42 consciously developed: Author's interview with Brown Johnson, August 9, 2006.

42 In 2009, Nick introduced: Marysol Castro and Taylor Behrendt, "Dora the Explorer Updates Her Look," *Good Morning America Weekend*, March 8, 2009, http://abcnews.go.com/GMA/Weekend/story?id=7033295&page=1.

44 I'm projecting my own: See Brian Sutton-Smith, *Toys as Culture*, pp. 247–253.

44 playthings were expressly intended: Cross, *Kids' Stuff,* pp. 9, 24, 50–53.

45 couples no longer felt compelled: Ibid., p. 78.

45 less than 25 percent: Miriam Forman-Brunell, *Made to Play House*, p. 30.

45 campaign against "race suicide". Cross, *Kids' Stuff,* p. 78.

45 When women "feared motherhood": Theodore Roosevelt, *The Strenuous Life*, p. 4.

45 Baby dolls were seen: Cross, *Kids' Stuff,* pp. 77–78.

45 Miniature brooms, dustpans: Ibid., pp. 11, 16, 51.

45 "companion" dolls: Ibid., pp. 75–76.

45 Boys, by contrast: Ibid., p. 4.

45 That division continued: Ibid., p. 9.

45 when she was introduced: Ibid., p. 171.

47 baby boomers and Gen Xers: Author's interview with Gary Cross, February 2, 2009.

47 A headline-grabbing: Alexandra Frean, "Barbarism Begins with Barbie, the Doll Children Love to Hate," *The Times*, December 19, 2005, www.timesonline.co.uk/tol/news/uk/article767739.ece. See also University of Bath, "'Babyish' Barbie Under Attack from Little Girls, Study Shows," press release, December 19, 2005, www.bath.ac.uk/news/articles/archive/barbie161205.html.

48 the lower her sales fell: Nicholas Casey, "Mattel Profits De-

spite Barbie," *The Wall Street Journal*, February 1, 2008, p. A11. See also Joseph Woelfel, "Mattel Earnings Fall 46%, Sales Drop 11%," *The Street*, February 2, 2009, www.thestreet.com/story/10461260/mattel-earnings-fall-46-sales-drop-11.html.

49   gobbling up a full 40 percent: Margaret Talbot, "Little Hotties," *The New Yorker*, December 4, 2006, p. 74.

49   in 2008, Mattel struck back: "Barbie's Mattel Sues Maker of Bratz Dolls," *Morning Edition*, NPR, June 3, 2008, www.npr.org/templates/story/story.php?storyId=91098062.

50   With Bratz on ice: Andrea Chang, "Mattel Earnings Rise on Robust Sales and New Product Lines," *Los Angeles Times*, April 17, 2010, http://articles.latimes.com/2010/apr/17/business/la-fi-mattel17-2010apr17.

50   MGA rolled out Moxie Girlz: Ruth La Ferla, "Losing the Limo: New Fashion Dolls," *The New York Times*, November 8, 2009, p. ST1.

52   an annual survey: Lloyd B. Lueptow, Lori Garovich-Szabo, and Margaret B. Lueptow, "Social Change and the Persistence of Sex Typing: 1974–1997."

Chapter 4: What Makes Girls Girls?

55   "X: A Fabulous Child's Story": Lois Gould, "X: A Fabulous Child's Story," *Ms.*, December 1972, pp. 74–76, 105–106.

56   a Swedish couple: Lydia Parafianowicz, "Swedish Parents Keep 2-Year-Old's Gender Secret," *The Local*, June 23, 2009, www.thelocal.se/20232/20090623/.

57   rocking a blanket-wrapped Tonka: As early as age two and a half children have absorbed basic stereotypes about the sexes, including those involving appearance and activities. That influences not only how they see themselves but their assumptions about other children's behavior and preferences. What's more, children often distort or misremember information to conform to their stereotypes: over half of five- to nine-year-old children, after watching a TV commercial in which a boy

played with a doll and a girl with a truck, later recalled the reverse. So merely exposing children to examples that counter their expectations does not change stereotypes; more proactive measures have to be taken. Carol Lynn Martin and Richard Fabes, *Discovering Childhood Development*, p. 304.

57   Several cited the classic: For more on David Reimer, see Lise Eliot, *Pink Brain, Blue Brain*, pp. 33–34; John Colapinto, *As Nature Made Him*.

58   more like Canadians and Americans: Or, as Kathryn Dindia, Professor of Communications, University of Wisconsin–Milwaukee, put it in an article of the same name, "Men are from North Dakota, women are from South Dakota."

59   Male fetuses, she explained: Author's interview with Lise Eliot, Associate Professor, Department of Neuroscience, Chicago Medical School, May 13, 2009; see also Eliot, *Pink Brain, Blue Brain*, pp. 45–48.

59   There is another hormonal spike. Ibid.

59   in the beginning: Author's interview with Lise Eliot, May 13, 2009; see also Eliot, *Pink Brain, Blue Brain*, p. 107.

59   Then the whole concept: Author's interview with Lise Eliot, May 13, 2009; see also Eliot, *Pink Brain, Blue Brain*, pp. 117–118.

60   There is a legendary story: Jeremy is the son of Sandra Bem, professor of psychology at Cornell University. She writes about this incident in her book *The Lenses of Gender*, p. 149. It has become a favorite anecdote among women's studies and psychology professors everywhere. Eliot also relates this story; see Eliot, *Pink Brain, Blue Brain*, p. 118. See also Judith Elaine Owen Blakemore et al., *Gender Development*, p. 234.

60   until around age five: Psychologists call that gradual revelation "gender stability." It is also sometimes called "gender continuity." The recognition that others don't change sex by changing superficial appearance, which children arrive at around six or seven, is called "gender consistency," "gender constancy," or "gender immutability." Eliot, *Pink Brain, Blue Brain*, p. 116; au-

thor's interview with Carol Lynn Martin and Richard Fabes, Department of Family and Human Development, Arizona State University, June 25, 2009; Diane N. Ruble et al., "The Role of Gender Constancy in Early Gender Development"; Martin and Fabes, *Discovering Childhood Development*, p. 302; Blakemore et al., *Gender Development*, pp. 205–206, 236–242.

61   That's why four-year-olds: Author's interview with Carol Lynn Martin and Richard Fabes, June 25, 2009.

62   boys hopped: Vivian Gussin Paley, *Boys and Girls*, pp. ix, 19.

62   the Big Kahuna: Martin and Fabes, *Discovering Childhood Development*, pp. 304–305; Blakemore et al., *Gender Development*, pp. 125–126.

62   You even see it: Satoshi Kanazawa, "Why Do Boys and Girls Prefer Different Toys?" *Psychology Today*, April 17, 2008, www.psychologytoday.com/node/447.

63   that finding was replicated: Ibid. See also Janice M. Hassett et al., "Sex Differences in Rhesus Monkey Toy Preferences Parallel Those of Children."

63   girls who are born: Eliot, *Pink Brain, Blue Brain*, p. 126.

63   Toy choice turns out: Ibid., p. 106; author's interview with Carol Lynn Martin and Richard Fabes, June 25, 2009.

64   A child's brain: Author's interview with Lise Eliot, May 13, 2009.

64   their brains are also: Ibid.

64   Boys from more egalitarian homes: Judith Elaine Owen Blakemore, "The Influence of Gender and Parental Attitudes on Preschool Children's Interest in Babies."

64   a study of more than five thousand: John Rust et al., "The Role of Brothers and Sisters in the Gender Development of Preschool Children."

65   mathematically inclined girls: Janis E. Jacobs et al., "'I Can, But I Don't Want To': Impact of Parents, Interests, and Activities on Gender Differences in Math."

65   David was nearly two: Eliot, *Pink Brain, Blue Brain*, pp. 34–35.

66   a third of girls aged seven to eleven: Author's interview with Carol Lynn Martin and Richard Fabes, June 25, 2009.

68   the church-and-state separation: Author's interview with Carol Lynn Martin and Richard Fabes, June 25, 2009. See also Carol Lynn Martin and Richard A. Fabes, "The Stability and Consequences of Young Children's Same-Sex Peer Interactions"; Eleanor E. Maccoby, "Gender and Group Process"; Eleanor E. Maccoby, "Gender and Relationships"; Blakemore et al., *Gender Development*, pp. 306–315.

68   By the end of the first year: Author's interview with Carol Lynn Martin and Richard Fabes, June 25, 2009. See also Blakemore et al., *Gender Development*, pp. 306–315.

68   When they do have cross-sex friendships: Author's interview with Carol Lynn Martin and Richard Fabes, June 25, 2009. See also Blakemore et al., *Gender Development*, pp. 322–323.

68   self-segregation, like toy choice: Author's interview with Carol Lynn Martin and Richard Fabes, June 25, 2009. See also Maccoby, "Gender and Relationships."

68   The threat of cooties: Author's interview with Carol Lynn Martin and Richard Fabes, June 25, 2009. See also Martin and Fabes, "The Stability and Consequences of Young Children's Same-Sex Peer Interactions."

68   Every cliché I have: Author's interview with Carol Lynn Martin and Richard Fabes, June 25, 2009. See also Martin and Fabes, "The Stability and Consequences of Young Children's Same-Sex Peer Interactions"; Maccoby, "Gender and Group Process"; Maccoby, "Gender and Relationships"; Blakemore et al., *Gender Development*, pp. 306–308. All that said, there are cultural differences in children's sex-typed behaviors, such as conflict resolution. At ages four and five, African-American and Latina girls tend to speak more directly than Caucasian or Asian-American girls. Girls in mainland China at that age also have a more assertive communication style; see Blakemore et al., *Gender Development*, p. 311.

69   children who have friends of the other sex: Children who have

friends of the other sex in elementary school also appear to have better social skills. Blakemore et al., *Gender Development*, p. 323.

70   boys hear less well: Elizabeth Weil, "Teaching Boys and Girls Separately," *The New York Times Magazine*, March 2, 2008, www.nytimes.com/2008/03/02/magazine/02sex3-t.html. See also Leonard Sax, *Why Gender Matters*, pp. 16–18, 24.

70   Girls, by contrast: Weil, "Teaching Boys and Girls Separately."

71   sex-based hearing and vision differences: In their ground-breaking work *The Psychology of Sex Differences*, Eleanor Maccoby and Carol Nagy Jacklin write that one of the most serious problems with research on sex differences is that it is, in fact, skewed toward *differences*: research showing how slight differences are, or that shows similarities where differences were expected, does not get published; see Blakemore et al., *Gender Development*, p. 35, and Eliot, *Pink Brain, Blue Brain*, pp. 61–64.

71   assigning kids to classrooms: Weil, "Teaching Boys and Girls Separately."

71   the number of single-sex: www.singlesexschools.org/schools-schools.htm.

Chapter 5: Sparkle, Sweetie!

82   in 2007, we spent: Jayne O'Donnell, "As Kids Get Savvy, Marketers Move down the Age Scale," *USA Today*, April 13, 2007, www.usatoday.com/money/advertising/2007-04-11-tween-usat_N.htm.

82   Close to half: NPD Group, "NPD Reports Tween Girls Increase Their Beauty Usage," press release, April 29, 2010, www.npd.com/press/releases/press_100429.html.

82   the percentage of: Ibid.

82   "Tween" girls now spend: Ibid.

82   No wonder Nair: Andrew Adam Newman, "Depilatory Market Moves Far Beyond the Short-Shorts Wearers," *The New York*

Times, September 14, 2007, www.nytimes.com/2007/09/14/business/media/14adco.html.

82 And who, according to: NPD Group, "NPD Reports Tween Girls Increase."

82 As a headline: "How Many 8-Year-Olds Have to Get Bikini Waxes Before We Can All Agree the Terrorists Have Won?" Weblog entry, Jezebel, March 27, 2008, http://jezebel.com/373096/how-many-8+year+olds-have-to-get-bikini-waxes-before-we-all-agree-the-terrorists-have-won.

83 it was conceived of: Sree Roy, "Very Important Princesses," *Display and Design Ideas,* March 1, 2005, www.allbusiness.com/retail-trade/miscellaneous-retail/4165383-1.html; Susan Chandler, "Retailer Courts the 'Princess Set,'" *Chicago Tribune,* February 10, 2002, http://articles.chicagotribune.com/2002 02-10/business/0202100006_1_tween-girls-american-girl-place-chain; "Saks Incorporated Acquires Club Libby Lu," *Business Wire,* May 6, 2003, www.allbusiness.com/retail/retailers-general-merchandise-stores-department/5774038-1.html.

84 Marketers call that KGOY: Paul Kurnit, "Kids Getting Older Younger," interview, Advertising Education Foundation, 1999, www.aef.com/on_campus/classroom/speaker_pres/data/35; Lisa Bannon, "Little Big Spenders," *The Wall Street Journal,* October 13, 1998, p. A1.

84 That's why the cherry-flavored: O'Donnell, "As Kids Get Savvy."

84 girls are going through puberty: Denise Grady, "First Signs of Puberty Seen in Younger Girls," *The New York Times,* August 9, 2010, p. A11; Tara Parker-Pope, "Earlier Puberty in European Girls," *The New York Times,* May 4, 2009, http://well.blogs.nytimes.com/2009/05/04/earlier-puberty-in-european-girls/?scp=1&sq=Aksglaede&st=cse; Susan Brink, "Modern Puberty," *Los Angeles Times,* January 21, 2008, p. F1.

84 pediatricians no longer consider it: Brink, "Modern Puberty."

84 although they are physically more advanced: Ibid.

85 imposing any developmental task: Stephen Hinshaw with Rachel Krantz, *The Triple Bind*, p. 112. For more on academically accelerated kindergarten and preschool, see Edward Miller and Joan Almon, *Crisis in Kindergarten.*

85 the ways pageant moms: Martha Heltsley and Thomas C. Calhoun, "The Good Mother."

86 The routine sparked: *Fox and Friends*, May 15, 2010, http://video.foxnews.com/v/4197785/sexual-dance-sparks-controversy; Michael Winter, "'Single Ladies' Dance by Young Girls Is Kicking Up a Storm," Weblog entry, "On Deadline," *USA Today*, May 14, 2010, www.usatoday.com/communities/ondeadline/post/2010/05/single-ladies-dance-by-young-girls-is-kicking-up-a-storm/1; *Rick's List*, May 13, 2010, http://edition.cnn.com/video/#/video/showbiz/2010/05/14/sbt.too.sexy.too.soon.cnn?iref=allsearch.

86 best known for the faux pas: DeNeen L. Brown, "First Lady Assails Use of Daughters' Images for Dolls," *The Washington Post*, January 25, 2009, www.washingtonpost.com/wpdyn/content/article/2009/01/24/AR2009012401854.html.

90 Historically, girls' bodies: Joan Jacobs Brumberg, *The Body Project.*

91 Back in the 1960s: Kareen Nussbaum, "Children and Beauty Pageants," 2002, www.minorcon.org/pageants.html.

91 A woman who did not: Camille Sweeney, "Never Too Young for That First Pedicure," *The New York Times*, February 28, 2008, www.nytimes.com/2008/02/28/fashion/28Skin.html. See also Camille Sweeney, "A Girl's Life, with Highlights," *The New York Times*, April 3, 2008, www.nytimes.com/2008/04/03/fashion/03SKIN.html.

91 Parents in San Francisco: Meredith May, "Kids Escape to Spa Camp," *The San Francisco Chronicle*, August 12, 2007, p. B1.

94 One prominent former: Andrea Canning and Jessica Hoffman, "Former Child Beauty Queen Speaks Out," *Good Morning America*, August 13, 2009, http://abcnews.go.com/GMA/

beauty-queen-takes-gma-scenes-pageants/story?id=8315785;
for video, see http://jezebel.com/5336807/former-child-beauty
-queen-says-pageants-led-to-emotional-problems.

Chapter 6: Guns and (Briar) Roses

98 there is virtually no research: Author's interview with Diane Levin, Department of Education, Wheelock College, Boston, May 18, 2009. See also Diane E. Levin and Nancy Carlsson-Paige, *The War Play Dilemma*, p. 30.

98 violent play is useful: Author's interview with Diane Levin, May 18, 2009. Levin and Carlsson-Paige, *The War Play Dilemma*, pp. 25–28, 37–39, 46.

98 children's television advertising: Author's interview with Diane Levin, May 18, 2009; Levin and Carlsson-Paige, *The War Play Dilemma*, pp. 3–5, 15–17.

99 rather than engaging in creative play: Author's interview with Diane Levin, May 18, 2009; Levin and Carlsson-Paige, *The War Play Dilemma*, pp. 3–5.

100 Allied commanders banned: Thomas O'Neill, "Guardians of the Fairy Tale: The Brothers Grimm," *National Geographic*, December 1999, www.nationalgeographic.com/grimm/article.html.

100 we avoid the Grimms' grimness: Bruno Bettelheim, *The Uses of Enchantment*.

100 the brothers' gore: Ibid., p. 19.

100 John Locke, disagreed: Ruth B. Bottigheimer, "Fairy Tales and Folk-Tales," p. 154; John Locke, *Some Thoughts Concerning Education*, pp. 189–190.

100 fairy tales and *only*: Bettelheim, *The Uses of Enchantment*, pp. 35–41.

100 In their tiny minds: Ibid.; see, e.g., pp. 24–27, 39–40, 57–58.

100 the solutions to life's struggles: Ibid., pp. 4–5, 25–26.

102 Calling the Grimms': Maria Ibido, "Reading the Grimms' *Children's Stories and Household Tales*," pp. xxvii–xlvii.

102 Before the Grimms: Ibid., pp. xlii–xliii; Giambattista Basile, "Sun, Moon, and Talia."

102 the porn of their day: Maria Tatar, *The Hard Facts of the Grimms' Fairy Tales*, pp. xiii–xiv.

102 They were also rife: Ibid., pp. 10–11, 20.

102 The brothers' delicacy: Ibid.

103 There are at least: Some scholars put the number at 345, others at "thousands." For a list of some of them (and links to online texts), see "Tales Similar to Cinderella" at www.surlalune fairytales.com/cinderella/other.html.

103 The Chinese Yeh-Shen: This is the first known recorded version of a Cinderella story. See also Jacob Grimm and Wilhelm Grimm, *The Annotated Brothers Grimm*, p. 114.

104 splitting the mother: Tatar, *The Hard Facts*, p. 223.

105 she demands that he: Joan Gould, *Spinning Straw into Gold*, p. 70.

107 In the Andersen version: Hans Christian Andersen, *Hans Christian Andersen: Eighty Fairy Tales*, pp. 46–63.

108 the heroine shrewdly foiled: Jacob Grimm and Wilhelm Grimm, "The Robber Bridegroom," in Grimm and Grimm, *The Annotated Brothers Grimm*, pp. 187–193.

108 a feisty girl saved her sisters: Grimm and Grimm, *The Annotated Brothers Grimm*, pp. 201–207.

108 a princess fearlessly: Ibid., pp. 291–300.

109 a seven-year vow of silence: Ibid., pp. 224–231.

109 I loved Diane Wolkstein's: Diane Wolkstein, *The Glass Mountain*.

109 an Algonquin Indian legend: Katrin Tchana and Trina Schart Hyman, "Nesoowa and the Chenoo," in Tchana and Hyman, *The Serpent Slayer*, pp. 13–18.

109 imagined in a "vivid dream": Stephenie Meyer, "The Story Behind Twilight," www.stepheniemeyer.com/twilight.html.

109 more than 100 million copies: John A. Sellers, "New Stephenie Meyer Novella Arriving in June," *Publisher's Weekly*, March 30, 2010. The Harry Potter series has sold more than three times

as many volumes, but though the books are fantasy, I do not consider them to be fairy tales.

109 films based on the first two: Global grosses for *New Moon*, which broke opening-day records, were nearly $710 million as of June 8, 2010. Global grosses for *Twilight* were nearly $410 million. http://boxofficemojo.com/movies/?id=newmoon.htm; http://boxofficemojo.com/movies/?id=twilight.htm.

109 No wonder it has been: Sara Vilkomerson, "Why Is *Twilight* Such Crack for Girls?" *The New York Observer*, November 20, 2008, www.observer.com/2008/02/why-twilight-such-crack -girls; Sarah Hepola, "'Twilight' of Our Youth," *Salon*, November 16, 2009, www.salon.com/life/feature/2009/11/16/ twilight_of_our_youth; Tracee Sioux, "Empowering Girls: Twilight, Female Crack Cocaine."

111 "some fear they can't": Cited in Hepola, "'Twilight' of Our Youth."

111 "some things, it seems": Laura Miller, "Touched by a Vampire," *Salon*, July 30, 2008, www.salon.com/books/review/2008/07/30/ Twilight.

Chapter 7: Wholesome to Whoresome: The *Other* Disney Princesses

114 Until the publication: Bruce Handy, "Miley Knows Best," *Vanity Fair*, June 2008, www.vanityfair.com/culture/features/ 2008/06/miley200806.

114 Miley was quoted: Ibid.

114 releasing a formal: Brooks Barnes, "Revealing Photo Threatens a Major Disney Franchise," *The New York Times*, April 28, 2008, p. C1.

115 Bruce Handy asked: Handy, "Miley Knows Best."

116 Anne Sweeney: Karl Taro Greenfeld, "How Mickey Got His Groove Back," *Portfolio*, May 2008, www.portfolio.com/news -markets/national-news/portfolio/2008/04/14/Disneys -Evolving-Business-Model; Julia Boorstin, "Disney's 'Tween

Machine," *Fortune*, September 29, 2003, http://money.cnn.com/ magazines/fortune/fortune_archive/2003/09/29/349896/ index.htm.

116 Within a year: Boorstin, "Disney's 'Tween Machine."

117 Duff quit: Stephen M. Silverman, "Lizzie McGuire Star Divorces Disney," *People*, May 27, 2003, www.people.com/ people/article/0,26334,626089,00.html.

117 Disney simply replicated: Boorstin, "Disney's 'Tween Machine"; Greenfeld, "How Mickey Got His Groove Back."

118 200 million viewers globally: Stephen Armstrong, "Teen Queen Is a Global Brand," *The Sunday Times*, May 21, 2009, cited on www.dispatch.co.za/article.aspx?id=316998.

118 *Billboard*'s top five: Ibid.

118 some were later scalped: Stephen M. Silverman, "Possible *Hannah Montana* Ticket Scalping Probed," *People*, October 4, 2007, www.people.com/people/article/0,,20137827,00.html.

118 The limited-release: http://boxofficemojo.com/movies/?id =hannahmontanaconcert.htm.

118 more than $155 million worldwide: http://boxofficemojo.com/ movies/?id=hannahmontanamovie.htm.

118 Cyrus is on track: Greenfeld, "How Mickey Got His Groove Back."

119 By age eleven: Kristin Mcmurran, "Shirley Temple Black Taps Out a Telling Memoir of Child Stardom," *People*, November 28, 1988, www.people.com/people/archive/article/ 0,,20100608,00.html.

120 MGM forced: Christopher Finch, *Rainbow*, pp. 134–135.

120 a navel-baring swimsuit: There is a picture of said event at www.beachpartymoviemusic.com/TheMythoftheHidden Navel.html.

120 Hilary Duff appeared: See the cover of *Maxim*, August 2007.

120 "your favorite witch": Stephen Schaefer, "Tarted-up Hart Draws 'Sabrina' Fire," *USA Today*, November 17, 1999, www .usatoday.com/life/enter/leps004.htm.

120 she has been accused: TMZ Staff, "Vanessa Hudgens Attacks over Naked Pics," August 6, 2009, www.tmz.com/2009/08/06/vanessa-hudgens-nude-photos/.

120 a film starring: Roger Ebert, "Review: Freaky Friday," *Chicago Sun-Times*, August 6, 2003, http://rogerebert.suntimes.com/apps/pbcs.dll/article?AID=/20030806/REVIEWS/308060301/1023.

121 "a sleazy, inept and worthless": William Booth, "Critics Everywhere Agree: These Were the Stinkers of Summer," *The Washington Post*, September 12, 2007, www.washingtonpost.com/wp-dyn/content/article/2007/09/11/AR2007091102208.html.

121 Lohan, who admitted to drug use: Jennifer Vineyard, "Lindsay Lohan Admits Eating Disorder, Drug Use in *Vanity Fair* Interview," MTV News, January 4, 2006, www.mtv.com/news/articles/1519731/20060104/lohan_lindsay.jhtml.

122 publicly insisted on her chastity: "Britney's Boast Busts Virgin Myth," July 9, 2003, http://news.bbc.co.uk/2/hi/entertainment/3052143.stm.

122 she appeared on the cover: www.mirror.co.uk/celebs/news/2009/05/28/lady-gaga-appears-semi-naked-on-rolling-stone-and-more-controversial-nude-front-covers-from-the-last-twenty-years-115875-21396496/; see also John Harris, "Britney Spears: This Baby Doll Means Business," *The Independent*, May 14, 2000, www.independent.co.uk/news/people/profiles/britney-spears-this-baby-doll-means-business-717538.html.

122 in an *Esquire* interview: Chuck Klosterman, "Bending Spoons with Britney Spears," *Esquire*, October 1, 2008, www.esquire.com/women/women-we-love/britney-spears-pics-1103?click=main_sr.

123 "slore": Melanie Lowe, "Colliding Feminisms: Britney Spears, 'Tweens,' and the Politics of Reception," *Popular Music and Society* 26, no. 2 (2003): 123–140.

123 Over the course: See "Britney Spears Biography," www.people
.com/people/britney_spears/biography.

126 she chooses clothing that: Tim Nudd, "Miley Cyrus: Being
a Role Model Starts with the Clothes," *People*, December
20, 2007, www.people.com/people/article/0,,20167543,00
.html.

127 "any parent's antidote": *The Barbara Walters Special*,
ABC, February 24, 2008, video at www.youtube.com/
watch?v=NfJ0wV6TjL8.

127 Once again, controversy: See, e.g., Katherine Thomson, "Miley
Cyrus' Teen Choice Pole Dance (Video)," *The Huffington Post*,
August 10, 2009, www.huffingtonpost.com/2009/08/10/mi
ley-cyrus-teen-choice-p_n_255338.html.

127 lying on a table: Holly Millea, "Miley Cyrus Cover Shoot," *Elle*,
July 27, 2009, www.elle.com/Pop-Culture/Cover-Shoots/Mi
ley-Cyrus2/Miley-Cyrus-Cover-Shoot.

128 Bridgit Mendler: Belinda Luscombe, "Making New Mileys:
Disney's Teen-Star Factory," *Time*, October 22, 2009, www
.time.com/time/business/article/0,8599,1930657,00.html.

129 A *Wall Street Journal* profile: Amy Chozick, "Creating the Next
Teen Star," *The Wall Street Journal*, August 28, 2009, http://
online.wsj.com/article/SB10001424052970203706604574374
561767358856.html.

129 Although she is actually: Ibid.

129 "true love waits" ring: Katherine Thomson, "Miley Cyrus
on God, Remaking 'Sex and the City' and Her Purity Ring,"
Weblog entry, *The Huffington Post*, July 15, 2008, www
.huffingtonpost.com/2008/07/15/miley-cyrus-on-god
-remaki_n_112891.html; "Disney Tween Selena's Vow of Ab-
stinence," *Extra*, June 9, 2008, http://extratv.warnerbros
.com/2008/06/disney_tween_selenas_vow_of_ab.php.

Chapter 8: It's All About the Cape

135   nearly half of girls: For an overview of research on preadolescent girls' body image, see Dohnt and Tiggemann, "Body Image Concerns in Young Girls." See also Jessica Bennett, "Say 'Cheese!' and Now Say 'Airbrush!'" *Newsweek*, February 16, 2008, www.newsweek.com/2008/02/16/say-cheese-and-now-say-airbrush.html; Peggy Orenstein, *Schoolgirls*, p. 97.

136   pinups of mid-nineteenth-century: Peter N. Stearns, *Fat History*, p. 9.

136   Those not blessed: Ibid., p. 80.

136   Children were considered sickly: Ibid., pp. 140–148.

136   overweight was first linked: Ibid., pp. 25–47.

136   Fat did not take on: Ibid., pp. 48–70.

138   has become the single: Orenstein, *Schoolgirls*, p. 94; Brown et al., "Changes in Self-Esteem in Black and White Girls Between the Ages of 9 and 14 Years."

138   must be derived: Self-esteem is defined as "the value an individual attaches to the mental picture of himself or herself." Patterns of self-esteem are made up of combinations of competence and worthiness: Carol Lynn Martin and Richard Fabes, *Discovering Childhood Development*, p. 301. If what makes a girl feel "high worth" is looking sexy and she achieves that, her self-esteem may be great but perhaps not derived from the most appropriate or most sustainable of sources. What's more, as the psychologist Jean Twenge has pointed out, self-esteem without basis breeds narcissism. "Study Sees Rise in Narcissism Among Students," *Day to Day*, NPR, February 27, 2007, www.npr.org/templates/story/story.php?storyid=7618722&ps=rs.

138   an article I recently saw: "Stars Who Make over 40 Look Fab," *More*, October 2009, www.more.com/2049/9377-stars-who-make-over-40#1. To be fair, the magazine also ran groundbreaking pictures of the famously fit actress Jamie Lee Curtis, then forty-three, posed in her underwear, without benefit of stylists, makeup, or Photoshop. She looked as bulgy as any of

us. The next page showed Curtis glammed up like a star—a transformation, she said, that took thirteen people three hours to achieve. Amy Wallace, "Jamie Lee Curtis: True Thighs," *More*, September 2002, www.more.com/2049/2464-jamie -lee-curtis-true-thighs.

138   "Should women simply": Cited in Catherine Saint Louis, "Appreciating Your Value as You Age," *The New York Times*, March 18, 2010, p. E3.

139   Most of the 9.3 million: American Society for Aesthetic Plastic Surgery, *Cosmetic Surgery National Data Bank Statistics*.

139   a new picture book: Michael Salzhauer, *My Beautiful Mommy*; the recommended reading level for this book on Amazon .com is four to eight years of age; www.amazon.com/Beautiful -Mommy-Michael-Alexander-Salzhauer/dp/1601310323.

139   Nearly 43,000 children: American Society for Aesthetic Plastic Surgery, *Cosmetic Surgery National Data Bank Statistics*.

139   That does not include: Ibid.

139   the 12,000: Catherine Saint Louis, "This Teenage Girl Uses Botox. No, She's Not Alone," *The New York Times*, August 12, 2010, p. E1.

140   for girls growing up: Joan Jacobs Brumberg, *The Body Project*, p. xxi.

141   try not commenting: A 2004 survey of 3,000 women in ten countries commissioned by Dove's "Real Beauty" campaign found that only 2 percent of women said they would describe themselves as beautiful, while two-thirds said they avoided basic activities—including going to work or school and voicing opinions—on days they felt unattractive. Nancy Etcoff, Susie Orbach, Jennifer Scott, and Heidi D'Agostino, "The Real Truth About Beauty: A Global Report," www.cam paignforrealbeauty.com/uploadedfiles/dove_white_paper_ final.pdf.

142   I took the quandary: Author's interview with Catherine Steiner-Adair, director of eating disorders education and pre-

vention at the Klarman Eating Disorders Center at McLean Hospital, Belmont, Mass., May 2, 2010.

146 Consider a 2007 survey: Catalyst, *The Double-Bind Dilemma.*

147 40 percent of men: J. Walter Thompson, "Millennial Women Face Gender Issues," press release, April 24, 2008.

148 "Excellent question!": Marc Santora, "Pointed Question Puts McCain in Tight Spot," *The New York Times*, November 14, 2007, www.nytimes.com/2007/11/14/us/politics/14mccain.html.

148 Rush Limbaugh declared: Ellen Goodman, "Eek! It's a Wrinkle!" December 19, 2007, www.truthdig.com/report/item/20071219_eek_its_a_wrinkle/.

148 "aging and resentful female": Christopher Hitchens, "Identity Crisis," *Slate*, January 7, 2008, www.slate.com/id/2181460/.

148 the novelist Susanna Moore: Susan Morrison, ed., *Thirty Ways of Looking at Hillary. New York Times* reviewer Michiko Kakutani commented that the book underscored "this willful focus on the personal" in the analysis of Clinton; see "Candidate Clinton Scrutinized by Women," *The New York Times*, January 15, 2008, www.nytimes.com/2008/01/15/books/15kaku.html.

148 "The mind ... strays": Robin Givhan, "Wearing the Pants," *The Washington Post*, December 9, 2007, www.washingtonpost.com/wp-dyn/content/article/2007/12/08/AR2007120801502.html.

148 she used her position: Jo Becker, Peter S. Goodman, and Michael Powell, "Once Elected, Palin Hired Friends and Lashed Foes," *The New York Times*, September 14, 2008, p. A1; Katie Couric, "One-on-One with Sarah Palin," *CBS Evening News*, September 24, 2008, www.cbsnews.com/stories/2008/09/24/eveningnews/main4476173.shtml.

149 Palin had been dubbed: Carolyn Lockhead, "Who's Sarah Palin? She's Hot Where He's Not," Weblog entry, "Below the Beltway," *San Francisco Chronicle*, March 1, 2008, www.sfgate.com/cgi-bin/blogs/nov05election/detail?blogid=14&entry_id=24593.

149 a woman at a firehouse: Tony Plohetski, "Defacing at Fire Station Unsolved," *The Austin American-Statesman*, January 10, 2007, www.freerepublic.com/focus/f-news/1765197/posts.

151 the culture ultimately offers: Sharon Lamb and Lyn Mikel Brown, *Packaging Girlhood*.

153 the movement went alt-rock: Hole, in turn, paved the way for Alanis Morissette, whose 1995 album, *Jagged Little Pill*, a sometimes scathing—but endlessly catchy—ode to female coming-of-age, was one of the decade's top sellers.

154 something called "girlie feminism": See Jennifer Baumgardner and Amy Richards, *Manifesta (10th Anniversary Edition)*, p. 80.

Chapter 9: Just Between You, Me, and My 622 BFFs

160 A digital divide was looming: Matthew DeBell and Chris Chapman, *Computer and Internet Use by Children and Adolescents in 2003*, p. v.

160 35 million kids: Ibid., p. iii.

161 Girls spend the same: Ibid., p. v.

161 Girls, meanwhile, are: Amanda Lenhart, Mary Madden, Aaron Smith, and Alexandra Macgill, *Teens and Social Media*.

161 Doll sales have declined: Lini S. Kadaba, "Girls Abandon Dolls for Web-based Toys," *The Philadelphia Enquirer*, March 31, 2010, www.philly.com/inquirer/magazine/89579552.html #axzz0nvMSGtfF.

162 It chilled me: Ibid.

162 Children's Online Privacy Protection Act: For more on COPPA, see www.coppa.org/coppa.htm.

163 3.7 million teens: Mike Shields, "Kids' Virtual Worlds Gain Traction," *Mediaweek*, May 22, 2009, www.adweek.com/aw/content_display/news/digital/e3i9659c5aa3ebf28066173d de9ce1c5366.

165 young people's real-life identities: Author's interview with Adriana Manago, Department of Psychology and Children's Digital Media Center, UCLA, May 7, 2010; Adriana Manago,

Michael B. Graham, Patricia M. Greenfield, and Goldie Salim-khan, "Self-Presentation and Gender on MySpace."

166 scores of the 16,475: "Study Sees Rise in Narcissism Among Students," *Day to Day*, February 27, 2007, www.npr.org/tem plates/story/story.php?storyId=7618722&ps=rs; Associated Press, "College Students Think They're *So* Special," February 27, 2007, www.msnbc.msn.com/id/17349066/.

166 empathy, too, seems: "Empathy: College Students Don't Have as Much as They Used to, Study Finds," *Science Daily*, May 29, 2010, www.sciencedaily.com/releases/2010/05/100528081434.htm.

167 provocative photos: Author's interview with Adriana Manago; Manago et al., "Self-Presentation and Gender on MySpace."

168 the first high-profile case: Jennifer Steinhauer, "Verdict in MySpace Suicide Case," *The New York Times*, November 27, 2008, p. A25.

169 Phoebe Prince: Brian Ballou and John Ellement, "9 Charged in Death of South Hadley Teen, Who Took Life After Bullying," *The Boston Globe*, March 29, 2010, www.boston.com/news/local/breaking_news/2010/03/holding_for_pho.html.

169 Alexis Pilkington: Oren Yaniv, "Long Island Teen's Suicide Linked to Cruel Cyberbullies, Formspring.me Site: Police," *Daily News*, March 25, 2010, www.nydailynews.com/news/ny_crime/2010/03/25/2010-03-25_li_teens_suicide_linked_to_cruel_cyberbullies_police.html; "Cyber Bullies Harass Teen Even After Suicide," *The Huffington Post*, March 24, 2010, www.huffingtonpost.com/2010/03/24/alexis-pilking ton-faceboo_n_512482.html.

169 half of young people: Associated Press and MTV, "A Thin Line: Executive Summary," MTV, December 2009, www.athinline.org/MTV-AP_Digital_Abuse_Study_Executive_Summary.pdf. A report by the Pew Internet and American Life Project put the rates of cyberbullying at one-third of teens; 38 percent of girls in that survey experienced harassment versus 26 per-

cent of boys. Amanda Lenhart, *Cyberbullying*, www.pewinter net.org/reports/2007/cyberbullying.aspx.

170   39 percent: The National Campaign to Prevent Teen and Un-planned Pregnancy, *Sex and Tech: Executive Summary*.

171   the annual "slut list": Tina Kelley, "A Rite of Hazing Now Out in the Open," *The New York Times*, September 18, 2009, p. A13; Tina Kelley, "When the Cool Get Hazed," *The New York Times*, September 27, 2009, p. WK5.

172   Megan Meier, the girl: Steinhauer, "Verdict in MySpace Suicide Case"; "Cyber Bullies Harass Teen Even After Suicide."

172   Phoebe Prince seems to have: Emily Bazelon, "What Really Happened to Phoebe Prince?" *Slate*, July 20, 2010, www.slate .com/id/2260952.

Chapter 10: Girl Power—No, *Really*

180   café au lait variation: While young black women are not af-fected by exposure to idealized images of white women, they re-port higher levels of body dissatisfaction after viewing those of African-American women. Cynthia Frisby, "Does Race Matter?" See also Taneisha S. Buchanan et al., "Testing a Culture-Specific Extension of Objectification Theory Regarding African American Women's Body Image."

180   the first pass: Bobbi Misick, "Controversy over 'The Princess and the Frog,'" Weblog entry, *Essence*, November 30, 2009, www.essence.com/entertainment/film/critics_dispute_prin cess_and_the_frog.php.

180   Disney also miscalculated: Ibid.

181   by consulting Oprah Winfrey: Chuck Barney, "Disney's First Black Princess Has Parents Excited," *Contra Costa Times*, De-cember 11, 2009, www.popmatters.com/pm/article/117751 -disneys-first-black-princess-has-parents-excited.

182   marketing to children under twelve: Sarah Ellison, "Market-ing to Children Sparks Criticism in Europe," *The Wall Street Journal*, December 18, 2000, p. 1. Denmark, meanwhile, bans

ads aimed at children within ninety seconds of children's programming. State broadcasters in Belgium can't air ads directed at kids for five minutes on either side of a children's show. In Greece, there are no toy advertisements before 10 P.M. Norway, the Netherlands, Ireland, and Austria all have some restrictions.

184   squat thrusts in an oversized cage: See Miley Cyrus "Can't Be Tamed" video, released May 2010, www.youtube.com/watch?v=sjSG6z_13-Q. Cyrus also made headlines in 2010 for kissing a female backup dancer during an onstage rendition of that song. "Girl-on-girl" action between straight women is another example of female sexuality as a performance for others' pleasure.

186   Your attempt to deconstruct: Author's interview with Sahara Byrne, Department of Communications, Cornell University, May 28, 2010. See also Sahara Byrne and Philip Solomon Hart, "The Boomerang Effect"; Sahara Byrne, Daniel Linz, and James W. Potter, "Test of Competing Cognitive Explanations for the Boomerang Effect in Response to the Deliberate Disruption of Media-Induced Aggression."

186   the "forbidden fruit" effect: Amy I. Nathanson, "Identifying and Explaining the Relationship"; Nathanson, "The Unintended Effects of Parental Mediation of Television on Adolescents."

186   Meanwhile, a 2009 study: Byrne, Linz, and Potter, "Test of Competing Cognitive Explanations."

186   pointing out inaccurate: Nathanson, "The Unintended Effects."

186   talking to little girls: Byrne et al., "Test of Competing Cognitive Explanations."

186   Going all Amish: Nathanson, "The Unintended Effects"; Byrne and Hart, "The Boomerang Effect."

187   Lyn Mikel Brown: Lamb and Brown, *Packaging Girlhood*, pp. 263-294.

187   otherwise, your presence: Nathanson, "Identifying and Explaining the Relationship."

187   ones who are skeptical: Author's interview with Erica Wein-traub Austin, Edward R. Murrow School of Communication, Washington State University, May 8, 2010.

189   The studio's lack of interest: Manohla Dargis and A. O. Scott, "Memos to Hollywood," *The New York Times*, May 3, 2009, p. MT1.

189   *The Princess and the Frog*: Dawn C. Chmielewski and Claudia Eller, "Disney Restyles 'Rapunzel' to Appeal to Boys," Weblog entry, "Company Town," *Los Angeles Times*, March 9, 2010, http://articles.latimes.com/2010/mar/09/business/la-fi-ct -disney9-2010mar09.

189   *Pocahontas* grossed $346 million: http://boxofficemojo.com/ movies/?id=pocahontas.htm.

189   *Up*, released six months before: Chmielewski and Eller, "Disney Restyles 'Rapunzel.'"

189   Ed Catmull: Ibid.

190   merchandising blockbuster: "Disney's 'The Princess and the Frog' Merchandise in High Demand Weeks Before Film's Debut," November 18, 2009, http://fefwww.istockanalyst.com/ article/viewiStockNews/articleid/3647634#.

190   Disney shelved its plans: Chmielewski and Eller, "Disney Restyles 'Rapunzel.'"

191   neither maimed nor killed: See Bettelheim, *The Uses of Enchantment*, p. 149.

Bibliography

Acuff, Daniel, and Robert H. Reiher. *What Kids Buy and Why.* New York: Simon and Schuster, 1997.

American Psychological Association, Task Force on the Sexualization of Girls. *Report of the APA Task Force on the Sexualization of Girls.* Washington, D.C.: American Psychological Association, 2007. www.apa.org/pi/wpo/sexualization.html.

American Society for Aesthetic Plastic Surgery. *Cosmetic Surgery National Data Bank Statistics.* New York: American Society for Aesthetic Plastic Surgery, 2008.

Andersen, Hans Christian. *Hans Christian Andersen: Eighty Fairy Tales,* tr. R. P. Keigwin. New York: Pantheon, 1982.

Basile, Giambattista. "Sun, Moon, and Talia." In *Stories from the Pentamerone,* ed. E. F. Strange. London: Macmillan & Co., 1911. www .surlalunefairytales.com/pentamerone/29sunmoontalia1911.html.

Baumgardner, Jennifer, and Amy Richards. *Manifesta (10th Anniversary Edition).* New York: Farrar, Straus and Giroux, 2010.

Bem, Sandra. *The Lenses of Gender.* New Haven, Conn.: Yale University Press, 1994.

Bettelheim, Bruno. *The Uses of Enchantment: The Meaning and Importance of Fairy Tales.* New York: Vintage Books, 1989.

Black, Shirley Temple. *Child Star.* New York: McGraw-Hill, 1998.

Blakemore, Judith Elaine Owen. "The Influence of Gender and Parental Attitudes on Preschool Children's Interest in Babies: Observations in Natural Settings." *Sex Roles* 38 (1998): 73–94.

Blakemore, Judith E. Owen, Sheri A. Berenbaum, and Lynn S. Liben. *Gender Development.* New York: Psychology Press, 2009.

Bottigheimer, Ruth B. "Fairy Tales and Folk-Tales." In *International Companion Encyclopedia of Children's Literature,* ed. Peter Hunt and Sheila G. Bannister Ray. London: Routledge, 1996.

Brown, K. M., et al. "Changes in Self-Esteem in Black and White Girls Between the Ages of 9 and 14 Years: The NHLBI Growth and Health Study." *Journal of Adolescent Health* 23, no. 1 (1998): 7–19.

Brumberg, Joan Jacobs. *The Body Project: An Intimate History of American Girls.* New York: Vintage, 1998.

Buchanan, Taneisha S., et al. "Testing a Culture-Specific Extension of Objectification Theory Regarding African American Women's Body Image." *The Counseling Psychologist* 36, no. 5 (2008): 697–718.

Byrne, Sahara, and Philip Solomon Hart. "The Boomerang Effect: A Synthesis of Findings and a Preliminary Theoretical Framework." In *Communication Yearbook 33,* ed. Christina Beck. Mahwah, N.J.: Lawrence Erlbaum Associates, 2009, pp. 33–37.

Byrne, Sahara, Daniel Linz, and James W. Potter. "Test of Competing Cognitive Explanations for the Boomerang Effect in Response to the Deliberate Disruption of Media-Induced Aggression." *Media Psychology* 12, no. 3 (2009): 227–248.

Catalyst. *The Double-Bind Dilemma for Women in Leadership: Damned if You Do, Doomed if You Don't.* New York: Catalyst, 2007.

Cherney, Isabelle D., and J. Dempsey (in press). "Young Children's Classification, Stereotyping, and Play Behavior for Gender Neutral and Ambiguous Toys." *Journal of Educational Psychology.*

Cherney, Isabelle, and K. London. "Gender-linked Differences in the Toys, Television Shows, Computer Games, and Outdoor Activities of 5- to 13-Year-Old Children." *Journal of Sex Roles* 54 (2006): 717–726.

Colapinto, John. *As Nature Made Him.* New York: HarperCollins, 2001.

Cook, Daniel Thomas. *The Commodification of Childhood: The Children's Clothing Industry and the Rise of the Child Consumer.* Durham, N.C.: Duke University Press, 2004.

———. "The Rise of 'the Toddler' as Subject and as Merchandising Category in the 1930s," in *New Forms of Consumption: Consumers, Culture, and Commodification,* ed. Mark Gottdiener. Lanham, Md.: Rowman and Littlefield, 2000, pp. 111–130.

Cook, Daniel Thomas, and Susan B. Kaiser. "Betwixt and be 'Tween: Age Ambiguity and the Sexualization of the Female Consuming Subject." *Journal of Consumer Culture* 4, no. 2 (2004): 203–227.

Cross, Gary. *Kids' Stuff: Toys and the Changing World of American Childhood.* Cambridge, Mass.: Harvard University Press, 1997.

———. "Valves of Adult Desire: The Regulation and Incitement of Children's Consumption." In *Childhood and Consumer Culture,* ed. David Buckingham and Vebjørg Tingstad. London: Palgrave, 2010, pp. 17–30.

———. "Valves of Desire: A Historian's Perspective on Parents, Children, and Marketing." *Journal of Consumer Research* 29, no. 3 (2002): 441–447.

———. "Wondrous Innocence: Print Advertising and the Origins of Permissive Child Rearing in the U.S." *Journal of Consumer Culture* 4, no. 183 (2004): 183–201.

Davies, Paul, Steven J. Spencer, Diane M. Quinn, and Rebecca Gerhardstein. "Consuming Images: How Demeaning Commercials That Elicit Stereotype Threat Can Restrain Women Academically and Professionally." *Personality and Social Psychology Bulletin* 28, no. 12 (2002): 1615–1628.

Davis, Michael. *Street Gang: The Complete History of Sesame Street.* New York: Penguin, 2009.

DeBell, Matthew, and Chris Chapman. *Computer and Internet Use by Children and Adolescents in 2003.* Washington, D.C.: National Center for Education Statistics, 2006. http://nces.ed.gov/pubs2006/2006065.pdf.

Dohnt, Hayley, and Marika Tiggemann. "Body Image Concerns in Young Girls." *Journal of Youth and Adolescents* 35, no. 2 (2006): 135–145.

Douglas, Susan J. *Enlightened Sexism: The Seductive Message That Feminism's Work Is Done.* New York: Henry Holt, 2010.

Eliot, Lise. *Pink Brain, Blue Brain: How Small Differences Grow into Troublesome Gaps—and What We Can Do About It.* New York: Houghton Mifflin, 2009.

Finch, Christopher. *Rainbow: The Stormy Life of Judy Garland.* New York: Ballantine, 1975.

Forman-Brunell, Miriam. *Made to Play House: Dolls and the Commercialization of American Girlhood, 1830–1930.* New Haven, Conn.: Yale University Press, 1993.

Fredrickson, B. L., T. A. Roberts, S. M. Noll, D. M. Quinn, and J. M. Twenge. "That Swimsuit Becomes You: Sex Differences in Self-Objectification, Restrained Eating, and Math Performance." *Journal of Personality and Social Psychology* 75, no. 1 (1998): 269–284.

Frisby, Cynthia M. "Does Race Matter? Effects of Idealized Images on African American Women's Perceptions of Body Esteem." *Journal of Black Studies* 34, no. 3 (2004): 323–347.

Girls Incorporated. *The Supergirl Dilemma: Girls Grapple with the Mounting Pressure of Expectations, Summary Findings.* New York: Girls Incorporated, 2006.

Gould, Joan. *Spinning Straw into Gold: What Fairy Tales Reveal About the Transformations in a Woman's Life.* New York: Random House, 2006.

Grimm, Jacob, and Wilhelm Grimm. *The Annotated Brothers Grimm,* ed. Maria Tatar. New York: W. W. Norton, 2004.

Hargreaves, Duane, and Marika Tiggemann. "The Effect of Television Commercials on Mood and Body Dissatisfaction: The Role of Appearance-Schema Activation." *Journal of Social and Clinical Psychology* 21, no. 3 (2002): 287–308.

———. "The Effect of 'Thin Ideal' Television Commercials on Body Dissatisfaction and Schema Activation During Early Adolescence." *Journal of Youth and Adolescence* 32, no. 5 (2003): 367–373.

———. "Idealized Media Images and Adolescent Body Image: 'Comparing' Boys and Girls." *Body Image* 1, no. 4 (2004): 351–361.

Hassett, Janice M., et al. "Sex Differences in Rhesus Monkey Toy Preferences Parallel Those of Children." *Journal of Hormones and Behavior* 54, no. 3 (2008): 349–364.

Heltsley, Martha, and Thomas C. Calhoun. "The Good Mother: Neutralization Techniques Used by Pageant Mothers." *Deviant Behavior* 24, no. 2 (2003): 81–100.

Hinshaw, Stephen, with Rachel Krantz. *The Triple Bind: Saving Our Teenage Girls from Today's Pressures*. New York: Random House, 2009.

Impett, Emily A., Deborah Schooler, and Deborah L. Tolman. "To Be Seen and Not Heard: Feminine Ideology and Adolescent Girls' Sexual Health." *Archives of Sexual Behavior* 35, no. 2 (2006): 129–142.

Jacobs, Janis E., et al. "'I Can, but I Don't Want To': Impact of Parents, Interests, and Activities on Gender Differences in Math." In *Gender Differences in Mathematics: An Integrative Psychological Approach*, ed. Ann M. Gallagher and James C. Kaufman. Cambridge, England: Cambridge University Press, 2005, pp. 246–263.

Lamb, Sharon, and Lyn Mikel Brown. *Packaging Girlhood: Rescuing Our Daughters from Marketers' Schemes*. New York: St. Martin's Press, 2006.

Lenhart, Amanda. *Cyberbullying*. Washington, D.C.: Pew Internet & American Life Project, 2007.

Lenhart, Amanda, Mary Madden, Aaron Smith, and Alexandra Macgill. *Teens and Social Media.* Washington, D.C.: Pew Internet & American Life Project, 2007. www.pewinternet.org/Reports/2007/Teens-and-Social-Media.aspx.

Levin, Diane E., and Nancy Carlsson-Paige. *The War Play Dilemma: Balancing Needs and Values in the Early Childhood Classroom.* New York: Teachers College Press, 2005.

Locke, John. *Some Thoughts Concerning Education.* Cambridge, England: Cambridge University Press, 1989 (first published 1693).

Lueptow, Lloyd B., Lori Garovich-Szabo, and Margaret B. Lueptow. "Social Change and the Persistence of Sex Typing: 1974–1997." *Social Forces* 80, no. 1 (2001): 31–35.

Maccoby, Eleanor E. "Gender and Group Process." *Current Directions in Psychological Science* 11, no. 2 (2002): 54–59.

———. "Gender and Relationships: A Developmental Account." *American Psychologist* 45, no. 4 (1990): 513–520.

Manago, Adriana, Michael B. Graham, Patricia M. Greenfield, and Goldie Salimkhan. "Self-Presentation and Gender on MySpace." *Journal of Applied Developmental Psychology* 29, no. 6 (2008): 446–458.

Martin, Carol Lynn, and Richard Fabes. *Discovering Childhood Development,* 2nd ed. Belmont, Calif.: Wadsworth, 2008.

———. "The Stability and Consequences of Young Children's Same-Sex Peer Interactions." *Developmental Psychology* 37, no. 3 (2001): 431–446.

Miller, Edward, and Joan Almon. *Crisis in Kindergarten: Why Children Need to Play in School.* New York: Alliance for Childhood, 2009.

Morgenson, Gretchen. *Forbes Great Minds of Business.* New York: John Wiley & Sons, 1997.

Morrison, Susan, ed. *Thirty Ways of Looking at Hillary.* New York: Harper, 2008.

Nathanson, Amy I. "Identifying and Explaining the Relationship Between Parental Mediation and Children's Aggression." *Communication Research* 26, no. 2 (1999): 124–133.

———. "The Unintended Effects of Parental Mediation of Television on Adolescents." *Media Psychology* 4, no. 3 (2002): 207–230.

National Campaign to Prevent Teen and Unplanned Pregnancy. *Sex and Tech: Executive Summary.* Washington, D.C.: National Campaign to Prevent Teen and Unplanned Pregnancy, December 2009.

Orenstein, Peggy. *Schoolgirls: Young Women, Self-Esteem, and the Confidence Gap.* New York: Anchor, 1995.

Paley, Vivian Gussin. *Boys and Girls: Superheroes in the Doll Corner.* Chicago: University of Chicago Press, 1984.

Roosevelt, Theodore. *The Strenuous Life: Essays and Addresses.* Mineola, N.Y.: Dover Books, 2009 (originally published 1900).

Ruble, Diane N., et al. "The Role of Gender Constancy in Early Gender Development." *Child Development* 78, no. 4 (2007): 1121–1136.

Rust, John, et al. "The Role of Brothers and Sisters in the Gender Development of Preschool Children." *Journal of Experimental Child Psychology* 77, no. 4 (2000): 292–303.

Sax, Leonard. *Why Gender Matters: What Parents and Teachers Need to Know about the Emerging Science of Sex Differences.* New York: Broadway, 2006.

Slater, Amy, and Marika Tiggemann. "A Test of Objectification Theory in Adolescent Girls." *Sex Roles* 46, no. 9 (2002): 343–349.

Stearns, Peter N. *Fat History.* New York: New York University Press, 1997.

Sutton-Smith, Brian. *Toys as Culture.* New York: Gardner Press, 1986.

Tatar, Maria. *The Hard Facts of the Grimms' Fairy Tales*, 2nd ed. Princeton, N.J.: Princeton University Press, 2003.

———. "Reading the Grimms' *Children's Stories and Household Tales*." In Jacob Grimm and Wilhelm Grimm, *The Annotated Brothers*

Grimm, ed. Maria Tatar. New York: W. W. Norton, 2004.

Tchana, Katrin, and Trina Schart Hyman. *The Serpent Slayer.* New York: Little, Brown, 2000.

Tolman, Deborah, Emily A. Impett, Allison J. Tracy, and Alice Michael. "Looking Good, Sounding Good: Femininity Ideology and Adolescent Girls' Mental Health." *Psychology of Women Quarterly* 30 (2006): 85–95.

Wolkstein, Diane. *The Glass Mountain.* New York: Morrow, 1999.

Index

Damned if You Do, Doomed if You Don't (Catalyst), 146
Dangerous Book for Boys, The (Iggulden and Iggulden), 155
Daring Book for Girls, The (Buchanan and Peskowitz), 155, 156–57
DeCesare, Danielle, 175–76
DeCesare, Hilary, 174, 175–78
depression, 6, 16, 18, 76, 172
dieting, 8, 135, 143, 186
Diller, Vivian, 138–39
Disney, 8, 13, 14, 16, 22, 23, 24, 32, 36, 41, 51, 87–88, 102, 103, 107, 111, 144, 185–86
child stars launched and marketed by, 113–15, 116–19, 120, 124–25, 128–30
first African-American Princess of, 15, 179–82, 189–90
Disney, Roy, 13
Disney, Walt, 116, 120
Disney Channel, 7, 114, 116, 117, 128
Disneyland, 41
Disney Princesses, 3, 7, 8, 19, 20, 23, 31, 32, 33, 48, 49, 61, 62, 85, 111, 114, 115, 124, 135, 138, 142, 143–44, 153, 155, 187
marketing of, 13–15, 16, 23, 24, 26, 36, 104, 116, 125, 182, 189–90
Web site for, 162
Dora the Explorer, 7, 15, 42–43, 51, 161–62
Duff, Hilary, 115, 116–17, 118, 120, 129

eating disorders, 6, 76, 137, 141
education reform, 70–71, 85
Elenita (Campbell and Juan), 149–50

Eliot, Lise, 59, 60–61, 62–63, 64, 65, 69, 71
Eschberger, Tallon, 80–82
Eschberger, Taralyn, 73–75, 78, 79–81, 84, 89, 92, 93–94
Eschberger, Todd, 80, 82, 93, 94
Eschberger, Traci, 74–75, 79–82, 89, 90, 91, 92, 93
Everloop, 174–78

Fabes, Richard, 66, 67–68, 69, 71–72, 158, 215*n*
Facebook, 24, 163, 164–65, 166, 168, 169, 171, 174, 182
Face It (Diller and Muir-Sukenick), 138–39
fairy tales, 8, 12, 13, 14, 20–21, 23, 25, 101, 108–9, 115, 139, 145, 149, 181, 185, 190, 211*n*
by Brothers Grimm, 100, 101–7, 108–9, 183, 190–92
emotional development aided by, 100, 102, 104
rescue-fantasy and landing-a-prince theme in, 12, 20, 23, 101, 102, 103, 107, 144, 182
violent and gruesome imagery in, 100, 102–3, 105, 106–9, 191–92
Fairytopia Barbie, 88
fashion, 82, 86, 91, 117, 119, 123, 125, 139, 143, 152
female heroines and role models, 14, 36, 180–82, 187–91
in fairy tales, 12, 14, 20–21, 101, 102, 104–5, 107, 108–9, 185, 190–92
independent and nontraditional examples of, 30, 42, 46, 50, 101, 108–9, 112, 128, 144–45, 148, 149–50, 153, 185–86
marketing and merchandising

Index

Index

Wonder Woman, 144, 145–46, 148, 150, 158

Wonder World Tour, 124, 125–26, 130–31

Wood, Eden, 78, 79, 89, 90, 92

Wood, Mickie, 78, 90

World War II, 100

"X: A Fabulous Child's Story," 55–56

Yeh-Shen, 103

YouTube, 46, 144, 161, 169

Zoe (Muppet), 40

About the Author

Peggy Orenstein is the author of the *New York Times* bestselling memoir *Waiting for Daisy: A Tale of Two Continents, Three Religions, Five Infertility Doctors, an Oscar, an Atomic Bomb, a Romantic Night and One Woman's Quest to Become a Mother*; *Schoolgirls: Young Women, Self-Esteem and the Confidence Gap*; and *Flux: Women on Sex, Work, Love, Kids and Life in a Half-Changed World*. She is a contributing writer to *The New York Times Magazine*. Her work has also appeared in the *Los Angeles Times, USA Today, Vogue, Elle, Parenting, O: The Oprah Magazine, More, Discover, Salon*, and *The New Yorker*, and she contributes commentaries to NPR's *All Things Considered*. She lives in the San Francisco Bay Area with her husband and their daughter, Daisy. Visit her Web site at www.peggyorenstein.com; you can follow her on Twitter @peggyorenstein.

THE PARIS
DIVERSION

THE PARIS DIVERSION

A NOVEL

CHRIS PAVONE

FABER & FABER

First published in the UK in 2019
by Faber & Faber Limited
Bloomsbury House,
74-77 Great Russell Street
London WC1B 3DA

First published in the United States in 2018
by Crown, an imprint of Crown Publishing Group,
a division of Penguin Random House LLC, New York

Printed and bound by CPI Group (UK) Ltd, Croydon CR0 4YY

A CIP record for this book
is available from the British Library

ISBN 978-0-571-35187-9

Book design by Elina D. Nudelman
Interior photography credits: (title page) Getty, Sam Salek/EyeEm; (Part I: Louvre) Getty/Purestock; (Part II: Champs Élysées) Getty/portishead1; (Part III: Palais Royal) Istock: isaxar; (Part IV: Notre Dame) Istock: IakovKalinin; (Part V: Tour Eiffel) Rogdy Espinoza Photography.

10 9 8 7 6 5 4 3 2 1

THE PARIS
DIVERSION

What the eyes see and the ears hear, the mind believes.

—HARRY HOUDINI

PART I

LOUVRE

1

A siren wails, far away.

Kate Moore is lingering in front of school, her daily dose of sidewalk-swimming in a sea of expat moms, gossip and chitchat and a dizzying ping-pong of cheek kisses, usually planted on both sides of the face but sometimes three pecks, or for some lunatics four separate kisses.

It's an international school. All the parents are transplants from dozens of different countries, with different ideas about what constitutes the proper sequence. It's an etiquette minefield, is what it is. And etiquette has never been Kate's forte.

She cocks her head, trying to discern if the siren is approaching or receding, an instinctual habit—a professional obligation—of assessing potential levels of danger. Here in Paris, at this hour, sirens are unusual. This city is less noisy than other global capitals, London or New York, Mumbai or Hong Kong. And much less than where Kate lived before here: Luxembourg, perhaps the least noisy capital in the world; and Washington, which doesn't even make the cut of the twenty most populous US cities.

But Kate has traveled plenty. For her job, dispatching her to far-flung destinations in Latin America and Europe. And for the past few years for adventure, driving around the Continent in their aging station wagon, with their EU driver's licenses and bilingual kids.

Other metropoli have all seemed like more aggressive aural assaults than Paris, with more insistent car horns honked more frequently, more idling trucks and unmufflered motorcycles, jackhammers and pile drivers and bass-heavy music blaring from souped-up sound systems, fire trucks and ambulances and police cars in hot pursuit, the unmistakable urban sounds of urgency, emergency.

It's in the mornings when Paris feels especially hushed, and in particular this slice of the *septième,* sleepy cafés on the quiet corners of narrow streets, well-dressed women depositing well-groomed kids at the towering green door of the school's fortress-like façade, forbidding stone walls from which no sounds can escape, nor for that matter children.

The siren grows louder, nearer.

A curbside fence prevents the kids from running into the street, getting hit by cars. Every school's sidewalk is lined with these fences, festooned with locked-up bicycles and kick-scooters decorated with decals of football clubs, pop singers, flower petals.

The kids are absolutely safe in there.

After the *Charlie Hebdo* massacre, sirens began to take on a new significance, triggering more vital concerns. Then the November attacks ratcheted up the tension further, and then again the Champs-Élysées shooting, these events produced a permanent propensity to generalized panic.

Sirens no longer suggest a multicar pile-up on the *périphérique* or a gangland shoot-out in St-Denis—somebody else's problem, somewhere else. These days, sirens could mean a nightclub shooting, hostages in a grocery store, a madman in a museum. Sirens could mean that Kate should storm into school, drag out her children, initiate one of her emergency protocols, go-bags from the linen closet, the always-gassed-up car in the garage, speeding out of the city toward the secret farmhouse in the Ardennes, or the airbase in the Ruhr, or somewhere else, anywhere else.

These days, sirens could mean anything.

It's what everyone is talking about, the shopkeepers, restaurateurs, hoteliers. Tourism is down. Locals are wary. Customers scarce. Soldiers and police patrol the streets in threes and fours, heavily armed, flak-jacket clad. Not only near the ministries and embassies, the busy commercial boulevards and the famous monuments, but everywhere, soldiers are loitering even here, on sedate residential streets.

The military has become a permanent presence, the new normal. Sharpshooters have taken positions in the latticework of the Eiffel Tower, the flying buttresses of Notre-Dame, the neoclassical roof of the Arc de Triomphe. Everyone is getting used to it.

This is how a police state happens, isn't it? An emergency that never subsides. Everything is getting worse all the time, so the far-right steps in and promises to solve it all—the taxes, the unemployment, the poverty and immigration and terrifying violence out in *les banlieues,* Balkan gunrunners and Albanian drug dealers and Corsican mobsters.

The police suit up, and never stand down.

People are talking about getting out of town, buying a crumbling pile of château in the country, starting a biodynamic vineyard or an eco-friendly bed-and-breakfast. Or to hell with it, leaving France entirely, moving to Zurich, to Helsinki or Lisbon or Edinburgh, places that are immune, or seem to be.

Kate hears a second siren, coming from another direction.

The other moms seem to be oblivious to the noise, nattering about nothing. Kate tunes them out, scans the bulletin board next to her, push-pinned with notices for kids' activities, community meetings, nannies, holidays, the week's lunch menu—symbols for organic, for local, for vegetarian—next to the list of every kid's allergies, right out there on the sidewalk for anyone to see.

The goodbyes begin. With all this cheek kissing, it takes forever to say hello and goodbye. Like adding a whole new category of daily chore, now every morning you have to iron a shirt, mop the kitchen floor.

"What time would suit tonight?" asks Hashtag Mom. "And what shall we bring?" Hashtag Mom never lived anywhere except New Jersey until she was thirty-one, when she moved with her global-banker husband to London, then Singapore, then Paris. Somewhere along the way, she apparently started pretending to be British.

"Bring nothing," Kate says, "except your good company. Everyone's coming at seven."

"Lovely." Hashtag Mom leans in for her final air-kiss. For Hashtag Mom, everything, always, is hashtag lovely.

As much time as Kate needs to spend kissing all these women, she's increasingly unwelcome to kiss her own children, not in public, especially not the mortified older one. But Kate is confident that her younger boy is just going along with that pose because that's what younger siblings do;

she knows that Ben still wants his mother's kisses. So she sneaks them onto his head when Jake isn't looking, an open secret right there in a crowd.

The sirens are closing in.

Now other people finally begin to react, to tilt their heads, dart their eyes, searching for whatever proximate threat might be attracting the police.

Cautionary tales, the things you hear: the aroma that turns out to be a ruptured gas main, the staph infection that over the weekend becomes an amputated leg. Lessons in vigilance, the things you could've done, should've done, if only you'd been worried enough, if you hadn't been so lazy, so selfish, if you'd had the courage to follow your fear from the very first flush. But it's only in hindsight that you see it clearly: this was one of those moments.

Everyone turns in unison, to where the narrow street ends at a broad boulevard, glimpses through the gap of a convoy zooming past, motorcycles followed by squad cars followed by armored trucks then more motorcycles sweeping up the rear, all those dark-blue vehicles with lights flashing, a thundering herd galloping in the direction of the river, the museums, the presidential palace, it's all just over there, spitting distance.

Shooting distance.

It's terror that's amassing in Kate, a sense that something is very wrong.

Maybe it's finally here: payback for all her mistakes. Her parenting mistakes and filial ones, her professional mistakes, matrimonial, her wrongdoings in every segment of life. She wakes up every single morning prepared for it to happen, for her life to be assailed.

Maybe it's today.

2

The biggest concern is safety. A distant second is discretion. But if you are concerned with neither unintentional detonation nor with being noticed, your options multiply immensely.

There are so many different ways to build a bomb.

Mahmoud has occasionally wondered if he has hallucinated this whole thing, the past two years, everything. It all *seems* so real, but is that not what people think when they are hallucinating?

The bomb that Mahmoud is wearing under his windbreaker is the type that can be easily identified by any layperson, at first glance: bricks of Semtex and a battery-powered detonator connected by wires to a flip-phone, all of it duct-taped to a canvas vest, everything easily visible. Everyone knows what this is. That is the point.

This bomb can be delivered by foot, then detonated remotely, even if the delivery system is no longer functioning.

The world has become prepared for this sort of thing, in the sorts of places where it makes sense. Places like here.

Mahmoud is the delivery system.

This type of bomb is as close as possible to fail-safe. The only drawback: one person must be willing to die. But what is one death? Hundreds of millions of people die every year. We all, obviously, die. Nearly all of us before we think it is our time, many by surprise. So it is a luxury to know when, exactly.

Mahmoud will also carry a second device, not as easily recognizable. The police will have their suspicions: Why would a man wearing a suicide vest also carry a briefcase? What could be the point of the luggage? They will be prepared for various possibilities, they will have detectors, sensors, a mobile laboratory. They will guess just from Mahmoud's body language, from his location, what the most likely scenario is. They will use their equipment to make measurements. Then they will be sure.

He sits in the rear of the panel van, GOUPIL ET FRÈRES ÉLECTRICIENS on the dingy side.

After months of planning, the final arrangements were pulled together hastily. Mahmoud does not understand all the factors, or perhaps any; there is much more to this than anyone is telling him. For all he knows, he has been lied to repeatedly, more or less constantly, about everything.

Nearly everything. Some things he knows to be true. He has seen proof.

The problem with the van—although not, in the end, Mahmoud's problem—is that because the event will happen in a heavily monitored neighborhood, the police will have access to copious surveillance footage. It will take only minutes to procure the video of Mahmoud stepping out of this vehicle, then trace the van's movements backward through the various state-owned surveillance cameras that are affixed to the walls, streetlights, and traffic lights, as well as the private cameras at jewelers and banks and hotels and ministries, new cameras are mounted every day, ever cheaper and easier to install, to network, to identify a specific timeframe, compress the file, e-mail it to investigators.

There is no way to evade surveillance.

This necessitated complex logistics just to get Mahmoud into the vehicle. A system whose sole purpose was to deliver one man to one spot on one occasion.

Him, here, now.

This tradesman's van is hand-stenciled with a nonexistent address, a fictional phone number; there is no Goupil in Paris who is an electrician with his brothers. There are no tools in the rear, no supplies, no other passengers. The steel floor is hard, the shock absorbers ineffective. Mahmoud feels every bump and pothole in his tailbone, his spine, even in the back of his head as it clunks and thumps against the side, which he does not much try to prevent, even relishes to some extent.

Recently the concepts of pain and death have been consuming his thoughts, especially late at night, when he reaches to the other side of the bed. His hand always comes away empty.

There are no windows back here. It is weak light that comes through the front windshield, on the far side of the high-backed seats. Mahmoud's angle does not allow a view of any but the tallest or closest structures, difficult to identify in the whir of whizzing by, set against a small slice of sky.

Mahmoud cannot tell which direction the van is headed in, cannot keep track of the turns. Even the passing of time has become difficult to gauge. He does not know the exact destination, but he does know it will be in central Paris. All the same to him. He has lived here only a few years, but that has been long enough to learn to hate the whole beautiful place.

The van swings around a turn, too fast, and Mahmoud slides on his seat.

He tries to adjust his tight rubberized underwear. A very uncomfortable garment, but he understands the necessity. In fact he asked for it.

Mahmoud catches a glimpse of something through the windshield, a tall wide column, nothing on either side of it, just the bright blue sky pierced by this verdigris bronze. He recognizes this structure, it is . . . he knows this . . . ?

There are so many monuments here, statues, obelisks, fountains, the French are keen on memorializing events, celebrating themselves. What is this one called . . . ?

Mahmoud visited many of these sights back when they first moved here, dutifully trekking to one tourist attraction after another. He noticed the looks he received, he observed the security guards, many of them just like him, North Africans, Middle Easterns, dark-skinned men issued uniforms and badges and walkie-talkies, told to keep an eye on anyone who looked like themselves. Jobs to pay the rent, to feed their families, to purchase the things you need, maybe sometimes a few you simply want.

The driver shifts into PARK, hops out, then seconds later jumps back in.

Mahmoud wondered if these security guards lost sleep, wracked with guilt about how they earn their livings, about the types of men they had become, men who themselves were subjected to the same injustices and sleights and distrustful looks, all reliable constants, like the gray skies. It was only their absence that surprised—a sunny day, how glorious.

Today is a sunny day.

Ah! He remembers the name of this place, that square with the column in the middle, perimeter lined with the most expensive of jewelers, the fanciest of hotels: the place Vendôme.

It is a relief that he has not completely lost his memory. But then, what does it matter?

It was not Mahmoud who had wanted to move to France. That had been Neela's desire, her dream. He had been swayed by her passion, her conviction. For the children, she said. For me.

And then look what happened. What they did to her.

3

Hunter Forsyth doesn't register the sound of the siren.

Later, when he's second-guessing his decisions, he'll understand that he did hear this first-wave siren but failed to acknowledge it, standing on the balcony off the formal dining room, which during the year that he has owned this apartment has never, not once, been used for formal dining. He's ignoring the spectacular view of the Eiffel Tower in favor of the ordinary little screen in his palm, index finger swiping, and swiping, reading this message, dismissing that one, deleting, deleting, responding with single-syllable answers, *yes, no,* trying to project not only his general level of importance but also his extra-impatience with matters that are below his purview, decisions people should make without consulting him, problems they should solve on their own.

Today, of all days, nibbled to death by minnows. It's important to retaliate. Controlled rudeness can be an effective tool.

Hunter hears a car ignition turn over, and sees the police cruiser pull out of its customary space. The car's lights start to flash as it accelerates, then the sedan tears around the corner.

This penthouse is a spectacular apartment—high ceilings and tall windows, herringbone floors and marble fireplaces, the romantic ideal of a Parisian home. On the other hand, it's just off the Champs-Élysées, with the attendant riffraff crowd, and who the hell wants that? Not Hunter. But when he was looking to buy, he discovered that at any given moment there are only a handful of quality apartments available for people like himself—American businessmen with no titles of nobility or royalty, no above-the-title film credits.

Compromises were necessary. This place is just a few minutes from the downtown office, which is the European headquarters of Hunter's multinational conglomerate. There's another Paris office with far more employees, way out in La Défense, which he visits much less frequently. He doesn't like it out there.

With all his long-haul travel, Hunter tries to minimize his commutes. For the on-and-off month per year that he spends here, he'd much rather be somewhere else, maybe out in Passy amid all the Art Nouveau and ossified old ladies, or the Left Bank, not so artsy-fartsy anymore, perhaps now even welcoming to people like him, the kinds of people who can arrange for the local police to serve as private security.

So why did the cop car just leave?

⚜

"Colette?"

Hunter's efficient, officious assistant hurries from the kitchen, heels clickity-clacking. Colette wears monstrously tall heels that make her legs—her entire figure—look spectacular. The shoes seem impossible to walk in, but she does it with aplomb, as everything. Colette is the most competent human Hunter has ever met. That's one of the reasons—one of many—that he is utterly, helplessly in love with her.

"*Oui Monsieur?*" Phone in hand, ready to answer his every question, cater to his every whim, solve his every problem, those big hazel eyes gazing at him expectantly. It wasn't until last year when he realized just how beautiful Colette is, and since then he hasn't stopped kicking himself for how long it took.

"Do you know why our police just left?"

"I will find out" is what she says, what she always says, and what she always does.

In all other aspects of his life, Hunter is supremely confident. But with Colette he feels like a scrawny sophomore with a crush on the prom queen: flustered, hopeless. The more he becomes convinced of her perfection, the more he envisages all that could go wrong. Beginning with his wife finding out, prematurely. Or Colette's husband.

She hits a button on her phone, which connects her to the woman out in La Défense whose job it is to find answers for other people.

Hunter steps back out to the balcony, just in time to see a new car pull up, a strobing blue light on the roof. Both front doors open, and a couple of uniformed policemen climb out of the unmarked car, looking around.

"Colette?"

"Oui Monsieur?"

Of all the mistakes he'll make today, this one is perhaps the stupidest, for the most irresponsible reason: he doesn't want Colette to go to the bother of calling the office, then dialing the police station, then connecting to the operator, then a supervisor, then whoever arranges for Hunter's not-exactly-legal security detail. . . . He wants to save her these half-dozen conversations. Why? Because he can't stop thinking of her as his true love, instead of one of his five assistants. He's putting Colette's interests ahead of his own, the inverse of their professional relationship.

"Forget it," he says. "A new police car just arrived."

"Parfait."

She types into her device—fingers flying, greasing the various wheels of her boss's life—while walking back to her perch at the kitchen counter.

Then he hears her gasp.

The small television on the counter shows police cars amassed in front of a train station, MENACE À LA GARE in big red letters across the screen.

"A bomb," Colette explains. "At the Gare de Lyon."

His mind jumps to how this will impact him, his today, his tomorrow, when he'll be flying to Hong Kong. A bomb in a train station on the other side of Paris is not his problem. Not with the police stationed out front, and his bodyguard in the hall, in a neighborhood teeming with military, police, the presidential palace, the US Embassy. He's safe.

Tomorrow's flight will be brutal. What Hunter needs—it's so obvious— is his own plane. Not some chic little Gulfstream for short hops to vacation spots, but a big jet that could get him from anywhere on the planet to anywhere else.

After today, he'll be able to buy one of those planes. After today, he'll be able to buy anything. Have anything. Maybe even Colette.

4

Kate watches another pair of police cars zoom through the intersection, breaking the peace of the rue du Cherche-Midi still in the process of waking up for business, doors unlocking, signs being turned over to OUVERT.

It's easy to become uneasy these days, there's a general foreboding in the air, plus an extra dread that's special to Kate: the specter of her career imploding. She keeps hoping that she'll be able to relegate it to the background, stop seeing it in the stark foreground at four A.M.

Flashes flood her consciousness, all her worst visions parading through. The life going out of Santibanez's eyes, slumped against the tree trunk in the dark park in Oaxaca. The surprise of a woman's pleading face in New York, her blood blooming into the carpet. The hateful, determined look on Julia's face, drenched in the pounding rain atop the medieval wall of Luxembourg, the muzzle of her gun just inches from Kate's forehead.

That seems so long ago, when they were still new to Europe.

Until she moved to Luxembourg, Kate didn't have any experience with this variety of high-street retail, the same clerks working the same schedule for years, for lifetimes, closing up for lunch hours, for a whole month during *les fermetures annuelles;* half the people are gone in August, the other half in July. Back in DC, Kate did her shopping in supermarkets and big-box stores, a hazy blur on Saturday mornings, driving from this parking lot to that in the rain, waiting with other sensible cars in left-turn lanes, the household chores a halfhearted afterthought to distracted parenting and autopilot marriage and faltering career, one that had once been rewarding, exciting, and invigorating but recently had become frustrating, terrifying, and ultimately untenable.

One night, Dexter came home from another dispiriting DC day and asked, "What would you think of living in Luxembourg?"

Just like that: a whole different life. Expats.

There's even a name for those traditionalists who take their holidays in August, and another for the upstarts who prefer July. *Aoûitiens* versus *juilletistes.*

Around the corner from home is a squeaky-clean, brightly lit new supermarket, but Kate prefers to shop the traditional way, beginning at the farmer's market on a boulevard's shady meridian, the fish guy and the fresh-fruit guy, the onion stall, the potatoes, the olives, the rotisserie meats, the butcher's yellow chickens and quartered rabbits. Kate is buying a fistful of flowers when everyone pauses to watch a tight caravan of *gendarmerie* people-movers tear past, big blue vans with red-and-white-zebra-striped accents, blue sirens, ten *flics* ready to leap out of each, with riot gear and assault rifles over their shoulders plus automatic pistols in their holsters, a lot of armor, a lot of firepower.

Her phone chimes with an alert, an explanation for all this activity: a bomb threat reported at the Gare de Lyon.

Another day, another threat.

She continues her rounds of the commercial street, everything anyone needs, pharmacist and housewares, *fromagerie* and *boucherie,* a veritable explosion of health-food stores, *bio* this and *nature* that and fresh-pressed juices that all incorporate ginger or echinacea. With the bike-shares and smoking ban and electric-car chargers, the place is becoming California, there's even a rash of burger joints, the type of fad that Kate thinks of as an American phenomenon, outsize passions for pit barbecue, for craft beer, for stuffing ducks into turkeys into cauldrons of deep-frying oil.

The longer she lives away from America—has it really been five years?—the less she identifies with her increasingly foreign homeland. The less she can imagine working her entire career for the American government. It was different when she had supreme confidence in the system, in its mechanisms for sorting leaders, for choosing the people entrusted with the privilege—the responsibility—of making decisions. But recent events suggest an institutional failure of epic proportions.

Yet still she remains over here, following orders from back there. And still she doesn't know who, ultimately, is giving her the orders. That makes her increasingly uncomfortable.

What Kate does know is that her position is growing more precarious by the day, as her past failures are not offset by new successes. As Hayden continues to be disappeared. Peter too. As every day it becomes more possible that her career is over, it's just that no one has yet bothered to inform her.

She takes her place on line among the women in the *boulangerie,* catches sight of her reflection in the store's window. She's a well-put-together woman on the early end of middle-aged, a working mom who hasn't yet succumbed to the inevitable short haircut that French women all seem to adopt somewhere in their forties. That haircut isn't something she's willing to admit about herself, not yet.

Kate wants to look to other people the way she sees herself. She wonders if anyone, ever, has attained that goal.

Maybe tomorrow she'll find something new to do for a living. Maybe tomorrow she'll need to.

Kate's work begins first thing every morning by checking on a handful of persons of interest scattered across Europe, their homes under surveillance, their devices hacked, wifi networks penetrated. She scans these updates before even getting out of bed.

Then she breakfasts her kids, clothes them, escorts them to school. Kate's end-of-day professional hours are unpredictable: meetings with assets, with sources who want to be bought a drink, with snitches in need of cash. These obligations tend to arise beginning late afternoon; nobody stumbles across valuable intel when they're asleep.

So her mornings are for householding, for making the rounds of her *bonnes addresses,* for meeting her husband at the café, an important component of her marriage-rehabilitation program. After Dexter's betrayals, and her own behavior, Kate realized that she couldn't continue to be a passive participant in her marriage. She couldn't assume that everything would work out, as if marriage were a perfectly engineered rocket hurtling through the infinite expanse of outer space, with no friction, no resistance, no reason to slow down or veer off-course, to crash and burn.

There's ample friction. Also plenty of foreign bodies that exert their own gravitational forces, magnetic attractions, repulsions.

Somebody needs to be active about keeping this marriage moving forward, on-course. Kate has lived with Dexter long enough to know that he isn't going to be the pilot. So she instituted these semi-regular morning dates, eased into their schedules subtly, one proffered invitation after another, until it became a habit.

Kate is the pilot.

❖

She glances at her watch, a guilt-induced anniversary present from Dexter. Are all men so transparent? Or just her own feckless husband?

The workday ahead of her will probably be uneventful—futile, even. But her dinner party tonight won't. There's a point to these relationships, working at them. It has been Kate's turn to host for a while, a responsibility dodged too long. The guests will be school couples: the inevitable Hashtag Mom and her Hashtag Husband; the charming Dutch couple who look like siblings; the quiet Norwegian banker whose garrulous wife once drunkenly shared that he has a colossal penis— she held up her hands, staggeringly wide—and this subject now comes up every few months, during that portion of a girls' night when someone invariably admits to some level of dalliance, an innocent crush on the math teacher, a not-so-innocent tryst with a bartender, backroom blowjobs and a brief pregnancy scare—though never Kate's indiscretion, that never comes up, not to anyone, not ever—and sooner or later someone will ask, straight-faced, "So has anyone seen Olaf's cock lately?" and they'll all crack up, double over, trying desperately not to laugh wine-bar pinot noir through their nostrils.

It's not a bad life.

5

Dexter Moore hears sirens, somewhere in the distance.

He glances at his wristwatch: just past the dot of nine o'clock. He looks over his shoulder: once again, no one is waiting. Throngs used to queue up for these half-dozen tennis courts, everyone wearing whites, sipping coffee, leafing through newspapers, chattering away.

Not today.

Dexter has played badly this morning, distracted, his mind wandering unproductively around unpleasant subjects, building up his anxiety, degrading his play, a vicious cycle.

He suspects that the reason these courts have become unpopular is their proximity to the Sénat. Nobody wants to be playing tennis here if a bomb goes off at the legislature, possibly lethal and—worse—deeply shameful, to be killed that way, your Lacoste'd body found under an umpire chair, a sweatband around your wrist. *Insupportable.*

"*Bon match,*" he says to Luc, in what he knows is a poor accent. Dexter has lived in French-speaking countries for a half-decade now, and he really did try his best—private lessons, vocabulary memorization, verb-conjugation exercises—but with limited success. Which is another way of saying: failure.

"You sure you don't want to come tonight?"

Luc looks up from unwrapping his knee brace. "It will be four married couples?"

"That's right."

Perhaps nothing seems like a bigger waste of a night to a guy like Luc, a divorcé constantly on the make, always hyper-aware of every woman within striking distance, who isn't wearing a ring, who's most attractive, who's most likely to sleep with him. Luc never stops collecting phone numbers and drinks dates and notches on his belt, morning-after regrets and disappointments and exes. He sees his kids only on Sundays, after kicking out Saturday night's date, burying the condom wrappers deep in the bin where the children won't see them when they're tossing away the wrappers of the chocolate bribes, ticking off every divorced-dad cliché in one fell swoop.

"*Merci,*" he says with an indulgent smile, "*mais non merci.*"

Dexter doesn't expect Luc to accept. But it's the invitation extended to the lonely person that's the nice thing, not the occasion itself. Dexter doesn't even want to go to his own dinner party, he doesn't especially like those people from school. And certainly not tonight, with so much on the line today. He'll be lucky to make it through the afternoon without throwing up.

"You are ready for today, Dexter?"

"Yes, I think so." He looks up from his tennis bag, navy canvas, racquet handle sticking out. "I hope so. Thanks again for the tip."

The Frenchman laughs. "Do not thank me yet, *mon frère.* I promise nothing!" Luc too is a self-employed investor. They met online via a message board, then in person at a freelancers-in-finance meet-up where everyone was too young at a bar in Oberkampf, a whole neighborhood where everyone is too young. "Can I ask, what size position you have taken?"

"Enough to be worth it." Dexter smiles, a look that he hopes is light-hearted, untroubled. "Not enough to break me."

If only this were true.

There are plenty of people in the world who spend most of their waking hours—maybe their sleeping ones too—thinking about money, about margins, about currencies and credit and equity and debt, market share and cost ratios, different ways of considering relative valuation. Dexter never imagined he'd become one of them.

His path hasn't been straightforward. There was the ultimately disappointing Silicon Valley sojourn, then the more satisfying DC years, the complicated detour in Luxembourg. He wonders if Paris will be the longest stage. With their kids in their cosmopolitan school, Dexter in his home office day-trading, his wife doing . . . what, exactly . . . ?

Doing whatever the hell Kate does.

Dexter has been forced to accept that she's entitled to her secrets. He's had plenty of his own.

⚜

His day: first tennis, now coffee with his wife, then his computer for London's opening, a couple of hours of trading before lunch, then New York's bell followed by a tense afternoon, late pickup of the kids from school, and somewhere in there he must scour the city for Ben's birthday present—something Dexter should've bought weeks ago, but didn't—and finally the dinner party.

A normal day, just a bit busier. And hopefully a bit more profitable.

Scratch that: a shitload more profitable.

Dexter has too much riding on today's outcome, he understands this in the rational part of his brain, knows that this investment is not a level-headed solution to his myriad and mounting financial problems, and the not-unrelated personal ones. He's reluctant to even acknowledge the extent of the problems to himself, unwilling to write off his bad choices, situations that continue to deteriorate on an almost daily basis—

He fights back the sense of doom, the tsunami, the hurricane, the uncontrollable force that threatens everything—

It's *not* uncontrollable, he tells himself. It's *not* doom.

Everything is going to be fine.

Fine.

He looks around at the manicured trees and shrubs, the neat tan-pebbled paths, the thoughtful orderliness of it all. When they first moved to Paris, this park was the kids' favorite place in the world, queuing up for the zip line, scaling the tension-rope climbing pyramid, stopping at the café for juice, for candy, for ice cream. Dexter used to purchase playground tickets by the ten-pack, earning a tiny volume discount. French culture does not embrace discounts, and any markdown sales are generally illegal, except during specifically delineated periods—*les soldes*—when a blanket of ads proclaims the sorts of modest percentages that wouldn't even convince American shoppers to slow down on their way to Walmart.

Then at some point the kids simply stopped asking, "Can we go to the park? Please? *Please?*" Just like that. Finished not only with this particular playground but with all of them, with slides and swings and seesaws and sand pits, that whole stage of life was concluded; done and done, no sentimentality.

Dexter quickens his pace through the tall wrought-iron gates, and turns to watch a police car zoom by at an unusual speed, a terrifying speed, from which he turns just in time to crash sideways into a woman— where the hell did she come from?—her groceries spilling, apples tumbling, potatoes, even her cheese is round, everything in her shopping bag seems to be rolling in different directions across the sidewalk, and Dexter is apologizing profusely, jettisoning his tennis bag, lunging for errant produce.

"*Je suis desolé,*" he says, depositing the grapefruit into her bag, one of those big sturdy recycled-material things. Nobody uses plastic anymore.

"*C'est pas grave.*"

"*Ça va?*" he asks. "*Sûr, ça va?*"

Most mornings Dexter doesn't interact with anyone except his family, sequestered alone in the apartment with his computer. But today there has been Luc and the old man who spoke to him while waiting for the traffic light and now this woman, who stands up, her hands full of round fruit.

"*Oui Monsieur.*" She smiles at him. "*Merci bien.*"

It's a nice smile. She's an attractive woman, in fact she's beautiful, and Dexter has a vague inkling that he's seen her before, though he can't place where, and realizes that he's trying too hard to figure it out.

6

The van pulls to another stop. This one, Mahmoud suspects, is the final. This one is his.

Mahmoud was never told the ultimate destination, and he did not object to being kept in the dark. But in the minutes since he identified the place Vendôme, he has been trying to guess where he will end up.

He has no idea what other elements are involved, what other people, in what other parts of the city, of Europe, the world. He could be one piece of an immense puzzle; he could be a solo operator. In the end, it makes no difference, not to him.

The driver is dressed like any other Frenchman, the type of outfit that can step out of a van and merge into the pedestrian flow, anonymous, unnoticed. Mahmoud does not even know his name.

The man turns around. *"Nous sommes arrivés."*

Mahmoud had been told that it would be a familiar shape, something well known to everyone, and even more well known to him than to most others. Like a riddle. He worried that he would not understand this riddle, that these people had overestimated the breadth of his knowledge, his powers of deductive reasoning, his overall intelligence.

"Là-bas"—the driver points at the pedestrian passageway through the sturdy building. "Do you know it?"

Mahmoud nods, of course he knows it, everyone knows it. Now that he is here, it is completely obvious, and he cannot believe he did not figure it out beforehand. Maybe he really is, after all, an idiot, just like his father used to yell at him.

"Bonne chance."

That is what this guy is telling him? Good luck?

When he met the driver for the first time this morning, Mahmoud was surprised that he was not from the Middle East, nor Africa, nor Asia. In fact he seemed like an American; spoke French like one too. And he was not the only American involved. For a mission that really did not seem like an American thing.

Mahmoud does not know how to respond to the man's good-luck wishes. Thanks? He simply turns away.

"Hey!"

Mahmoud looks back. The driver is now facing the other way, reaching toward the passenger seat, then back, extending something through the window—

Ah, of course! How could he have forgotten?

This heavy reinforced-steel briefcase is supposedly the only thing that will give Mahmoud any chance of surviving the next few minutes.

He reaches up, takes hold of the smooth handle of the shiny case. His palm is sweaty, wet—he is growing more nervous with each second—and the metal handle slips through his slick fingers, and both men gasp as the thing falls, clatters to the sidewalk—

One second—

Two—

Three—

Nothing happens.

They both exhale.

⚜

It is just a few steps from the van to the gold-tipped gates at the entrance to the pedestrian *passage,* where it is cool, dark, moist, echoing with the sounds of footfalls, which are suddenly drowned as a city bus enters one of the roadway bores, filling the space with roars.

On the far side he steps out into the bright light of the expansive vista, the little arch, the carousel, the trees and flowers, all under a tremendous sky, the Eiffel Tower on the distant horizon. The sky is often visible in Paris, there are many open spaces, the buildings are not tall. It is unfortunate that all this sky is so often gray.

People had once tried to explain to him about the weather in Northern Europe, but he could not understand it, not until he lived here.

Large marble spheres line the sidewalk, as well as square concrete blocks, protection against attack by car, by truck. But there are no closed fences, no police, no security guards, nothing to impede a pedestrian's progress on this walkway.

Mahmoud pauses at the lightweight movable fence. This is his last chance to turn around, to wade back into the scrum of vendors from sub-Saharan Africa selling Eiffel Tower keychains and water bottles and selfie-sticks, of pedicabs and tour guides, of every species of hustler preying on tourists who are lost in guidebooks and phones, double-checking the opening hour, wondering why there is such a long queue.

Mahmoud knows: the queue is for security, which everywhere is increasingly tight these days, with everything that has happened in Paris, in France, in the rest of the world.

It is a dangerous time to be alive.

In truth it is always a dangerous time to be alive. But now it is dangerous for Western Europeans and Americans, not merely for the overwhelming majority of the world's people who live and die all over the earth in places that are pretty much always dangerous, places where sizable populations are exterminated in genocides, in famines and epidemics, in floods and earthquakes and hurricanes, in civil wars and counterrevolutions and political purges and sectarian strife and tribal feuds and deeply ingrained religious conflicts that have been going on for decades, for centuries, for millennia.

Yes, these metal detectors make people feel safer. But it is just a feeling, not a fact. In reality, none of these people are safe. There is no such thing as safety for anyone, anywhere. Not anymore.

7

Her arms are growing tired, with the big bunch of flowers, and the bag filled with a heavy dome of bread and a box of assorted *gâteaux apéritifs* for the obligatory cocktail hour, and fresh fruits and ripe cheeses and a bottle of Armagnac. She dutifully marinated her chicken in red wine, braised it last night, ready to reheat.

Kate cooks, it's now something she does, she even owns an apron, which was a birthday present supposedly selected by the kids, though it was probably a not-so-subtle gesture by Dexter; Kate pretended to be overjoyed. She has even started teaching the boys to manage for themselves, nothing complicated, no fingertips shaved off by a mandoline, forearms scalded by burbling oil. Just marinara sauce, grilled cheese sandwiches, those sorts of things.

She spots Dexter across the boulevard, already installed with an espresso and *Le Monde*, still wearing his tennis clothes. As he crosses his legs, he kicks over the racquet propped against a chair, then bends to retrieve it and bangs his head.

Jesus.

She can't help but smile. If she didn't know better, she'd think it was an act.

They've been in a simmering feud for the past few weeks—no, it's months now, but it was that recent trip to Champagne that really put her over this edge. It was Dexter's idea to go see the cathedral in Reims, go on a winery tour. Evincing an appalling lack of awareness of how his children want to spend a Saturday. This ill-conceived trip came fast on the heels of a recurrence of Ben's health crisis, reminding Kate of Dexter's role in failing to mitigate it, to manage it. Also her own disappointment with herself for not being home to prevent it. Her reason for not being home.

But day by day, Kate's anger has been ebbing away. She is once again willing to be amused by her husband. Though not yet willing to let him know it.

The traffic light changes. Kate steps off the sidewalk, not especially paying attention—

A flash of danger, coming fast on her left, it's a truck swerving in her direction, turning onto the rue de Rennes, clearing out of the path of a pack of police cars speeding past, lights flashing but sirens silent, there must be a dozen of them. Kate leaps back, just barely not getting hit by the truck, which careens into the crosswalk, braking but not quickly enough, not before a few people scream as the tires screech and—

Kate drops her shopping bag, her flowers, and sprints over, ready to help, her mind running through first-responder checklists, don't move any neck or back injuries, examine pupils, apply pressure to lacerations, tourniquets—

It's a dog.

It's a brown-and-white springer spaniel, still tethered to its leash, whose other end is held by a natty old woman whose mouth is wide open in horror.

The driver jumps out of the delivery truck, leaving his door open, and looks around like he's coming upon the scene as a curious bystander, not his problem.

The old woman starts to yell at him.

People are converging from every direction. A young woman kneels to the dog, puts down her motorcycle helmet, wearing tight jeans and tall boots and a distressed leather jacket, cigarette dangling from the corner of her mouth. She examines the dog, who with no warning clambers to his feet and shakes himself off, a full-body electrocution shake, as if he has just emerged from the cool lake, ooh that felt good.

The old woman bends over to stroke her pet gingerly, checking for injuries, the legs, paws, skull. Staring into the dog's eyes, as if for signs of a concussion, asking the spaniel to count backward from ten, what's today's date, who's the president.

A few people have begun to berate the driver, and Kate can hear a hysterical woman phoning the police. But the dog is now wagging his tail, thrilled with all this attention from strangers, normally the morning walks are so uneventful, we just go get the newspaper and then return to the apartment, plop down at the door and wait for something fun to happen, maybe today is cleaning-lady day.

Kate feels sorry for this truck driver, who's trying to explain that the police were swarming in his rearview, it was his civic duty to get out of the way, the dog impossible to see down there . . .

The guy's points are valid; some people are nodding in agreement, others are still livid. A middle-aged man with a terrifically hooked Gallic nose has anointed himself moderator, he's wearing magenta jeans and a puffy vest over his tweed jacket, the outfit of a man who sees his rightful place as the center of anything.

Kate is finished here. She's not going to get involved in any police reports about an uninjured dog.

"What's all that about?" Dexter exchanges a peck with his wife.

"Spaniel got hit by that truck. Dog fine. People up in arms. How was tennis?"

He grunts, then turns back to the paper, studying up for another day at the computer, in this new career of his, which is not really so new. Kate thinks anything in the past decade is new—new to be a parent, new to live in Europe, new that Dexter is a day-trader. The Internet is new. Cell phones.

"Hey," she says, "what's with this?" She points at his new cap, made by the preferred brand of French outdoors enthusiasts, the requisite head-to-toe outfit to *faire de la rando* in the Pyrenees or the Dolomites. This brand doesn't really belong in the wardrobe of the man who's Kate's husband; Dexter doesn't hike, he's not French, he's not trendy. "What happened to your tennis cap?"

In Luxembourg he'd belonged to a club built on the grounds of a noble family's old estate, a place where the whole village used to come every year for a hunt, back when that things like that went on. The land eventually evolved into a suburban development surrounding a tennis club whose logo is a kneeling rifleman, which makes a small amount of sense if you know the club's history, but otherwise suggests that the club is a hunting one.

"That's a good question," Dexter says. "I can't find it."

Kate's phone vibrates. She doesn't like being a person who jumps to attention at every electronic interruption, but with all the police zooming around, today is different. Many days, she tells herself something similar.

It's a text-message from someone who's identified in her contacts app as Pierre, at the butcher shop, telling her something she already knows: *Undetonated bomb at Gare de Lyon.*

The guy's name isn't really Pierre. He's not a butcher.

8

T he driver is trying to look like any other guy killing time in a tradesman's vehicle, window down, arm on the door, waiting. His orders are to give it one full minute, in case the other man needs to return, for some unarticulated reason.

He glances at the phone resting on the passenger seat, next to that bag that he sometimes has to carry around. Forty seconds more.

This is a risky minute, perhaps the riskiest. He can hear sirens, a whole chorus of them, rushing somewhere. But he knows that it can't be here that they're coming, not yet.

Deep breath.

Remember the money. That's what he's been telling himself, over and over, ever since he signed on to this op. Except there was no signature, obviously. No contract. No record of any sort.

It'll be just another few hours. Then he'll be rich. Or at least no longer broke.

His phone beeps: the minute is up. He quickly types out the no-nonsense text—*Departing Louvre*—then shifts into gear. He restrains himself from peeling away from the curb in a scream of burning rubber, and focuses on adding gas incrementally, accelerating slowly, merging into traffic without swerving around too-slow cars, puny Peugeots and effete Fiats, wimpy little cars on their way to nowhere, driven by nobodies, in no rush.

He sure as hell is in a rush.

Remember the money, he tells himself. Remember why you need it.

❧

Even after his discharge—four long years in Afghanistan and Iraq—he'd continued to spend much of his life abroad, three months here, six there, East Africa, Central Asia, places where his skill set was highly valued in the private-contractor environment. He was decently compensated, and for a long time he'd spent all his income freely. Wastefully. A tricked-out Hummer, which he almost never got to drive. Long weekends in Vegas, in Mauritius; full weeks in Jamaica or Bali. Any new weapons that caught his eye. Doing his part to maintain America's 1:1 gun-to-person ratio.

He merges right, into the thick rush hour on the rue de Rivoli, then right again, then takes the first available turn.

Another turn, and another. He can recite this route from memory, starting at any point along the tight streets of the first *arrondissement* and into the second and then the ninth, putting distance between himself and the Arab's drop-off point, away from the confluence of law enforcement and military, from cell-phone cameras and cable-news reporters, from all the potential problems back at the Louvre and the landmarks that surround it, venues where the police are stationed, the army also showing up, erecting roadblocks any minute now, checkpoints, lockdowns.

They'd plotted this out—they'd plotted everything out, beating it to death—but now that it's upon him, the route feels improvised, slapdash. He sticks to the minor streets, the sorts that won't be blockaded. In Paris, minor streets aren't long-distance ones. So the straight line that he's attempting to drive isn't all that straight, the quick escape not terribly quick.

But straight isn't the goal. Fast isn't the goal. Undetected, that's the goal. Unimpeded.

The eyeglasses are distracting him, encroaching on his vision from every direction. There's no prescription to these lenses, yet it still feels like his vision is altered. To acclimate himself, he'd worn these frames a few times around the little apartment, and out in the street, even driving a stolen car along this very route, making all these same turns, at this exact time of day, headed to the same destination.

But practice is practice. Now, in the real moment, the glasses are bothering the shit out of him. Everything is bothering the shit out of him.

The eyeglasses weren't the only thing that had been foisted upon him. He'd been painstakingly wardrobed, precisely haircut and groomed, all choices he would not have made himself.

Wyatt is aware of the figure he normally cuts, buff and bicep'd and heavily inked, jaw muscles twitching in stoic toughness, a lean mean fighting machine, a force to be reckoned with; he thinks of himself in these tough-guy tropes, always has. But this whole getup hides his assets, disguises his bearing, makes him look like any other French fag.

Which he supposes is the point.

He's worried, irrationally, that he's going to run into someone he knows, some hot chick who'll give him a once-over and ask, "Dude, the fuck happened to you?"

Remember the money.

He did what he could do. He emptied his cash box. He liquidated this and that. When people are selling something to you, they talk about value retention and resale demand; when they're buying back, though, it's all depreciation, it's excess inventory, it's market downturns, global economic conditions. It's fifty cents on the dollar. If you're lucky.

On the other hand: the hospital costs, the specialists, the medications, none of that is discounted. There are no sales on life-saving surgeries.

One minute he was swimming in it—trucks and guns, gambling and liquor and coke and carefree casual sex—and the next, nothing.

Desperate times, they descended in an instant. So he started searching for drastic measures.

The job was in Paris. Big European cities were not the type of locale with which Wyatt had operational experience, but thanks to the grandparents who raised him, he did speak some French, which was one of the job requirements. And the payday was an awful lot of cake for a few weeks' training and waiting, then one day of actual work.

Today. It would be a long and perilous day, no doubt. Already was, and it was barely nine in the morning. But he'd worked plenty of lengthy dangerous days in his life, and every single one of them had earned him a fuckload less money.

He'd already been paid the first installment. But that moment—seeing proof that fifty K had been transferred to his Cayman Islands account—

turned out to be the saddest of his life. Because it was when he saw that balance that it hit him: the only way he was going to stop paying—ever—was if his little girl died.

And no, not if: when. *When* she died.

In that dark apartment in Paris, laptop in lap, he cried like a baby, tears splatting down onto the trackpad, wiping them away with the bottom of his T-shirt, until a window popped up on his screen, informing him that he was going to be logged out of his account due to inactivity.

"No," he muttered. "I am definitely not fucking inactive."

9

Hunter sees another unmarked sedan pull to a stop, a blue light on its dashboard. Two uniformed patrolmen had emerged from the first car, and now a business-suited man climbs from the second, greets the cops. All three men swivel their heads around, scanning every direction, on alert, looking for something. What? Trouble.

They turn in unison and march to the building's door, their heads still swiveling.

A window has popped up on Hunter's phone: *Unable to connect to server.*

"Colette? I'm having a problem with my phone."

She squints down, then consults her own device. *"Moi aussi."* She shakes her head in disappointment; Colette takes things personally. "Both are not working. I will find out."

"And the police seem to be coming inside."

"Pardon? Coming inside where? *Ici? Maintenant?"*

Hunter nods. He worries that there's a relationship between the two, the phone problem and the police arrival. He certainly hopes not. Any telecom issue that involves law enforcement is much more serious than rebooting the router. He doesn't have time for serious French problems, telecom or otherwise.

His first phone appointment is in ten minutes. His plan is to take this morning easy, slowly, carefully. His jetlag is severe, his nerves are frayed, he's exhausted. So he's going to spend the whole morning here, making calls away from the office, giving himself the space to focus on the conversations, alerting VIPs to the news. Trying to stay calm.

Then he'll have a light lunch and head to the office, where the press conference is scheduled for three P.M., thirty minutes before New York's opening and while London is still trading and the rest of Europe still working, ensuring attention across all the financial institutions and media of the Western Hemisphere, and thus maximal trading volume.

And maximal profit. Today Hunter expects to increase his net worth by hundreds of millions of dollars; today is the day when he finally becomes a billionaire. But it's going to be a hard day; he'll be earning every penny. In fact he has been earning the billions of pennies his whole life, but it's only now that he'll be able to collect them.

The sun never sets on Hunter's empire, thousands of employees in a dozen countries, no time of any day when he does not have active business.

This is something that poor people—and most Democrats of any socioeconomic strata—don't seem to understand about extremely successful businessmen like himself: being this wealthy doesn't mean you can relax. The opposite.

"*Monsieur?* The television, now it also does not work." Colette looks disgusted. "Everything is *en panne.* I am sorry, I—"

Ding.

✤

What Hunter hopes is that the police are here because of some simple misunderstanding, something that Colette will take care of without even telling him about it. She'll shake her head, not willing to waste even one second of his time explaining it. Hunter relishes the way she shields him; that's part of the whole attraction.

He can hear the guard's voice on the far side of the closed door. Hunter maintains a twenty-four-hour security detail everywhere, and here at the apartment that means a big stoic guy on a barstool in the hall. His global security chief hires local talent in every country, an interchangeable assortment of beefy men who all seem to wear close-cropped beards or goatees, and skulls that are some level of shaved, and automatic pistols strapped into shoulder holsters. It's difficult to tell them apart, to keep track of their names.

At first, the minor *comtesse* who lives in the other penthouse was scandalized by these thugs who were so presumptively occupying their small shared hall. But Madame was also titillated. She still makes the occasional show of complaining, but probably because she thinks these protests will entitle her to some other concession, some favor, at some future point. She's the type who has spent a lifetime trading in favors and obligations. Also the type who believes that surviving till old age entitles you to be a complete asshole whenever you want, a quality that Hunter recognizes from his own mother.

Now he hears heated words from the foyer, an unfamiliar man speaking firmly to Colette, her protests. Then Colette's heels clacking on the wooden floors.

Six months ago, the downstairs neighbor complained about the noise, demanded that carpets be installed to muffle footsteps. But Hunter likes the look of the bare wood. Another problem solved by a timely transfer of a reasonable sum of money.

"*Monsieur,*" Colette says, approaching quickly. "These men, they are insistent. It is one member of the Parisian police, and one man from your embassy."

"The US Embassy?"

In the foyer, the strangers are standing in uneasy poses around the security guard—Guillerme? Gustave?—who's glancing from intruders to Hunter to Colette and back. Hunter's guards have a specific protocol for what to do if the French police ever show up; that's a foreseeable circumstance. But not in conjunction with an American official.

"*Bonjour,*" Hunter says, in French to be polite. Then "I'm Hunter Forsyth" in English, to clarify that this interaction will be on his terms. Everything is on Hunter's terms; he makes that clear to everyone, all the time. "What can I do for you gentlemen?"

"Mr. Forsyth, I'm so sorry to bother you. My name's Tom Simpson." The guy reaches into his pocket, extracts something. "I'm with the Department of State." He extends his hand, an identity card. Hunter looks from ID to person to ID again.

"I'm sorry to inform you, Mr. Forsyth, that we have a, um, situation." The guy is nervous. "Credible terrorist threats against heavily populated landmarks in central Paris."

"You mean the train station?"

"Well, yes. But additional targets as well. The threats are immediate and active."

Hunter instinctively glances toward the windows, the balcony . . . The sirens.

"The police informed us that your regular, um, security detail would be redirected to one of the target sites. The department has assigned two replacements—one has secured the lobby—to come here." Simpson gestures at the Parisian uniform, still at the elevator. It's a crowd of large men in a tight space. "We at the embassy thought it would be prudent to join. And perhaps to wait inside?"

"Inside my apartment? For what?"

"For the situation to be resolved."

There's something Hunter isn't getting. "What does any of this have to do with me?"

The American looks uneasy. "Just a precaution."

Bullshit, Hunter thinks. And speaking of bullshit: there's no way this guy is really from State, is there? No. This must be a CIA officer who's standing in Hunter's foyer. Should that make him feel better? Worse? At this point, hard to tell.

"Okay, I guess. Come on in." He glances at the phone glued to his palm. Still no signal. Still no wifi. "Colette?"

"*Oui Monsieur.* I will try again."

10

"*Bonjour Madame.*" It's one of the morning waiters, in shirt and tie and tightly cinched apron.

"*Bonjour Julien. Comment ça va?*"

Julien shrugs; he's a fatalist. "*Café crème?*" He asks every time, a standing invitation for Kate to change her mind, to order something else. But she never does.

Here on the boulevard St-Germain, waiting tables is not a holding pattern, a job for young people trying to do something else, or figuring out what to try, or for mothers who need to be home in the mornings, or for downsized people, for anyone hoping for something better. At this café, being a waiter is a career, a destination in and of itself.

"You get everything you need?" Dexter indicates the bulging cloth shopping bag, which when empty Kate carries folded into a little packet in the bottom of her handbag.

"Not quite. Could you pick up cocktail napkins?"

"Cocktail napkins?"

"You know. Little square things."

"Where am I supposed to find those?"

"Probably at that place on the rue Jacob."

"Which place?"

"The place with all the paper napkins in the window."

Kate knows where to find things, how to do things, meet people, have a life. Here in Paris, she has made every attempt to fit in. Back in Luxembourg, one of the sources of her discontent was that she hadn't. She'd held herself apart, and not just apart but above, superior to all those other homemakers, their aggressive parenting, fanatical nesting, competitive entertaining. She'd made no secret of her rejection of it all.

Not this time around. Hence the tennis league, the coffees at the café next to school, sitting around, accomplishing nothing more than going to a place for the sake of having a place to go. A concerted campaign to make friends, connections, resources. To be a full human being, complete with all the components of a full life.

She used to invite people out to breakfast—quick, inexpensive, conducive to her late-starting workday—until she realized that breakfast is not a social occasion in Paris; the only defensible breakfast invitation is actually one to have sex the night before. So she stopped doing that.

But despite her best efforts, Kate eventually had to acknowledge that she didn't want to be a stay-at-home parent. It was driving her nuts.

Maybe two years hadn't been sufficient to make the momentous adjustments, the wholesale redefinitions. Maybe in those two years she hadn't been patient enough, dedicated enough, flexible enough. Maybe if she would've stuck it out—another year? two?—she could've found more fulfillment, more joy, less frustration, less resentment. Maybe she could've been happy as a full-time mom, if only she'd tried harder, longer.

She didn't. Instead she found part-time work, like many women in her situation, graphic designers, social-media consultants, the types of positions that accommodate unexpected visits to the pediatrician, and standard workdays that must routinely end in mid-afternoon, and the expanded holiday breaks that correspond with school schedules and amply compensated husbands.

Kate's, though, is different. When she's working, it's sometimes out of town, it's twenty-four hours per day, and occasionally people try to kill her. And it has been going downhill ever since her boss went on a mission to America and disappeared. Presumed, by many, to be dead.

But not by Kate.

When she returned to the working world, Kate no longer had the luxury of frittering away days with three-hour lunches and recreational-retail expeditions to the *grands magasins.* She had become a rarity in her milieu: a working mother, with a working husband. A two-career household.

But she didn't want to withdraw entirely. She'd taken satisfaction in this community, a normal person who drops her kids at school, hosts dinners, meets her husband at the café, everything she's doing today, this regular life, the life she wants, everyone does.

Kate's phone dings: a text-message group chat, a shuffling of responsibilities for a school event next week. Organized, as ever, by Hashtag Mom. Kate can't help but wonder if—hope that—the woman's popularity is illusory, nothing more than a projection of her social ambition, her self-aggrandizing missives punctuated with a barrage of three or four and sometimes as many as ten references, as if the woman dropped a hand grenade into a barrel of hashtags and they came exploding out hither-thither, #Paris #autumn #Saturdays #BlessedLeftBankLiving #matin #fashion, all concluded—always—with #ExpatMom.

Kate occasionally has to remind herself that Hashtag Mom is not the woman's actual name.

It's not really the hashtags that eat at Kate. They're just a symptom. The disease is superior parenting—humble-brags and name-drops and condescending advice that all elicit this stream of positive reinforcement from HM's so-called friends, hollow affirmations and validations, *omg so beautiful!* and *u r the best mum ever!!* and *couldn't agree more!!!*

These posts accuse Kate that she herself is an inadequate #ExpatMom. That she doesn't lay it all out there, her love for her children, her pride in her kids and husband, her rented villas and reupholstered chaises and adventure safaris.

Kate isn't immune—is anyone?—to wanting to be a perfect mom. And all these valedictory hashtags are reminders that she isn't. But Kate reminds herself that this isn't Hashtag Mom's fault. Also that Kate's own priorities are a lot more consequential than social-media likes.

Her phone dings again: *Anyone know why all the police????!!!!*

It's not just hashtags that Hashtag Mom uses with reckless abandon.

"*Merci,*" she says to Julien as he delivers her café.

"*Je vous en prie.*"

The waiters here know everyone in the family, their coffee preferences, evening drinks. They are regulars, just like Sartre and Camus had been, de Beauvoir and Brecht, Picasso and Joyce and Baldwin and Wright, Julia Child. And now Ben and Jake and Dexter and Kate, the Moores. These waiters have watched the kids grow, become fluent in French, Jake now corrects Kate's pronunciation—"No, Mommy, it's *rrhhhobbb-eh*," a guttural *r* sound from deep in his throat, a noise that Kate will never be able to get quite right.

They'd come to Paris licking their wounds, somehow having survived the disaster of Luxembourg and emerging even stronger. Or maybe that's just how they choose to spin it to each other, to themselves. Though not to anyone else, they won't ever be able to explain any of it, to anyone. There were too many illegal aspects, clandestine operations, the CIA and FBI and Interpol, a whole mess.

And maybe the tale they tell themselves is a lie; maybe they're not stronger. Maybe they're just pretending, because that's what you do, that's how marriage works, how life works: you pretend everything is fine. Even in the face of overwhelming evidence to the contrary, a preponderance of evidence. But you convict only if the evidence is beyond all reasonable doubt. The burden of criminal court, not civil.

It's still possible—it will always be possible—that Dexter's past will eventually sneak up and attack him. Or Kate's.

But that hasn't happened, not yet. Their life is placid. So Kate comes to the café with her husband, and she watches Paris stroll by, *les hommes d'affaires* in their slim-silhouette suits and pointy shoes and seven-day stubble, the women in their perfectly tailored skirts and deftly knotted scarves. Kate herself is wearing a scarf, tied the way that Parisian women do, a thing she had to learn.

Kate has grown out of her tourist love of the city, sees this place more plainly for what's wrong with it. She still loves Paris, but now it's a mature love, clear-eyed with no illusions, no misconceptions. No shortage of disappointments, resentments, grievances.

Not unlike her marriage. Not unlike any marriage.

Another flock of police cars comes flying up the boulevard, and everyone watches for a few seconds before returning to their everyday concerns, a little less comfortable.

11

The baby is gurgling, a sound that could be a prelude to crying, or could be harmless. At the moment, no action is required.

She turns her attention back to the computer on the ornate rolltop desk, the barrage of financial-market information bombarding her. She's trying to hear the various squawk boxes of the world at once, her ear attuned to a few specific developments. A handful of bank sites are also loaded onto her screen, plus a dozen brokerage accounts, representing trades she made over the past weeks, all using different aliases, executed at different times of different days for different amounts, eighty here, one-thirty there.

There will be thorough investigations. She's taking thorough precautions.

There are dozens of windows open in front of her.

Each account has its own regimen of security protocols—bot-combating interfaces, triple-encrypted user names, random-character passcodes generated by a battery-powered remote device. A rich tapestry of multilayered defenses against the ever more aggressive, sophisticated, relentless intrusions of hackers.

She of all people is well aware that hacking pays lucratively, and anything that pays lucratively attracts high-caliber talent. Smuggling, drug-trafficking, arms-dealing, bond-trading, hedge-funding, all these legal and illegal methods of skimming, of chiseling a cut between production and consumption. All immensely lucrative. The more original the idea, the more lucrative.

You don't need to have a lot of great ideas to get immensely rich. Just one, really. As long as you also manage to consider all the angles and get there early, preferably first. Plenty of people have great ideas, lying on the couch. The trick is getting up.

She'd already had her one great idea, and she'd executed it with full vigor. But she'd been overconfident, and this hubris had cost her everything. Almost everything.

This is her second great idea, and she probably won't get a third chance. She's not making the same mistakes this time.

❖

She tries to relax. Inhales slowly, deeply, lets her head fall back, stretching out her tense neck muscles.

This living room is huge, with three different seating areas, two fireplaces, French doors to a balcony perched over the *campo,* half-shaded at this hour by the low angle of the sun. She stares up at the coffered ceiling, they're all spectacular in this apartment, different in every room. The master bedroom has a fantastic fresco painted onto a plaster oval, mountains and streams, blue skies and puffy clouds and chubby cheerful cherubim. Lots to look at when you're fucking in missionary position. But recently there'd been precious little of that in the king-size bed with the brocade cover, not with the copulatory consequence in the adjoining bedroom, screaming and shitting up a storm.

Nothing is quite as desexualizing as parenting an infant.

Plus her husband has slept in this bed a grand total of three nights in the past month.

She keeps refreshing one window, keeping herself logged into the account that holds the greatest volume of put options. Waiting for the signal.

This old building is one of many in Venice whose ownership has recently changed hands. The new owner is awaiting permits to renovate, to transition the building from long-term rentals into much more enriching short-term tourist housing. In the meantime everything is falling apart, walls crumbling, electricity fizzling, pipes leaking. At first glance this place looks like luxury, but after ten minutes the decay becomes evident. Just like the entire city, increasingly unable to provide the things that residents need but tourists don't, groceries and hardware and fresh fish.

Venice may have once been a world capital, but that was a thousand years ago, Marco Polo's day. In the past few decades the population has fallen by half, and within another twenty years basically no one will live here anymore, it'll be just tourists who sleep on the main islands, in hotels and hostels and apartments like this one, while every night all the Italians will sleep across the lagoon in Mestre, which is nobody's idea of a pretty place.

The baby's noise has become louder. It's touch-and-go.

For all the fanny-packed visitors discharged from all the mega–cruise ships, for all the rising fetid waters and skyrocketing rents and disappearing services, the beauty is still beyond compare. Venice is a spectacular place to wait it out, to meld into the mass of foreigners, the constant churn of a city whose population turns over every single day, tens of thousands of new faces. A place where familiar faces are noticeable. If someone shows up here, looking for her, she'll know it.

She packed her bag last night, then stopped by Lorenzo's shop just before closing to confirm that he'll be available to give her a ride. Family problems, she said. She might need to leave on short notice. Tonight.

"*Certo,*" Lorenzo said. She paid him a hundred euros per month, for various favors. For reliability.

Off to the side, a few prepaid mobiles are plugged into their chargers, lights glowing, awaiting different pieces of information. One of these phones chimes, delivering the expected update. She turns back to her larger screen, the trackpad, the little cursor blinking, winking at her, in on the whole scheme.

She hits EXECUTE, and waits for the screen to refresh. Then she needs to move the cursor to another spot, where she clicks another button: CONFIRM.

She stares at the little animation that signals that something is in the process of happening, but hasn't yet happened . . .

Not yet . . .

Not yet . . .

Then it does. Your transaction is complete, here is the confirmation number, thank you for your business.

That's done. It's not until she exhales that she realizes she'd been holding her breath.

Even in a modest boat like Lorenzo's, you can get to dozens of countries, the Balkans, even North Africa, the Mediterranean Mideast. Down to Sicily or over to Greece. Or instead you could drive up into the Alps, to Switzerland, Liechtenstein, the Black Forest. Or fly anywhere. Venice presents a lot of options, to a lot of destinations. A lot of ways to lose a trail, or create a false one. An easy place from which to escape.

12

The crowd is large at this hour, with the eager hordes who showed up early plus all the people showing up now as the doors open, streaming in from all directions, everybody wants to be here bright and early, go get a glimpse of that famous smile.

Mahmoud walks through the opening in the temporary fence, which is perhaps no longer temporary. Portable, but permanent.

There is no one at this fence to challenge him.

Sculptural-looking concrete blocks are scattered around the central plaza. Tourists stand atop these sturdy forms, balancing themselves in silly positions, or holding up thumbs and forefingers to create a trick of perspective for the benefit of cameras, a novelty shot that is not so novel when thousands of people take it every day.

These protective bollards are another layer of fortification to prevent attack by vehicle, the manner of assault that happened in Nice, in New York. Or to prevent something even more devastating: an armored vehicle delivering a bomb, or an armored vehicle that itself is a bomb. Or a whole fleet of vehicles. Perhaps not even for the purpose of mass killing, but for mass theft, or mass destruction. The treasures here are, literally, priceless. That is why all these people have come. That is why Mahmoud has come.

Yes, these concrete pillars are for protection.

Ha.

⚜

The crowd's collective energy is impatient. Mahmoud feels the humanity thrumming around him, enveloping him, all these heartbeats, all this flesh. He pushes past people, not worried about seeming rude, and suddenly finds himself on the periphery of a large group of children, it is obviously a school group, there must be a hundred little kids, paired off, holding hands.

When he was approaching, this area looked like a depression in the crowd, perhaps a roped-off section, or another big fountain, someplace where it would be impossible for people to be standing. But there are plenty of people standing here, they are just small people, so Mahmoud could not see them.

Back home, he had been an average-size adult male. But here in well-fed Western Europe he is a short man, slight, narrow-shouldered and pencil-armed, even his hair seems thinner here. Everyone in Paris looks like they could beat him up, even the women.

It had not occurred to Mahmoud that there would be little kids here, but of course there are. Probably to see the mummies, overseen by these young women, schoolteachers.

Mahmoud has two little children himself. And his wife, she is a schoolteacher.

He surveys the plaza, the familiar shapes whose most famous incarnations preside over a stretch of desert not far from where he was born, where he lived most of his life, in the southern sprawl of the largest city in the Arab world. Those three immense structures in Giza are made of stone. The four here in Paris are much smaller, and made of glass.

Was, he has to remind himself. *Was* a schoolteacher.

Mahmoud arrives to his assigned destination, the only statue in the courtyard, King Louis XIV on his rearing horse. Mahmoud stops walking and waits, strapped into one bomb and carrying another, in the epicenter of Western civilization.

13

"Dex?"

He doesn't look up from the paper. "Hmm?"

"You're going to remember Ben's present, right?"

An inflexible little-boy birthday request, a much coveted toy—a set of movie tie-in Lego—that has proven hard to find. Dexter should have bought it long ago, or ordered it online; neither the birthday nor the request snuck up. Now he's out of time. A small chore, something he promised to take care of, then didn't. It infuriates her.

"Yes."

"Really, Dex?"

"Trust me."

Kate sighs audibly, a huff of unambiguous displeasure. Dexter chooses to ignore it, and she chooses to leave it at that, unwilling to escalate, at least not at the moment. Maybe later. Especially if it turns out that he'll be unable to find the right box of Danish plastic, which is an outcome that Kate might even be rooting for, it will serve him right, and she will be justified in her sanctimony. There's very little as satisfying as irrefutable spousal self-righteousness.

They sit silently, stewing in the kind of spat that's undetectable if you're not in the marriage, not exhaustively versed in its history, the prior mistakes and misrepresentations and errors of judgment and honesty, the full set of luggage that comes with sharing a life.

Dexter hands the French newspaper to Kate. It's a small gesture, but better than nothing. He moves on to the *International New York Times*.

They sip their coffees, read their papers, in silence. Dexter has never been the most talkative of men, but for the past days he's been especially uncommunicative. Which makes Kate wonder, worry: again?

She tries to brush aside that thought. Again.

But her ire is up, and she refuses to say thanks for the paper. Punishing him, is what she's doing. But he probably doesn't realize he's being punished. In fact—in *fact*—he might even think he's being *rewarded*, afforded a little peace and quiet for once.

Goddamn it.

She flings aside a page without having finished the article she was in the middle of not reading.

❧

Like Kate's, Dexter's workday skews late. Some days they barely overlap. This led to problems back in Luxembourg, where neither had much idea what the other one did all day.

When she took this new position, she tried to be more up-front. There would be travel in this job, she told Dexter, for indefinite duration, to destinations that she wouldn't necessarily be able to divulge. There would be secrets. She couldn't answer most questions, so she'd appreciate it if he wouldn't ask. She didn't want to have to lie to him, she didn't want him to have to pretend to believe her lies. Wouldn't they be better off if they just skipped all the lying?

But he did need to know her cover story. Enough to be able to answer casual questions, or, in a dire situation, noncasual ones. He needed to know enough to be credible.

"You're a consultant?"

"That's right."

Most people in Paris don't talk about work, at least not cocktail-party acquaintances; too *bourge.* But that French anti-bourgeois sentiment doesn't fully penetrate the expat bubble, so Kate needed to be prepared for people to ask her "What do you do for a living?" and not be content with a one-line answer. They might ask Dexter too. And it might not always be casual chitchatters.

"And what is it you consult about?"

"Political-economic issues in France."

"Really?"

It was a ludicrous question. She didn't answer.

"And who are your clients?"

"Large US-based multinationals."

Kate had planned for this conversation. She'd made an occasion of it, a favorite bistro, dark wood and yellow walls and old brass sconces. She sat on the red velvet banquette, the same color as the restaurant's name in extravagant script decorating the china.

"Such as?"

"I'm not at liberty to divulge the identity of my clients."

"Why not?"

"NDAs as a matter of blanket policy. To prevent any misunderstandings."

The menu featured all the greatest hits. Kate was having coq au vin, trying to figure out how to make it herself. Following a recipe wasn't always enough.

"And what is it that these clients expect from your consultancy?"

"That, too, is something I've promised not to dis—"

"Okay, I get it. But just between us."

"Just between us? What does that even mean in this situation? Seriously?"

Dexter looked past her, to the rear wall with floral wallpaper. The tablecloths were white, the silver old and slightly tarnished, the waiters wearing black and white, formal yet discrete and agreeable.

"Listen, Dex, I wouldn't answer that question, so you wouldn't know the answer. Let's just keep it that way. Let's not invent more lies than we need to."

"But do you have an answer?"

"Yes, I obviously know who my clients are, I know what services I provide to them, I know what they pay me, and I keep records to document all this."

"Records." Kate could see it dawn on Dexter: she was advancing the same arguments now as he had, back when they'd moved to Luxembourg, when he'd fabricated his own fake career—fake job, fake office, fake clients.

But unlike Dexter in Luxembourg, Kate in Paris actually generates real reports for real clients—people who could be contacted, files that could be double-checked, verified. The work is not dissimilar to what Kate did as an analyst in Washington, except here she pays anonymous freelancers to do it for her.

This is the difference between Dexter's sham job and Kate's: he's an amateur, and she's a pro.

"Where are these records?"

"My office."

"Where's that?"

"The sixteenth."

"What street?"

"You can't remember."

"I can't? Why not?"

"You don't really go to that neighborhood, the streets are unfamiliar, I told you but you forgot. The street name begins with *M*, maybe. Or *N*."

Sooner or later, Kate suspected, her husband would try to find out. Just as she had. Back in Luxembourg, she'd succeeded; here in Paris, he would not.

She told herself that these lies of hers were for Dexter's own good. His own safety. The street begins with neither *M* nor *N*.

"So I have to be an idiot."

This was an inane simplification, and he knew it. No reason for Kate to counter the argument, which would only lead to a bigger argument.

"Are all these secrets really any better than lies?"

He was trying to be reasonable, but he didn't have the right to be assertive, and they both knew it. Dexter didn't have the luxury of occupying any moral high ground; the opposite. He was in a low, precarious position, powerless.

"Yes," Kate said, though she didn't have any confidence that this was true, or even if she believed it. But secrets were her métier. She was less comfortable with lies.

"Why do you want to do this?"

That was a valid question. She should have a better answer, but all she had was: "I don't know."

"Do you really think that's good enough?"

"I'm sorry. It's . . ."

She didn't want to explain it, not aloud. That she was worried it was too late for any other options. That she was a mid-forties woman who wasn't educated or trained to do anything else. That she couldn't bear the idea of starting from scratch, she didn't have the humility for it. That it was this or nothing, and she'd already tried nothing, and couldn't handle it.

"This is all I've ever done, Dex. This is what I'm good at."

Some people are able to try a few different careers, hopping around interrelated fields. Not Kate. She'd made her choice long ago, and now it was too late. At a certain point in life, you are what you are.

⚜

"We could also use something for the kids to drink. Orangina."

"Okay."

"Maybe you want to make a list?"

Dexter peers at her over the top of his newspaper. Cocktail napkins and soda. Does he need a fucking list?

"Fine," Kate says, and turns back to speed-reading the paper, a skill she'd developed in her old analyst job, when it had occasionally been necessary to consume imposing volumes of information very quickly. Then when she started living in France, she transferred this habit to scanning the French newspaper—key words, general ideas, proper nouns.

Like this one, right here.

"Oh my God," Kate says, angling the newsprint toward Dexter. "Did you see this?" There's even a picture, a handsome man who's perhaps too well groomed, too smooth looking.

"*Mm-hmm.*" Dexter turns back to his own paper.

"This is a surprise."

He doesn't respond.

"Dex? Are you surprised about this?"

"Um, no."

"Your old friend—"

"We were never friends. You know that, Kate."

"That was sarcasm. Your old *boss* is here in Paris, and you don't care?"

"I'm not saying I don't care. I'm saying I'm not surprised. I've known for a while that some big announcement was coming from him, and that it would involve Europe. So it makes sense that the press conference would be here." Dexter shrugs, trying to dismiss the whole subject, an ineptly feigned indifference. Acting isn't one of Dexter's core competencies.

"How?"

"How what?"

"How did you know about this announcement?"

Dexter screws up his mouth. "It was a while ago. Probably a tech newsletter, or even just the paper . . ."

Kate maintains eye contact with her husband, waits it out . . .

Waits . . .

Dexter breaks his gaze away. He turns back to his newspaper, resumes reading, too studiously.

He's lying.

❖

She should drop it.

But when Dexter lied to her before, it was a whole series of life-defining lies that almost ruined them, ruined everything. Now he's lying again, she's sure of it. What she doesn't know is why, at what magnitude. She really hopes that it's not his career that Dexter is lying about; the family needs that to be lucrative, and secure.

Because Kate is lying too. She's more and more worried for her job every day, but hasn't mentioned a word of it to her husband. Every day her silence grows harder and harder to defend. Every day she promises to break it, but doesn't.

Another police car goes flying by, this one in a different direction, responding to a different emergency. Just because there's a bomb at a train station doesn't mean all other problems disappear.

14

Hunter looks at his phone again. Still no reception, no wifi.

"Colette."

"*Oui,* I will try again." She heads off to reboot the router.

He should've finished a couple of calls already. He has a list of important staff in Hong Kong, Mumbai, here in Paris; later, after noon, America too. Hunter also has a second call list, this one purely mental, no record of it. People in London, New York, the Bay Area. Two different call lists, using two different phones—

That's the solution. He hurries to the kitchen, through it, to the utility room. "Colette?"

She spins from the electrical panel, startled to find him back here, in the behind-the-scenes mess of wires, meters, fuses, logistics.

"The other phone? Do you have it?"

She looks confused, then realizes. "The Belgian?"

"Yes."

Colette gives him that smile of hers that means no, I am sorry, I am disappointed to need to disappoint you, but I simply must. It's a very expressive smile. "*Non Monsieur.* It is at the office."

Colette had ridden the TGV from Paris to Brussels and back for the express purpose of buying a Belgian burner. Hunter himself has never set foot in Belgium. That was the point.

He returns to the living room. The guy from State, or the CIA, he's facing the window, gazing out at the city. After the initial conversation, the Parisian uniformed cop returned to street level. Now one cop is sitting in the car, the other standing in the lobby. This is not the usual arrangement; there's never an officer inside. This is a change that definitely does not make Hunter feel more secure. But the important thing is not to feel secure; it's to be it.

"Your name is Simpson, right?"

"Please call me Tom."

"You still have no cell service?"

The man looks down at his own phone, presses a button, another. Shakes his head, holds out his hand. "Mind if I take a look?"

Hunter hands his device to this American official, then takes a seat on a velvet sofa that Colette picked out, along with nearly everything else in the apartment except his personal things—a few suits, shirts, ties, toiletries, electronic chargers. He has similar supplies in the other apartments, which is why he prefers them to hotels: so he doesn't need to pack. Doesn't need to wheel a bag through airports. Doesn't need to plan. He always carries his passport, and that's all he needs. At any given moment, he can decide it's more important for him to be somewhere else, and go there.

"What are you doing?" Hunter asks.

He also keeps a couple of Krugerrands in his wallet, always.

"Seeing if I can connect you to another server. Or to someone else's wifi, if there's any other network functioning. Doesn't look like it." Simpson continues to stab his pointer finger at the touch-screen, then finally shakes his head, and hands back the device. "Sorry. Do you think I could take a look at your assistant's phone? Sometimes these problems affect—or don't—different devices in different ways."

"Sure. Colette?"

She exchanges a look with Simpson, something between them. Hostility? Fear? Distrust? *"Oui Monsieur."*

"Could I ask you to unlock your phone, please?"

Colette lets a beat pass. *"Bien sûr."* She taps at a few buttons, then relinquishes her device, and steps away from the American quickly, as if afraid of catching a communicable disease.

"What do you think is going on here, Simpson?"

The guy doesn't look up from Colette's phone. "I don't want to speculate."

"Sure," Hunter says, "I get that. But can you, Simpson? Will you?"

The guy cuts his eyes up to Hunter, then back to the screen, continues pressing and swiping. Then he shakes his head, and walks over to Colette. "Nothing worked."

She doesn't say anything as she accepts her phone, doesn't look at the guy. Just nods curtly. An uncharacteristic lapse in manners.

"Look," Hunter says, taking a conspiratorial tone. Just one guy to another, what can we do about this. "I'm giving a press conference this afternoon. Big announcement. I should be making calls right now. It's going to be a huge problem if I can't get in touch with these people before my announcement."

The guy scrunches up his mouth.

"What does that mean?" Hunter asks. "That face?"

"Um . . . I'm not . . ." The guy trails off, looks away.

"Come on."

"Listen, Mr. Forsyth, you may not be holding any press conference today."

"Why? What do you know?"

"I don't *know* much, Mr. Forsyth, not for certain. I've related to you what I *do* know: there's a widespread attack against Paris. And for the past"—he looks at his watch—"ten minutes, there's been no mobile service here, no electricity. This situation doesn't sound promising, does it?"

No, it certainly doesn't.

"And I suspect it's not a simple problem with a quick solution. Whatever's going on in Paris, I'd be very surprised if everything was resolved by three o'clock."

Hunter doesn't remember telling this guy anything about three o'clock. But that's public knowledge, isn't it? The morning papers. Google.

"Our goal right now—*my* goal—is not to facilitate your business, as important as that may seem to you. My goal is to keep an American citizen safe."

"Safe from what?"

"From getting *blown up*, Mr. Forsyth. From getting shot. *Kid*napped."

"What makes you think I'm in danger of any of those things? What are you not telling me?"

"There's a lot of chatter."

"Chatter? About what? Come on, man. Tell me what the hell is going on."

"Specifically targeting Americans. *American capitalists* is the phrase."

"But not specifically me, right?" Hunter had been threatened before, more than once. He has plenty of enemies, personal ones and professional, corporate, international labor, maybe even organized crime, he isn't completely sure. Hence the bodyguards.

"We're aware of a number of prominent American businessmen currently in Paris."

"*A number.* Like two? Or like a hundred?"

"You know I can't tell you that, Mr. Forsyth."

This conversation has taken a much worse turn than Hunter could've anticipated. This whole day. "It's just two French cops we've got downstairs?" That doesn't seem like sufficient manpower to prevent any professional team intent on—what? On anything.

"Backup should be arriving soon, Mr. Forsyth. Within two hours. Or three."

"Three hours?" A lot of bad things can happen in three hours.

"You have to understand that this is a very fluid situation, an environment that's not under any normal level of control. And as you're well aware, we are not in the United States, we can't just do whatever we want. But I want to assure you that we have procedures for this category of scenario. Protocols."

"Are you armed, Simpson?"

"I understand your concern, Mr. Forsyth, I really do, but sheltering in place is the best option at the moment."

Sheltering in place? What is this, a fucking tornado?

"What about the embassy?" The oldest American diplomatic mission in the world is just a few blocks away. "The embassy has its own networks, right? And secure landlines?"

There have been American diplomats in Paris since Benjamin Franklin arrived in 1776, before there was an American constitution. But the more recent representative doesn't respond.

"The embassy must have its own generators," Hunter continues, his argument building up a head of steam, yes, this is the solution. "And backup generators, it—"

"Mr. Forsyth, let me stop you right there: I can*not* take you to rue Gabriel. The embassy is on total lockdown, even I couldn't get in, and that's where I work. I certainly couldn't bring in a civilian."

I'm not just any civilian, Hunter wants to say, but even in his mounting frustration he realizes this is a dead end. *Don't-you-know-who-I-am?* never gets positive results.

"Is there somewhere else?"

The guy looks away again. He sure is one reticent son-of-a-bitch.

"There is, isn't there? There must be. A safehouse?"

"You've seen too many movies, Mr. Forsyth."

"You're telling me there's no such thing? Come on. All I'm asking for is phone service. Or a wifi signal."

Hunter is a person who's used to getting what he wants, has been getting anything he wants his whole life. His power doesn't derive from his good looks, or his fine clothes, or even his money, it's everything together—the way he holds his body, the way he walks and talks, the way he maintains eye contact and a firm grip, the way he accepts the ministrations of the servant class, the people who do things for him, not merely because they're paid to but sometimes just because they understand, innately, that this is how the world works.

"Mr. Forsyth, I really do want to help you. I'm *here* to help you."

"Then do it."

The guy sighs. Purses his lips. He's really drawing this out.

"Okay," he finally says, followed by a phrase that Hunter hears all the time, the phrase that people always use when confronted by men like Hunter Forsyth who are dissatisfied with something, with anything, men who are not in the habit of accepting their own dissatisfaction. How many times has Hunter heard this phrase? Thousands?

"Let me see what I can do."

15

The sniper rests his elbows on the parapet atop the Richelieu Wing, and sweeps his binoculars across the far side of the cour Napoléon. Dozens of people are milling around in that quadrant, maybe hundreds, doing all the normal things, nothing unusual except perhaps that pair of blondes who are exploding out of their clothing, both wearing T-shirts and miniskirts that do not leave much to the imagination.

Ibrahim Abid adjusts the focus, gets a nice sharp image. Oh, goodness.

He pushes the spyglasses away from this unacceptable distraction, scans back toward the center, where the crowd is denser. It is more difficult to concentrate on one individual at a time, with each person surrounded in close proximity by so many others. But that is what he forces himself to do.

The sniper's great-grandparents both emigrated from Morocco right after the First World War. All of his grandparents were born in Nice, both his parents here in Paris. Himself too, his siblings. Ibrahim is more Parisian than most Parisians, a city bursting with people from somewhere else, from Cairo and Dakar, Saigon and Bangkok, New York and San Francisco, from West London and central Stockholm, sent over from corporate headquarters in Bonn, in Moscow, in Rio de Janeiro, migrating here from the crowded slums of Marseille and the sleepy farmland of the Loire, the gritty industrial towns in Lorraine, Dijon, Pas-de-Calais, people flocking from all over France, all over the world.

Ibrahim is more Parisian than all those carpetbaggers. Though not necessarily as French. But French enough to do six long years of military service, then to join the *préfecture de police,* to become one of the department's top snipers.

He has been assigned to this Louvre posting for only six months. Which is a very long time to do a job in which nothing happens, ever.

Regulations forbid the use of the rifle's sights for routine surveillance. This is Paris, after all, not Tikrit, not Kabul, the ten million annual visitors are not accustomed to being monitored from rooftops through the scopes of high-powered rifles. So Ibrahim continues his sweep with binoculars, pushing the lenses up through the courtyard, back toward the far side of the—

Wait. What was that?

He aims the binoculars back toward the middle, to a densely occupied area, looking for . . .

There.

That man, wearing a windbreaker. He is standing stock-still, arms hanging at his side. Something is not right, but it takes Ibrahim a second to recognize what: his head is at the wrong angle. The man is not scanning the crowd, looking for a friend, a sister. He is not admiring the palace, or staring off at the view. He is facing the sky. And . . . is it . . . ?

Ibrahim adjusts the focus, his fingers spinning nervously.

Yes, the man's eyes: they are closed.

"Command," Ibrahim says into the mic on his headset, "we have a suspicious man in the cour Napoléon."

Ibrahim puts down the binoculars. He picks up his rifle, aligns the sight, locates the man in this different lens just in time to see the guy bend over, deposit a briefcase on the ground. A metal briefcase.

"Position four, precise location of target?"

This lens has crosshairs.

"Five meters north of the Louis XIV statue."

"Patrol is en route." This is the four-man paramilitary team that sweeps the courtyard constantly, one circuit after another, watching everyone from ground level, being visible, a deterrent. At this moment they are as far away from the Louis XIV statue as possible. This, Ibrahim realizes, is not a coincidence. He feels the hairs on the back of his neck stand up.

"Description?"

"Gray jacket, black jeans. He, uh . . ." Damn. Ibrahim does not want to say this part. This is what he wakes up every single day hoping not to have to say: "He appears to be North African. Or Middle Eastern."

"Copy." Pause. Crackle. "Position seven, are you seeing this?"

"One moment . . ." This is the plainclothes officer standing at the café on the terrace, elevated a few feet above the courtyard level, a good angle to see faces. "Yes, got him. I agree, he does look suspicious. Patrol, approach carefully."

"Does anyone see a weapon?"

"Negative."

"Negative."

"Anyone?"

No one says anything.

Ibrahim is growing increasingly anxious. "Awaiting orders, Command."

"Hold."

"He is unzipping his jacket," Ibrahim says.

"Repeat?"

"He just opened his jacket. He is now taking it off . . . Oh *merde*."

"Repeat? Position four, status?"

Ibrahim adjusts his focus, though the image is already sharp enough.

"Position four, please clarify."

Ibrahim is irrationally hoping that maybe refocusing the lens will transform the contents of the vest into something it is not. Into water bottles, perhaps. Fly-fishing lures. Iron-on ski-mountain badges. Anything else, anything whatsoever.

"He is wearing—" Ibrahim's voice catches, and he clears his throat.

"Repeat, please?"

"He is wearing a bomb vest."

16

"Do you know anything that's not in the newspaper, Dex?"

He takes a sip of coffee before answering. "Forsyth is buying his largest European competitor."

"Wow. That must be a big deal."

"I guess."

"You guess?" Kate knows that Dexter isn't guessing any damn thing. He has probably calculated what the deal is worth to a penny. "You participating, Dexter?"

"Uh . . . sort of." He takes another sip. Either buying time or trying to avoid the topic entirely, to wear down his wife with tedious pauses. But he should know better. Kate does not wear down. "I'm shorting it."

Shorting. Dexter had explained this before: betting against a company's performance by borrowing shares, then immediately selling those borrowed shares, then later buying back the same quantity of shares, hopefully at a lower price. Sell first, buy later.

To Kate, stock-market speculation has always seemed more like a game than a legitimate profession. Especially short-selling, which doesn't seem terribly different from poker, or sports wagering, I'll take the Redskins plus points. Is this really the way the world works? Should it be?

Judgments aside, this betting is how her husband earns his comfortable living, and Kate's job has never been lucrative. She can't be sanctimonious about how her good life is provided. Rather: She can't act sanctimonious. She can *be* as high-minded as she wants, within her own high mind.

Hers is not a unique predicament. How many wives volunteer at homeless shelters to atone for their husbands' predatory professions? But then again, Kate doesn't volunteer. And her own career has not exactly been a model of moral rectitude.

❧

A phone is ringing, Dexter's. He glances at the number, hits IGNORE.

"You're not going to answer?"

"It's a robocall. I get them every day."

"Since when?"

"I don't know. A couple of weeks?"

"What are they selling?"

"Car insurance? Life insurance? Some insurance. I listened for only a few seconds, then I blocked the caller. But they keep finding me. What do you care?"

"Just curious. Aren't you?"

He shrugs. There's plenty about modern life that's inconvenient, annoying, offensive. Dexter doesn't seem bothered by most of it. It's one of the things Kate admires about her husband.

"Is this a rational decision?"

"Ignoring robocalls? Why would it not be?"

"No, Dexter. The short-sell." Or maybe he's lying about this too. That's the thing about lying: if you're a liar, when do you not lie? "Is this based on a rational assessment of 4Syte's prospects? Or is this an emotional choice?"

Dexter tilts his head, as if genuinely thinking. "Mostly rational." He obviously doesn't want to discuss this. But he has reluctantly come to accept that silence is not a viable mode of marital communication. He knows he needs to explain himself, sometimes.

"The share price has been inching up for weeks."

He puts down his paper, giving up the hopeful pretense that they're not going to talk about this.

"Immediately after the announcement, I think the share price may rise dramatically. But Hunter is *way* overextending, and I'm sure the acquisition is going to encounter regulatory resistance. A few days from now, a week maybe, the EU is going to start hemming and hawing. Bankers will grow skittish. Then either the deal will fall apart rapidly, and the stock will tank, or the deal will limp through, but with the price slowly eroding. Either way, I'll come out ahead."

And if you're wrong? she wants to ask. But that's a line she shouldn't cross. "How much?"

"How much what?"

She gives him a look, *Are you kidding?*

"Don't worry about it."

"You understand, Dex, that this is a phrase that *ensures* the opposite?"

"Not too much."

"*Dexter.*"

"Two-fifty."

"Two-fifty what? Tell me you're not betting a quarter million dollars on a grudge."

"Euros, not dollars." So it's more. "And it's not a grudge. Plus, wrong tense. I already made the deal."

"Excuse me?"

"This is an exhaustively researched move that I'm in a privileged position to assess."

"What the hell does that mean, *privileged position*?"

"You know: my history with Hunter."

This is so clearly horseshit.

Kate's spirits plummet. For the past couple of years she's been telling herself that she could trust Dexter again, that she should. That the lies he'd told hadn't been so bad. That he was, at heart, a good, trustworthy man. That she loved him. She could tell this to him too; indeed she had. But once trust is destroyed, can it ever be entirely rebuilt?

And now look: he's lying to her again.

"Obviously it's possible to lose money, as with *any* investment," he continues, but Kate doesn't even want to listen. "And, yes, the exposure on a short-sell is far greater. No risk, no reward."

"Don't placate me with platitudes." She's getting angry. What's the good in asking questions if she can't expect truthful answers? "I'm not a moron."

"And I'm not reckless."

She arches an eyebrow, a reminder, enough said.

"And I've learned some important lessons." Sounding apologetic, but not overly, he doesn't want to give an excess of validity to the long-term accusation in that arched eyebrow of hers. "You know that, Kate."

She takes a deep breath.

"Trust me."

"Again, Dexter, you're *completely* misunderstanding the effect of that phrase."

He sighs, clams up, jaw tight. This has always been his response to spats: to shut down. He knows that Kate hates this—all women do—and it's a tactic that has no hope of accomplishing what he wants to accomplish. But he can't seem to help himself.

"Seriously, Dexter: tell me you're not being irrational."

"Seriously: I know what I'm doing here."

She wants to tell him—she *needs* him to know—that now is really not a good time for him to be reckless. Telling him is obviously the responsible thing to do. There are good times to take risks, and bad times.

But she can't bring herself to broach the subject. She'd have to admit too many things that she really does not want to admit.

It's not just Dexter who'd spent a long time lying to his spouse about fundamental facts. It's not just Dexter who'd needed to rebuild trust.

⚜

Kate is proud of her career. Of her expertise, her experience, her execution. But that doesn't mean she's free of regrets, of guilt, about the things she has done to other people in the name of professionalism, of patriotism. Plus a different sort of guilt about her personal decisions—about how she treated her sister, how she lied to Dexter so much for so long, how she betrayed Julia.

At the time, Kate had been convinced that it was the right thing to do, the legal thing, the ethical thing. But she eventually realized that it was something else: she'd done it because Julia had lied to her, and had enlisted Dexter too to lie to her. Because Kate had been gullible enough to believe them both. She'd done it because she could; she'd done it out of anger and spite. This wasn't the high road she'd taken. It was low. Petty.

This guilt isn't the worst sort. It's more like the guilt for flying off the handle with the kids. Or for her relationship with Peter. Not a cold-sweat-in-the-middle-of-the-night guilt, just a shiver down her spine in broad daylight, right here, right now, sitting beside her husband in the warm morning sunshine at a famous café in St-Germain-des-Prés.

⚜

What she should tell Dexter is this: it could happen any day now. I'll be summoned to a meet, somewhere open and public—a bench in Parc Monceau, maybe, or the Tuileries. A paunchy officious man will arrive, someone I've never met.

This man won't say hello. He'll take a seat and gaze into the mid-distance; he won't say anything for a few seconds, making me wait, making me anxious, a small display of power, wielded by a small man.

Then he'll begin to speak in a slow monotone. The decision has been made—he'll use a passive construction, as if the decision came from a computer—to terminate the operation. To close down this risky, unorthodox initiative. The Paris Substation had been Hayden Grey's project, and Mr. Grey, as you know, has been missing for a long time. There's no reason to think that he will ever reappear. And without Mr. Grey . . . ?

The Agency thanks you for your service. Best of luck in future endeavors.

There will be no apology. No talk of references, of assistance finding a new situation. He'll walk away without saying goodbye. She'll never even be told his fake name.

17

Out past Gare St-Lazare, where traffic grows heavier, Wyatt pulls the van to a stop at a red light. He reaches over to the canvas bag resting on the passenger seat, another prop that had been foisted upon him, along with the clothes, the glasses, the haircut.

He plucks a pair of surgical gloves from the bag. The tight rubber isn't easy to handle, not with his nerves, and he has time to pull on only the left glove before the light changes, and he returns his hands to the wheel. It would be disastrous to crash now, even a fender-bender could be devastating, a rear-end tap, a soft brush against a parked car. He can't afford to interact with anyone, not while associated with this van. Certainly not police.

Only a couple more minutes now. The blue *P* beckons ahead, the final stop of this leg of his journey, thank God—

But what's this?

Fuck.

Stick to the plan. This is just a street cop, preventing street crime, out on patrol, a leisurely stroll. No reason for any patrolman to pay any attention to some tradesman's van pulling into a public garage. And Wyatt shouldn't create one.

He keeps his eyes trained straight ahead, ignoring the cop's gaze. The two men pass within a couple of yards of each other, nearly face-to-face, but Wyatt refuses to glance in the cop's direction. Then he second-guesses himself—maybe he should've met the cop's eye, nodded hello? Would that have been less suspicious?

Too late.

Wyatt turns into the garage, keeps the bill of his cap angled low; he knows where the camera is. He reaches with his rubber-gloved left hand to press the button, collect the ticket. The barrier rises, and he rolls the van down the incline, makes a hairpin turn to descend another level, and another. The bottom.

Down here, most of the parking spaces are available, as expected. His instinct is to pull into the most isolated spot, but he needs light to clean up. He takes a well-illuminated space in the middle, and kills the engine.

He pulls on the second rubber glove. There's a thin plastic film that covers the steering wheel, the gear shift, the directional-signal arm, the door handle, the key—everything he'd needed to touch. He peels off all these car condoms, rolls up the garbage, stuffs this plastic ball into the bag.

It's important not to rush. Not to panic. Not to forget anything.

Wyatt reaches into his pocket, extracts a piece of paper. A checklist. Fourteen items. He scans the lines, mentally ticking off the minor milestones. Parking ticket on seat . . . Key in ignition . . . Wipe down exterior door handles with disinfecting cloth . . .

He reads the checklist one final time, to reassure himself: done. Then he walks away, toward the backlit icon of a man climbing stairs, SORTIE, just thirty yards away, a few seconds' walk. One foot in front of the other, keep breathing.

Remember the money.

Twenty yards.

Everything is fine, everything is going according to—

Click.

He spins around, eyes darting around the dim-lit space. What the fuck was that?

There, on the other side of the low wide room: a guy is getting out of a car, a little black Cooper. That click? That was the door latch disengaging.

Fuck.

And now a woman too, she's emerging from the passenger side. What have these people been doing in that car? They didn't arrive while he was here, which means they were here before he was. Here the whole time, they saw everything, they watched him wipe down the vehicle, consult his checklist, behavior that's explicable only in the context of the commission of crime. What they saw was a man behaving like a criminal.

He feels the weight in his jacket's pocket, the heaviness, the no-slip grip. It suddenly seems like a hammer, and these people are indistinguishable from nails.

No, he tells himself: They were not watching him. They were not paying attention, they could not have seen much, and what's more they could not have cared. Who are these people? They're no one. They're not police. Not military. Just two randoms, nothing to do with him. Sitting in a car having a marital spat. Or prepping for a meeting. Or fucking—yes, they're having an affair, stealing a few minutes for desperate but uncomfortable early-morning sports-car sex, the shift stick digging into somebody's thigh. If you're planning on using a car for intercourse, a Mini is not the best option. But that's probably not how anyone chooses a car. Not unless you have a pretty serious fucking-in-cars fetish.

Wyatt turns back toward the exit, takes another step away.

That's when he remembers: the bag. It's still on the passenger seat.

Fuck.

He turns back again. He must look like an idiot, back and forth. But an idiot is okay, he's willing to look like an idiot. What he doesn't want to look like is a terrorist.

If he returns to the van now, he'll have to walk right past these people, and the man is going to look him in the face, say *Bonjour.* Not good. Or Wyatt can continue to the stairwell, ascend to a higher level to lurk until these people climb past, then return. Nothing lost except a couple of minutes. No risk, unless he has the bad luck of running into someone else up there, but that's a solvable problem. The trick is to not be startled. To not be stupid.

Yes, that's what he'll do.

He turns back again—he's spinning like a lunatic, isn't he?—and takes a step, and—

"Monsieur?"

Oh fuck. He takes a second step, pretending he didn't hear. A third.

"Monsieur!"

Can he ignore this guy? What would the consequences be?

He glances over his shoulder, but doesn't turn all the way around.

"Vos phares," the man says.

At first Wyatt doesn't understand what this can mean.

"Ils sont allumés."

Phares? He left the headlights on? "Ah," Wyatt says, looking at the van, sure enough. *"Merci."*

Fuck. Was that on the checklist?

He doesn't have a choice, does he? He can't ignore this. That policeman might still be up on the street, it would be easy for this guy to approach him, almost inevitable. *"Pardonnez-moi, officer, there's a man acting strangely, he left his headlights ignited and then he fled—look! There he is, running!"*

"Vous êtes très gentil," Wyatt says. He starts walking toward the van, which is also in the direction of this couple. Their paths will converge. In three seconds. In two.

The man has stopped walking.

One.

"Ça va?" The man looks concerned.

"Oui," Wyatt croaks, a bundle of exploding nerves now, his mind increasingly muddled, looking from Monsieur Cooper's face to Madame's, she too is staring at him with a furrowed brow until she realizes she's staring so looks away, not wanting to maintain eye contact with this possibly crazy or dangerous person in a dark garage three levels underground. She even takes a step away. It's just a tiny step, but not unnoticeable.

These people are scared of him, of course they are. They should be.

These people are going to walk upstairs, they're going to see the policeman, make a report. They will not hesitate, especially if they are aware of the larger situation in the city. Maybe they were sitting in that car listening to the radio, news reports, *Police warn everyone to be on the lookout for a white panel van,* GOUPIL ET FRÈRES ÉLECTRICIENS *on the side—*

"You understand that you cannot allow yourself to be caught?" That's what the man with the big beard asked, the man who has run this op. "Not under any circumstances."

It was a beard that could look like many things, depending on context. A rugged mountain man. Or a hipster. Or an orthodox Jew, maybe a rabbi. Or a devout Muslim. Or a jihadist planning to blow up Paris. A lot of competing types.

Wyatt accepted the familiar handgun.

"But do not use this unless absolutely necessary."

"Sure," Wyatt agreed reflexively, the instinctual response of a trained soldier to an order. But he didn't understand this one, didn't see why he should restrain himself from freely dispensing with witnesses, with obstacles, with challenges, with inconveniences. Many innocent people were going to die anyway. Wasn't that the point?

At the very first meeting, Wyatt suspected that the big beard did signify jihadist. That's the thing that would've made sense, given what it seemed they were planning. But the more he learned, less so.

Wyatt still wants a full explanation of whatever the hell this is, but he doesn't really need one, and doesn't expect one. "That," the man told him, "is what all the money is for."

The man was serious, the type who exudes competence, confidence. A man to be reckoned with. Even in repose, clearly a dangerous man, a lethal man. A man with a scar on his cheekbone that looks like a memento from a knife fight.

Wyatt has spent his life with such dangerous men. His father was one, the sadistic fucker. Wyatt himself is one. You either are or you aren't, and you know it. Though some men turn out to be mistaken, and don't discover their error until it's too late.

But not Wyatt, he's not mistaken: he's definitely a lethal man. An untrustworthy man too, an untrusting one, a man who takes his own precautions. Wyatt is a double-crosser. Which makes him always ready to be double-crossed.

He clears his throat, says "*Oui*" again, trying to sound soft, trying to reassure these scared people. "*Merci, ça va bien.*"

Wyatt musters something that he hopes approximates a smile, aiming his bared teeth in the general direction of M. and Mme. Cooper. He probably looks like a snarling wolf.

He's not going to assuage these people, it's too late for that. All he's trying to do now is prevent them from panicking too early, from running, from making too much noise, too much commotion, before he has time.

18

"Do not engage." This is what Ibrahim hears in his headset, a blanket order delivered to everyone, to Ibrahim and the other sniper atop the opposite wing, to the four-man patrol closing in on the bomber's position, to the plainclothes officers, to the uniformed police.

"Repeat, do not engage."

Nearly every soul has fled the cour Napoléon, except a couple of guards, the guys who manage the crowds at the ticket queues, at the doors, more like ushers than security, empowered to prevent only the most casual of disturbances—line cutters, aggressive panhandlers. This situation is well beyond their pay grade; they do not even wear badges, just laminated ID cards. They exchange looks, a quick conversation—"Should we get the fuck out of here?" "Definitely"—and back away, into the big glass pyramid and down out of view, out of the most obvious harm.

The only other people who are still in the courtyard are the four members of the tactical patrol team, wearing body armor and combat helmets, assault rifles at the ready.

"The target has no visible firearms, but is wearing what appears to be explosives."

The crowd had dispersed quickly, giving these soldiers a clear view of the man before they were anywhere near him. They immediately understood that it was not advisable to simply shoot him, which would neutralize only one part of the threat, a possibly insignificant part compared to that vest, that luggage.

The four soldiers separate from one another, form a staggered line of advancement, different angles. They close in carefully, their target always sighted at the ends of their weapons. Fifty meters away, one of the soldiers holds up a fist, and they all stop.

For a few seconds, they are all absolutely still.

Then the two soldiers on either end begin to move laterally, not getting any nearer to the target, but skirting him. Then the other two also begin to reposition, everyone walking slowly, maintaining ready stances. It takes a couple of minutes before they establish a full containment ring at the four cardinal points.

The bomber is surrounded.

❖

First things first: all the exterior doors are secured, the main doors at the pyramid, the ones under the place du Carrousel, the employee entrances, the supply routes.

Wings are sealed off from one another, rooms locked down, like a ship hit by a torpedo, or crashed into an iceberg: you isolate the compromised sections to prevent water from flooding everywhere, killing everyone.

Guests are instructed to stay calm, take seats on the floor, make themselves comfortable.

The authorities are called, so many different authorities: the army, the national police, the mayor, the president, ministers, senators. Plus museum staff, foreign ambassadors, the director of the Métro, on and on, like a phone tree for an international football league, canceling dozens of games at once, due to natural disaster.

The surrounding streets are closed, the nearest Métro stations too, bus service, river traffic. None of this is simple to effectuate.

The museum's *président directeur–général* leaves his office facing the Seine, and crosses to the other side of the building, to a window that overlooks the courtyard. He stares with wide eyes in broad daylight at his worst nightmare.

They run annual drills. Not just abstract plans that are debated in meetings, modeled on custom-designed software, but real-world real-time simulations using live human beings to test response rates, logistical controls, unanticipated challenges. Some tasks have proven easier than expected; some harder. There is a lot that must be mobilized to secure this capacious site in the middle of the most visited city on the Continent.

No, this right now is not the director's worst nightmare. Just the prelude.

The Palais du Louvre is relatively well protected from attack by vehicle, by car or truck, even armored military vehicles would be thwarted by the layers of hardened bollards. Attackers would need a tank to get through. And if anyone rolls a tank into central Paris, the Louvre is not their target.

But the exercise is like whack-a-mole: you close off one method of ingress and others pop up. There are virtually unlimited locales where crowds gather, and so many options for killing large numbers of people. There is no way to make people safe everywhere. The only thing you can do is make them feel safe, with the metal detectors, the security guards, snipers, enabling everyone to go about their lives believing that every precaution has been taken.

But there has always been this, and always will be: you can never entirely protect against a person who is willing to sacrifice his life in order to kill others.

Ibrahim keeps the target squarely in his sites, finger on the trigger.

19

Dexter steals a glance behind him, the street, the bins, the cars, the hotel on the corner . . . Everything is still, except a small garbage truck passing at the far end of the block, the sanitation workers' outfits in different shades of vibrant green that match the green bins with yellow lids all in a row, looking like the Green Bay Packers offensive line.

Paris is an empty sort of place in the mornings, without people jogging everywhere, scurrying to and from gyms, twenty-four-hour delis and overnight shifts, the morning convergence of enterprise and exercise that you see in American cities. Not here.

He's startled by movement over his shoulder, and spins to see a crow—a huge one—fluttering onto the roof of a parked car. The big black bird seems to stare at Dexter for a second, then herky-jerks its head down to peck at something. That's one scary bird.

Dexter shifts the shopping bag and flowers to his other hand, his tennis bag to his other shoulder, a double-switch.

"Can you take this home?" Kate had asked, in front of the café. She was headed to whatever passes for her office. Dexter doesn't know where it is, or what goes on there.

A few months ago, when curiosity had gotten the best of him, he attempted to follow her; he could no longer live with his failure to even try. Unsurprisingly, Kate was difficult to tail, changing Métro platforms, doubling back on sidewalks, and eventually striding through the wrought-iron door to the Galerie de la Madeleine, one of those marble-floored *passages* that smell of musty old paper, they all do, the covered arcades strewn around the Right Bank, lined with tiny boutiques and artisan workshops and cozy cafés, all with giant plate-glass windows, nowhere to turn, no way to hide.

The *galerie* looked like a trap, set to catch a tail.

Dexter gave up, walked back to his side of the river, dejected. Wondering if he'd ever again know what the hell his wife did for a living. Wondering if it mattered.

He never did find out if Kate realized it was her husband following her that day, or anyone; maybe she went through that evasive rigmarole as a matter of everyday habit. He was too ashamed to ask; she was perhaps too restrained to mention it.

There are some things best left unsaid, even in a marriage. Perhaps especially in a marriage. The dirty things, the shameful things, the taboo sexual fantasies, the fleeting suicidal tendencies, the petty jealousies and juvenile revenge scenarios, things you're more likely to admit to a drunk stranger in an airport lounge, someone you don't have to wake up with for a half-century, don't have to worry if she'll now look at you in a new, horrid light.

Secrets are not unusual. But what is unusual is that "What do you do for a living?" and "Where is your office?" are questions that can't even be asked, much less answered.

Whatever it is that Kate does, at the moment Dexter is thankful for its steadiness, its reliability, the wire-transferred paychecks that replenish their account twice per month.

Dexter thinks of himself as a modern man, a progressive man. He'd be absolutely thrilled for his wife to earn more than he does. But the burden of providing for the family has always sat on his shoulders, and they're not especially macho shoulders—no big muscles, no tattoos, no MBA. It's a heavy weight, uncomfortable. Failure to provide for your family is a pretty big failure. Maybe the biggest.

Kate doesn't know it, but her income is what's keeping them afloat.

Dexter never loops his wife into his trades. Sometimes afterward he'll share wildly positive results, he'll come home with vintage Champagne and a small tin of caviar. He has learned to celebrate, not just the regularly scheduled annual dates, the anniversary, the birthdays.

He was even less inclined than normal to mention this 4Syte position, so reluctant that he stopped talking shop entirely a couple of weeks ago, when he made the decision. Because if he avoided the subject of work entirely, he'd have plausible deniability, later. "Why didn't I mention it? I don't know, Kate. We weren't discussing *any* of my work."

Dexter knows that his wife never, ever stops worrying that it can all be lost in an instant, any instant, tomorrow, today. She grew up with even less than he did, and she can't escape feeling that they don't deserve this life. That it's only temporary, the world will come to its senses and take it away, everything. And the way that Dexter earns his living makes Kate plenty anxious.

It's for her own good that he keeps her in the dark about the details, that he occasionally—very occasionally—needs to lie to her. Mostly lies of omission. Such as: Dexter had been monitoring 4Syte's stock long before Luc's tip. For a decade, in fact.

Also: this short-sell is definitely a hugely risky endeavor, and it is without question an emotional decision. Yes, Dexter has a perhaps unhealthy receptivity to nefarious gossip about Hunter Forsyth, to vicious rumor, to illegal inside information. Some of which have been copious. Because the more success Hunter achieves, the more people want to take him down, want to see him taken down, want to benefit if his take-down eventually happens.

Dexter is one of them.

It's not because there's a sizable population who are so envious that the guy is so successful. No, it's because Hunter Forsyth is an unremitting bastard. There are plenty of successful people who don't step on everyone else as they climb their ladders. And Hunter does it with so little humility, so much arrogance, entitlement. Born on third base, believing he hit a triple.

So many people are defined by their bootstraps, by the lowliness of their origins, people who have no choice but to try to climb out, climb up. Dexter. Kate too. But by the sheer luck of birth, Hunter had been afforded the choice to do absolutely anything. Instead of using that immense good fortune to do something positive for the planet, for mankind—or at least something creative—the guy chose as his goal simply to get richer, to slide through life with the greased ease of an aristocrat.

Dexter hates Hunter's guts.

No, this trade is not entirely rational. It's not unemotional.

Yesterday, in anticipation of today's press conference, 4Syte's stock hit its all-time high. This was exactly what Luc's inside source had predicted. It was real, and it was now.

While the kids did homework and Kate did dishes, Dexter closed himself into his office. He still wasn't entirely comfortable with the information, its circuitous route from somewhere inside 4Syte to that German trader to Luc to Dexter. Not to mention the discomfort endemic to any short position, which entails unlimited downside: if the share price rises dramatically instead of falls, it's even possible to lose more than your original investment, to swing past zero. Way past.

But that's the nature of risk, isn't it? That's when risk is most worthwhile, most profitable: when the outcome is least certain.

This was what Dexter had been working toward for years, this type of move based on this type of info, betting against this particular person. A perfect storm. It was irresistible.

He took a deep breath, then executed the trade. Twice.

Dexter punches in the security code, pushes open the heavy red door. There's always an extra chill in this breezeway, a dampness that clings to the stone walls. He walks past the bicycles into the courtyard, a little garden with a wooden shed that houses the supplies. It's a simple garden, not much in the way of direct sunlight, but well tended by the concierge. Last Christmas, the residents chipped in to buy Madame a chic set of tools from that exorbitant place on the rue du Bac, she was nearly overcome. Madame hasn't been able to bring herself to sully this gift with soil; she gardens with her old tools, while the new ones hang in their canvas belt from a wooden peg on the shed's door, pride of place, like the university graduation picture of a grandchild.

As Dexter hustles through the courtyard, he catches a glimpse of something white peeking from behind a corner of the shed.

He strides over. Peeks around and down, and—*yes.* He kneels, picks up the missing cap from his Luxembourg tennis club. He looks around, hoping his eyes will stumble across some explanation of how it got here. He'll have to ask Madame.

Dexter rides up the slow, loud elevator, clanging and groaning, forever suggesting imminent breakdown. At his apartment door, he pauses, uneasy. He leans over the railing, looks down the stairwell . . .

Nothing.

He stands still, listening for footsteps, for breathing, for anything . . .

Nothing.

He unlocks his front door, and steps into the darkness.

20

Kate has many rules.

One is that she alternates the routes she takes across the river. Some days she'll walk the pont des Arts, other days the pont Royal or pont du Carrousel. Or she'll ride the 68 or 69 bus up the rue du Bac. Or take the number 12 Métro, get off at Madeleine, melt into the maze of *correspondance* tunnels, up and down the stairs, pause at an exit, double back.

Kate had never before been a regular subway rider, it wasn't convenient to her home in DC—saved neither time nor money—and it didn't exist back in Connecticut. But she adores the Paris Métro, the Art Nouveau entryways, the different styles of benches, the manually operated doors. And the subway facilitates extremely effective countersurveillance.

Sometimes she rides her bicycle to work, and very rarely her Vespa, which she keeps parked on the private street in front of her office. She doesn't want the moped to be easily identifiable as hers. When the time comes when she needs it, she wants the scooter to be clean, unidentified, unmonitored.

Kate never takes the family car to work. Their apartment building doesn't have parking in the courtyard, which is instead dominated by a garden—flowers, foliage, a few tomatoes in August, thyme and rosemary for anyone who wants it, limitless mint. When they were looking for a place to live, they didn't realize that courtyard parking was an option. They'd probably do it differently now. They'd probably live in a different neighborhood too, a more livable one, with fewer tourists and students and art galleries. St-Germain is a formal, buttoned-up quarter of *ancienne* nobility who aren't much interested in arriviste expats.

There are many things she'd do differently.

When it's raining, Kate tends to walk. Especially when it's raining hard, because almost no one else does.

The European weather used to get her down, the long months of everyday grayness, it seemed like the sun never shone from September till April, day after day of cloud cover, spitting rain, bone-chilling frost. But Kate got used to it, as you get used to anything. Bad weather couldn't be avoided, it wasn't viable to stay indoors whenever it rained; for half the year you'd never leave home. So she acquired the proper gear, one item at a time—rubberized hat, slicker, comfortable boots—to manage the wetness. Like any other rational adult solution to any other problem. Not ignored, not dodged. Managed.

What drives her crazy about Dexter is that he tries to avoid the unavoidable, ignore the unignorable. It makes her wish she were the kind of wife who could stand in the kitchen and scream at her husband, spewing profanity at high volume, accompanied by projectiles—teacups, produce, hardcover novels. But she isn't.

Another of Kate's rules is that she keeps a log of her routes, to ensure that she doesn't unintentionally fall into a pattern, a predictable sequence. The log is coded—it looks like a list of household reminders, scrawled in a handmade notebook she picked up in Venice—even though there's no danger if this information falls into other hands. It's a record of the past, not a plan for the future. It's nothing.

But using codes is another of Kate's rules, and she adheres to it even when the codes are 99.9 percent superfluous. It's a discipline, she tells herself. It's not the details that matter. What matters is the general state of mind, a state of being: careful. Always.

This is how she was trained, how she has lived. This is her identity, this careful person who maintains coded records of her surveillance-detection routes and countermeasures, of dead-drops and blind passes. This is what Kate knows how to do. This is all.

What could she possibly do next?

During their long year living in Luxembourg, Kate tried having no job; for their first year in Paris too. Then when she finally rooted out the full extent of her husband's duplicities, Kate realized that she had leverage. Leverage with Dexter, who'd nearly wrecked their lives with a combination of ambition, amorality, dishonesty, and gullibility; he owed Kate, they both knew it. She also had leverage with the CIA, courtesy of the huge sum of untraceable money that Dexter had stolen—dirty money, free money that could be used for anything—as well as the prospect of making the FBI look inept, corrupt. And leverage with herself, an argument that Kate could now advance to justify the increasingly uncomfortable feeling that had tainted her first couple of years as an expat: she was not cut out to be a full-time homemaker.

What did Kate want in return for all this leverage? To be young again. But instead she asked for something that was actually possible.

Today she takes the pont des Arts, which affords her her favorite vantage in Paris—the pont Neuf bisected by the Île de la Cité, with the towers of Notre-Dame looming behind, and the grandeur of the Louvre, and the Musée d'Orsay and the Grand Palais, and the top of the Eiffel Tower. You can see it all from one spot, right here.

This city is unrelentingly gorgeous, everywhere Kate turns, the broad boulevards and their neat apartment blocks, the grand *hôtels particuliers* and gothic churches and medieval houses, the wide green river traversed by all these splendid bridges, the quiet little *places* and leafy little parks, the Machine Age railroad terminals and Art Nouveau Métro stations, the incessant materialization of majesty around any corner, a constant barrage of world-famous landmarks. It seems unreasonable, an unfair distribution of assets.

Kate feels the soft give of the wooden walkway beneath her feet, worn and uneven, mossy and damp, the sheen of wetness creating a mirror effect, reflecting the old lampposts and the clouds rushing by in the bright blue sky.

The pont des Arts is a pedestrian bridge, and at this moment nearly all its pedestrians are coming toward Kate, away from the Louvre on the far side. Which is not the typical flow, not in the morning, with the museum just opening, the crowds converging.

The last time Kate was in a museum was a year ago, what she hoped would be a manageable little visit with the kids to the Orsay, an hour tops. Take advantage of the culture; they might not live in Paris forever. She gathered her rosebuds from school, stopped at the bakery for *le goûter*:

a *pain au chocolat* for Jake, a *brioche au sucre* for Ben, who asserts that chocolate croissants are too chocolaty. The same snack every afternoon, no dissatisfaction, no experimentation. Children are creatures of happy habit. Something needs to go awry to sway them to change.

Kate was accustomed to the crowds in central Paris, but they were usually easy to circumnavigate. The multitudes at the Musée d'Orsay, though, were inescapable, unavoidable, holding up their phone cameras, their tablets, amassing in front of each painting to take a photo and then move on, an assembly line. Or—worse—blocking everyone's view to stand directly in front of paintings, facing away, to take selfies with blockbuster backdrops.

Teenage girls were the worst offenders. Posing was second nature for these kids, selfie smiles rehearsed in mirrors, poses perfected after thousands of variations in body angle and head tilt, hair fluff and lip purse and peace sign, a permanent regimen of fine-tuning, akin to practicing piano or laying down a sacrifice bunt, skills never attempted by these kids, who instead know how to do mainly this one thing: look like they're having a great time in social-media photos, exposure and exclamation points compulsory, soliciting other exclamation points, an ouroboros of manufactured enthusiasm.

Kate looks off to one side of the bridge, then the other. The houseboats are sitting there, as ever, but not the *bateaux-mouches* that should be plying the river, laden with tourists on this rarity of a perfect sunny day, thick throngs leaning over the gunwales.

She herself had once been a teenage girl with a water-lily poster thumb-tacked above her dorm-room bed. She understood the attraction, wanting to possess the art. But not the impulse of adding yourself to it. Why? Proving you'd been there? Or something more insidious?

Not only are there no sightseeing barges on the Seine, there are instead police boats.

Kate's little children were too short to see above the packs of auto-paparazzi in the Orsay. The only thing her boys could see were other people taking photos, of themselves. It was the opposite of appreciating art. It was unbearable.

Now Kate also notices that there aren't any cars on the far quay's roadway. Traffic must be diverted.

What the hell is happening?

21

"So Mr. Forsyth, I've got good news and bad news."

"Isn't that always the case."

"The radio in my car is working, so I was able to get in touch with the embassy. Which is definitely on complete lockdown. No one in, no exceptions."

"I'm assuming that's not the good news?"

"There *is* a place we can go where the electricity appears to be functional."

"Okay. I guess that is good. What about a phone?"

"It's not plugged in, so I'm not sure if it's working."

That doesn't seem so bad. "Is that the bad news, Mr. Simpson?" Hunter knows that the guy's name isn't Tom Simpson, and he doesn't work for State. But Hunter has decided to let it slide. Proving to everyone how smart you are can be counterproductive.

"Er, no. There are a few bits of bad news. The first is that the cellular networks are all compromised, there's no service anywhere in Paris right now. And it's possible that there won't be any wifi where we're going. We'll have to see once we're there."

"Are there any other places I can go?"

"Not at the moment, no."

"Well then that sounds perfect. Can we get going immediately?"

"There's one other thing, Mr. Forsyth: it'll just be you. Your security can't come with you. And your . . ." He cuts his eyes in the direction of Colette.

"My assistant? She's absolutely coming with me."

"*C'est pas nécessaire,*" Colette protests. But Hunter knows that she really does want to be rescued by him, plucked from her middle-class life as a professor's wife, he'll propose at Le Jules Verne, the ceremony will be on St-Jean-Cap-Ferrat, the honeymoon will be a glamping safari in Kenya. He has planned it all.

It took Hunter a good long while to come around to the idea of marriage, at which point he proposed to a girlfriend who wasn't any more marriage-worthy than the preceding ones; she just happened to be the current one. Since his wedding, he has also become attached to the prospect of fatherhood, which is a much more compelling concept than being a husband. But he has also realized that it's not Jen who he wants to be the mother of his children.

"I'm sorry, Mr. Forsyth. But Mademoiselle, um . . ."

"Benoit. *Madame* Benoit."

"Excuse me, Madame Benoit is not an American citizen. We can't—"

"I'm not going anywhere without her." Hunter is going to bluster his way through this, as he does everything. "Grab your things, Colette. Let's go."

Tom Simpson from State has a quick conversation with the Parisian cops on the sidewalk. Hunter feels like he should hear whatever it is they're discussing, but Simpson told him—ordered him—to wait in the lobby. Hunter understood that there was a dire warning in that instruction, a concern about being in plain sight on the sidewalk. Is it really possible that someone is going to take a shot at him?

Simpson returns, looking serious. "Here's how this is going to work. I'll walk first. Mr. Forsyth, you'll follow immediately behind me. And Mme. Benoit, you'll walk directly behind Mr. Forsyth, flanked by these police officers, with the rear brought up by your security guard . . . ?"

It's something with a *G* . . . Gérard? . . . Gérome? . . .

"Didier," Colette supplies.

Didier?

"Didier will return upstairs to keep your apartment secure. *Comprenez-vous,* Didier?"

"*Oui.*"

Didier. Hunter never bothered to learn the name of this security guard. Has he really become that asshole? It seems like just yesterday when he accepted the necessity of full-time security. An uncomfortable conversation, like estate planning, contemplating your demise, the different ways that it could—would—come about, and when, and how people would move on afterward.

"*Merci Didier,*" Hunter says, but he's not fooling anyone.

"Please keep your heads down, and walk directly through the car's rear door without slowing. Get yourselves onto the floor quickly. I'll cover you with a tarp."

"A tarp? Is that really necessary?"

"I certainly hope not. But I don't want to discover the contrary due to a bullet in your head."

"Um . . ." Hunter looks over at the sedan. "You don't have bulletproof glass?"

"Or an RPG through the windshield."

How the hell does a role-playing game come through the windshield? "RPG?"

"Rocket-propelled grenade. We don't want you to get shot, we don't want you to be seen, we don't want anyone to be able to observe that there are any passengers. Just me. And no one knows me, I'm nobody. Okay, are we ready?" Nods all around. "Let's do this."

He's all business, this Simpson character, striding across the narrow sidewalk, just a few steps to the car, the guy's head swiveling left and right, left and right, then he reaches to open the door, fingers on the handle, but something diverts his attention—

He holds up his left hand. His right hand is in his jacket pocket.

"What?" Hunter asks.

Simpson gazes off to the right, the direction from which cars would come down this one-way street. Nothing is moving.

"It's okay. Get in."

Hunter bends into the backseat, scooches across the leather on his knees, and folds himself onto the floor. Colette joins him, limber, flexible. He can't help but watch as her skirt is pushed up, up, high up her thigh . . .

Oh my fucking God: her stockings are held up by *garters*.

How did he not realize at their very first meeting that this was the sexiest woman in the world? Missing that has shattered his faith in his own powers of perception.

Their faces are just inches apart, down here on the floor. It's a new car, very clean carpets. It's possible that there's never been a backseat passenger.

Hunter is plenty used to slipping in and out of car doors that are opened by other people, driven by other people, chauffeurs holding umbrellas, assistants carrying bags, doormen and porters and lawyers and publicists, leading him this way and that, intervening on his behalf. Hunter's is a life set apart, buffered by bodyguards and hired cars, first-class cabins and private jets, three-star restaurants whose astronomical prices segregate the elite like him from the envious masses who want to be.

But he's never been hustled into a car like this. Except that one time in Kuala Lumpur, the political demonstration, who the hell knew what was going to happen, Southeast Asia.

"This is something, isn't it?"

Colette smiles first with her eyes, then the smile migrates to her mouth, her whole face. It's a beautiful smile. "An adventure, *Monsieur. N'est-ce pas?*"

"*Oui,*" Hunter says, "an adventure."

In the end, KL turned out okay. This too will turn out okay.

Hunter would definitely prefer if he had some way of confirming Simpson's identity, his affiliation, their destination, anything. But he doesn't. And he isn't hampered by a dogmatic attachment to certainty. Hunter's competitive advantage has never been fact-based. It's his intuition, and his speed: Hunter acts quicker than everyone else, and has never been proven wrong, not on anything that matters. Except women. But those misjudgments have never really cost him much.

"Maybe for today, Colette, you can stop calling me *Monsieur*? Hunter will be fine."

"*Oui Monsieur,*" she says. They both laugh, and that's when Simpson drapes the tarp over the two of them, a fluttering descent of dark, and the last Hunter sees are Colette's hazel eyes, replaced by the after-burned image of her garters, seared in his memory.

The car pulls away, and his stomach immediately starts to roil. He's going to have to concentrate on not getting sick here. Their romance definitely wouldn't be hastened along by that humiliation.

22

First it was just a single sound of alarm, one woman who said something shrill to her companion, who responded in an urgent tone that was overheard by an adjoining family, and within seconds everyone in Mahmoud's immediate proximity was fleeing in every direction, radiating waves of panic, people dragging each other by their hands, their wrists, falling and trampled and rising with ripped pants and bloody elbows, losing grips on phones and cameras and bottles of water, making a mad dash to nowhere, they had no destination in front, just trying to put distance behind, as much as possible, because no one knew why exactly they were running except those few who had the presence of mind and took the time to look back over their shoulders, to focus through the chaos on the expanding emptiness at the center, and these were the most terrified people of all, these were the ones who understood, who were calculating when exactly all that Semtex was going to be detonated, what magnitude of blast radius, and what in the name of God Almighty was with that briefcase?

"There will then be a long period of waiting," the man had explained. "You will stand there, alone. For a few hours, or all day, into the night."

"Just waiting?"

"We will make demands. There will be negotiations, back and forth. Our demands, theirs, concessions. Lines of communication will be established, credentials confirmed."

"Why will they not simply shoot me immediately?"

"Good question. Two answers. One: it will be obvious from the design of the vest—with the phone—that the detonator is not controlled by you, so even if you are dead, the device can still be detonated. You are not in control; they have nothing to gain by shooting you, and possibly something to lose. Two: the briefcase. At the outset, they will not know exactly what the case is. Why would a man like you have such a thing?"

A man like you.

"They will realize there can be only one reason."

Mahmoud nodded, expecting more of an explanation. He did not get one. But he figured it out, on his own.

After just a few minutes, the soldiers who surrounded him begin to retreat, walking backward, then sideways, until they step through the gap in the fence. Then Mahmoud is all alone.

Except for this earpiece in his ear, and a microphone pinned to his collar. "Everyone is gone," he says into the mic.

"You will have the gratitude of your people," the man says into Mahmoud's ear.

There will be no further instructions for Mahmoud, no updates from him. No decision for him to make, no actions to take.

"Of your family."

There will be nothing.

"You will have the thanks of Allah."

23

She would know if a world leader were in town, a European president, the pope, the type of dignitary whose presence would shut down traffic on the streets and the river too. Those visits are difficult for any run-of-the-mill Parisian to overlook, and impossible for Kate.

So that's not it.

Plenty of large-scale demonstrations occur in Paris. *Jours de grève* pop up regularly; some population of French workers is pretty much always on strike. Large crowds march to support social security, or on the other hand to decry *la sécu.* On any given day, some group is protesting something. But these demonstrations don't arise out of nowhere.

There has been no civil unrest, no overt religious strife, no outrageous incident of police brutality. There's no current, recent, or upcoming election.

This is not a culture inclined toward martial law, nor random displays of military might. Bastille Day is one thing, but the police here don't flex their muscles merely to show off.

There's no volcano within hundreds of miles, earthquakes don't happen here, nor hurricanes, tornadoes, the sorts of natural emergencies that can necessitate large-scale mobilizations of security forces.

No, the sort of catastrophe that happens in Paris is something else. The specifics of each attack have come as a surprise, but not the general fact of them, it's an ever-present possibility. And Kate's job is knowing such things, if not in advance then at least once they've begun, when the circle of secrecy expands to include someone or other in her wide network of paid informants, pink hundred-euro notes handed out liberally across Western Europe. But she has heard of nothing happening today. Is this another failure of hers?

They're mounting. Ever since Copenhagen, from which Hayden fled, chasing a lead to America, where his blood was found on a rocky beach. It wasn't a huge amount of blood, not a lethal volume. And no body. But still.

Then there was the operation in Seville, the missed opportunity. Followed by Palermo, when Kate overcompensated for her failure in the first, and lost an actual person. And not just any person.

Since then, no new assignments, nothing to reassure her that she still directs an active concern. It's hard to avoid the conclusion that she blew it. That after her ongoing ops conclude, the Paris Substation is going to be folded. Which at this point in her career will mean the end of. Like a ballplayer: at a certain point, another surgery is no longer sensible, and there's nothing to be done but hang up the cleats, buy a car dealership.

A few years ago, in Luxembourg, Jake quizzed her about her job. They were in the car, on their way to one of the big playgrounds, three-thirty in the afternoon. The little boy listened to her cover story with no skepticism, nodding along, trying to understand the grown-up world, and his mother's place in it. He considered her explanation for a few seconds, then asked, "Mommy, you're quite young to be retired, aren't you?"

It wasn't until then that she considered the possibility that her unemployment was permanent. "I'm not retired, Sweetie. I'm just taking a break."

While she waits for the hammer to drop, Kate still goes to work most days, even when there's basically nothing to do. Every day might be the day that she can save her career.

In Kate's mind, there are definitely other people who could be blamed. In the ultimate court, she'd be able to call witnesses in her defense, there'd be an argument she could advance, appeals to the judge. But you never do get to defend yourself, explain your decisions, justify your missteps. Certainly not to anyone who can make any difference; the only people who would listen are the people who can't do anything about it.

And in any court there'd be cross-examinations, a solid case could definitely be made against her. "What about Seville?" they'd ask. "What about Palermo? What about Julia MacLean? How do you explain all that?"

❧

Kate plants herself in front of a family of four rushing toward her, parents and a pair of teenagers wearing scandalously short skirts, obscenely tight tees, dance-clubby makeup.

"Excuse me," Kate says. The mother has been crying. The father meets her eye, so Kate addresses him: "What's going on?"

"A man is in the middle of the Louvre, wearing a suicide vest."

They rush past, scurrying back to their hotel where they'll hole up until their flight home, no more museums, no Métro or public places, not with their worst fears about international travel confirmed. Why didn't the CIA see this coming? Isn't that what they're for?

Kate has tried her case herself—over and over, usually in the middle of the night. She knows that in a just world she'd be found not guilty. But that's not the same thing as innocent.

24

This isn't something you know until you've done it: moving dead bodies is extremely awkward. Wyatt hadn't needed to move around any of the previous dead bodies in his life, just let them lie where they fell. These two are also the only completely innocent people he's ever killed, as far as he knows. Maybe the hard work is his penance.

He tries to work quickly, dragging them across the concrete floor, back behind the little Cooper. The man weighs at least two hundred pounds, surprisingly difficult to drag forty yards. When Wyatt finishes he's winded, arms burning, back aching.

He climbs back into the van to catch his breath, gather his wits, collect his bag. This damn bag. If only he hadn't forgotten it.

Though what does that even mean, innocent? Innocent doesn't mean you don't deserve to die. We all die, there's no deserve or don't deserve about it. Just a question of when, and how. His daughter doesn't deserve to die. But she will.

It's possible he's going to vomit. He fights it back, swallows. And again.

Wyatt takes a deep, slow breath, trying to bring his digestive system under control, to halt the reverse peristalsis—

Fuck—he can't help it—he flings open the door, and leans over, and *splat,* it's all coming up, last night's dinner, absolutely disgusting, orange and brown chunks bound up in unctuous slime. He can't stop staring down into this repugnant puddle of sick.

His DNA is all over the goddamned place.

He climbs out of the van, scans the walls, there must be a hose here somewhere, a spigot, a way to clean the pavement, sluice away oil slicks, broken bottles of mango nectar, drunken-relief urine, a long pleasant *aahhhhhh*. He'll hose down this mess, it won't take more than a minute or two, then get—

What's that? Jesus H., will it never end?

Another car is coming down the ramp, he can see the headlights, so he launches himself back into the driver's seat, pulls the door closed, ducks down and leans his body across the gearshift, the side of his head hitting this bag—this *fucking* bag—in the passenger seat, he shoves it to the floor, giving himself room to hide his head.

The new car's wheels squeak around a turn. Wyatt can see headlights flash across his truck's roof, then on the opposite wall, another squeak, then the lights stop strobing, aimed *right here* at the wall in front of him.

Damn.

He can feel the new car pull up just beyond his head, it can be only a few feet that separates him from this other driver.

The new car's engine dies. The click of another door unlatching, a creak as it opens, then slams shut, loudly, echoing. A rustle of movement, clothes, and then nothing. No footsteps. Why? Why no footsteps? Is this fucker looking through the van's window?

Wyatt is lying on his right side, which makes it awkward to shift the angle of his right arm, reach his right hand into his pocket, where the gun is.

Now he notices the glow, it must be a screen, this newly arrived person is standing right here between his car and Wyatt's van, typing a text-message, checking a map, doing something that might seem urgent, with no idea that it might be the biggest—the final—mistake of his life.

Wyatt is going to hyperventilate. He focuses on taking in a breath slowly, carefully, quietly.

This glow persists, right here, just inches from his face.

Wyatt's right hand finds the grip in his pocket. His palm settles, fingers find their positions. He takes another controlled breath.

Then movement—what's this?—it's the light, the phone's glow, the angle shifted, and then the dim light extinguishes.

Footsteps recede.

Another door creaks open, shudders shut, then: silence.

Wyatt counts to ten. Then to ten again. Then he sits up. Looks around, his eyes drawn to the Cooper on the far side. He can just barely make out one of the woman's feet, peeking out from behind a rear wheel.

He can't be here anymore.

⚜

As he hustles down the sidewalk, Wyatt tries to locate the policeman, but can't. The Métro station is right up here, around this corner, which he turns—

Fuck.

Of course that's where the cop is, standing at the top of the steps, in the crisscross shadows of the latticework Métro sign, looking vigilant, alert, like a policeman should during a terrorist siege. *Of course* the patrolman would be dispatched to the subway station. Why didn't anyone think of this? Why didn't Wyatt?

Do not stop walking, he tells himself. Do not slow down. Do not look around. Just one foot in front of the other, step off this curb—

Fuck! What the—?

"Fou!" It's a cyclist screaming at him, cursing. *"Connard!"*

"Désolé!" Wyatt calls out, too late. *"Désolé,"* he repeats the apology, quieter, but that doesn't put the genie back in the bottle: the cop is now staring straight at him.

Wyatt can't turn around now. He continues toward the subway, shaky, God he's nervous. He has to walk right by this policeman, here in broad daylight. Any blood spatters will be clearly visible. The smell of his exertion, his sweat, his fear. And he's carrying this pistol, there's gunshot residue on his clothing, the aroma trapped in his nasal passages.

Stop it, he tells himself. Stop thinking of all that shit. Just put one foot in front of the other, just a few more steps, just one more.

The cop looks him dead in the face, and Wyatt can't help but cut his eyes away from this confrontational gaze, a mistake, what can he do to compensate . . . ?

"Bonjour," he mutters.

"Bonjour."

Now he has passed, and taken one step down the stairs, a second—

"Monsieur?"

Oh my fucking God! What now?

He freezes absolutely still for a second, then turns, looks up at the cop.

"*Votre sac,*" the cop says. His bag? "*Il est ouvert.*"

"*Ah oui?*" Wyatt looks down at his open bag. He zips it closed, and a half-second too late realizes he's still wearing latex gloves. "*Merci.*"

"*Faites attention, aujourd'hui,*" the cop says, already turned away. He didn't notice the gloves, did he?

Be careful today. Indeed.

25

They're moving at a decent clip on a straightaway, probably one of those broad Right Bank boulevards. At this higher speed the bumps hurt more, the chassis jarring into Hunter's sides, his ribs, shaking the contents of his skull.

Maybe this wasn't such a great idea. What does he really know about this so-called Tom Simpson? What facts did Hunter check? None. He was bullied into blind trust.

"Listen, Mr. Simpson," he says from under the tarp. "Tom."

But what's he going to say? I'm not having fun, please take me home? Can I speak to your supervisor? Show me your ID again? I want my mommy?

He almost says *Forget it,* but then chivalry occurs to him as a viable alternative to cowardice. "Could I ask you to slow down? I think you're knocking Colette's marbles loose." Or pretend chivalry. Hunter suspects that all chivalry is pretend, just as he's convinced about all religion. Everyone must know, on some level, that there's no fucking way. But maybe if you pretend long enough, hard enough, you forget that what you're doing is pretending.

⚜

The car comes to a stop.

"Just a minute more," Simpson says. "Please remain still."

Hunter hears the driver's door open, but not close. Another noise, a high-pitched creak, a hinge that needs oiling. Then a similar noise, but not exactly the same.

Big doors. Two of them.

The driver plops back into his seat, shifts gears. The car moves forward slowly, then stops again, and the transmission shifts into reverse, turning, then forward again. Hunter realizes what this is: Simpson just turned the car around, so it faces the direction whence they came, the exit.

Hunter congratulates himself on figuring this out. But is it a good thing for them to be ready for a quick getaway? Or bad? What does it suggest about this predicament? About the safety of this location? About the confidence that Simpson has in—

The tarp is yanked off.

"Sorry for the discomfort," Simpson says. "You can get out now." He walks around to open Colette's door, reaches out his hand.

"*Merci.*" She extends her arm, her blouse disheveled, quick glimpse of lace bra, hot pink. Christ. She's got some weapons-grade lingerie under there. Hunter wonders if this is normal, if she wears lace garters and hot-pink bras every day, or if today is an occasion, date night, an anniversary. Or is it possible that she wears special underwear for Hunter's benefit?

"In here." Simpson ushers them toward the building's door, a keypad, a long string of digits that the guy shields from view. "Sorry, there's no elevator."

They trudge up the stairs, one flight, two. They pause on the landing, catch their breath. Then up another long flight.

"I guess we must be in the penthouse," Hunter says. No one responds.

There's a single door up at the top, steel-plated. A few locks, top, bottom, middle.

Something is tugging at the corners of Hunter's consciousness. What? He glances around the short hall. Should there be another door up here? The locks look high-tech, and three seems like a large number of them. But isn't that what you'd expect from a CIA safehouse? The steel reinforcement too?

Simpson unlocks the final mechanism with a loud click, turns the knob, pushes open the fortified door.

It's dark in here, heavy curtains on the windows. Simpson flips a switch that turns on a few floor lamps; there's no overhead. "Come on in."

Hunter allows Colette to step inside first, then follows tentatively.

Simpson reengages the locks, one of which requires a key to secure from the inside. "It's not much to look at, but it's safe." He slips the keys into his pocket.

Maybe nothing's wrong. Maybe Hunter is just nervous. As well he should be. Nothing wimpy about that, just a sensible response to what's obviously a highly fucked-up situation, spirited away by the CIA to protect him from murder, kidnapping. If he weren't nervous, he'd be a moron.

But Hunter is used to trusting his gut. And his gut is telling him that it isn't just nerves.

26

Kate is frozen in the middle of the pont des Arts, a boulder in a stream, people flowing around her like fast-moving currents.

Her first instinct is to spin around, to join the panicked mob fleeing danger, to return to school and reclaim her children, just as it crossed her mind an hour and a half ago, when she heard the first sirens, when the threat was unknown. But then what? Where would the family go? Traffic will be a nightmare, roads closed, maybe train stations, airports. All she'd accomplish would be to panic the children. And the apartment wouldn't be any safer than school. Less so: home is closer to a greater number of higher-value targets. Plus proximity to Kate Moore doesn't necessarily make anyone safer.

Paris is replete with noteworthy terrorist targets—dozens, hundreds, they're everywhere, but the International School of St-Germain is not one. There are no celebrity children there, no presidential daughters, no reason for the school to interest anyone. The kids are as safe as they can be, in that school.

That's the logical assessment. But parenting isn't always logical, and Kate is having a hard time beating back the emotional impulse, convincing herself to do what she knows she needs to do: continue to the Louvre, see this situation firsthand. Kate is the boots on the ground. If she's still a useful intelligence resource, she needs to prove it today.

And if she can't? Well then, that conclusion is inescapable, the sort she wouldn't even need to explain to her younger kid, who'd recently dubbed himself Incompetent Ninja. Like a superhero, but the opposite. "Because, Mommy, I *like* being a ninja, but I'm not *good* at it." Ben executed a wild leg kick and karate chop. "I am! Incompetent!! *Ninja*!!!"

These things are obvious, if you can manage to do what little kids can: suspend your pride, and see yourself clearly.

It was a few years ago when Kate saw clearly what she wanted, at a once-in-a-lifetime moment when she was in a position to get it. She cut a deal with her ex-mentor Hayden Grey, the CIA's chief of Western Europe. She'd hand over to Hayden the bulk of Dexter's stolen fortune, and also facilitate a recorded admission of guilt by the mastermind of the conspiracy, who happened to be an ex-FBI agent. Hayden looked forward to the impending scandal with uncharacteristic glee; the animosity between the Agency and the Bureau was apparently a strong motivator.

What Kate wanted from Hayden in return was two things: immunity for Dexter, and a job for herself. She wanted to be a spy again.

Hayden obliged. He used the 24 million untraceable euros to establish the Paris Substation, a clandestine, agile little outfit whose day-to-day Kate would manage. The fieldwork would be done by freelancers—informants, sources, criminals. The mandate would be the types of extra-curricular activities that the Agency didn't want on their books, or in their meetings, in their reports, their congressional oversight. These were not traditional intelligence-gathering operations, but rather active measures—supporting, undermining, influencing. Sometimes illegal, or close to it: the gray areas of character assassination and scandal manufacture, of destabilizing enemies and propping up friends, the illicit business of interfering in the internal affairs of sovereign governments.

First Kate hired a Paris fixer who could find the strays—plumber, electrician, cat burglar—that you always need. Then a cadre of techs who could hack into police departments, newsrooms, corporate e-mail servers. Bribable low-level officials in customs, in immigration, in tax authorities, people who could be paid modestly to part with modest information, the kind of data Kate could use to extract more meaningful disclosures, an infinite ladder of trading up, each extorted secret building upon another, an edifice of shame.

The irony was not lost on Kate: she had traded her husband's secret criminal enterprise for her own.

This work involved frequent travel for Kate, usually for same-day meetings, away and back between breakfast and dinner, the TGV to

Brussels, a shuttle to Frankfurt, the Eurostar to London. Sometimes an overnight, a week here and there for a cleanup in Capri, or a Basque crisis in San Sebastián, or an extortion of a German industrialist on holiday in Mallorca, as German industrialists do.

She was effective at running her network of journalists, bloggers, influencers, as well as drug dealers, thieves, prostitutes, and cops, plus diplomats and soldiers, maître d's and concierges and bartenders and shopkeepers; it's surprising how much you can learn from the eagle-eyed owner of a well-sited bodega. All these assets, the fabric that holds society together, recruited so Kate could identify weaknesses and exploit them, manipulating reality to one that's a more hospitable environment for the security of the USA and the health of its global corporations, its banks, its exported culture, Coca-Cola, ExxonMobil, the films of Steven Spielberg.

Kate had been thrilled to return to this work, to this world. She got the Paris Substation up and running quickly, ahead of her own self-imposed schedule. Everything was working just fine.

Until Copenhagen.

❧

Kate's first clue that something was wrong was that Hayden handed her a gun. She'd thought this op was supposed to be a simple stakeout, and there's nothing more boring than a stakeout. Until it isn't.

"What's going on here?" She examined the weapon, the type of locally procured, untraceable gun that means not only that you're expecting trouble, but also more trouble for solving the trouble.

"Kate, I need to explain what steps you'll take, in the event of my, um, *indisposition*."

"I know the protocols, Hayden. Why are we talking about this?"

He gestured at the building across the street, their operation. He swept his arm: all of this, he was saying. Anything. "Things happen, Kate, you know what the *if*s are. *If* ever I turn up, um, dead. *If* I'm missing for more than a few days. Or a week. Use your judgment."

Hayden had never before broached the subject of succession plans, and he'd never imposed a weapon upon her. She was worried.

"You'll go to this address."

He scribbled something that she read quickly, then closed her eyes, repeated the address to herself, invented a mnemonic, and repeated that a couple of times too. Then it was done. The Paris address was now, as Jake had been taught to say in math, a known fact.

"It's a travel bureau, not far from your office. You'll see any available representative, and say you're Kathy Anderson, wife of me, Harry Anderson." Hayden took out a cigarette lighter, set the paper afire, dropped it to the floor. "You're collecting my itinerary. The first time, there won't be anything. You'll ask the rep to check with her supervisor. She will. Then she'll assure you that *no,* there's nothing waiting for Monsieur Anderson. You'll leave a phone number—a burner—in case something appears. Sooner or later, it will."

"How long?"

"*I* don't know, Kate. A day? A *month*?" He handed the binoculars back to her. "Looks like another visitor."

Kate raised her binoculars. "The same pizza guy as yesterday."

"Yes. He should get a different drug dealer, one who delivers something else. *Sushi,* maybe. *Falafel.* The guy's going to have a cardiac arrest any second. Keel over."

Kate put down the glasses. "Then what?"

"Then? I guess we'll call an ambulance; it's dialing 112, I think. Is that right?"

Kate shrugged. She didn't know how to dial emergency services in Copenhagen, and she couldn't fathom why Hayden would.

"Or maybe it would be better if we let him die? Then someone else will be forced to show up, and things will clarify?"

She never ceased to be amazed at Hayden's ability to find distorted angles, which is probably what made him such a successful spymaster. "No, Hayden, I mean: what will happen when I eventually get this call?"

"You'll probably be summoned to a meet."

"Probably?"

"Again, Kate, it's hard to say."

"Why not the standard protocols?"

"Listen." He turned to face Kate, held her eye for a few seconds. "It's time for me to level with you, Kate. This operation—me, you, your team—we don't, *technically,* report into Langley. In any way, shape, or form."

She was too surprised to respond.

"Actually, that's not all true: *I* of course do report to Langley."

"But I don't?"

"Your whole substation, Kate, is our little secret, yours and mine. We operate completely outside CIA's chain of command. Our orders don't even come from Langley."

"Then where?"

"The other side of the Potomac."

Kate's mind raced through the possibilities. Secretary of state . . . of defense . . . national security advisor . . .

"Are you going to tell me?"

Vice president . . .

He shook his head. "Sorry."

President.

"It's called the Travelers International Booking Service, and it's affiliated with the American magazine called *The Travelers*. That's where you'll go for assignments."

"You're kidding."

"I'm not."

"It's a real magazine, right? I've heard of it. I've *read* it."

"It even wins awards, I'm told."

"And is it a real travel agency?"

"Yes. The agency is part of the parent company's *revenue* stream. Or a *profit* center." He shrugged. "Whatever they call it."

"And the whole thing is an Agency front?"

"The *whole* thing? No, that's not how fronts work, Kate, you know that. The travel agency is a legitimate business, affiliated with a legitimate magazine, which is a division of a legitimate American conglomerate. But *behind* the front, it's also a couple of other things. One is a clandestine courier service, and that's primarily what you'll be using it for."

"How?"

"Every other week, you'll call in, ask if there are any tickets for me." Hayden didn't need to tell Kate to use pay phones in assorted neighborhoods, to call at different hours on different days, to avoid any pattern, any suggestion of routine. "If the answer is yes, go there yourself. Collect the envelope, like anyone else picking up travel documents. There may be other clients around, you always need to be behaving as if you're one of them."

"Does the staff know?"

"No, not the people in the agency; those people are just travel agents."

"So what's in these envelopes?"

"The names of targets, encrypted using the Berlin code. Usually no other information or instruction. It's completely at our discretion to figure out exactly how, and when. If there's any required timeframe, that too will be obvious. The reasons will also make themselves obvious, once you start looking."

"Such as?"

"Such as an upcoming election. Or a diplomatic summit. A trade deal. But other than the name, there will be no incoming information. And outgoing from you, also nothing. You won't provide any updates, *ever*. If your operation is successful, the necessary reporting will come through other avenues within the Agency, and from the press. Briefs will make their way to the right people. You don't need to worry about reporting successes."

"I'm assuming I also don't need to report failures?"

"You see, Kate? I've always known you're a genius."

"And no specifics about the mission?"

"It's always the same: ruin the target. Discredited. Fired. Arrested."

"Killed?"

Hayden shrugged.

She understood: whatever it took. "And what's the other thing Travelers does?"

Hayden turned back to Kate, and gave her a big smile. "You're going to love this."

"Hi Dex," she says.

"Kate? Everything all right?" It has been only a few minutes since they parted.

"No. There's apparently a suicide bomber at the Louvre. A guy wearing a vest."

"My God."

"Dex, you're planning to stay home all day, right?"

"Well, I still need to go find that Lego. But I guess not if the city blows up."

"Not funny, Dexter."

"You're right. Sorry."

"Listen: please answer any calls, from any phone number, even if you don't recognize it. It might be me calling from another line, or school, or a teacher calling from a mobile, or another parent."

"Gotcha."

"I don't think we should do it right now, but we should be prepared to get the kids."

"And what are you going to do?"

What should Kate say? She wonders where Dexter imagines her office is. Maybe the embassy? Or the American Club? Someplace easily identifiable as American, flag flying out front, a fleet of black Escalades?

"I have work to do."

"Work?"

She doesn't elaborate.

"You're kind of scaring me, Kate. What's going on?"

"I don't know, Dex. But first the bomb threat at the train station, and now . . ." She trails off, pursuing a line of conjecture that she doesn't want to share.

"Should I be worried?" he asks.

"Well, yeah. At least a little."

"About what?"

"I'm not sure exactly."

"Are there other bombs? Let me . . . Oh God, I'm now seeing this on TV. The courtyard has been evacuated, except for one guy. Yes, he's definitely wearing a vest, and he's also got a case. Kate, where exactly are you?"

"On my way there."

"*There?* What the hell do you mean by that? Tell me you're not going to the Louvre."

"Calm down, Dexter."

"*Calm down?* What do you think is *in* that case? The guy didn't detonate immediately, when he was surrounded by victims. And now that the courtyard has been evacuated, what's a bomb going to accomplish? Shatter the windows? Who gives a shit?"

Dexter is right. If it were only a conventional explosive that was going to be detonated, it would make sense only in a big crowd, when there's flesh to pierce, people to injure, maim, murder. But if all the people are gone, there's no one left to kill except the bomber. So what's the briefcase for?

"But even the *tiniest* nuclear detonation? The radiation?"

"There's not really any such thing as a suitcase nuclear bomb," Kate says. "Not one that fits in an actual suitcase." It's a halfhearted objection. She knows that it's only a matter of semantics, and magnitude.

"But a case like that could contain radioactive material. A dirty bomb."

A dirty bomb wouldn't create the same type of blast, no mushroom cloud; downtown Paris wouldn't be leveled. But it could produce plenty of long-term lethal radiation; for all intents and purposes, everything in the Louvre would be destroyed—the Rembrandts and Vermeers, Raphaels and Caravaggios, the artifacts from Greece, Rome, Egypt, the largest repository of art and artifacts in the world.

And it would kill everyone within the primary blast zone, if not immediately from the explosion then within a matter of days from the radiation. Definitely Kate. Dexter too? And the children, are they far enough away to be spared? Every inch might count, when it comes to radiation. Every minute that you get farther away, every second, might save your life.

"Or," Dexter says.

Or. Kate's mind is catching up to other possibilities, worse even than nuclear radiation at the Louvre.

"Biological," Dexter continues.

Worse for whom? she asks herself.

"Chemical."

Worse for her. Worse for her family.

She picks up her pace, breaks into a run, dodging among all the people who are fleeing in the other direction. Kate is the only one who is rushing toward the bomb.

PART II

CHAMPS-ÉLYSÉES

27

t would be unthinkable, if there still were such a thing. But nothing is unthinkable, not anymore.

There's a suicide bomber at the Louvre.

Kate pushes her way through the chaotic crowd in the plaza, most people still fleeing in terror but some inching forward in curiosity, or milling about in confusion, or inquiry, or simply hovering with smartphones aloft, citizen-reporters eager to document anything, even if it turns out to be their own demise.

Police are securing a perimeter across all the access points—the *passages* through the palace's ground level, the big open space of the Tuileries, the heavily trafficked two-way street that runs through the place du Carrousel, the wide sidewalks, the buses and trucks and abundant volume of pedestrians, a huge space to seal off, requiring a lot of personnel and vehicles, all still in the process of arriving.

The grand U-shaped courtyard itself is relatively easy to secure, with its sole open facet already lined with fencing. Choke points have been closed, checkpoints established. No one in. No one out.

A few uniformed officers are trying to reason with hysterical people—my wife is inside, my grandparents—while also making sure that no one comes bursting through intent on who the hell knows, an accomplice, an unrelated psychopath. There's no accounting for psychopaths.

Kate finally elbows her way into a position where she can see—

She gasps. She's surprised at her reaction, like an amateur. She has never before seen anything like this. No one here has.

What she sees: a man is standing all alone in the middle of the vast open space, looking tiny. He's wearing a bulky vest, and a briefcase sits at his feet, the sort of luggage that in action-adventure films follows around the president of the United States, a shiny case lugged by a tall square-jawed man wearing a military uniform, a handsome extra with no speaking lines. The nuclear codes.

In real-world non-POTUS life, this case is the sort of thing that can be outfitted with foam insets and thick padding and reinforced super-structure to prevent accidental damage or premature detonation, tidy packets of TNT or nitro or Semtex surrounded by ready-made shrapnel, construction screws or ball bearings, little bits of lethal.

Yes, Dexter was right: that's a suitcase bomb.

⚜

Is this an SOS situation?

Kate's cover isn't compromised, her substation isn't blown, her network isn't being rounded up, there's no high-visibility op imploding. Those are the valid reasons for her to send an SOS; those are the potential problems of hers that her superiors might be willing to help solve. Or at least be willing to hear about.

Then again, she doesn't know exactly who her superiors are, so it's hard to tell.

But someone blowing up the Louvre? That doesn't present any immediate risk to Kate's personnel or office or the CIA or the USA. It wouldn't lay bare anyone's diligently covered ass, wouldn't cost anyone a job, a promotion. This attack is not the Agency's failure of intelligence, not its problem to solve. Perhaps even the opposite: this attack could help further the CIA's agenda, could advance a rationale for some action, a policy shift, a realignment of resources. Perhaps it's an opportunity.

Either way, it's not something Kate can ignore, just a bystander, like that truck driver tried to pretend with the dog. He looked like a fool, and Kate would too. No: worse than a fool. She'd look like a neglectful, incompetent fraud. On the heels of her other recent failures, Kate would appear worthless.

She turns her back on the bomber, scans the crowd, the police mobilizing, crowd-controlling, looking for other signs of trouble. This bomber can't be a simple lone-wolf attack; that situation would be over already, the police would have shot him, or he would've blown himself up. There must be a bigger picture, and Kate needs to insert herself into it.

If it turns out that this attack does have something to do with American interests—and at this point in geopolitical history, what doesn't—and Kate has chosen to spend the day watching cable-news coverage? If something preventable is happening in Paris and she fails to prevent it? If there's a plot to crack and she fails to crack it, if American lives are going to be lost and she fails to save them?

Then today will be the last operational day of her career. It won't happen a few weeks from now, with some marginally rude guy on a park bench. No, it'll be immediate, persona non grata. Or worse.

Kate reaches the far end of the *place,* and turns to take one last look at the man who's standing there in the middle of the courtyard, strapped into oblivion.

She knows that this has nothing to do with her. Except that everything in Paris has something to do with her.

Most of the post-Agency options for people like Kate are not available to the actual Kate. Private contracting work in conflict zones, or high-value security details, the types of jobs you can't have if you're a parent, if you need to come home alive every night. Management or consulting jobs in Langley, or in Washington, or on the rural campuses of paramilitary training camps in North Carolina, in Honduras, in Sudan, the types of jobs you can't have if you're married to Dexter Moore, and you've had their shared life experiences, their entanglements, and you live in France.

She could do something completely unrelated, something entrepreneurial, maybe launch one of those businesses like Hashtag Mom, who supposedly designs necklaces, though mostly she seems to make so-called strategic expenditures—the studio in Montparnasse, the personal assistant who's "*so* indispensable," the research trips to India, to Thailand; they're Eastern-inspired, Hashtag Mom's necklaces. #Inspired.

Or she could again try full-time householding, older and wiser, planning the vacations and inspecting the car, paying the bills and filing the taxes, cleaning and cooking and educating and shopping, plus all the personal maintenance, it's like being a professional athlete, constantly training with one exercise obsession after another, plus the manicures, the teeth-whitenings, the haircuts and blowouts and colorings, the depilatorizations, and the fashion—the jeans, the boots, God all the shoes—

amassing the requisite tribal insignia, the logos and patterns and patches and badges that sort you, that identify your clan.

Could Kate do it? Could she compete for firmest ass and strongest triceps and widest gap between her thighs, for the latest this and chicest that, the most original and attractive conversions of the money her husband earns into documentable manifestations of the good life, Instagrammable and Facebookable, eminently enviable, the best of everything, we all want the good life, don't we, and look—I have it! I win.

Could Kate win?

⚜

She unlocks a Vélib' bike and pedals away on the rue de Rivoli, completely empty on this section alongside the Tuileries, with squad cars blocking the intersecting streets, traffic jams already formed, drivers standing beside the open doors of their fuel-efficient little *citadines*—Renaults, Citroëns—on the rue de Castiglione, the rue Cambon, smoking cigarettes, complaining into their mobiles. They don't know what exactly the problem is. Rumors are flying.

Kate passes the larger of the English-language bookstores, which reminds her of the other shop, closer to home, another resource developed, just in case.

She glances over her shoulder. It's impossible that any cars are following her, but there are also no mopeds, no motorcycles, no other bicycles. Just streams of pedestrians, some more frantic than others, but none paying any attention to her. No one is following Kate.

She fights the urge to look up into the sky; you can't see the satellites, not with the naked eye in daylight. But they're there, watching. Drones too.

At Concorde she cuts diagonally across the broad expanse of unoccupied lanes, a rare moment of calm in what's usually a madhouse mega-roundabout. But now it's just her bicycle headed in one direction, and a trio of cop cars zooming in the other.

She barely glances at the US Embassy on her right; she's not going there. Nor is she going home. Nor school. Nor the musty safehouse out behind Père Lachaise in the *vingtième*, a ground-floor unit with a private street-level entrance in an apartment building occupied mostly by North Africans.

Kate continues onto the Champs-Élysées. The grand boulevard is almost entirely empty, as if the bomb had already detonated.

Suddenly she's facing into a phalanx of police cars with their lights flashing, and behind the cops here comes the army, a few jeeps and a couple of armored personnel carriers and—yes—here they are, a half-dozen of them.

That really didn't take long, something she never thought she'd see in France.

Tanks.

Tanks are rolling down the Champs-Élysées.

28

Shreve looks at his watch. *Fuck.*

He rushes by that awesome sign—PLEASE DON'T WAIL AGAINST THE FLOW—while bounding down the Central–Mid-Levels escalator-walkway that transports pedestrians up and down the steep foothills of Hong Kong Island. Shreve loves that fucking sign—Wail Against the Flow! He wants that on a T-shirt. Or start a band, this could be the title for their debut.

Though the thing is: however you interpret Wail Against the Flow, Shreve doesn't do it. He's more of a wail-*with*-the-flow guy. Maybe that's why he finds the sign so appealing.

Like, what was that band? Rage Against the Machine.

He looks again at his Rolex. Fuck. He's going to be *so* late.

Okay, so, yes, things did get out of hand. It was just supposed to be a quick bite after the gym at that Italian in the Hollywood mall, Dougie and Frenac and the hot arbitrage chick Veronica, they'd already opened a Barolo before he arrived, then Dougie offered a bump, which turned into a few, and soon they were all shuttling back and forth to the unisex as if digging out the final stretch under the prison walls using soupspoons.

So now, yes, he can't deny it: he's pretty fucking high.

But these are *clients;* this is his *job.* Not just chiseling his commission off the intersection where someone else's idea meets another someone's investment, but recruiting and massaging and servicing these clients. They'd all agreed to meet again later, at Kau U Fong, Jell-O shots and beers down in the street, then the elevator up to Ping's, where Dougie could re-up, everyone on sofas, the balcony for cigarettes, Veronica in that skintight skirt, what he'd really love to do is lean down to snort some blow off her back while fucking her from behind, bent over a leather sofa.

Shreve has arrived at the end of the escalator-stairs, and now he's running over a sky-bridge and through the shopping plaza, onto an elevated sidewalk, nothing is on ground level here, you're constantly getting on and off escalators, elevators, even the *sidewalks* are in the sky, like the Jetsons, bars on the fifth floor, restaurants on the tenth, everything in vertical malls built into hillsides, you never know where you are in relation to street level, which isn't even that clear of a concept. Car level.

Even from up here on one-above-car level, Shreve still needs to dash up another escalator to the soaring glass-walled lobby with all the corporate signage, his own bank and a few others, plus media, and that American-based tech company that just expanded onto the fortieth and forty-first, they're obviously growing, maybe he should get in on that, but right now he's frantically searching for the ID card, not there, nor there, patting down his chest, swinging his gym bag off his shoulder, and *fuck* where's my goddamned card?

There. Whew. He looks at his watch again, fourteen minutes late and still in the lobby, Harrison is going to *ream* him.

Shreve drops his corporate-logo'd little duffle—everybody at his gym uses these canvas bags, they're like sports uniforms, they announce what team you play for, HSBC or UBS or BNP, the occasional Morgan or Citi dude—onto the conveyor through the X-ray, and he swipes his key card through the slot and strides into the turnstile, waits to collect his bag, which hasn't come through the belt yet, and the security guards are staring at the monitor, then one of them yells at him—what did that dude say?—while the other jumps off his stool, and draws his gun, and that's when all fucking hell breaks loose.

29

unter holds the newly powered-up phone to his ear, depresses the switch hook. Nothing, not even a hiss. Just silence.

"There's no dial tone," he says. Depress and release, depress and release. "Nothing."

"No?" Simpson walks over. "I'm surprised."

Simpson reaches out his hand, and Hunter gives him the landline. Why? Does this CIA guy have a magic touch? Or is he just the kind of man who doesn't trust anyone else to do anything right? Hunter is himself one of those men.

"Huh," Simpson says, depressing the plastic button himself, releasing, depressing. He examines his mobile too. "Nothing. You?"

Hunter already checked. He shakes his head.

"Sorry about that," Simpson says. "I was told—Well, you know what I was told. I bet you don't like hearing excuses. I'll try rebooting."

It's clear that Simpson knows this effort will be purely ceremonial.

Hunter stifles the urge to explode at this guy, who obviously does not understand the magnitude of the shittiness that's confronting Hunter.

You work your whole life for something. You study. You cram. You pull the late nights and early flights, you beg and connive, you plot and scheme, you lie and cheat and maybe even steal, you do *everything*, all to create a specific opportunity at a particular time—your moment. Only to discover that all the things you could control aren't nearly enough, too much is uncontrollable, beyond your influence. The world doesn't give a fuck about your plans. About you.

Okay, Hunter thinks, this is definitely bad on some level. But *bad* is a large, abstract thought. Let's break it down into specific practical considerations.

First, he doesn't need to worry about San Jose, where everyone is still asleep. The people in California won't be a concern for—Hunter checks his watch—another seven hours, maybe eight. And if this whole Paris situation isn't resolved in eight hours? Then the high-level staff in San Jose will be the least of his problems.

So what about Asia? It's the middle of the afternoon in Mumbai, and the business day is almost over in Hong Kong. Both are problems. The people who were awaiting Hunter's call are sitting at their desks, increasingly worried, maybe even panicked, they're calling one another: "Have you heard from Forsyth?," "No. You neither?," "What do you think is going on?" They know that a big announcement is coming, they know Hunter is supposed to be calling, and then *no one* hears from him? *No one* knows where he even *is*?

If it were just internal, that could be managed. His people aren't going to go blabbing; no one in any of his offices would respond to any inquiry by saying, "Sorry, Mr. Forsyth seems to have vanished off the face of the earth. Good luck finding him! If I were you, I'd certainly sell any 4Syte stock you're holding, asap."

But it's not just internal. There are favors owed. A discrete call here and there, using a burner phone with an untraceable number from a country he's never in his life visited, providing a quick update: the merger is on, no regulatory problems, banks committed, all clear. *Guaranteed.*

An hour's head start, or two. For some people, this will mean tens of millions in profit, even hundreds of millions. Not just by the early purchase of 4Syte's and their acquisition's stock, but also by shorting others, their competition's, those companies' suppliers. By making big complicated trades, taking heavy positions, accepting what looks like irresponsible risk in the hope of generating stupendous reward.

These are not the types of investments that these people—that any sane, rational people—would make without assurances. Not just the untrustworthy scripted assurances of blustering from a CEO at a carefully orchestrated press conference. But iron-clad assurances, made by a longtime associate, in a private call.

While speaking obliquely. Because, no, this is not, technically, legal.

But if none of these people hear from Hunter—if this day continues to erode minute by minute, the hours mounting, while he continues to not place call after call—then sooner or later, someone somewhere is going to get worried, and change his mind.

Maybe any minute now, some trader dude who was expecting the call after Hunter's call that doesn't arrive, this dude decides to sell instead of buy.

Maybe this has already happened.

Then someone further up the food chain notices. Does the same thing, in a bigger way.

Then some nerd at a financial news service will catch wind, then mention it to someone else, then the share price will fall infinitesimally, then a cable-news producer will post the activity to the chyron.

Then the share price will inch down further.

Then everyone will notice.

Then calls will be made, increasingly urgent and panicked.

Then it will become clear that no one in the world has seen or heard from CEO Hunter Forsyth all day.

Then the speculation will start, the rumors—drug overdose? kidnapped? hiding in the dark paralyzed with fear because his huge deal is falling apart?—will spread like wildfire.

Then the stock price will fall off a cliff, it'll turn into a fire sale, a bloodbath, and meanwhile Hunter won't even *know* it, because he'll be trapped here in this blackout.

Then when "beleaguered 4Syte CEO Hunter Forsyth"—that's what he'll be called—eventually reemerges, blinking in the daylight, his personal net worth will have reduced by tens of millions, the company billions in valuation, plus he'll have alienated some of the most powerful bankers in the world, he'll have burned his network, ended his friendships.

Then not only will he be broke, he'll also be a pariah. An abject failure.

Then he might as well be dead.

So if some violent death—by assassination, or bombing, or who-the-hell-knows—is what's waiting for him out there on the Paris streets, fuck it, at least he'll die dramatically, while he's still at the height of his success. He'll die famous.

He has worked himself up into a frenzy, sitting here on this musty sofa. He turns to Simpson, tries to wipe the panic from his face, but not the urgency. "Listen," he says, "I have to get to my office. I really do."

Simpson nods. "I can understand why you'd feel that way, Mr. Forsyth, but it's just not a good idea. I'm sure you recognize that."

"Well, good idea or bad"—Hunter stands—"that's what I need to do."

Simpson sighs. This seems to be one of his main methods of communicating. Hunter is really beginning to hate this guy. "I'm sorry, but I have to insist. It's too dangerous out there."

It takes a second for Hunter to understand what Simpson is saying. It's so improbable. "Excuse me?"

"I'm sorry, Mr. Forsyth." Another unapologetic apology. "I can't let you leave."

"Can't *let* me leave? What exactly do you mean?"

The guy doesn't elaborate.

"You're going to forcibly *detain* me here, Simpson?"

"You shouldn't think of it that way."

"By whose authority? In case you haven't noticed, we're in *France*. You don't have any authority here."

Simpson nods, as if in agreement.

"And what about Colette? She's not even American. You, an American— what? What are we calling you? An American diplomat? Or should we dispense with that charade, and say *CIA officer*? An American *spy* is going to detain a French citizen, in France?"

The guy doesn't rise to the bait, doesn't say anything at all.

"Come on, Colette. We're leaving."

Hunter walks past Simpson, brushing him on the shoulder, purposefully but lightly, like a teenage boy in a high-school hall, attempting to start a fight.

He takes only a couple of firm strides before he remembers—

Damn it: for one of the locks, Simpson used a key. From the inside.

"I'm sorry, Mr. Forsyth. It's for your own safety."

Hunter turns around.

"Your own good."

30

Wyatt fumbles in his pocket, locates the Métro ticket, jams it into the turnstile, whisks through with a thump. He collects his validated ticket, pushes through the doors, tries to remember which train in which direction.

He descends to the platform. Looks left, right. Walks to the map, confirms that he's waiting for the correct train, headed in the correct direction, and the stop where he'll get off.

The train arrives in a warm whoosh, packed, newspapers and backpacks and people staring at their phones, earbuds, headphones, everyone in their own private worlds. He wedges himself uncomfortably, arm raised to hold a pole. At the next stop, many people exit, many more board, then the train sits for a long delay. He wouldn't be surprised if the system gets shut down entirely. Wyatt has a contingency plan for that. For everything.

Just a couple more stops.

One more.

Only a few people disembark with him. He walks slowly, allowing the others to outpace him until he's the last on the platform, and the train has pulled out, and the arrivals board refreshes itself: the next train is due in three minutes, the following one in seven.

Three minutes is plenty of time.

He climbs the stairs, turns into an exit-only passage that will remain empty for those three minutes. He checks the photo booth—it's always possible there's a tourist, or a pair of teenagers necking. There isn't.

He drops the bag with a thud, unzips it quickly. He removes a folded-up piece of green nylon, fluffs it open: another duffel bag. He takes off his sport jacket, puts it in this new duffel. Unbuttons his blue shirt, shoves that in too; now he's wearing a white tee. Tosses in the eyeglasses, good riddance. Switches out the brogues for running shoes. He can't help but notice the bloodstains in the treads of the leather shoes.

Almost finished, still more than a minute to spare.

He pulls on a black cap, the bill low over his brow. Places the blue canvas bag into the green nylon one, closes the bigger bag.

Now he's a completely different person, carrying a completely different bag.

He slings the duffel over his shoulder and walks around the corner, where a surveillance camera is mounted from the ceiling. This camera is supposedly disabled, but better safe than sorry: he keeps his head down, face hidden. He descends to the platform for the train heading in the other direction, back toward his origin.

There are more cameras down here, but he knows that if he waits at the front end of the platform, he's out of their range.

Wyatt has a theory about why he came all the way to Odéon just to change his clothes and switch bags, but he doubts it'll ever be confirmed. "You're not going to be told much," the bearded American had told him. "Thus the large bonus. You all right with that?"

"Honestly? I prefer it that way."

He switches trains at a busy hub, navigates the throngs shuffling through the *correspondance* tunnels, the platforms where everyone listens to the service announcements, moaning and groaning, sending texts and making calls, *Sorry, running late, please don't wait . . .*

He lunges onto the new train, just one more anxious body in a heaving mass of frustrated commuters. A fresh force boards at the following stop, each station more crowded than the last, with different routes converging, all these lines forced to take up the overflow from the suspended line that runs under the rue de Rivoli. The number 1 is closed temporarily, due to a security issue.

Security issue. That is one drastic understatement.

Wyatt checks his watch. This is taking longer than anticipated. But this part of the schedule has built-in padding. It's okay.

After a mass exodus at Opéra, the crowd remains relatively sparse for a couple of stops, then gathers again at Strasbourg–St-Denis, where the subway meets the commuter rail. Then even thicker at the multi-line convergence at République, sardines now, everyone too uncomfortable, too delayed, too scared. It's a buzzing mass of negativity here in this steel cylinder lurching through a burrowed-out tunnel underneath a panic-stricken metropolis.

Wyatt is relieved that there are all these other passengers, the sweaty press around him, the jostling elbows, the inconsiderate backpacks, the roll-aboard bags clogging the aisles, everyone in everyone else's way, short-tempered and impatient and unobservant, lost in their own inconveniences, their own multiplying problems. It's too crowded for anyone to see much, to notice any bags that might be resting down on the floor, or under seats.

As the train slows into the next station, Wyatt nudges the bag under the seat at his feet. He gives it a toe-shove, wedging it far under. He darts his eyes around, but no one seems to have noticed.

The train stops.

"*Pardonnez-moi,*" he says, making his way, "*Pardonnez-moi*" again, a chant on this pilgrimage to the exit, as much to keep himself calm as to be unnoticeable. No one notices normal courtesies. What's noticeable is rudeness.

He mumbles a final "*Pardonnez-moi*" and then he's through the doors, onto the platform, and he forces himself not to glance back to see if anyone has noticed his abandoned bag, calling after him, "*Monsieur, votre—*"

No one would do that. No one would imagine that the green bag was his, no one would have even noticed the thing, not yet, not with so many people surrounding the duffel, so many potential owners. The orphaned luggage won't be remarked upon for at least a half-dozen stops, after the crowd thins as the train heads toward Créteil, it'll be way past city limits before someone in uniform finally takes possession of it, opens the zipper . . .

What will he find? A change of clothes, unremarkable. What will be suspicious is the phone, with a handful of numbers programmed into the contacts. One number is named Gare. Another Vendôme and another Triomphe and another Louvre. Also a contact for PDG—*président-directeur général,* what the French call a CEO. This number is the only one that has ever been called. Every day, in fact. Just a few seconds per call, each made using a special app that disguised the phone number.

How long before investigators compare this bag's contents to the surveillance footage of Wyatt at the bomb sites? Tomorrow? Next week? At that point, they will conclude that the bag was lost, something went wrong, that's why the negotiations never commenced. Criminals are stupid; that's why they're criminals. That will be the moral of the story.

If they ever start to search for the man in the footage, Wyatt will be long gone, back in Louisiana, straightening out McKayla's past-due bills, looking like a completely different person. No one could connect this American military veteran to these surveillance images, this body of evidence, this terrorist plot. If it's an American, it's not terrorism.

31

The convoy rumbles by.

How did the army respond so quickly? Did French intelligence have advance warning of the attacks? Were they already on heightened alert? Battalions pre-deployed in the city?

Or is it possible that the bomb threats are something completely different. A false-flag operation? An excuse to impose martial law, to suspend civil rights, to purge the government, to expel the immigrants, to round up the usual suspects?

When the tanks have passed, Kate cuts across the boulevard. She turns onto a quiet street, then again onto an even quieter one, narrow, tidy.

She deposits her bike at a docking station, looks around, walks away. No one in sight. Kate doubles back to the corner, crosses the street in the other direction.

Still no one.

The entrance to the private street is barred with two gates, one for pedestrians, the other just wide enough for a single car lane, drop-offs and pickups only, no parking allowed, no way for anyone to lurk in a parked car, watching her. No way for anyone to lurk, period.

The lock's code is a number that Kate knows only in French. She memorized the string of digits in French, she tells it to people in French, it's a sequence that's lodged in her brain in this second language of hers, an expanding vocabulary of ideas that she expresses primarily in French, like the backup player who comes off the bench and, sometimes, is stronger. When Kate meets new people, even in English, she says *"Enchantée"* with a straight face. Enchanted to meet you.

There are a few private residences on the short street, but mostly it's professional—a psychoanalyst, a law office, *cabinet de dentiste.* It's both busy and quiet.

Finding this office space had been Kate's first task for the Paris Substation. Someplace where freelancers and sources could come and go without attracting too much attention, somewhere private yet accessible, and convenient for Kate to meet the people she'd need to meet—a quick drink in a café, a blind pass in a park, a discreet encounter in a boutique.

At that point she'd been living in Paris for more than a year, she thought she knew the city well. But looking around for the perfect spot, Kate discovered that she really knew only the same Paris that Dexter knew, the other expats too, a few finite sections of the central *arrondissements* and a couple of select suburbs. She wasn't familiar with the greater city of working-class quarters and commercial ones and the residential *faubourgs* far from her own. She also couldn't have told you the location of the Greek Embassy. Now she can.

Downstairs in the small building, the *rez-de-chaussée* is occupied by an OB-GYN, pregnant women constantly coming and going. Kate is not concerned with pregnant women.

Upstairs, the Paris Substation occupies a couple of rooms, a few desks, computer monitors, a landline that no one uses. Installing all the electronics was not simple, making sure everything was secure and would stay that way.

Thierry, already at his desk, looks up when the boss enters. Kate raises her eyebrows, asking: do you know what the hell is going on? He shakes his head in reply, then turns back to his screen.

More than a dozen items are strewn atop Kate's desk, which at first glance—or second or third—doesn't look particularly neat, keyboard and mouse, in-box and stapler, pencil cup and notepad and tape dispenser, all the normal things you find on a worktop. They're not equidistant from one another, they're not aligned in a grid, they're not arranged in any noticeable fashion.

Except they are.

Moving from the front of the desk to the rear, each item is one centimeter farther away than the distance between the two previous items, as measured at their shortest gaps. Always. Every time Kate takes this seat, the first thing she does is check all the distances, using a tape measure in her top drawer. No one has touched anything, not today, not ever.

Now she can start looking for answers.

Her first call is to a man listed in her app under a different name, with a different address, as the proprietor of a catering outfit. "I cannot talk to you now," he says. No *bonjour,* no nothing. "You know that."

She's not surprised.

Another call, to a supposed hairdresser: this one doesn't even pick up.

Another, another, another, almost no one picks up, and Kate doesn't leave messages. Everyone has caller ID, so it's clear that her sources don't want to talk to Kate now, not on the telephone, not so she can ask questions. On a day like today, the only thing anyone wants from Kate are answers. She has none.

The only people who answer are those who don't know anything; "I don't think" and "I don't know" are how their sentences begin; "Sorry" is how they end.

She's getting nowhere, accomplishing nothing except proving to herself that she's exhausting every possible resource before escalating to the next level. Sometimes that's what you need to do.

Public transportation is going to be unreliable, cars won't be productive, bicycles may not be fast enough. Today is one of those circumstances for which Kate saves the moped, which she now takes down the Chaillot hill, toward the river, where the luxury is a bit louder, the conspicuous-consumption flagships and five-star everything, a neighborhood catering to people who want—who demand—something special, if just anyone can have it they don't want it, their cultural currency is unique experiences. Even though the hotels here, the restaurants, are mostly the generic variety of five-star posh that could be anywhere, menus indistinguishable, linens, obsequious staff, and everyone speaks English, it's all the same, could be Mayfair, could be Madison Avenue.

The old mansion is an imposing pile of blinding white limestone on a quiet side street that's off the path beaten by most tourists. The business plan never anticipated much in the way of walk-in customers, casual browsers, people wandering in to buy group tickets to Versailles. Well-heeled globetrotters come here on purpose, looking for something specific, something special.

One side of the street level is dominated by a plate-glass window,

TRAVELERS INTERNATIONAL BOOKING SERVICE in black lettering with gold outline. Kate puts her hand on the doorknob, turns, pulls. The glass rattles, but the door doesn't budge. She turns the knob the other way. Pushes. Still nothing.

Through the window, Kate meets the eye of the woman sitting at the first of three desks, who reaches down, *buzz,* the door unlocks.

"*Bonjour Madame Anderson.*"

Kate catches a sound bite of news before the young woman mutes her computer's speakers, then turns to Kate wearing a professional smile and a nametag that reads MANON. This office has already been open for a half-hour, but on a day like today Manon probably wasn't expecting any customers yet.

Manon taps on her keyboard, squints at her screen. "I do not believe we have anything for you?" She uses a key to unlock a drawer filled with boarding passes, travel dossiers, long itineraries with contact numbers and addresses and instructions, opera tickets, backstage passes, SIM cards, the occasional passport stamped with foreign visas. And for special clients like Mme. Anderson, the agency is willing to provide extra services that cost the office practically nothing while generating ample goodwill. Like accepting international courier packages, envelopes of various shapes and sizes that are delivered by mail, by messenger, sometimes by the inscrutable woman who works upstairs.

"I want to arrange a new trip," Kate says.

"*Très bien Madame.* To where, please?"

"Beirut."

The smile remains on the woman's face, but she doesn't say anything. Beirut has not been a popular tourist destination recently. Plus this travel agency is owned by a New York magazine conglomerate, and its mostly American clientele doesn't tend to book trips to Beirut from Paris.

"Do you have a colleague who is familiar with Beirut?"

Manon's smile sags, but doesn't disappear entirely. "*Oui.*" She's wearing a headset connected to a keypad, which she jabs using the eraser end of a pencil, protecting her perfectly manicured nails. She rotates in her chair, spinning away so the customer can't hear this in-house interaction, low voice, an economy of words.

"*C'est bon,*" Manon says, rearranging her smile. Everything is very good. "*Un moment.*"

❧

"*Madame*?" It's another woman standing back there, young and dark-haired and attractive, though not as put-together as Manon, not as blown-out and made-up, not as consumer-facing. This more serious-looking woman assesses Kate from across the room, and Kate in turn sizes her up.

"*S'il vous plaît*," this woman says, indicating the open door.

They don't shake hands or introduce themselves. It would be impossible for anyone to tell whether or not these two women have met before. Kate steps into a small office, its walls lined with international travel posters—*Afrique, Suède, Brésil, Italie.* No windows. A modern, functional desk.

"How can I help you, Madame Anderson?"

"I would like to arrange a trip to Beirut," Kate repeats. She can smell the woman's cigarettes coming off her hair, her clothes.

"How many people?"

They are still standing, awkwardly, next to the desk. Kate wonders if she's going to be offered a seat. "There are five of us," Kate says. "Myself, my husband, three children." This fabrication—she has only two children—is one part of the code.

"And do you have a preferred hotel?"

"I do. The Kempinski."

And this is the other. The codes are for the benefit of other people who might be in this quasi-public space; you never know. There are no other customers in this room, but the codes are the protocol, and the protocol is sacrosanct.

"*Très bien.*"

This woman opens a deadbolt at another door at the far end of the office, and Kate follows her out of the grim little space into a grand one, the mansion's polished lobby of marble floors, ornate moldings, soaring ceiling, crystal chandelier. Up a sweeping staircase to the *premier étage,* a wide hall lined with glossy black doors. She unlocks the first of these doors using a key card.

This room is extremely large and cluttered, a few desks strewn around, filing cabinets everywhere, screens and keyboards and a dusty typewriter wedged into a corner, maps and posters and corkboards and even a couple of oil paintings, all hung with no apparent plan. It looks like a small-town newsroom run by an eccentric, thirty years ago. Kate had imagined something else, something twenty-first-century, high-tech.

The woman shuts the door behind her, says, *"Je m'appelle Inez."*

"Kate." They shake hands.

It's not just the room that's defying expectations, it's this person too. Is this young Frenchwoman really running the Paris bureau of an American clandestine service? Kate had envisaged a middle-aged man from the East Coast. Then again, Kate too is someone who runs the Paris bureau of an American clandestine service.

Inez turns back to the door, reaches up to the locks. As a matter of habit, Kate glances at the woman's ring finger, and notices that she isn't wearing a wedding band. What Inez is wearing is a shoulder holster, and it isn't empty.

"Please, Kate, take yourself a seat."

A wall-mounted television displays an anchorman sitting at a desk, a crawl that proclaims TERRORISME À PARIS, a screen that's split with video from a helicopter at a great distance, an overhead image of the Louvre that communicates practically nothing, not unless there's a large explosion, which is probably the point of this angle: to record the explosion.

"Okay," Kate says, taking a narrow wooden chair. Inez's own chair is a large curvy plastic-mesh affair that suggests ergonomics, lumbar support, chiropractors, science. "What can you tell me about all this today?"

Inez nods curtly, down to business. "At 8:41, the police received the following telephone call from a mobile." She taps on her keyboard, clicks an icon and then another and another.

A digitally scrambled voice speaks in a monotone: *"A remote-detonated bomb has been placed in the main hall of the Gare de Lyon. If you attempt to disable the bomb, we will detonate. Await further instructions."* The recording ends. "And again, from twenty-four minutes later." Inez cues up the second track: *"A bomb has been placed at the Arc de Triomphe. Await further instructions.* Another on the subject of place Vendôme, and finally Notre-Dame."

"Are there actually bombs at these locations?"

"There are bags confirmed at the locations that could contain explosive devices."

"Or?"

"Or the bags might not contain explosive devices."

"Why would anyone do that?"

"I am not suggesting that anyone has done that. I am saying that it is not yet confirmed that these bags are . . . *comment dit-on?*—weaponized."

This is a very precise woman.

"*Ensuite,* as you know"—Inez indicates the TV—"a man arrived to the Louvre wearing a suicide vest, also carrying what has the appearance of a bomb in a briefcase."

Inez clicks around some more, opens a video feed from a camera that's positioned high above the Louvre, aiming down at the man who's standing between the pyramids. The scene appears unchanged since Kate was there an hour ago.

"This is a livestream?"

"*Oui.* The camera is from the police on the roof of the Louvre. The police are in command of the scene, but I do not doubt that at this moment self-important men are making arguments on the subject of who should make the decisions. *Comme toujours.*"

"No group has claimed responsibility? No demands?"

"Not that I know."

Kate stares at the monitor. She isn't surprised that Inez managed to intercept the phone recordings, which had probably been forwarded to hundreds of people, sprayed out to law enforcement and national intelligence, the mayor and his deputies, local politicians and national ones, foreign embassies, even the CIA. A very wide and hasty distribution, with potential leaks aplenty. No way to keep it all secure.

But this real-time video is not being e-mailed to anyone. This feed represents an impressive level of intrusion into the police's security.

Kate has no idea what size facility is here in this mansion, what resources, what personnel. This office doesn't look like much, but it's a big building, and Kate has seen only a small portion of it. There's more.

"How did you obtain this access?"

"*C'est pas important.*"

Of course it's important. But Kate is a guest here, doesn't have the right to make demands. In this business, everyone deserves to keep their own secrets, and everyone else knows it.

These two strangers have been thrust into a position where they're supposed to trust each other, in the same way that civilians are supposed to trust their bankers, their lawyers. But in Kate's world the blind trust is not with some of your money, or elective surgery, but like trusting someone to catch you when you've made the deliberate choice to fall backward, without a net, off a cliff.

⚜

Hayden had let her dangle there in that Copenhagen apartment, grinning while Kate's curiosity mounted.

"*Tell me,*" she pled.

"You're going to *adore* this, Kate."

"Oh for the love of—"

"The Travelers section is, in addition to being a courier service, also a complete parallel intelligence service. With officers, agents, assets, the whole shebang. This cadre occupies a thoroughly separate reporting structure, like us. But unlike us, their bureau chiefs report directly to someone in New York."

"New York? That's nuts. What's in New York?"

"The editor of the magazine. He in turn reports directly to the DCI."

"The director himself? God. And did you say bureau *chiefs,* plural? There's more than one of these bureaus?"

"There are dozens."

Kate was having trouble grasping this. "How long has this been going on?"

"The program began right after World War II, as solely the courier service. It evolved."

"That's incredible. But how is this related to us?"

"It's not, other than our unusual level of independence from Langley. But we both operate out of Paris, so we've agreed to pool resources, in a pinch. If you ever find yourself in one, go there. Say you want to arrange a trip to Beirut . . ."

That's when Hayden explained how to make contact with the head of the Travelers' Paris Bureau. But then he got pulled away by an urgent call, and the next time Kate saw him was when the action was beginning across the street in the hacker's apartment, which spiraled out of control—a shootout followed by a frantic chase, a failed mission and dead bodies. Nørrebro turned out to be the last place Kate ever saw Hayden. He never did get around to telling her who it was back in America who provided Kate with her targets.

In the weeks and months that followed Hayden's disappearance, Kate began to suspect that he'd known exactly what was going to happen across the street, and then across the ocean. She kept remembering a piece of his advice, something he'd taught her when she was new and still figuring out how to make her way in the Agency, how to make things happen in the world: a carefully orchestrated disaster can be the perfect diversion.

32

She's staring out at the sun-drenched *campo,* trying to appreciate the beautiful surroundings instead of the horrific noise. She's failing.

The boy's midday nap was supposed to begin a half-hour ago, but Matteo is refusing vociferously, going red in the face, then purple. If she didn't know better, she'd think that the baby was suffocating. But she does know better. That's apparently what motherhood is: learning to know better.

The kid doesn't want to eat. He doesn't need a new diaper, doesn't want to be held or rocked. He doesn't want anything that she can provide, and her attempts at soothing him serve only to antagonize.

The decibel level is brutal. Like an enhanced interrogation technique, something outlawed by the Geneva Conventions.

At least she doesn't have to worry about bothering the neighbors. The apartment's walls are thick plaster, the under-flooring solid beneath the elaborate parquet, everything efficiently soundproofed as a side effect of old-fashioned workmanship, a building that dates back at least six hundred years, maybe seven, it's hard to be exact for some of these structures, which have undergone so many transformations over the centuries, transfers of ownership, major renovations, lost records.

You wouldn't think that such a tiny animal could make such a racket.

How many babies have cried in this room? Renaissance babies, Baroque babies, Fascist babies. Thirty generations? Forty? Hundreds of babies have wailed here in this well-constructed room, each and every one of them driving their mothers up a tree.

One of the things she has learned about the child-screaming sound is that it erodes rationality, compromises your ability to make lucid, purposeful choices. An evolutionary mechanism that prevents mothers from ignoring distressed offspring. Like the babies' cuteness, from the other direction. Cuteness is the carrot. This screaming, this is the fucking stick.

The kid screams yet louder, if that's possible.

⚜

She bundles him up into a little pastel packet, a sweater that's beginning to strain at the seams, a matching cap. She binds her own long hair into a ponytail, puts on the oversize sunglasses that she wears for walks regardless of the weather, whenever she's going out in public for a while, visible in the narrow pedestrian lanes of Venice where everyone looks everyone else in the face, at close range. It's easy to be recognized here, if you're recognizable, and if you don't take precautions. If someone is looking for you.

As soon as she moved to Italy, she dyed her hair, her eyebrows too. She can't help but think she looks Italian now, from somewhere in the south. It makes her wonder if her Polish ancestry is more mixed than she'd been led to believe; almost everyone's is. And even after all this time, she's still not accustomed to this raven-haired look, still wonders *Who the hell is that woman?* when she catches sight of herself in a mirror. Not just the hair length and color, but also the big glasses, the absence of makeup, the loose flowing clothing. It would take a vigilant, focused eye for anyone to see under all that, to recognize her as the woman she used to be.

The truth is that she no longer is that same woman, and not just in appearance. The baby changed so much, especially after all she'd been through to carry to term. The husband too, he'd necessitated a lot of changes in her, after so many years without one. And the end of her career, the dissolution of her identity as a respected professional. The setbacks she'd faced—the immense failure, the public disgrace, the hasty relocations, the itinerant lifestyle. Every single aspect of her life.

But in some important respects, she's still exactly the same. Her fingerprints, for example. Her dental records, the bright white mouthful expensively aligned by aggressive American orthodontia. Her ambition, and willingness to bend rules and laws to serve it.

She double-checks that her primary phone has held its charge; now would be a terrible time to be unavailable. She jacks in the headphones, puts a little speaker into one ear, leaves the other free to hear the sounds of the world around her. Pats down her pockets for keys, wallet, the extra pacifier she always carries, diaper, wipes.

She straps the baby into the Swedish baby-carrying contraption, clips clicking, tugging taut.

Finally she pulls open the drawer of the small table next to the front door. She removes the tourism guidebook and the Italian-English dictionary, sets these heavy tomes atop the table, next to the bowl of coins, *vaporetti* tickets, a notepad whose top sheet is usually a shopping list.

With the drawer empty, she runs her fingertip along a seam where the bottom panel meets the side, until she finds the narrow gap, just wide enough for a fingernail.

Retrofitting this drawer was one of the first projects her husband tackled immediately after they moved into this apartment, fresh from their cleansing exile in the Wild West of southern Sicily, where she'd given birth to this baby boy. It was a carpentry job that took him a couple of days—sketching and shopping, sawing and sanding, gluing and clamping.

They have been extremely careful. Every piece of furniture in this apartment came with the lease; the bed linens, the bath towels, the kitchenware, everything. They paid cash for the small additional items they've needed; they established telecom and utility accounts using airtight aliases. They use a rotating assortment of burner phones, replacing them on a regular basis. It's fun, destroying phones. She uses a ball-peen hammer.

Rural Sicily was much more third-world than first, agrarian and analog, sparsely populated and mostly poor and corruptly governed, a place where official favors can be bought from bank clerks, from state ministries, from hospital administrators, favors that can be used to construct new identities with all necessary documentation.

Sicilians had become somewhat inured to illegal migrants, to undocumented people arriving by the literal boatload. But those were North Africans and Middle Easterns, desperate people escaping war-torn hellscapes, risking their lives on treacherous crossings in watercraft of questionable seaworthiness, with unknown prospects on the far shore. It was almost a relief for the Sicilians to be accepting substantial bribes from prosperous-looking Americans, even if these Americans were clearly up to no good. At least there weren't any humanitarian dilemmas to consider, war crimes, genocides.

She'd been gone from America for a half-decade now, except for that scant single year back in Washington when she discovered that while she'd followed her career out of the country, all her unmarried friends back home seemed to have stumbled into long-term relationships, and all her married friends had spawned children. Her college classmates, her work colleagues, her neighbors, everyone procreating all at once. A contagion.

Here in Italy, she gave her own baby an Italian name, a name that might make it less obvious that the adults were a pair of Americans, that might make people wonder if she was of Italian heritage, speculate on some excuse for Americans to be living here, a story they could tell other than the truth.

The drawer's bottom panel pivots upward from a rear hinge. A few items are arranged in the false-bottom recess, each occupying its own carefully proportioned niche, the whole arrangement constructed from balsa strips and crushed velvet to prevent the contents from sliding around and creating noises that might make someone wonder what the hell is in this piece of occasional furniture, and where exactly, and why.

She collects one of the items from its housing, slips it into the big pocket in her jacket, right there with the more usual things that a mom carries.

She pulls the door closed behind her, double-checks that the lock engaged. With this kid screaming in her ear, it's impossible to hear things like the clicking of locks. She squats to pick up a strand of her hair that's resting on the door's saddle. Licks the tips of her forefinger and thumb, and runs these moistened fingertips down the length of hair, which she saliva-sticks against the door and jamb, positioned at exactly the same level as the widest of five separate nicks in the wood.

Every time she leaves the apartment, she uses this discrete privacy seal. Sometimes it's hard to imagine that anyone would still be looking for her, but that's the sort of resigned, exhausted complacency that can lead to disaster.

She walks down the well-worn stone staircase carefully; she doesn't want to tumble herself and her baby headlong into the emergency room. Through the dark damp lobby, where the kid's crying sounds extra-shrill, bouncing off the tall ceilings and stone walls and floors. She pushes open the gigantic slab of door, and bursts into the bright sunlight of the *campo*.

If they ever move back to the United States—an unlikely eventuality—they'd have the option of shortening the kid's name to Matt without the transformation seeming absurd to him, without it being something they'd need to explain with a series of unsustainable lies. Or he could simply remain Matteo, which at that point might be just as common in America.

She still holds out hope that they'll eventually live some version of a normal life, settled in one place, using one set of names consistently, telling mostly the truth to most people, most of the time. But she knows it's a slim hope. Very slim.

33

"*Alors.*" Inez is staring intently at her screen. "Something in Hong Kong. A man was detained attempting to bring a bomb into an office."

"What type of man?"

"What is it you are asking?"

"Does he seem Muslim?"

While Inez turns back to the screen, Kate glances around the cluttered office, paper everywhere. In Kate's office, there's practically none.

"It seems he is American."

"Are you sure?"

Inez gives her a look, *What do you want from me?*

"Anywhere else, besides Hong Kong?"

Inez clicks open a new window, scans line after line of incident reports—street-crime gunfire, a prison break in Kenya, a bank heist in Saigon. It's still too early in the Americas for any law-enforcement alerts, although a hurricane is forming in the Gulf of Mexico. This time of year, a hurricane is almost always forming in the Gulf of Mexico. The opposite of news.

The Frenchwoman leans forward. "*Voilà*: Mumbai, a bomb threat is made to a building."

Another bomb in another office building? "Directed against any specific occupant?"

Click, and click again. "*Non*, it does not appear so."

"You have the Mumbai address?"

"*Oui.*"

"Of the building in Hong Kong also?"

Inez toggles to another window—"*Voilà*"—understanding what to do next, typing both addresses into a search, and it doesn't take even a second for the results page to load, and there at the top, the very first commonality—

✤

Kate feels the air sucked out of her through the hole in her soul that had been blasted open in Luxembourg, decimating the fortifications of truth and honesty and trust that we all rely upon to make it through the day. She'd thought that the hole had been repaired, but maybe it had been shoddy workmanship, bound to fall apart sooner or later.

"This has importance for you?"

Kate nods.

"It is an American company, *n'est-ce pas?*"

"Yes. Listen, would you mind?" She indicates the keyboard, the screen. Inez nods, stands, and the two switch places. Kate's fingers clatter across the keyboard. A new page loads, displaying two hits, one address in La Défense, another in the *huitième,* with map windows. One of the red stars is a kilometer away.

Kate can't wrap her mind around what exactly this means. But it's definitely not nothing.

"Are any of your phone lines clean?" A plan is forming, a way to find answers.

"*Évidemment,*" Inez says. "All of them."

Kate dials the main number of the company, and the line is answered before the first ring is complete. "*Bonjour,* thank you for calling 4Syte Paris, how may I direct your call?"

"I'm trying to reach the public-relations department."

"Hold one minute, please." But Kate has to wait only seconds before someone new comes on the line. "*Bonjour!* This is Schuyler Franks in community engagement?"

Kate's fingers fly, typing in *Schuyler Franks* and *4Syte* and *Paris,* and the young woman's photo pops up, her contact info, hits for a LinkedIn profile, Facebook, a college young-alumni association and a volleyball team and a high-school graduating class, an article in a local newspaper about where the graduates will attend college. There's so much information about everyone, so available, requiring so little effort.

"Hi Schuyler. I'm looking for Hunter Forsyth."

"I'm sorry, Mr. Forsyth isn't available? What's this regarding?"

"Is he in the office?"

"I'm sorry, may I ask who's calling?"

"Is Hunter Forsyth on your premises at this moment?"

"I'm sorry, ma'am, but that information isn't something I can just, y'know, *give out* to anyone? But if you help me understand why you're asking? That would be *super*-helpful?"

So: the staff are still in their offices, not evacuated; these women both sound calm, business as normal. Which means the Paris office is not under attack, no violent threat has been made against 4Syte's European headquarters. At least not yet. Or not in the same way.

Hayden had been right: after a few weeks, Kate was summoned to a meet. For the only time since the Paris Substation was established.

She spotted her contact right away, limping his way through the park, sidestepping the children darting about, smiling indulgently at the little ones flinging sand, their mothers gossiping on benches. This man was clearly a father himself, accustomed to the constant disarray, always prepared for crisis.

The place des Vosges was a well-chosen venue, large enough to be anonymous but small enough that from the right vantage you can see nearly everyone scattered around the park's well-groomed foliage, the square-cut trees, the conical shrubs.

The man collapsed onto one of those uncomfortable-looking high-backed wooden benches near a fountain. He didn't seem old enough to be so exhausted, so tottering. Injury, Kate guessed, maybe he'd blown out his knee in the weekly pickup game with guys from law school. He looked like he could've been from New York, as Hayden suspected. But then again he could've been from Washington, or Langley, or Moscow via an intensive English-language immersion program in New Hampshire. He could've been from anywhere. If someone makes a concerted, professional effort, it's impossible to tell.

Clusters of teenagers were nearby, sitting cross-legged, smoking cigarettes. A grade-school girl was doing a tumbling routine on one patch of grass, while on another a couple of boys were kicking a ball. Neither field was quite big enough for its activity, but the kids were making do. City kids, city life.

The American man unfolded a newspaper, crossed his legs gingerly. He lit a cigarette. After just a single drag, he tossed the butt, ground it out on the dirt path littered with leaves, with twigs, but with surprisingly few cigarette butts.

Despite appearances, those high-backed benches are surprisingly comfortable. Kate rose from hers, and made her approach.

⚜

"*Bonjour?*" Dexter answers tentatively. He doesn't recognize the number; Kate has placed this call on a Travelers' secure line.

"Hi Dex."

"Hello my wife. This is a lot of phone calls for us, isn't it?"

"Listen: where'd you get your information about 4Syte?"

"My information?"

"You know what I'm asking."

He pauses, then admits: "Luc."

"And where'd he get it?"

"We shouldn't be talking about this on the phone, should we?"

"Why not?"

He doesn't answer, which is all the answer she needs. Then he says, "An investor named Reinhard Jeckelmann. I think you met him, at Luc's party?"

A louche affair with an ill-conceived guest list, an embarrassing imbalance of single women, free radicals floating around the party, gravitating toward the men, many of them married. Kate remembers Jeckelmann as a disagreeable German, angular eyeglasses and poor manners, a general brusqueness.

"And where did Jeckelmann get *his* info?"

"Someone inside 4Syte, but I don't know who exactly. Jeckelmann didn't tell Luc, or Luc didn't tell me, and I didn't feel like I could press him. Or should."

"Why'd this person come forward to Jeckelmann with this leak?"

"They knew each other somehow. Earlier in life."

"But you don't know how?"

"That's not something anyone would share. To protect everyone else."

That makes sense. But that doesn't make it true. "And you just accepted this?"

"No, I didn't just accept this. I did exhaustive due diligence. I made dozens of calls, full days of research."

She sighs loudly enough for him to hear, on purpose.

"This information is not slam-dunk true, Kate, but I've executed far more speculative trades based on far less convincing intel, successfully. Profitably."

Profitability is no longer Kate's primary concern. But she doesn't want to share her suspicions with Dexter, at least not yet. She doesn't want him to flip out. "Has anyone ever given you info like this before?"

"Sure. Some people have shared tips with me. And vice versa."

"Anything illegal, Dex?"

A second of silence, two. "It's not always black-and-white."

Kate had been in command of the Paris Substation, temporarily, until Hayden returned; but he never did. So Kate was in command until a replacement was found; but a replacement was never found. So this man had come to Paris to tell Kate that she was now in command, full stop.

"This substation is yours," he said. "Are you ready for it?"

"I am," Kate answered quickly, trying to manufacture self-confidence by projecting it. She had no idea if she was really ready. But she definitely wanted it.

"I guess we'll find out," he said, pushing himself up with a wince and a low groan.

When she was young, Kate imagined that these moves happened by careful design, with exhaustive interviews and committee meetings and long training periods. But she'd come to understand that life doesn't work that way. So much is haphazard, one short-term problem solved after another, with scarcely a sideways glance at any big picture.

That's how someone like her can be thrust from a part-time position to full-time, from freelancer to manager of a secret substation that's subject to no chain of command, no oversight. Which unfortunately also meant no access to Agency resources, assets, networks, files, personnel.

Nothing except a tenuous connection to this other clandestine bureau, managed by a Frenchwoman, hiding above a high-end travel bureau.

This isn't the way anyone would deliberately design anything, but here it was, here Kate was, suddenly abuzz, more excited than she would've expected. She'd come to the place des Vosges fully prepared to be fired, she was already considering options on how to console herself. But instead she was leaving with a giant promotion bestowed by this man from New York, who despite the creaky limbs was sexy, and the thought of him flickered in her brain, a fleeting fantasy, or maybe it wasn't exactly her brain that generated this idea that propelled her homeward as fast as possible, pedaling across the Île St-Louis and then along the actual bank of the Left Bank, ditching the bike, rushing upstairs.

"Hey?" Dexter said, turning away from his computer, surprised to see his wife in the middle of the afternoon. "What are you doing here?"

"Let's make this quick." Kate unfurled her panties, dropped them to the floor. She was planning to keep everything else on, even her boots. Especially her boots. "I need to get back to work."

She stands at the mirror in the Travelers' small bathroom. She unzips an interior pocket of her handbag, removes a nylon packet. She extracts a couple of hairpins, and secures her hair tightly to her scalp. Then she pulls out a blond wig, a messy mop of coif, a distraction of a hairstyle. She tugs here, pushes there, good enough. She adds a set of thick-framed eyeglasses.

"Okay," she says to Inez. "Let's go. I'll explain on the way."

34

". . . and stocks are down *across* the board due to *massive* uncertainty regarding the ongoing terror attack in Paris, which is about to enter the *third* hour of a standoff between an apparent *suicide* bomber at the Louvre and the authorities."

Dexter looks out the dormer window, past the shutters that hang on hinges topped with finials that are little cast-bronze statuettes of men, tiny servants whose job it is to preside over hinges.

"We also have *un*confirmed reports—and let me stress, these reports have been neither confirmed *nor* denied by *any* officials—of *other* threats against high-visibility targets in Paris, beyond the Louvre and the Gare de Lyon. And we *just* learned, only moments ago, that there might be a threat in *Mumbai,* and that's where we go now, to our . . ."

Dexter listens to the Indian reporter for only a minute before he understands that she doesn't know anything. This is the sort of report that didn't exist until the advent of twenty-four-hour so-called news stations that need to fill every moment of every day with something, preferably alarming, to prevent viewers from changing the channel.

He lowers the volume of this report in one of the windows on his large screen, the one he uses to monitor the international broadcast-news stations to which he pays varying degrees of attention, plus the home-pages of a few media outlets that continue to be known as newspapers, despite the increasing irrelevancy of the actual paper.

Otherwise, Dexter's vision is filled with numbers, almost entirely red. Over the past hour, the share price of nearly everything to do with Europe has dropped, at least incrementally, and some of it dramatically. It's not a general panic, but it's getting close. And if the Louvre situation doesn't get resolved soon, who the hell knows.

This is both good and bad. Dexter obviously wants one particular stock to tank, but he's extremely motivated for some others to turn it around. Just thinking about it makes his chest tighten. He stands, stretches, takes a few purposeful breaths . . .

That's not enough; he needs a real break.

Some days Dexter doesn't even emerge from the apartment for lunch. He keeps the refrigerator stocked with yogurt, little glass jars of different combinations of fruits and spices and sweeteners. The nearby *supérette*'s largest section is yogurt, everyone in Paris seems to eat it with every meal. Yogurt or Nutella, sometimes both.

Something is tugging vaguely at his consciousness, pulling his concentration into some murky corner where he can't recognize what it is that his mind's eye is trying to look at.

Is it something he just learned, or should have? Or . . . ?

Dexter showers, dresses himself like a grown-up Frenchman. He's still a nerd, and will be forevermore, but he can no longer be identified as one as quickly, from as far away. Dexter is of that generation who embraced nerdiness as a badge of so-called authenticity, contriving to be uncool by exaggerating their awkwardness, shuffling their feet and slouching their shoulders and stammering, wearing shirts that didn't fit in colors that didn't flatter, a uniform of antifashion.

Then he turned forty-five, and realized he looked like an idiot. He stopped wearing sneakers except for exercise. Started wearing jackets—actually, *jacket* in the singular, the same navy canvas every day. Button-down shirts in a finite assortment of light blue or white, no more T-shirts. He has forsaken the geeky rimless Bill Gates look for tortoiseshell eyeglasses, and every six weeks he endures a proper haircut from a stylist, a concession to his wife, who had grown tired of looking at his walk-in-barbershop hatchet jobs.

He has even begun to clasp his hands behind his back, like any other middle-aged-plus Frenchman walking down the boulevard. Trying it out.

It wasn't just the bad haircuts that Kate had grown tired of. And she'd grown tired of keeping it all to herself. They'd had a tumultuous few years. It would be a mistake to pretend that the rough patch was over. Maybe it never would be. Maybe that's not how marriage works.

❖

When the realization makes a sneak-attack on his consciousness, Dexter runs back down the hall wearing only one shoe, rushing toward his computer, trying to figure out what this could mean . . .

He'd been taken advantage of before, exploited, while he'd been utterly convinced that he was being the genius, that he'd anticipated every possible problem. Afterward, he told himself: never again.

So now he sits at his terminal, staring at the news reporter, a stand-up shot in a busy city on another continent, trying to figure out if there can be any connection among terror threats here in Paris, and terror threats there in Mumbai, and himself.

Yes.

❖

For such a long time, Dexter and Kate had lived so responsibly, and he'd disdained the rampant profligacy he saw everywhere in America, consumerism amok, all the fossil-fueled toys—the SUVs and ATVs, the speedboats and Jet Skis—and the double-height foyers and picture-windowed great rooms and slate-surrounded swimming pools, every house twice as big as anyone needed, wall-mounted plasma TVs everywhere.

Even as Dexter scorned all this acquisitiveness, he also envied these people. Not their stuff, but the freedom they enjoyed to be so irresponsible.

Then his own money started to flow in. His trades were predominantly positive, and his confidence grew each week as he tallied the results on his obsessively maintained spreadsheet of realized gains and losses, of current valuations against purchase prices. So one decision at a time, they took on this increasingly expensive life: Paris, the international school, the apartment, matching luggage and Michelin stars, an incremental accumulation of comfort, restaurants three or four nights a week, Tuesday-night family suppers of nothing special—roast chicken, wood-oven pizzas—whose bill comes to a hundred euros.

Dexter had allowed himself to fall victim to the excess of confidence that can come with an insufficiency of experience. Something he'd been quick to notice in other people, but was awfully slow to recognize in himself. This isn't so hard, you tell yourself. That nincompoop over there can do it, so can I.

So perhaps this is what he has coming to him, like any other over-extended entitled American who thought he deserved everything.

There are so many awful aspects. The constant sense of dread, the nightmares, the panic attacks. The shame and embarrassment of having been so wrong; not only of being such a rank amateur, but of being unwilling to acknowledge it, even to himself. The intense loneliness, unable to share his problems with anyone, especially with his wife, who's not only the single person who'd care the most, the one person most affected, but also the only person with whom he'd want to discuss it.

He's reminded of Hemingway's line from *The Sun Also Rises*, Mike explaining how he went bankrupt: "Gradually, then suddenly." Dexter used to think it was funny.

He knows there have to be many commonalities between Mumbai and Paris, but at the moment he can think of only the one, and only one reason for it.

35

PARIS. 12:19 P.M.

Kate examines another of those huge doors that are everywhere in Paris, big enough for horse and carriage, doors that open up to schools, to courtyards, to private mews, to that surprisingly large segment of the city that isn't visible to the public. This set is wide open, and the broad archway between is barricaded with magnetic-card turnstiles, and a small hut where a guard sits, looking bored. It's an unusual level of security for a Paris office building, but Kate isn't surprised. Inside is an American tech company, and almost no one is more paranoid, except absolutely everyone in Kate's line of work.

Inez pulls up on her own Vespa, parks a few meters beyond Kate's.

A small crowd of young people is clustered on the sidewalk for their *pause clope,* each wearing an ID badge hanging from a lanyard, or clipped to a lapel. Everybody under thirty in Paris seems to smoke. It's like America a hundred years ago.

"Do you have any credentials?" Kate asks as Inez stows her helmet.

"Credentials?"

Kate cuts her eyes across the street.

"Ah," Inez says, seeing the security guard, understanding. *"Non."*

Kate herself doesn't have any authority here, no reason for anyone to let her in anywhere, to provide her with any information about anything. "Can you make a distraction?"

Inez cocks her head, running through the imaginary interaction, her line of dialogue, his. "Yes." She glances down at herself, her blouse. Unclasps a button. "I will have the guard open his door. It will be three, four seconds after, that is when you should be at the gate. *Ça marche?*"

"Yes."

"The mark will be when I sneeze. Then sixty seconds precisely. *D'accord?*"

Kate nods. She glances around, searching for any apparent problem, any reason not to do this right now—

Oh my God, look at that.

"One moment," Kate says. "I'll be right back."

Kate was the one who'd done everything. The research, the specialists, the pharmacies, the follow-ups, every medical assessment of her shirtless little boy, his bony shoulders and hollowed-out chest, he looked so fragile, so vulnerable, so quiet, so scared. This was the boy who used to laugh so easily, not just at the joke in front of him in the book or the movie, but at all the jokes in the world, the joke of life itself. Now he went entire days without even smiling.

And all the while, Dexter hung back, a dispirited spectator in the endeavor of keeping their child alive, like at a ballgame that wasn't going his team's way.

"Why aren't you doing any of this, Dexter?"

He looked confused, as if he didn't understand the point of the question, as if she'd asked, *What shape is the earth?* Everyone knows that, even the kids.

"Why is it me who has to take care of all of this? How did that become the default?" This wasn't about merely doctor's visits.

"Because you're the one who's best at this stuff," he said, matter-of-factly, as if this were a matter of actual fact, two plus two equals four. "You're in charge, Kate." Plain as day. "You've always been in charge."

But I never asked for that, she thought; we never agreed to that. And it wasn't even true! If Kate was in charge, why was it she who always did all the work? That's not what it means to be in charge.

Back when Kate didn't have a paying job, it made sense for her to assume all the household responsibilities. And when she first rejoined the workplace it was piecemeal, half-time, so they never reassigned the chores. That was her fault as well as his, this imbalance.

"You have to do more, Dexter. You have to care more."

"I care."

"Then you have to show it."

"I care plenty. That's a terrible thing to say. A terrible thing to think."

"I can't continue to do all this on my own. I can't come home from work trips to find actual litter on our floor. I can't collect every single prescription. I can't be the only one who ever serves the children a vegetable or puts away laundry or buys toilet paper or—"

"I buy—"

Her glare cut him off. "I don't know where the fuck you got the idea that this is how marriage works. But it's not, Dexter. Not one to me."

Is this how a marriage ends? Maybe it doesn't need to be a life-shattering betrayal, nothing explosive or dramatic, nothing cinematic, nothing filmable. Just an absence.

And that was exactly when Peter reentered her life. When Kate allowed him—invited him—back in.

That fault, that was hers, and hers alone.

The coveted box of Lego is right there in the *vitrine*. She could send a text to Dexter, letting him know it's here, saving him the trouble of searching. Or she could ignore it, leave her husband to fend for himself, and possibly fail, and suffer the boy's disappointment. Or she could walk into this store and buy it, solve her husband's problem for him, as usual.

It's not even really a decision. Ben needs something good to happen to him, and here it is.

"*Tout va bien?*" Inez asks.

"*Oui.*" Kate is wedging the box into her bag.

She composes a text to her husband. *Pls make sure bathrooms and bedrooms tidy.* She's not going to let him off the hook.

Then she turns to Inez. "*On y va.*"

Kate walks a few steps farther up the street, putting distance between herself and Inez, creating the appearance that they're not together. Just strangers who happen to be crossing the same street.

There's a gap in the traffic, a large truck that's lagging far behind a speeding taxi. Both women cross the street at different paces, alighting at different points on the opposite shore, where Kate comes to an immediate stop and watches Inez continue up the street, then turn into the archway, pause, push a button on her watch, and sneeze.

Kate starts a stopwatch on her phone.

Inez begins digging through her bag. She removes a wallet, sunglasses, a coin pouch. Kate can see the woman mutter to herself, shake her head, let out a frustrated huff. She drops her glasses, picks them up. Walks to the security hut, taps on the window.

Twenty seconds.

The guard looks up. Inez's mouth is moving, but Kate can't hear what she's saying.

Thirty seconds.

Inez makes a helpless gesture, palms up, please. The guard shakes his head, unmoved. *Non.*

Thirty-five.

Inez slips something out of her wallet, extends it toward the guard, who frowns, skeptical.

Forty.

Kate starts walking.

Inez extends her hand, shoving this thing at him, some irrelevancy.

Forty-five.

Kate is now close enough to hear him say, "*Désolé, Mademoiselle, mais c'est pas possible,*" the unremitting chorus of nay-saying that you hear whenever you try to get anything done, from every single representative of *l'administration,* the vast network of bureaucracies that underpins French society. *Sorry, but it's not possible.*

Fifty.

Inez beseeches, "*S'il vous plaît, Monsieur. C'est très important.*"

Now Kate is just a few steps away, perhaps getting too close too fast—

The guard relents, pushes open his glass door, and Inez steps toward him, and that's when her bag slips from her shoulder, slides down the length of her arm, past her elbow, her wrist, crashing to the floor—

"*Putain!*"

—fifty-five seconds—

—and as Inez kneels to collect her spilled belongings, her blouse billows, and the guard stares at the fabric's gape while Kate turns into the arch, and he steps forward toward this woman in distress, this attractive mess, while Kate slides behind him—

"*Oh, merci bien Monsieur . . .*"

—and hops the turnstile in one fluid motion, and strides forward as if she has every right in the world—

"*Merci,*" Inez repeats, gathering her things, tossing them back into the bag, then cutting her eyes up to the helpful man, giving him a small thankful smile.

"*De rien,*" the guard says with his own smile.

—and Kate disappears around the corner.

❧

The elevator opens onto a smoothly impersonal waiting room, right-angled and hard-edged, glass and chrome and large expanses of cold dark stone.

"*Bonjour,*" Kate says to the receptionist. "I'm here to see Schuyler Franks."

"*Bonjour.* Your name, please, Madame?"

"Lindsay Davis."

"*Un moment, Madame Davis.*"

The receptionist is wearing a headset, so Kate can't hear a thing, but from the woman's response it seems as if Schuyler is denying this appointment. It's taking longer than a quick dismissive "I don't have any appointment with any Lindsay Davis," so maybe Schuyler is searching her calendar, looking for this name, double-checking that she hasn't made some horrible mistake, because any mistake of any sort can be horrible when you work in PR, anyone you insult, any information you neglect to forward, any call you forget to return, any tiny thing can turn out to be a career-wrecking epic fail, this has been ingrained, the public-relations Hippocratic oath: first, do not offend.

"*Donc,* what do you want me to do?" The receptionist whispers. Then she turns back to Kate. "*S'il vous plaît,* Madame Davis. Mademoiselle Franks will be one minute."

There's already another woman waiting on a firm, uncomfortable-looking sofa, between end tables adorned with small stacks of magazines, tech and business, and a few of today's international newspapers. A security camera is suspended in one corner; Kate noticed a seeing eye in the elevator, and a pair of them at the security gates in the breezeway. Her presence here is being amply documented, she registers that now. But it won't be until later that she understands the magnitude of the threat this presents.

Pls get 6 candles, she types. *Plain white, no scent.* If there's one thing Kate hates, it's scented candles at the dinner table.

The other woman waiting is a middle-aged suit-wearing executive type, serious eyeglasses and sensible hair and a dour expression, constantly fidgeting with her collar, her neckline, as if worried that too much breast might be visible. She has smile-lines and crow's-feet and deep-set wrinkles across her forehead, the unmistakable look of someone who consumes a daily diet of recirculated office air and salad-bar lunches, too much work and too much stress, too little sleep and too little fun and far, far too little sex.

For a couple of years back in DC, Kate worried that she was on a path to becoming one of these women, officious and humorless, no room to project anything except hyper-competent professionalism, as if any chink in that armor would be fatal, the gap that would allow sexism and ageism to sneak in, to infect her career, lay ruin to it. Nursing the bunions from high heels and the hangovers from office parties, harboring deep resentments that her work kept her away from her children, and her children away from her work, everything always tugging in the other direction.

Her Washington office had even looked a bit like this one, the absence of personality its own kind of personality, institutional gray walls, loudly patterned wall-to-wall to hide soil and stains, chest-high cubicle dividers and glass-walled offices, women's room down this hall and men's down that one with the kitchen in between, decaf in the orange-handled pot and a plastic platter with leftover cake from a conference-room birthday celebration, the bulletin board with sign-up sheets for the potluck picnic and the softball squad, a list of the names and numbers of the fire-safety monitors, a long-ignored memo about recycling sent by an office manager who quit years ago.

This caught Kate by surprise. It's not what she'd imagined back when she'd first applied to the Agency, senior year of college, looking for a job that would take her far from her decaying hometown, far from the ghosts of her dead parents, from the mounting problems of her dysfunctional disaster of a sister. Far from a life she didn't want.

The CIA was Kate's first escape, her first reinvention. It would not be her last.

✦

"Madame Davis?" It's Schuyler, twenty-five and slender, pencil-skirted and long-haired. Her cell phone is in her palm, facing up; this is a woman who never misses a call, an e-mail, a text-message, a tweet, the alerts flashing constantly, the light igniting every few seconds, and never, ever failing to catch her attention.

"*Bonjour.*" Kate stands, extends her hand. Ready to head back to Schuyler's office, or a conference room. Ready for their meeting.

"I'm sorry, I don't *think* I have any appointment now? Are you sure it's me you're here to see?"

Kate does her best to look worried. "Oh crap, do I have the time wrong?"

She takes out her phone, brings up her calendar, into which she has entered a meeting with this woman—her address, phone number, job title. Kate extends this screen in front of her, here, look, I'll prove it to you, we have a meeting.

Schuyler glances at Kate's phone. Yes indeed, that's her name, right there. "I'm sorry, I see *you* have a record of it, but I don't? Maybe you can tell me what this is about?"

Kate takes a deep breath, as if bringing herself under the barest tether of control.

"Yes, of course." She glances at the receptionist. "But not out here, okay?" Kate leans in. "It's, um, sensitive," she says in a near-whisper, and places her hand on Schuyler's forearm. "*Please?*"

36

"We are getting a much more full picture of this man." It is someone new speaking, a voice that Ibrahim does not recognize. "Mahmoud Khalid."

"Finally."

"Oh give me a fucking break, François. Using nothing more than the long-distance visual, this has been an extremely fast response. And it must be said—"

"Do not—"

"—that I have not seen an *abundance* of information being supplied by military—"

"Oh go to hell."

"That *suffices*, you two."

"—intelligence."

"You are like children."

Ibrahim can imagine the bickering men behind him, glaring at each other, the third one standing there, shaking his head in disgust. The pissing contests are endless, it is just one after another, dicks hanging out all over the place.

"Everything we have learned so far indicates that Mahmoud Khalid is a secular Egyptian. No ties to radical Islam. Not him, not his relatives. He migrated here immediately after the Arab Spring. Accompanied by his wife and children. They were two and three when they moved here."

"And the wife?"

"Neela Khalid. A schoolteacher in Egypt, worked at a crèche here, not far from their home in the eighteenth. She appears to have died last year. Then a month ago, the children flew to Cairo, and it appears that they have not returned to Paris."

"The children traveled to Egypt by themselves?"

"No. They were accompanied by what looks like the wife's father."

"And what does Mahmoud Khalid do when not a suicide bomber?"

"For the past two years, he has worked full-time in a *quincaillerie*."

Ibrahim almost drops his gun. He fights the urge to spin around, to see who offered this bit of information, to ask for details. Is it possible . . . ?

He needs to know.

"Sir?" Ibrahim has not spoken in a while, his voice is croaky. He clears it. Then starts anew, "Sir, permission to ask a question?"

This is a surprise to everyone. A long pause. "Yes, Officer Abid. Go ahead."

"Could I ask, where exactly is this shop?"

"This is a strange question, Officer Abid."

"My parents, they are proprietors of a *quincaillerie*."

The hardware store is where Ibrahim worked his very first job, after school, stocking shelves, reorganizing the storeroom. Price-stickering was the first gun he ever used, back when guns were a completely different idea, when guns meant fun, games. You wore a smile on your face when you held a gun.

His parents limited his working to just a few hours per week; token employment. They said he needed time to do his schoolwork. But school was easy, homework minimal, he had plenty of time. It was not until years later when he understood that they were trying to give him a normal schoolboy's life—friends, football, girls. They did not want him stuck in a hardware-store basement. They were not immigrants, they did not want to live like immigrants, with the children working in the family shop.

Ibrahim often wonders if his parents would make the same decisions today. And his great-grandparents, would they still leave Morocco for France? Would they still be as eager to raise their families here, to make their lives in a country that is increasingly hostile toward people like them, increasingly intolerant? Or maybe this tendency is merely how it looks to Ibrahim now, because when he was a child, things seemed to be headed in the other direction.

He worries sometimes that he is living in a variation of Germany, 1932. That in five years, or ten, he will look back on this moment from a jail cell, or from an internment camp, or from some newly invented horror, and he will be furious at himself for his failure to anticipate what is so clearly the logical extension of everything that is coalescing around him now, and not just in France but in England too, in Russia, even in the United States, which is perhaps most terrifying of all. It is supposed to be the United States that prevents this from happening elsewhere. But then what do the Americans go and do?

Is that what today is about? Is that why this man is standing here, clad in explosives? This Muslim man from North Africa, this family man who works in a *quincaillerie,* this man who could be Ibrahim himself.

It is hard to understand what could bring a man to this. But Ibrahim is sure that it is not as simple as evil. Almost nothing is. Evil, in his experience, is a temporary subjective condition, not a permanent objective fact.

"Where is your family's shop, Officer Abid?"

Ibrahim wonders why the man is responding this way, then he understands. "In the sixth, sir. The rue du Cherche-Midi."

It is the man named François who answers: "It is not the same store."

"Thank you, sir."

Ibrahim returns his focus to the target, to the man who works in a hardware store that is not owned by Ibrahim's parents. Mahmoud Khalil is not a man whom Ibrahim has met. If Ibrahim needs to kill Khalil, it will not mean anything personally to him.

But if the opposite were true? What would François have said? He would, of course, have lied. Maybe he just did.

"Oh, here is something interesting. A new-patient record for a Mahmoud Khalid was opened at the University Hospital eight months ago. One guess: which department?"

A whole crowd has gathered on the Richelieu Wing's rooftop, men who had been arriving over the past couple of hours, one by one and some in twos. There is Ibrahim's commanding officer, who runs the Louvre detail, and his commanding officer, plus a couple of other serious-looking men from the police department, management types. There is a deputy mayor. A pair of uniformed military men. A couple of guys in suits who must be from intelligence; Ibrahim did not catch their names, their affiliations, or maybe they did not say.

Not one of these men has introduced himself to Ibrahim. The sniper is not here to give any input, discuss any options, make any decisions. He is here for one purpose.

"What do we have to lose, Édouard?"

"You mean if we take him right now?"

He is here to pull the trigger.

"That is a good question. Jean-Paul, what do you think?"

"Well . . ." Jean-Paul either does not have an opinion or does not want to share it. Instead he makes a noise like a harrumph. It is when all the options are bad that true cowardice reveals itself. "There is no evidence that he has been radicalized."

Ibrahim hears one of the men snort at the absurdity of that statement. *Evidence.* Ibrahim cannot turn around, but he does not need his eyes to see it clearly, the man pointing at the center of the *cour,* at the terrorist in a bomb vest. Evidence? There is your fucking evidence.

"You have to be firm with these people."

"These people?"

"You cannot just let them get away with this, cannot let them hold a whole city—a whole nation—hostage. Every minute that we wait serves only to embolden them, to legitimize this tactic. *Every* minute. I strongly urge we take action right now."

"Yves?"

"No. An unprovoked assassination could trigger a disproportionate response."

"Unprovoked? Assassination? What the hell are you talking about?"

"I am just trying to put myself in their position. If what they are trying to do is open a negotiation, and we preemptively end the negotiation before even *any* communication—"

"But there has been no communication, has there? And it has been three hours. So we have to consider the possibility that this is not a negotiation."

"It must be. Do we know anything more about the other devices?"

"The sites have been cleared, wide perimeters established around maximum blast radii. The explosive-ordnance disposal devices—"

"Eh? What does that mean?"

"Robots. The robots are in position to approach and investigate, which should take between thirty and sixty minutes. Each location presents different challenges."

"But that has not commenced? Why not?"

"Awaiting the final order."

"Really? Whose order?"

"Um . . . at this point, Édouard . . . ?"

"I believe we are waiting for the president of the republic."

"The *president*? That does not make sense."

"No, it does not, but who is going to tell him that? You?"

"I still say we shoot this bastard right now. Even if this is supposed to be the opening move of a negotiation, eliminating him establishes our position. Displays our strength. Our willingness to make a hard choice, even at high risk."

Ibrahim can feel the posturing behind him, like a cloud of indignation: we in *la police*, our hands are always tied, we never get to arrest anyone anymore, much less shoot the bad guys, everything is so PC, all the criminals are owed all the understanding, the immigrants too, one must have sympathy, *n'est-ce pas*?

No, damn it, and it would feel awfully good to just shoot one, blow his fucking head off.

Sometimes Ibrahim feels himself agreeing with this sentiment, with the frustration behind it, probably shared all across the world wherever the impartial rule of law butts against respect for human rights and civil liberties. On the other hand, most of the heads that get blown off look a lot like Ibrahim's, while the people who do the shooting do not.

"You are a lunatic, do you know that? An irresponsible lunatic. Does your wife know she married a lunatic?"

"And what if they call our bluff? If they are willing to detonate just because we shoot the messenger, then they are planning to detonate anyway. By waiting we are simply putting ourselves into a weaker position."

"Listen: is there any way to *prevent* the detonation from occurring?"

"Are you kidding? And we would have chosen *not* to do that yet?"

"Frankly, it is not even the suicide vest I am worried about. It is that briefcase. Yves, do we have the readings yet?"

"That team is still setting up the equipment. I am told that it is not so simple. Another few minutes."

Then they are all silent, perhaps waiting for those few minutes to pass.

"There are cell phones out there, you know. Look at all those people. News cameras too. It would be throughout the world, instantly. A cold-blooded assassination."

"Of a *terrorist*."

"Of one scared man who is standing still, putting no one in imminent danger."

"*Everyone* is in imminent danger. He is wearing a suicide vest! He has a suitcase bomb!"

"Maybe what they are *trying* to do is provoke us into shooting him. Have you considered that? Cameras everywhere, footage, they will be able to say, *Look what these French savages did.* And for all we know, this man is completely innocent."

"*Innocent*? What in the name of . . . ? How could he be *innocent*?"

"His family is being held at gunpoint. His children are huddled in some dark room at the business end of AK-47s. This poor sap here, he has been forced to walk into the cour Napoléon wearing this suicide vest or his kids are going to be beheaded by machetes."

"You have a fucked-up imagination, do you know that?"

"And if we blow this patsy's head off for eight billion people to see? Then they will be able to say that we forced their hands, they had no choice, so look, everyone, watch as we saw off all these little heads with a scythe?"

"A *scythe*?"

"They are barbarians."

"Who are you even talking about? We have no idea who is responsible for this."

"They are *all* barbarians."

Sudden silence. Ibrahim suspects that someone just realized that the sniper is one of the *they,* and probably held up a finger to lips, maybe inclined his head toward the man at the edge of the roof, creating a silent standoff.

"Gentlemen. Look at this."

"What is this?"

"A screen-grab from footage of the van that delivered the bomber here. We now know the vehicle make and model, the license plate. And, here, this image is a clear shot of the driver getting out of the van at place Vendôme. Depositing one of the bombs."

"He does not look, um . . ."

"Arab?"

A phone rings. One of the men answers tersely, listens for a few seconds, says thanks. "That was the tech team: the briefcase is definitely emitting radiation."

"Fuck."

"But that cannot really be a nuclear *bomb,* can it?"

"No. It is too small to be a fission device. I am pretty sure."

"*Pretty* sure?"

"But what it could be—in fact, what it *must* be—is a dirty bomb."

"Dirty. That could be nuclear dirt, right? What would we be looking at?"

"Depends on many factors. Too many. I cannot speculate about the likely extent of damage."

"What about minimum?"

"Without question it would make this immediate area a kill zone due to radiation poisoning. Radius of one thousand meters, at the absolute minimum. Possibly much more."

"Not to mention the contents of the Louvre contaminated for decades."

"A minimum of one thousand meters, you say? The radiation could reach l'Élysée?"

"Oh yes."

Everyone lets that sink in.

"Is he there today?"

"Yes."

"Someone needs to tell him."

Silence. No one wants to make this call.

"Yves?"

"*What*? Why me?"

"You know why. And it has to happen right now, this minute. The president needs to evacuate."

37

K ate pulls Schuyler's door closed.

"So, I'm sorry, but what's this all about?" Schuyler is still standing behind her desk, looking affronted.

"Listen carefully." Kate needs to put this woman on notice, to scare the shit out of her from the get-go. "You're having the hardest day of your career."

"Excuse me?"

"It may turn out to be the worst day of your entire life."

Now Schuyler has grown outraged, but speechless. And getting scared.

"Your company is under attack. *Physical* attack. Mortal, physical attack."

The woman's eyes dart to the closed door.

"Not by me, don't worry about me, I'm here to help."

"So says everyone who's not."

Schuyler Franks is a woman whose profession is to manipulate the public's perceptions of reality, to construct narratives, alternative facts. She probably confronts everyone else's narratives with a strong dose of skepticism.

"You're completely right, you don't have any reason to trust me," Kate says. "So I'm not asking for you to simply believe some woman—some possibly crazy woman—who has lied her way into your office."

"So let me get this straight: we don't have an appointment?"

"What I'm telling you is to check this out for yourself. Make a couple of calls."

"I'm sorry, who *are* you?"

"My identity matters a lot less than you might think."

"I'm sorry?" Shaking her head. "I'm going to need to call security?"

"No." Kate grabs the woman by the forearm, not gently.

"*Ow.*"

"You're not."

Kate doesn't like doing this, intimidating a woman who has done nothing wrong except appear accidentally in Kate's path. Getting bullied herself is something Kate still remembers intensely, viscerally. The CIA halls were suffused with the miasma of testosterone, and Kate was under a more or less constant threat of getting dismissed, getting ignored, getting rejected. She felt the sting well before it even happened, the aggression, the condescension, the subtle slights and hostile body language and flippant smirks.

She remembers how effective it was. How it kept her on the constant defensive, willing to do practically anything to avoid confrontation.

"Sit the fuck down," Kate says. "And for the love of God *stop* apologizing to me."

Schuyler Franks is not one hundred percent willing to accept Kate's authority, but she's awfully close.

"Right *now.*"

There, that does it. Just as effective as ever. The young woman takes a seat at the edge of her chair, back rigid, eyes wide. She doesn't know what defense is available to her—should she call security? Call her boss? Or should she hear out this intruder?

"Hong Kong and Mumbai, your offices there—those office buildings—both have bomb threats against them, at this minute. Please go ahead, check it out yourself."

"I'm sorry, what? How?"

"*Stop* apologizing. Just *call* someone over there. Anyone you want."

Schuyler nods, seems almost relieved to be told to do something so concrete, so straightforward. She looks at her screen, then down at her keyboard, her forefingers finding their positions at *F* and *J*. She types in a password, then clicks around with her mouse.

The speakerphone answers, "Hello, 4Syte Hong Kong, how may I direct your call?"

"Hi! This is Schuyler Franks in the Paris office? Do you work in reception?"

"Yes I do." This call to the other side of the world is very clear, to a woman with a very British accent. "How may I be of assistance?"

Schuyler is staring at nothingness, concentrating. Kate uses the opportunity to unlock her own phone and launch an app. Then she puts her device on the desk, just inches from Schuyler's cell. The process should take less than a minute.

"Sorry, may I ask you a strange question?"

"Erm . . ."

"Is there a *bomb* threat to your building?"

"Uh . . . One moment please."

Schuyler is put on hold with ambient music, or maybe this sound doesn't qualify as music, just a series of oscillating tones, hypnotizing—

"Yes." The Hong Kong receptionist says.

"Yes? Yes what?"

No answer.

"I'm sorry, I don't want to harass you?" Schuyler says. "But you just put me on hold to ask for permission to answer my question, right? You called someone in public relations? *I'm* in PR, check me out if you need to? Do you want me to spell out my name?"

"No, I've already verified you, your phone number."

"Awesome. Well, I received a query from the press, and my plan is to phone back and say I don't know anything? But that's not going to cut it forever, we're going to need a real response? So I'm sorry, but I have to know what's actually going on over there?"

That's a good story; Kate nods her encouragement.

Hong Kong pauses, then says. "Right. One moment please." Hold again, another half-minute. Then: "Right. Building management alerted all tenants that someone attempted entry with a potentially explosive device."

Schuyler's eyebrows shoot up her forehead, her mouth hangs open. She doesn't know where to go from here. Then she gathers her wits, says, "I'm sorry, may I have the name of the building management? A contact number?"

"Very well."

The Hong Kong woman rattles off some information, which Schuyler dutifully writes down, ends the call. Then she just sits there.

"Are you going to check with Mumbai?" Kate asks.

"Is it the same thing?"

"Similar, probably. Have you heard anything about this building? Evacuations, threats, anything?"

"No. Do you think *this* building is under attack?"

"I don't have any reason to," Kate says. "But other parts of Paris are. I understand that your CEO is holding a press conference this afternoon. Will that take place here?"

"Um . . . I'm sor—" Schuyler stops herself. "Listen: you need to tell me who you are, and what you're doing here, or I'm going to have to call security? I don't . . . I can't . . ."

Kate pushes past this. "Is Hunter Forsyth here right now? In the building?"

Schuyler doesn't answer.

"If this office is going to be attacked, Schuyler—if your boss is going to be attacked, abducted, *assassinated*—"

"*What?*"

"—do you really want to be the one who's responsible for *failing* to prevent it?"

"Why *me*? Why did you come to me?"

"You answered the phone."

"Wait, what? You're the one who called earlier?"

"Listen, I didn't choose you, that was just luck. But we're here now, you and I, and it's possible that something *very* bad is going on in your company today. Right now. You can either be a hero, and help me figure out what it is and how to prevent it, or you can be a villain, an obstacle. I'm sure we don't have an excess of spare time, so for fuck's sake tell me right now: is Hunter Forsyth here in this goddamned building?"

"I don't know."

"Well, can you find out? *Now?*"

A long second passes while the young woman makes her calculations, weighing one unpleasant possibility against another. She nods again, then stares down into her lap, thinking. Nods once more, this time agreeing with herself, with the plan she just hatched. She clicks her mouse again, and another speakerphone call goes through.

"*Allô* Schuyler."

"Hi?" She furrows her brow. "Colette?"

"*Non, c'est Dominique.*"

Kate leans forward, plants her elbows on the desk, listening carefully.

"Oh, okay? Has Colette stepped away?"

"Colette, she is not here."

"Sorry? Where is she?"

"She is with Monsieur Forsyth, at his home."

"Okay, well . . . um . . . I want to check if Hunter needs anything last-minute for the press conference?"

Dominique doesn't answer.

"Sorry, can I ask you to check for me? With Hunter?"

Dominique pauses before answering, "*Oui*. I will try."

Schuyler is put on hold again. It takes longer than expected, while Schuyler stares down at her desk, avoiding Kate's gaze.

Dominique comes back on the line. "Monsieur Forsyth, he does not answer."

"Can you try Col—"

"*Oui,* she also does not answer her mobile. And no one answers the telephone at the apartment. *Personne* answer *rien*."

"That's strange, isn't it? When is Monsieur Forsyth expected to the office?"

"Another hour."

"Aren't you worried?"

"Worried? *Non*. Why should I be worried?"

"Because no one answers the phone?"

The other woman laughs, a humorless staccato burst.

"What's funny?"

"What do you think, Schuyler?" Pronounced *skee-LAIR*.

"Sorry, I really don't know? Please, what are you talking about?"

Dominique sighs. "Why would a man and a woman together in an apartment not answer their phones? Can you imagine a reason?"

Kate knows how it can happen: an everyday relationship that exerts pressure, builds toward something, momentum without friction, acceleration. Like physics.

Part of the appeal was her growing resentments at home, a long-term amalgamation of little slights, minor inconsiderations. Dexter's parental neglects, educational, social, recreational, spousal. Kate could group them on a spreadsheet, sorted by category, ranked by orders of magnitude.

This is apparently how you can get to a spot where you can't stand your spouse.

The title of the spreadsheet would be: GRIEVANCES.

That was the push. The pull happened in Seville, the way these things happen. Kate and Peter had a typically late Andalusian dinner accompanied by vermouth and then *tinto* and then sherry—all told, perhaps too much to drink, though it didn't look that way at the time. It never looks that way at the time, especially when you're having great fun, sharing jokes, smiles, intimacies, a long slow walk through the sexy Spanish streets, the tapas bars spilling tipsy patrons onto the sidewalks, an air of permissiveness.

It was the type of night that looks a lot like a romantic date, one that ends in bed.

"So," she said to him in the hotel lobby, "what now?" Peter seemed like a man with something on his mind, a man who wanted to unburden himself, but needed to be given permission. Kate wanted to give him that permission, wanted him to open up, she wanted to be that sort of boss, that sort of friend, that sort of woman. She wanted to hear what it was he needed to say.

What else did she want? Yes, she did: she wanted him to make a pass. She didn't want to accept it, no, she was sure of that. But she wanted him to try.

Kate already knew the risks people could take, the damage these risks could do. Her career in exploiting people often hinged on the discovery of extramarital affairs, or the invention of them, which could happen even when—especially when—they could be most damaging. There are so many ways it can turn out badly.

And badly is the only way it can turn out, isn't it? In the end—and there's always an end—it's just a question of who ends up most hurt. But make no mistake about it: everyone ends up hurt.

"What," he said, "are my options?"

She'd asked for that, hadn't she? Kate turned away, fought a smile, felt herself blushing. She hated blushing; it made her feel exposed.

"Okay, I'll tell you what I want," Peter said. He took a step closer.

She kept her eyes averted, down at the floor, over by the door, anywhere else.

"I want you to come upstairs with me."

That's when she looked up. His eye was firm, he was absolutely sure of himself. This didn't come as a surprise to her, neither his desire nor his declaration. She knew him pretty well at this point.

"I want you to come to bed with me." He smiled. "Again."

Absolutely sure of her.

It has to be admitted: at that point in her life, Kate preferred a good flossing to having sex with Dexter. She'd been doing everything possible to avoid him short of saying no point-blank; she didn't want to create that rift in her marriage, possibly irreparable, a wife who denies sex to her husband. It was temporary, and she didn't want to impose a permanent solution onto a temporary problem. This is what she told herself, staring in the mirror, wearing her most matronly nightgown, shapeless plaid flannel.

"I want you," Peter said. "That's what I want."

38

Two knocks in quick succession. Pause. Then three knocks. Pause. Four. Then Simpson unlocks the various mechanisms, pulls the heavy door open just wide enough to collect a bag from the uniformed policeman. "*Merci*," he says, and shuts the door quickly. Re-engages all three locks.

They have a code, this CIA dude and a local cop? That's odd. Is this something they worked out just today? Or is it a standard spook-cop thing? If so, wouldn't all the bad guys also know the code?

Bad guys. Did he really just form that phrase in his mind? Jesus.

"Sandwiches," Simpson says. "And coffee. Water too." He sets the bag on the table, begins unloading little wax-paper packets. "*Jambon-beurre,* I hope that's okay with everyone."

Hunter doesn't want any damn ham-and-butter sandwich. He remains in his seat, dejected, slouched in this lumpy futon, with an out-of-date American gossip magazine in his lap. He has already leafed through all the more substantive publications; next is going to be fashion. Which will at least have the benefit of plentiful pictures of pretty women.

He watches his own pretty woman walk across the room. Though *walk* isn't the right word for what Colette does. *Saunter.*

She picks up a bottle of water, sparkling. Hunter has been making an effort to catalog Colette's preferences—whites from Burgundy, grilled *loup de mer,* triple-crème cheeses, swimming in the Mediterranean, Prada shoes. Sparkling, not still. He's laying the groundwork to be an attentive, considerate husband.

It's true that at this moment Colette already has a different husband, a guy—named Guy!—whom Hunter has researched exhaustively, exhaustingly. This Guy guy, a professor, apparently wrote the definitive biography of some long-dead French novelist—not Balzac, but another dude with a *z*—which makes him a writer who writes about other dead writers, which: for fuck's sake. Guy's headshot—turtleneck, long wavy hair, staring off into the distance—has Sensitive Guy written all over it, like a watermark in stationery.

Other than their mutual affection for the same woman, Hunter and Guy don't seem to have anything in common. Hopefully Colette's taste in men isn't completely consistent.

Hunter has considered different strategies for wrecking her marriage, a few very different schemes. Weighing practicalities, challenges, likelihoods of success. He always comes back to his first, most obvious concept: entrap Guy into having an affair, and make absolutely sure he gets caught.

The main stumbling block to this scenario is super-ironic: the person Hunter would entrust to find the right seductress? Colette. She solves all the problems that aren't the express domain of someone with a different specialty, and no one has this specialty.

In whatever way Hunter is going to ruin Colette's marriage, he'd better start soon. It's not as if he has forever. His sperm is fine—he had himself checked, that's not the concern—but the rest of his body is definitely aging, and he wants to be able to play catch with his son, hit fungoes, toss a football. Who knows how many more years he'll be able to rely on his body? Hunter's own dad tore an ACL at age forty-eight, and never skied again; never did much of anything physical again. By that point, Hunter was sixteen and no longer wanted to do anything with Dad, except that one trip to the brothel near Tahoe, which he'd never before realized was an option as a father-son activity. And it turned out to be just the one time, not an ongoing hobby.

Hunter watches as Colette unscrews the water-bottle cap and tips the bottle into her mouth, her lips open and pursed, barely touching the plastic, certainly not engulfing it, not wrapping her mouth around the shaft of it—

Oh, *God,* it's a physical ache he has for her, an actual generalized pain.

It really wasn't supposed to be this way. For this Paris assistant, he'd made a special point of asking HR to send over an older woman. Not *old,* per se, but at least well into her thirties. Labor laws being what they are, sexual harassment suits, who knows about French customs; Hunter didn't want to run any risks. This is a country in which every employee is guaranteed the right to *not respond* to work e-mails on vacation, of which everyone is guaranteed at least *five weeks per year.* Everyone! It's insane.

He was already well aware of his own predilection for French women, and for twenty-five-year-olds. He was, frankly, terrified to combine the two.

For her job interview, Colette had worn a roomy pantsuit, her hair strangled up in a bun, thick eyeglasses. She barely smiled. She was clearly a good-looking woman, but not in any distracting way, nothing to worry about. And she was obviously a hyper-competent, super-efficient person. Maybe a bit of a pill, but that was okay. Hunter wasn't trying to hire a friend. He'd learned that lesson already, more than once.

But it slowly became clear how obscenely clever Colette is. She's unfailingly pleasant to everyone, without ever seeming insincere. Every once in a while she even displays a flash of a sense of humor, which Hunter never could've anticipated from that brittle, joyless interviewee.

Then that night last year.

It came out of the blue: Colette accompanied him for the short walk over to his drinks date, as she does. The street in front of the hotel was lined with luxury cars, including a matching pair of cherry-red Lamborghinis with Qatar plates, an ostentatious display of wealth that made Hunter feel downright middle-class. He'd heard that a sultan rented out the presidential suite for an entire month on the mere chance that his family would want to come to Paris for a few days. *And then never did.*

Boss move.

That's the sort of money Hunter wants. The sort that makes it okay to throw away hundreds of thousands of dollars for basically no reason.

He made his way to the terrace while Colette stepped inside to check for his guest. As she was reemerging, she came face-to-face with a friend— *Mon Dieu,* big hugs, big smiles.

Hunter was sitting at a table under the red awnings that matched the red blooms that cascaded from the flower boxes of every red-awninged window. At the next table, a Pakistani guy wearing a bright-pink jacket was reading a London paper. That type of crowd, of place, exuding money. Across the wide tree-lined street, exorbitant fashion boutiques beckoned. Come over here, they called. You belong here.

In places like this, Hunter hated staring at his phone. So instead he watched Colette, who was only thirty feet away but hadn't seen Hunter sit, didn't know how close he was. So she was interacting with this person from her private life as if out of her boss's sight.

She was a completely different person. Her face was lit up in a wonderful smile, one that Hunter had never before seen. Those deep dimples, the rosy glow of her cheeks, the affectionate way she caressed her friend's arm. Her eyes were twinkling. She pushed a wisp of errant hair away from the side of her neck. Her long, incredibly sexy neck.

It was like a flash of lightning, the immediacy of this epiphany, the drama of it, the irrefutability of this violent bolt of electricity exploding in the sky, making everything else look minor, irrelevant: Colette was the most beautiful woman he'd ever met. His assistant! How had it taken him three years to realize this?

Now it was like looking back on a time when he believed that the world was flat, that politicians were honest: inconceivable, from this vantage, to fathom how he'd been so completely wrong, for so very long.

"Can we get some light in here?" Hunter asks, flinging aside the heavy drapery—

He freezes, staring. Turns back to face Simpson. "What the hell?"

Simpson holds up a finger while he finishes chewing his ham sandwich, swallows. "Sorry," he says. "I told you this place wasn't much to look at."

"But boarded-up windows?"

"For safety."

Hunter's first thought is about fire safety; there was an issue last year with inaccessible windows at the plant in Guangdong Province, six people died, or maybe it was eight? Some small, even number of dead Chinese people.

But this wasn't the type of safety Simpson was talking about. "In today's age of electronic intrusion, Mr. Forsyth, windows are too porous.

With directional microphones, portable telescopes, night-vision goggles. Not to mention high-powered sniper's rifles."

Hunter's mind roams to the bathroom, the small window there. Is that one boarded up too? The bedroom? "This is a super-cheerful place, isn't it?"

"It's not meant to be cheerful, Mr. Forsyth. It's meant to be safe."

Hunter has given up asking Simpson to call him by his first name. He prefers Mr. Forsyth anyway.

"Is there anything I can get for you? *Try* to get for you? To make you more comfortable while we're here?"

Hunter fingers a section of sandwich, but doesn't pick it up. "Can you please find out what's going on out there?"

"The police who accompanied us have instructions to bring me any news immediately." He shrugs. "They haven't brought any news."

Hunter examines this so-called Tom Simpson, a guy wearing a forgettable outfit, an unflattering suit and oxford shirt with repp tie, cap-toes that could use a shine, like a bureaucrat's uniform. Maybe it is an actual uniform, guidelines in some handbook. But any guidelines would probably prohibit these grooming choices—the big beard, the large square eyeglass frames with amber lenses. Like a character from an old cop show, *Kojak* maybe, *Columbo.*

Plus there's that scar on his cheek. Maybe the beard is there to hide others.

Barney Miller.

"You don't seem particularly concerned. Or interested."

"I'm concerned, Mr. Forsyth. And plenty interested. I understand that this situation is inconvenient for you, I really do. Today is not going how you planned, and it's an important day. That's true for lots of people. I hope for everyone's sake—including my own—that we can normalize as soon as possible. But my job right now is to keep you out of harm's way. In the meantime, we have to accept that everything else about the situation is out of our control."

Do we? Acceptance is not Hunter's style.

He looks around again, the boarded-up windows, the triple-locked steel-reinforced door, the magazines, the TV hooked up to a DVD player, the small stack of American movies, the shelf's worth of paperback books.

The bathroom has a bare-bones supply of toiletries, the single bedroom a queen-size bed. And that landline, plugged into the beige plastic box of a wall jack. It looks like an old piece of hardware, that box. Something from ten years ago, maybe more. Fifteen. Pre–fiber optic.

The phone unit also looks like it's not especially new. He walks over to the console table, picks up the handset, checks that there's still no dial tone. There isn't.

It's a model with two lines, an integrated digital answering machine. The kind of outdated phone you find in a mom-and-pop roadside motel, neither mom nor pop willing to invest in the latest communications systems, their clientele not in a position to care. Hunter has used a couple of those motels, once or twice.

This device is something that was bought from a consumer-electronics retailer, for your home office, for your kitchen counter. This handset wasn't one element of a big network buy with a purchase order, a complex install sequence, coordination between IT and HR, a temporary outgoing message for everyone, memos, complaints . . .

It never ceases to amaze Hunter how *anything* can become a royal pain in the ass.

But this phone wasn't. This was a quick inexpensive purchase, a one-minute install. He turns the base over, where MADE IN CHINA is die-cut into the beige plastic. He puts this down, walks away.

China . . .

Made in China . . . ?

This phone was made in *China*?

39

"Schuyler? Is Forsyth married?"

Schuyler is staring off at nothing, in stunned shock. She nods.

Kate retrieves her phone from the desk, glances at the screen. Yes, her intrusion has been successful.

"Happily?"

The woman looks at Kate. "Are you kidding me? How would I know?"

It's certainly not unheard-of, especially in France, where extramarital affairs are practically a requirement, especially for powerful men. Perhaps Schuyler thought her boss was different—a visionary, a genius, a whatever, above all that. No one is above all that.

So, yes, that could be a possibility: an affair plus blackmail. But how could this garden-variety shakedown fit into a coordinated terrorist attack on multiple continents?

Though there haven't been any *actual* attacks so far. No hostages taken. No networks breached, no systems crashed. No violence of any sort, physical or cyber. Although explosives have been planted at the Gare de Lyon, Arc de Triomphe, place Vendôme, and Notre-Dame, plus a suicide bomber in the middle of the Louvre, there have been no detonations. No trucks plowing through crowds. No deaths. No demands. No claims of responsibility. Just threats, strung like a necklace of menace across the city's neck.

Kate brings to mind a map of Paris, and drops mental pins at the bomb sites. They surround this office.

"Where's Forsyth's apartment?"

The young woman doesn't answer.

"Listen, I know you don't want to—"

"No, that's not it: I actually don't know where it is?"

"You need to find out."

"Sorry, and then what? *Go* there?" The young woman shakes her head. "No way."

"You have to."

"I *have* to? I don't think so."

"Then get me the address, and I'll go."

"*That's* out of the question. Listen, Miss ... What *is* your name anyway?"

"Lindsay."

"Well, *Lindsay,* I have no clue who you are? Or what you're doing here? Or what business this is—*any* of this—of yours? Seriously, who *are* you? A reporter?"

Kate doesn't answer.

"Are you CIA?"

Kate remains silent.

"For all I know, maybe *you're* involved in these attacks? Maybe you're a Trojan horse? Maybe this whole thing is orchestrated to trick me into taking you to Mr. Forsyth's apartment? Maybe *you're* the enemy?"

Kate opens her mouth to explain how wrong this is, but then changes her mind. This young woman is better off not knowing Kate's theory.

"Okay." Schuyler gets up. "I'm going to have to ask you to wait in reception?"

"Come on," Kate says. "What do you think I'm going to do in here? Steal your press releases?"

Kate holds up her phone, pretending to read messages so she can surreptitiously take a photo of the young woman.

"I can't guess what you want to steal? But if you're not planning on stealing anything, you'll be just as happy to wait out in reception?"

She follows Kate like a prison guard back down the gray hall. Kate sends Schuyler's photo to Inez, with instructions to follow her to Forsyth's apartment.

"This woman is going to wait for me here? I'll be back in fifteen minutes?"

"*D'accord.*"

"Hey," Kate says. "Take my phone number. In case you need help."

"What help am I going to need that you can provide?"

"You never know."

Schuyler seems to consider what possible threat it might be to take possession of this strange woman's number. "Write it down?"

"Let me call you, then you'll have it in your phone."

"No, I don't want your number in my phone? And I certainly don't want you to have mine?"

"Why not?"

"*Why not?* Because I don't trust you?"

Good for her. Kate scribbles down her number.

"Don't follow me?"

"Of course not."

Schuyler smiles at Kate's naked display of disingenuousness, turns to the receptionist. "If this woman leaves, please call me immediately? And then call security too?"

⚜

Did Kate debate it? Not really. As soon as Peter said it, she knew how she was going to respond. It just took her a few seconds to do it.

"I'm sorry," she said.

He didn't argue. He just left it there, hanging between them in the hotel lobby, the invitation, reiterated in his silent stare.

"I can't."

She could. And she wanted to. The one night they'd shared fifteen years ago had been spectacular. But at the time, neither was in a position to pursue a relationship with the other. The next time Kate saw Peter, they were both married to other people.

"I'm sorry," she said again, and before she changed her mind she aimed her good-night kiss unmistakably at the air beside his cheek, with her face angled away, for the avoidance of doubt. She marched to the elevator, to her room, she flung herself on the bed, her fingers working manically, her fantasies exceptionally vivid—this bed, now, me, him—and she came quickly and then again, fantasies intermingling with memories of that night in Morelia in the cheap hotel room where everything was done up in red and black and Gothic typefaces, Peter's tight taut body, a clump of soft threadbare sheet in her mouth—

Then she lay sprawled in the bed, panting, one hand on a breast and the other between her legs, sticky thighs, the cool of the soft sheet on her hot skin. She gathered her breath, then her phone.

She was still debating, still had time to change her mind . . .

Kate typed quickly, paused. Should she say something more? Or something else? Or just keep it simple?

Yes, simpler is better.

Good night. Wish you were here.

She hit SEND, and waited for a reply, which came quickly:

Miss you too.

Then the symbol that meant he was still typing . . . more to come . . .

Come home soon. D.

Kate felt a bit righteous, then felt guilty for feeling righteous about something that shouldn't even have been a question, taking candy from a baby, stealing from the collection jar, it goes without saying that you don't do it, and you don't congratulate yourself for not doing it.

Then she heard the knock on her door.

40

"Okay, listen, seriously: why would I do this?"

The policeman doesn't respond.

"It doesn't make any sense, surely you see that, I mean . . . Look." He takes a deep breath. Slow down, Shreve. Sound rational. "I'm successful here. I'm well-compensated, believe me. I have no debts. I'm loyal."

"Loyal? Interesting word to use in this situation. You are an American citizen. Born in America. Correct? You are loyal to America?"

"Sure."

"Yet you choose to work for a German bank? Why?"

"*Why?* What do you mean?"

"Why work for Germans, not Americans?"

"That's a crazy question. Because it's a good job. Because they pay me a lot."

"Do you *hate* Germans, Mr. Shreve? Perhaps you are Jewish?"

"I'm not."

"You hold grudges against the Nazis?"

"I'm not a *fan,* but seriously? Are you suggesting—"

"Do you have another reason to be anti-German?"

"I don't have *any* reason to be anti-German. *I'm not anti-German.*"

"Then you are angry at another business in this building? Which is it?"

With each passing question, Shreve feels more and more like he has fallen into the twilight zone, an increasing sense of disorientation that began when he was lying on the marble floor, hands behind his head, someone's foot in his back.

"The French bank? Or the expanding company?" The cop glances at his notepad. "4Syte?"

Shreve can't handle this conversation. He's crashing. "I want to speak to a lawyer." Didn't he say that already? "Didn't I say that already?"

"A solicitor? Mr. Shreve: are you . . . how shall I put this? Are you *altered*?"

Oh, wow, no, Shreve really doesn't want to go there. He's not sure, *precisely,* what crime it is, in Hong Kong, cocaine use, possession, though he's not in actual possession of any blow—is he?—no, so that doesn't matter. But could the Hong Kong police forcibly drug-test him? And is *using* cocaine an actual crime? Or buying it? Selling it, obviously, sure. But he doesn't do that. Almost ever. Never professionally.

Regardless of the criminal status of cocaine use, it obviously wouldn't *look* good, not from a law-enforcement perspective, not from an employment one. Nor for that matter from a personal one.

Christ: his mother.

But embarrassment aside, how much of a legit disaster is this? Is it possible that Shreve is going to *jail*? In Hong Kong?

The police have gotten a lot less understanding with young Anglo-expat finance guys ever since Occupy Hong Kong, and that call-girl incident with the super-disturbed Brit dude. For the entire time Shreve has lived here, local law has sadly been a lot less willing to turn the traditional blind eye toward expats' debauchery.

Shreve is sweating something fierce. The thing about Hong Kong that he didn't realize beforehand: it's tropical. Not just like South Florida, it's not Miami Beach tropical, not San Diego. It's Costa Rica tropical, equatorial. Here in this police station, it's hot as fuck.

"Lawyer," he repeats. He wouldn't be surprised if a goddamned tarantula appeared, crawled across the table. A scorpion. "Or embassy." He doesn't know which. He wants the cop to choose. "Listen," Shreve says, trying again to adopt a reasonable tone. "Listen." He has to focus here. "That thing—whatever it is, I never even *saw* it—was *not* in my bag when I left the gym. Someone must have put it in my bag when I was at the restaurant."

"Yes, you asserted that before. Why would anyone do such a thing? Explain that to me. Please. I want to understand."

"*I* don't know. I guess to get it into the building?"

"But the X-ray machines are not a secret, Mr. Shreve. The failure was foreseeable."

It's true, it doesn't make any fucking sense, nothing does, Shreve hasn't been able to come up with any plausible explanation since those first seconds lying on the lobby floor with his face pressed against the marble, an entirely new perspective on the space, the architecture, on the whole world, when your eyes are just inches off the ground, from there absolutely everything is up. Shreve was accustomed to looking down on things.

He inhabits that lobby for a few minutes every day, yet could not until today have been able to tell you what color the floor was.

"I don't know, man." Is this a *Midnight Express* scenario he's facing?

It's a peachy, rosy marble streaked with brown and magenta veins, the lobby floor.

Shreve sniffles—of course he sniffles, he's been sniffling for hours. "I really don't." And he realizes that this sniffle is a different sort, not the sniffle of someone who'd ingested eight fatties of high-grade blow, but the sniffle of someone who's being interrogated by the police halfway around the world from home, without his passport, without a lawyer, without any understanding of why someone—why anyone—would plant a bomb in his gym bag, would leave him literally holding the bag. The sniffle of someone who's crying.

41

It's good to be outside, in the semi-fresh air, surrounded by the ambient noise of Venetian life, drowning Matteo's sobbing into the purring of the *vaporetti* motors, and the water glurping in its currents and eddies, splashing against the canal banks, and the low-pitched rumble of the tradesmen's wheelbarrows laden with mortar and bricks and big bags of sand, and the tinkle-rattles of hand-trucks delivering cases of beer to the *tabaccheria*, and the scratch-scratch of a wide wicker broom against stone as the woman in the blue work-shirt sweeps the plaza, she's here every day, greeting all the other municipal workers and shopkeepers and waiters, the collective staff of the *campo*.

Around the corner, the stonemason keeps a soprano beat, chiseling away at a façade, another structure undergoing prettification. Nearly every surface in this city is visibly damaged, or eroded, chipping, falling apart, plaster giving way to the brick underneath, the brick to wood, cracks in everything, iron welts fastened to marble plinths to forestall expansion, mottled paint jobs, weeds growing from walls, peeling paint and water stains and soot streaks, the accumulated grunge of centuries, of millennia, all these blemishes somehow appealing, shabby chic.

A stroller is counterproductive here, with all the steps of all the bridges, up and down, up and down, every bridge an opportunity to jostle a child out of sleep, which is often her point in being outdoors in the first place. This is exactly why she's wandering these narrow streets now, with the baby harnessed to her chest, trying to get the little fucker to nap.

The only time she ever brings the stroller is to go to the Coop, using the thing as a dual-purpose baby carrier and shopping cart. It's a five-minute walk with two bridges to cross, six steps times two at the first, seven times two at the second, not easy, but easier than lugging groceries with the dead-weight of a child hanging off her shoulders, straining her lower back, which hasn't completely recovered from the strain of being pregnant. One of the many strains of being pregnant.

She is no whiner, no stranger to difficulty. She has done a lot of hard things. But until this baby, none of the difficulties had been surprises. She'd had no illusions about what she was attempting in her career, what adversities she'd be facing. She was prepared for all of it, she diligently managed her expectations, she always erred on the side of over-preparation, anticipating that things would be harder than they turned out to be.

There, she always thought: *that wasn't so bad.* Until this baby.

She turns off the street into a *sotoportego,* one of those low dark passageways burrowed through buildings' street levels. This one ends at a quiet narrow canal, alongside which she walks for a minute before it too ends at a small bridge, where she crosses to the other side of the canal, turns another corner.

It's quiet here, off the main *calle,* away from the tourists thronged on the banks of the Grand Canal, hanging off the Rialto. There are no landmarks here, none of Venice's top-ten must-see attractions, just normal life, small churches and modest *piazzi,* grocery stores and this *tabaccheria* here, whose owner Lorenzo lives in the neighborhood, she has met his wife, he has met her husband, they all shared a drink in the *campo* a few months ago.

Lorenzo is the type of shopkeeper who knows everyone in the neighborhood, who keeps a watchful eye on everything; the type of local who can be a real asset. He collects packages for her, important mail—her apartment's mailbox is insecure, she explained. This is one of the favors she pays him for, but mostly it's an arrangement whose main purpose is merely to have an arrangement, for the eventuality when she will really need someone to rely upon. Tonight.

"*Ciao* Susanna!" Lorenzo calls out. She waves back.

Susanna. Not exactly the name she was given at birth, but it's close, the Italian version. It's what she has been going by, here. It's her new name, part of her new life, her new plan.

What do you do when none of your schemes pan out? When everything comes crashing down—when you lose a fortune, a career, and a baby all within forty-eight hours? How do you come back from that?

Here is what she told herself: coming back is what makes you you. Coming back is how you get to deserve it. Coming back is everything. So stop your whining, get off the couch, and get the fuck back to work.

❖

Two weeks ago, in a moment of what she now realizes was fatigue-induced delirium, she started researching babysitters, nannies, options that they'd already discussed and dismissed, decided they shouldn't pursue, couldn't do. But she was falling apart, losing confidence in her certainties.

It was then, at her weakest point, when her faith in humanity was restored, because the kid finally relented: Matteo fell asleep quickly, then slept soundly for eight hours straight. And so did she.

She awoke refreshed, amazed that it was past dawn, double-checking her clock against her watch against her phone, unwilling to believe that it was really seven-thirty in the morning.

Yes, she could make it. No need for babysitters, no strangers in this household, no way, no how. It won't be long now, and then her husband will be back, this time for good. And they will, finally, be rich.

Today is it. If all goes well, he'll be back with her tomorrow. And at this moment all seems to be going well. There's still plenty of time for everything to go sideways, but she's prepared for that too. She's prepared for everything, even the things she doesn't know to be prepared for.

She sometimes has trouble identifying what it is that she actually wants, versus what she believes she's supposed to want. In an ideal world, they'd be the same. But she doesn't live in an ideal world. No one does, though some people choose to pretend. She has never been one of them. Which is why she's walking through the streets of Venice, with her newborn snuggled against her chest, and a semiautomatic handgun in her pocket.

42

Kate waits. Office workers are pouring out on their way to lunch, the three-course prix fixe, out and back within an hour.

It shouldn't be long before Schuyler returns with the CEO himself, a guy who thinks he'll be making a fortune today. Not if Kate is right about what's going on here.

She sends another request to Dexter: *Also check to see if we have bday candles.*

He responds quickly: *Yup.* Is that snarky? Is he tired of the to-do list she's scattershooting into his day? Well, she thinks, fuck you too.

She can feel the receptionist appraising her. Kate is increasingly aware that she's illegitimate here, exposed, sitting alone with this suspicious sentinel, in an office that any second now may discover that they're being assailed, and she may look a lot like an assailant.

A new message, this one from Inez: *She is ringing bell.*

It had taken nine minutes for Schuyler to get to the apartment.

Still outside. With a woman, I believe concierge.

The previous text in Kate's stream is from school, a wordy one; the head of school is new to texting, doesn't make any attempt at brevity. *Despite today's events, we are trying to have a normal day. However, we do understand if any family would be more comfortable collecting their children, so as to be together during this stressful time. If so, please be sure to ring the main office before arriving, to facilitate a minimum of disruption. Thank you so very much.*

Normal school day.

Another ding: *She went inside.*

The kids are scratching away at math problems, they're memorizing verb conjugations, they're doing all the normal things, running around the courtyard at recess, kicking a ball, playing tag. Not huddled around screens watching footage of an ongoing terrorism event, freaking them out about a danger that's looming outside the high stone walls. It was the right decision, leaving them at school.

Kate's phone buzzes. She picks it up, listens.

"Hi Dominique, it's Schuyler?"

This is an intercept of Schuyler's phone, transmitted to Kate's line. As if Kate is on a conference call, muted: she can hear the connection, but can't participate in the conversation.

"Schuyler, ça va?"

The other call participants don't know she's listening in. This was what Kate accomplished in Schuyler's office: cloning the young woman's cellular line. You think your phone is safe, just sitting there in plain sight, home-screen locked, password-protected? You're wrong.

"No. I'm at Mr. Forsyth's apartment, talking to the security guard? He says that at a quarter after nine, a man from the US Department of State showed up, with a pair of Parisian police? The official stayed in the apartment for a half-hour, then they all left? Mr. Forsyth told the guard—his name is Didier—that they were taking him someplace secure? For his protection?"

Protection? Is that possible? Would the embassy send someone to retrieve an American executive during a terrorist attack? Maybe. But not solely because of a generalized threat. At any given moment there are tens of thousands of Americans in Paris.

"Et Colette?"

"Elle aussi, she went with Mr. Forsyth." The assistant who might be fucking him. That makes sense. *"Didier says that his instructions were to remain at the apartment, to keep it secure, for Mr. Forsyth's return? Once the attack is over?"*

If this purported protection guy isn't really State, but is actually Agency, that's more plausible. Especially if the CIA has a particular interest in Hunter Forsyth. Why would they? Maybe Forsyth's business dealings are a matter of national security. Or maybe there's a specific threat against Forsyth.

"Dominique, has anyone from the American government called Mr. Forsyth's office?"

"Non."

Or maybe Forsyth is an asset.

"Anyone unusual at all?"

"Ah . . . non."

Or maybe there's no truth whatsoever to this cockamamie-sounding explanation.

The line is silent for a few seconds, while the two 4Syte employees try to figure out what each should do next.

"We have to loop in legal, don't we?"

Kate wasn't going to answer his knock. Peter knew, obviously, that she was in the hotel room. She couldn't pretend that she wasn't there, nor that she was asleep, nor that she didn't hear it, nor that she couldn't get to the door. She was just going to not answer.

That's what she should have done; that's what she tried to do.

She failed.

Kate rose from the bed. She crossed the room. She leaned against the door, put her hand on the knob, debating, wavering . . .

She opened the door.

Peter didn't look surprised, not even relieved, it was simply what he expected. He glanced at her disarrayed blouse, her mussed-up hair, her smeared lipstick. He could see it all, the past five minutes; he could smell it.

She didn't say anything. Neither did he.

He leaned toward her, and she couldn't stop it, wouldn't, his tongue was in her mouth and hers in his, and he leaned into her, she could feel him firm against her thigh, and she grew hot again, he was pressing against her harder, and then his hand was on her leg, he had snuck up her skirt, and she felt a finger slip inside, they were standing *in the hallway,* and she thought, no, we can't do this here, not in public like this, and then she thought—no!—it's not the location that's the problem, you idiot, it's the whole thing, you can't do this—

"I can't." She pushed down her skirt, expelling his fingers, his hand. "I'm sorry."

How long were they kissing? A minute? Two?

She kept trying to give herself over to it completely, but all these other scenes came rushing at her like a collage, the stolen afternoons in out-of-the-way hotels, and the coded messages on encrypted apps, and secretly holding hands under restaurant tables, kissing in elevators and tears in taxis and ignored phone calls, cover stories about the account being hacked, *No I don't know who that is . . .*

Kate could see it all so clearly. Even though she'd never done it, and never will.

She left Seville the next day. It was a few weeks before Kate and Peter had an opportunity to be alone, truly alone, with a chance to discuss what had happened. What hadn't happened. Kate wondered if they ever would get around to talking about it, or if instead it would hang there undiscussed, uncommented upon, a sexual sword of Damocles, ready in perpetuity to fall.

Then Palermo put them in a car together, alone. They arrived two hours before the meet, to ensure that no one could get the drop, also to give them—to give Kate—plenty of time to vocalize her myriad objections. Saying them aloud made the reasons more real, transformed the solo ideas into a shared reality, this discussion building a consensus, a bulwark for a state of no-ness. Though it wasn't a discussion so much as a monologue.

"This is not a rejection of *you*," she said.

"I don't think I could live with myself," she said.

"I couldn't have you working for me," she said.

"I don't think I'd be able to talk to you ever again, or even to see you," she said.

"I couldn't do that to my husband," she said.

"I've already done too many things that were wrong," she said.

"That's not the person I want to be," she said.

"I don't think I could live with myself," she said again.

She had a lot of reasons. Some were so compelling she counted them twice.

"I *know* that this is the right path for us," she concluded. "You see that, don't you?"

"I do," he said. "You're completely right. About all of it."

And she chose to believe him, although she knew he was lying. Because so was she.

It's impossible to be certain that she didn't put Peter in harm's way purposefully. Maybe, subconsciously, she wanted to prove that she wasn't playing favorites. That this man was not her lover, just another operative, expendable, no special treatment.

Maybe it was worse. Maybe she actively hoped for something bad, something that would remove this temptation, would bury this secret forever, from everyone.

She was parked a half-block from the café where Peter would meet the asset. It was a busy street, mid-afternoon, broad daylight, plenty of witnesses. There was even a policeman at the far end of the block, staring at his phone. A safe environment.

The first thing that happened was a beat-up Skoda double-parked next to her, trapping her. The driver killed the ignition and jumped out.

"Hey!" she called, but the man ran across the street, into a shop.

Not only couldn't she pull the car out of the spot, she couldn't even open her door.

This could've been benign, but Kate knew it wasn't.

She strained her neck to see through the sidewalk crowd. Peter was in front of the café now, about to turn, but then there was fast movement from a minivan parked at the curb, its door flew open and a man emerged, and Peter turned to confront this potential menace, unaware that another man was closing in rapidly from the other direction—

"*Fuck,*" Kate muttered, trying to climb over the gear shaft, into the passenger seat—

What *is* a thought? An infinitesimally small electrical charge jumping among synapses in the brain's frontal lobe. What the hell is that? Plenty of these electrical charges were hopping around Kate's brain in the space of the second it took for her to cross to the other side of the car. Intervention scenarios, rescues, shootouts on the streets of Palermo.

Plus this: maybe it's not such a bad thing, for me—for my marriage, for my life—if Peter disappears forever.

—and she reached for the door handle while this second man shoved Peter from the side, knocking him off-balance, allowing the first man to easily grab Peter from beside the van's door, and these were both big men, Kate could see they were businesslike and calm, these weren't panicked irrational hotheads, these were professionals, and it took at most two seconds before the door slid closed and the van was pulling away, while the policeman was still staring at his phone, and Kate had never even gotten herself out of the car.

This is what haunts her the most. Not the things she did, but this thing she didn't, this inaction. This shot she didn't take. This life she didn't save.

What does *deserve* mean? Who does the measuring, the meting out? What does Kate's scorecard look like?

What is she? She's a woman who has killed people, and at least one of them was innocent. She has ruined lives because it was her job. She has destroyed marriages, she has taken husbands from wives, parents from children, money and security and peace-of-mind from dozens of people. All over the world there are people who can't sleep at night because of what Kate did. Because someone told her to, and she didn't say no.

Has she been a good worker, using her employer's resources for her own agenda? A good parent, actively choosing not to stay home with her children, perhaps even putting them in peril because of her professional choices? A good wife, standing in a hotel hall, another man's fingers bringing her to the brink?

Kate had stayed in Seville for too long—longer than had strictly been necessary. By the time she came home to Paris on a Sunday night, Ben had fallen sick again, his medications run out. She hadn't been around to prevent it.

She took her little boy straightaway to the hospital, and sat there in the waiting room, wondering: what does a person like Kate Moore deserve?

Kate shifts the phone to her other ear. She has noticed that her hearing is no longer as strong in one ear, but sometimes she forgets which.

A double-whammy of hearing loss exacerbated by memory loss. It's humiliating, and no one even knows about it. She almost told Dexter, but something held her back.

She wishes some doctor would present her with a chart, or a timeline: which bodily functions she can expect to fail, with what speed and level of discomfort and inconvenience, beginning when, lasting for what duration, and ending with what level of incapacitation.

"Sans doute, we must cancel the press conference, Schuyler." This is a new call that Schuyler is on, with the lawyer.

Eyesight, hearing, knees, lower back, libido, hips, hair loss, menopause, breast cancer. It's all just a matter of time, isn't it?

"We cannot have la presse here and Monsieur Forsyth does not arrive. Even if it would be possible to keep the fact of his disappearance secret— which I do not think would be possible—it would still be a large problem to cancel when reporters are here, asking their questions, with their recording devices."

"Agreed, Aurélie."

"We must inform the board of directors, immédiatement." The woman sighs. *"Mon Dieu."*

There are legal ramifications to a situation like this, a missing CEO during a terrorism event. Responsibilities that employees have to their boards, to shareholders, perhaps to police, to other authorities.

"When the stock market opens in New York—"

The ramifications are immense, for 4Syte's employees, its investors, shareholders.

"—ça sera une catastrophe."

Yes, it certainly will be a catastrophe.

But that's when Kate realizes: not for everyone.

She has to get the hell out of here—

43

Think, Hunter tells himself: is it possible that the CIA would use a phone that had been manufactured in China, embedded with who knows what hidden technologies, or compromised microchips, or surreptitious recording mechanisms, or remote-activation triggers, or fiber-optic splices?

It seems so unlikely. But that's not the same as impossible.

He looks around at the curtains that hide the boarded-up windows, at the triple-locked door, at the American sitting at the small dining table, leafing through a newspaper. The guy looks like he knows his way around a fistfight. That cheap hopsack suit isn't hiding a spare-tire belly, his hands look like they've never met a manicure.

Think this through again.

Okay, yes: it does make sense that a CIA babysitter wouldn't allow a man like Hunter Forsyth to walk out this door, into a dangerous environment, when the Agency has been tasked with keeping him safe. If something awful happened, the babysitter would lose his job. Maybe end up investigated by the Senate, his own Benghazi, a public outcry, talk-show humiliations, criminal charges.

But what could be the excuse for detaining Colette? She's not a kidnapping target. Sure, the CIA would be worried about her blowing the location, but how important is that? Couldn't they just shut down this safehouse? Or hustle Colette out the same way they hustled her in?

She shouldn't be here. Hunter shouldn't have insisted that she come, that was selfish of him, greedy. He put her in harm's way.

But then again, he can't help thinking: Colette makes it two against one.

And: Hunter will have the element of surprise on his side.

And: Hunter is a strong man, he's fit, he has fast reflexes. Plus he knows how to throw a punch. Or at least he did, twenty years ago. Twenty-five.

And: maybe Colette can be useful, at the very least a distraction. She sure as hell distracts Hunter. She could distract any man, couldn't she?

But, on the other hand: Simpson is probably armed, and the cops outside too.

But, without a doubt: Simpson is trained in hand-to-hand combat.

But: if the CIA wouldn't buy a Chinese-made phone, that means that Simpson is not CIA, so what the fuck is he?

Every answer is more terrifying than the last, all variations on the same theme: Hunter has not really been taken under the protective embrace of an American diplomat or intelligence officer.

Hunter's pulse is racing, brain growing fuzzy with increasing panic.

What has happened to him is something much less outlandish, much more predictable, a contingency that he has foreseen, for which he has planned. His security chief, his international bodyguard teams, the motion-detector alarms, the armored cars, the whole thing, hundreds of thousands of dollars per year that Hunter Forsyth spends to try to prevent this very thing from happening.

He's almost sure of it now. Because he just realized what it was that was bothering him three hours ago, when they first arrived at this ostensible safe-house: how the fuck did Simpson get its keys?

PART III

PALAIS-ROYAL

44

"*M*adame?"

Kate pretends to be startled. "*Oui?*"

"I am *directeur* of communications. Can I be of some assistance?"

"I'm waiting for Schuyler Franks."

"*Oui.* And you are who, please?"

"My name is Lindsay Davis." Behind Kate, in the hall, the elevator door dings. She should've left already, when it was easy. Now it's going to be harder.

"Please, what is it you are doing here?"

"I told you, I'm—"

"Yes, *mais pourquoi?* Why, Madame, are you here to see Schuyler Franks? *Why?*"

Kate can feel the air pressure change as the glass door is opened. She doesn't need to look over her shoulder to know who has arrived. "It's personal."

"Sandrine?" The woman cuts her eyes toward the receptionist. "*Appelle la police.*"

"I'm sorry." Kate turns toward the door, which a security guard is now blocking. "There must be some confusion."

The guard takes a lumbering step forward, asserting his presence. He's a big guy, but not a hard-looking one. He's big and soft and slow moving, the type of large animal that looks a lot like prey to a smaller, agile, more vicious species.

"Perhaps I should leave," Kate says, smiling at the guard. He doesn't smile back. She reaches down to collect her bag, filled with sunglasses and wallet and lipstick and keys, and this box of Lego, and a packet of the biscuits that Ben likes, because you never know.

The guard is holding a walkie-talkie in one hand, a phone in the other, neither hand anywhere near his holster, both engaged in something that's not protecting himself. Maybe he's too dim-witted to think Kate could be a threat, or too dim-witted to do anything about it. Either way, his wits are not luminous. Kate feels sorry for him. It's possible that she really does have an enemy out there, intent on doing her and her family grievous harm, but this security guard isn't him. Or her.

"Please tell Mademoiselle Franks that I'll return when it's more convenient."

Kate can't allow herself to be detained by this rent-a-cop, to be questioned by the genuine police. She has a cover story, of course, a legend that will stand up to casual questioning, a set of rehearsed answers that paint a perfectly credible picture, as long as there's no compelling reason to believe otherwise, no conflicting evidence. But if the police and intelligence coordinate on a deep-dive into her life? Dexter's? On a matter of terrorism? Her legend might be able to withstand that level of scrutiny, but her husband would not be able to withstand that sort of interrogation.

Kate takes another step toward the guard, slowly, nonthreatening, continuing to wear a placid smile.

What at first looked like a holster is on second glance just a tool belt. A place to hang a walkie-talkie, a flashlight, a nylon pouch that holds whatever, but not a gun. Probably snacks. He's a potbellied man who seems to push out his stomach purposefully, accentuating his roundness, proclaiming, *That's right, I'm fat. What's it to you?*

And she's just a woman! The guard doesn't sense any challenge here, he's a big man in uniform, an authority, there's no way that she'd—

Kate lands her punch directly on the front of the nose, and he never even twitches a muscle to defend himself. After the fact, he now raises both hands to the pain in the middle of his face, protecting against a further onslaught of the same. But this is a counterproductive instinct, because not only does he conk himself in the middle of the forehead with his walkie-talkie, he also leaves his entire body exposed.

She now has her choice of unmissable targets, an embarrassment of riches. But this one's a no-brainer, the blow that she knows has zero chance of failure.

The noise he makes is subhuman.

The reassuring thing about perpetrating violence with your hard knee against someone's soft crotch is that you're in no danger of injuring yourself. Punching is risky; people break their fingers all the time. Kicking too, if you don't know what you're doing, an unrehearsed swift kick could land you on your own ass.

The guard doubles over, totters, then collapses.

Kate is coiled, her whole body tingling with tensed muscles, with adrenaline. She looms above the writhing pile of a person, ready to strike again. But it's clear that this guy isn't getting up anytime soon, he can barely breathe. Kate doesn't want to kill this innocent sap by mistake, doesn't want to send him to the hospital, doesn't want to give the police any additional motivation to go looking for her too hard, tomorrow.

So that's enough.

Kate realizes that she's disappointed. It has been a while since she hit anyone. This felt good. She wants to do more of it.

The director of communications is standing a few feet away, hand held up to her aghast mouth; the receptionist too is frozen. Kate doesn't want to hit either of these women. But there is a specific woman Kate suddenly wants to punch in the face.

"*Désolée*," she mutters at the guard, then rushes to the elevator, hits the call button, thinking that if the elevator isn't waiting here she'll take the stairs, but the door does open immediately, because the guard arrived only thirty seconds ago.

Life would be a lot easier if the things that felt good were also the right things. But Kate is pretty sure that the truth is closer to the contrary.

45

Hunter's stomach sinks with a whoosh, as if in a roller coaster's front car that has crested the apex and is now free-falling, and you're wondering if the descent is going to continue to accelerate forever, or if you'll discover some alternative explanation, backing up from terminal velocity, some other answer to this question, an answer that doesn't mean that something horrible is going on here.

Simpson should not have the keys to this apartment. If this guy really is from State, or CIA, the only reason he'd already be in possession of these keys—on their own key ring—is if he knew he'd be using this safehouse today. Yet it was supposedly only after Hunter's pressure that he reluctantly agreed to come here. Which meant he'd been dishonest to Hunter. Which in the abstract is fine with Hunter, he's not anti-lie, there are plenty of legitimate reasons for dishonesty. He himself lies often. But always for a clear purpose. What purpose did Simpson's misrepresentation serve? Why did he pretend to need to search for a safehouse, when he was already carrying the keys to one?

If it were just the keys, or just the Chinese-manufactured phone, Hunter could discount it. One misgiving could be a fluke, paranoia, misunderstanding. Two is a legitimate suspicion. Three pieces of corroborating evidence? That's not a coincidence; that's a conspiracy. That's what he needs to test, right now.

⚜

He runs through it again, his rationale, the rebuttal, the counterargument for one or another of Simpson's responses, the credibility of Hunter's replies, the viability of the whole plan. It's like a logic problem, a chess match.

He certainly hopes he's wrong, he has never in his life hoped so fervently to be so wrong.

Hunter's phone is still useless as a communication device to the outside world. Is it really possible that there's no cell service anywhere in Paris? All carriers? For hours on end?

Maybe. All the towers could be somehow compromised. Or all the networks breached, disabled. Or all the signals scrambled by some EMP. Hunter is looking for reasons, he wants to believe in them. Because if not? What are the other possibilities?

One: there is no Paris-wide telecom outage, but just something specific to him—to his phone, or to his physical environment. What? An exterior signal-jamming device could have been used at the apartment, and another here in the safehouse.

Two: his phone has been disabled from within. Simpson did take possession of Hunter's device, back at the apartment, supposedly trying to help. But he could have been installing malware, disabling cellular, he could have done so many things that would render the phone inoperable in ways that Hunter wouldn't be able to observe.

And yes, the guy did something with Colette's phone too.

And yes, of course—*of course*—the wifi service here would not work. Nor would this landline, this piece of consumer electronics manufactured in China, of all the unlikely origins for telecommunications equipment procured by an American intelligence service.

So, okay, let's say that this is what did happen: it's specifically Hunter and Colette whose communications have been cut off. With no way to find out what's going on in the world. No way to tell anyone where he is. No way to reassure anyone. Why?

Is there more than the one obvious explanation?

Hunter's chest grows tight again, this panicky feeling, this unfamiliar sensation. Hunter is not a panicky person, never has been. That's the essence of him: *not* panicky. Ask anyone, that's what they'll tell you: Hunter Forsyth, dude has balls of brass.

He tries to take a deep breath, but it doesn't work, he's not getting enough oxygen.

"Monsieur?" Colette is standing over him, concerned. She puts a hand on his shoulder, a soft touch.

"I'm okay," he says, even though he isn't, and she didn't ask. "How are you doing?"

"*Pas mal,*" she says. That's the worst that Colette would ever admit: not bad. And when the French say "not bad," what they usually mean is: pretty damn good. Colette is not a complainer. She's a pillar of strength, Colette is.

Christ, he loves her so much.

He wonders what she thinks is going on here, if she's imagining the same scenarios he is. Maybe she got there long ago, even before Hunter. Maybe she has known all along, and has somehow remained poised, placid, unpanicked—

Wait a second—

No. There's no way. That's a ridiculous thought.

But is it? Is it *really* impossible?

No.

Okay, what if she is? What if Colette is in on this whole thing? And he tries to enlist her in this plan to escape? Then what?

Then, obviously, Hunter will be fucked. But will he be any more fucked than he is already?

No, he literally shakes his head at himself: she can't be, not Colette.

Get your shit together. This is your company that's in danger, your future. Maybe even your life, and the woman you love. *Everything* is at stake. Now is not the time to start being a wimp, not the time to devolve into stress-induced paranoia. Now is the time to man up, as Forsyth men have always done.

Hunter's grandfather went to law school after Korea, then joined the same firm where his own father had worked, then moved to in-house counsel at a multinational, where he eventually rose to CEO. Albert Forsyth had chosen the right path in the 1950s and '60s.

Hunter's dad Thatcher embarked on his career in the early '70s in the fledgling investment-banking sector, a wave he rode through the obscene '80s to its residential apogee in Greenwich, Connecticut, where his cohort of robber barons headquartered their hedge funds, built their trophy houses where trophy wives raised trophy children, trophy cars in the driveway, trophy everything.

Trophy son Hunter Forsyth was vaguely aware of the tech boom even before it existed. After Yale he went West to business school and then one startup after another until pay-dirt. Just a matter of time. Not a question of if, but simply when.

All the Forsyth men had been in the right places for their times. They'd all made their own fortunes in their own ways, and though none would deny that they were helped by the successes of their forebears, they'd all deem that help to be incremental, incidental.

They all learned, as boys, to box. Hunter remembers his first lessons at Grandpa's greenhouse, which had been transformed into a gymnasium, with a rowing tank and a lap pool, a weight room and a basketball half-court and the leather-scented boxing corner with a speed bag, a heavy bag, a canvas ring, pairs of red-and-white gloves in various sizes hanging from wooden pegs.

How old was he? Six? Seven? He remembers not being able to reach the speed bag, Grandma helping get the gloves on and off. He remembers it was fun.

As a teenager, Hunter boxed in a gym out in White Plains; boxing was no longer something that went on in the types of schools he attended, no longer a gentleman's sport. Everyone else he met at Power Boxing was a minority or poor, mostly both. These guys were—still are—Hunter's main exposure to ethnic and economic diversity.

When he was a teenager, Hunter used to have fantasies that boxing would one day be real-world useful. That he'd find himself cornered by bullies at school—never happened—or confronted by muggers in a dark alleyway—ditto—or he'd be a senator, or maybe even president, and they'd kidnap him—the Soviets, the Colombian cartels—and they'd never suspect that he possessed this secret lethal skill, which is what he would use to save himself, and the beautiful woman too.

In this fantasy, there was always a beautiful woman. In every fantasy.

"Colette?"

"Oui Monsieur?"

"May I borrow your phone? I'd like to give you some notes on calls for you to make, when we're finally finished here. We're going to have a lot of catching up to do."

"Calls?" This is not really what Colette does.

Hunter meets her eye, trying to communicate that this isn't a debate, she just needs to obey. "That's right." His gaze is level and unwavering, and he hopes she understands what he's communicating.

"*Très bien.*"

He sees her cut her eyes to Simpson, then back. She unlocks her phone, hands it over.

"*Merci,*" he says, with a gentle nod, trying to soften the exchange.

He tells himself again that this is a smart thing to do. He starts to type, using more words than normal, being less economical. He needs to be clear more than he needs to be quick.

"Here." He extends the device. "Why don't you look this over now? Let me know if you have any questions."

At the very bottom, he'd typed, *DO NOT ask any questions. If you have not understood something, type your question, then hand back to me.*

Hunter stands above Colette. After she has read the opening lines, she's going to look at him with a question in her eyes, and he's going to nod in confirmation.

Do not panic, his note begins. *I think we may have been kidnapped.*

46

They tried, using a bullhorn, first in French, then English, then Arabic and Farsi and maybe Urdu, he stopped paying full attention. It could not matter, anything they were saying. Later, they tried Arabic again. He never responded to any of it.

There is no way to be ready for this, Mahmoud knows that. He might have told himself that he would be prepared, convinced himself that he knew what it would eventually feel like. But he always understood, on some level, that he had been deceiving himself.

He has now been standing here for four hours. He has taken thousands of breaths in this courtyard, with so many weapons pointing at him, the long-range rifles on the rooftops, the assault weapons, the automatic handguns. He is just a split-second from being blown to smithereens by the twitch of some stranger's finger. Then again, so is everyone.

Any of these breaths may have been his last, but turned out to not be. Maybe the next will be.

Or the next.

Or the next.

He tries again to focus on the good that will come. On the bad that will be avoided. Both sides helped make his decision, that late afternoon, sitting in the quiet room alone with the bearded American.

"A boy and a girl," Mahmoud said. "As I indicated on your questionnaire."

The man nodded, looking sympathetic, saying nothing, as usual. This was their fifth meeting.

The paperwork was something Mahmoud had been handed in front of the hospital, where an attractive woman stood near the entrance that was used by his ward's patients. She was offering fifty euros for nothing really, just an initial survey, it would take only a few minutes. Then another five hundred—five hundred euros!—for participating in the full study, long-term.

Or as long-term as possible. Given the obvious limitations.

The survey was highly personal: physical questions, medical history, even religious beliefs, philosophical, sexual. It was being conducted by an American institute, an organization that Mahmoud researched for a few minutes to satisfy himself that it was not an identity-theft scam. Mahmoud could not imagine why anyone would want to steal his identity, or what such a theft would entail. But this had become a subject people discussed, without knowing what they were talking about. As with many things.

The institute was headquartered in Boston; the European outpost was in Geneva.

"How old?"

"Four and six."

"So, after . . . what is going to happen to your children?"

"My wife's family, in Egypt. We have already made the arrangements."

"Do your in-laws have money?"

Mahmoud was sure that this man already knew the answer. He did not like this type of question, this conversational game. He did not answer.

"No, I do not suppose they do." The man sighed, as if disappointed in the answer that he himself provided. "But they could, Mahmoud."

"They could what?"

"They could have money, your in-laws. Plenty of money. Enough to ensure that they will be comfortable. That your children will be educated, have opportunities."

Their previous meetings had focused on Mahmoud's illness, his prospects. But the conversations had also veered into politics, into religion. It was an unusual relationship they had been developing for a few weeks.

Then one day the man had a proposition. Something Mahmoud could do, before he died, that would benefit his family immensely, after he was gone. The man had not explained immediately, had left Mahmoud wondering for a week. Dreaming. Wanting. Trying to guess what this man could possibly want that Mahmoud might be able to provide. There were not many explanations.

"Could my children live in America?"

"Perhaps. But that is not something we can arrange. We cannot offer papers. What we can offer is money."

Mahmoud was becoming increasingly convinced that this man was going to propose something illegal, something immoral, something horrible. But Mahmoud was reluctant to confront that obstacle head-on.

"How much?"

"Well, that depends. How much do you think you need?"

Mahmoud did not want to commit to anything—he did not even want to frame the negotiation—until he had a better idea of what was going on. "What is it that I would have to do?"

"As I have said, it will be only one day's work. Some training beforehand, but that will be incidental." The man made a dismissive face. "It is not a complicated job, physically. There is nothing you need to know how to do. Nothing you need to learn."

That was when Mahmoud began to understand. The most obvious answer is usually correct. Occam's razor, he had learned about it in school.

"You will not suffer a long, painful decline. Your children will not watch you wither away. You will not spend all your family's money buying yourself tortured extra days. You will not lose control of your body. You will not endure one sleepless night after another. You will not spend months in and out of hospitals, and hospice. You will not leave behind a mountain of debt."

Those were very compelling points.

"Instead what you will leave behind, Mahmoud, is a fortune."

"That sounds too easy. Too good to be true."

"Well, yes. It is not all going to be easy."

They sat in silence for a moment. This man was comfortable with silence.

"I am not a violent person," Mahmoud said, eventually.

The American nodded.

"I do not believe in violence."

The American remained silent.

"How many?" Mahmoud asked.

"How many what?"

"How many people would I need to kill?"

47

At the foot of a bridge she comes to a sudden stop, and spins around, starts walking back quickly in the other direction, as if she'd just realized something urgent, she left the stove on, the door open.

Susanna scans the faces in front of her, but doesn't see him. He's gone, the man she thought might be following her. She's relieved, but also a bit frustrated. If someone were following her, she could elude him, solve the problem. But if there's no one there, the problem is simply her nerves, her mind. Less easy to solve.

She has no one to blame but herself, not even her husband, and she has come to understand that being able to easily assign blame is one of the chief advantages of having a husband. But she knows that all this is her own doing. She's the one who desperately wanted to have a child; he was ambivalent about parenthood. She's the one who thought they should settle here, live this life. She's the one who came up with the new complicated plan, not to mention the old complicated plan. She's the one who put everything at risk, again.

For a while it looked as if childbearing was going to pass her by. That too was her own fault. She hadn't taken any of her relationships seriously, hadn't been attuned to the ticking of her clock. It turns out that if you wait until your career is fully established, your window is small, and it was nearly shut by the time she found the right man, almost by mistake.

And, being completely honest: he isn't necessarily the right man. Plus: they didn't find each other so much as they were thrust together by happenstance. Theirs was a professional partnership, arranged by management. They lived together, they shared a home, meals, vacations, sometimes they even shared a bed, though not conjugally; they both knew that sex would be a mistake. All the while, he was more than happy to find his outlets elsewhere—other men's wives, or young women in bars, one-night stands that didn't even last a whole night, stumbling home at two A.M., smelling like women who weren't her. But what did she care.

Except she did, a little bit.

She couldn't bring herself to behave the same way. She told herself that it could compromise her cover, jeopardize her mission, but that was only partially true, and became less true over time, until the night when she crept into his bed in the middle of the night, when their mission was near its end, at its most exciting, and she just couldn't help herself anymore. She knew he'd be good in bed; she didn't know how much she'd enjoy it.

She slows her pace. Is it? Yes, it's silence that she hears. Golden silence, silken silence, the warm-bath embrace of silence, better than Champagne and caviar, better than the famous duck at La Tour d'Argent, better than the very best sex. Nothing compares to the onset of silence from a crying baby.

Three years ago, if you'd have asked her what she'd be doing today, she'd never in her wildest dreams have predicted this. Married to that hopefully reformed cad, wandering the streets of Venice with their napping baby. The handgun in her pocket was the only predictable element.

She stopped walking in the middle of a narrow lane, became one of those pedestrian obstructions that makes her want to throttle heedless tourists.

With the baby asleep, and currently no crisis, she should eat, take care of her own physical needs while she has this chance. Another lesson from parenthood. There have been many teachable moments.

"*Ciao Susanna.*"

"*Ciao Guido.*"

"*Aperol spritz?*"

She would love to have her regular drink, sitting here in the Campo de la Pescaria, facing the Grand Canal, sun in her face, beautiful baby sleeping in her lap, net worth skyrocketing by the second.

"*No, grazie.*" No alcohol today, not even a sip. There still might be plenty of action in front of her. She orders mineral water, seafood risotto.

Her phone buzzes, an incoming text: *All ok?*

Richie Fucking Benedetti. Who'd have thought he'd turn out to be a pussy?

She's had enough of him, and his ilk. She's been interacting with scum for her whole life, she can feel the film of it coating her, she can't wash it off, it has seeped into her bloodstream, infected her, she recognizes this, an awareness that has heightened since Matteo was born, after so much effort, so many tears.

It's amazing that there's any path from being this innocent baby to becoming a Richie Benedetti. Or to becoming herself. She can't let either happen. This has become her primary goal, the organizing principle of her life from now on.

Starting tomorrow.

Yes, she types her reply, *all ok,* and hopes it's true.

When everything had been figured out, the final hurdle was securing the investment capital. If they landed just one big fish, others would fall into place, buoyed by someone else's confidence. That was the way these things worked.

This wasn't an opportunity they could take wide. The opposite. There was a very finite population of individuals who'd be willing to participate in this endeavor, and an even smaller subset she'd be willing to trust with it.

For better or worse, both her and her husband's careers had afforded a broad acquaintance with exactly the sorts of people who'd be interested in this investment. But the first candidates had declined, and she was losing confidence.

"Are you sure about this guy?" her husband asked, just steps from the hotel's revolving door.

They were running out of money, which is the same as running out of time, living on an ever thinner cushion of savings. Sicily had been an inexpensive place to live, and they'd been comfortable enough there, and for logistical reasons they'd wanted their kid to be born there. But they didn't want to raise a child there; they didn't want Sicily to be their permanent home.

"Am I *sure*? No. Obviously."

"It's not too late. We could . . ." He raised a hand to indicate the network of canals, boats, escape to other places, other possibilities. Her husband wore the cloak of a supremely confident man, a handsome man, a man who was good at everything; he had no doubts about his abilities to ski a steep bumpy slope, repair simple machinery, get a woman into bed. Trivial matters. It was the larger challenges that made him doubt himself.

"This is going to work," she reassured him. That was one of her roles in their relationship. Their partnership.

That was all he needed. He nodded, turned to the revolving door, which a navy-suited man had already launched into motion. Guests here didn't even need to push a door, the staff would do anything you wanted, fetch anything, arrange anything.

Upstairs, Richie Benedetti sat in a wingback chair, facing the terrace over the Grand Canal. He'd draped himself in a big British newspaper, and crossed his legs the tough-guy way, displaying every contour of his ball sack in his tight custom-tailored suit pants, a long expanse of brightly patterned socks, suede loafers with a garish logo.

Richie was small-time wiseguy from South Philly who'd turned into a halfway-connected mobster, then he stumbled first into a fortune and then into a quagmire and subsequently into the witness-protection program in North Carolina, from which he grew bored and skipped out to reunite himself with the money he'd squirreled away in a diverse portfolio of Italian real estate, Swiss numbered accounts, and Monacan safety deposit boxes. Richie wasn't a devotee of traditional market-based securities. This was going to make the pitch both easier and harder. Because this opportunity was both a traditional security and the complete opposite.

"Hi Richie," she said. "Long time."

Richie looked her up and down, took in her distended belly, her new hair. "A pleasure. Who's your friend?"

"This friend is my husband Chris."

Richie didn't stand to shake the new man's hand. "That's quite a beard you're sporting. What are you, some kinda hipster?"

"Something like that."

Richie turned back to her. "You won't mind if I have Gianna check you both out, will you?"

Susanna glanced at Gianna, bee-stung lips and jet-black hair and gravity-defying tits.

"No problem," Susanna said. "But we're going to have to check you too."

"You're fuckin' kiddin' me."

"Nope."

Richie contemplated the situation, shrugged. He wasn't wearing a wire, wasn't carrying, there was nothing to find. He didn't love the prospect of sacrificing his dignity by submitting to a pat-down, not at this stage in his life, but he understood the necessity. No one could trust anyone, not in his line of work. Not in anyone's. And he'd long ago relinquished his dignity to this woman. He no longer gave much of a shit.

"Phones?"

Everyone handed their mobiles to the bodyguard, who left the room.

"How's life treating you, Richie?"

Benedetti adjusted his heavy silk tie, one of those unmistakable patterns that certain men recognize, it's like a secret handshake, hey, look, we're both guys who spend a couple of hundred dollars on neckties.

"Can't complain."

He looked like part of the décor, decorated in that maximalist Italian fashion of velvet and silk, gold-leaf and marble.

"You enjoying life on Lake Como?"

Richie was a fourth-generation Italian-American whose ma cooked tuna casserole and meatloaf, not Sunday gravy. He learned everything he needed about being a guinea gangster from *The Godfather* and *The Sopranos,* and spent four decades fake-rhapsodizing about the old country that he'd always avoided visiting, too worried that reality would disappoint, that he'd be mocked for not speaking the language.

When he needed to start a new life, he finally made good on his supposed fantasy. He bought a modest villa on the lake, probably thinking he'd be hanging out with George Clooney.

"Sure, it's a nice place. But what are we doin' here?"

"No pleasantries, Richie?"

"You know I ain't that pleasant a guy. And you were never that pleasant to me, were you? So." He turned up one corner of his mouth, a sneering smile that's laughing at you, not with you. She really despised assholes like Richie. But that's how the world works, isn't it? For anything involving big money, you have to deal with big-money assholes.

"Okay, Richie." She was about to launch into it, but just then the bodyguard reentered, delivering their *espressi,* swiping lemon peels across the rims of the glasses, one, two, three of them. Then the factotum retreated.

"How much money do you have?"

Richie sneered again. "You fuckin' kiddin' me?"

"I'm going to guess somewhere between twenty and thirty mil." She used to have surreptitious access to Richie's financial situation. Not recently. "Am I right?"

He shrugged.

"That's certainly enough to live on for the rest of your life, I guess. As long as you don't go doing anything stupid like buying jets." She knew for a fact that he'd recently bought a jet. "But you're continuing to hustle, aren't you? Putting your neck out. Juggling this, juggling that, exposing yourself to people you don't—"

"We here to go over my whole, what, résumé? That's not so interestin' to me. I'm already familiar with the particulars. So why don't you tell me the fuck you want?"

She leaned forward. "How'd you like to double your money, Richie?"

He rolled his eyes. "Sure, I'd like that very much."

"In a couple of months."

His eyebrows shot up.

"Without hurting anyone. Or lifting a finger."

⚜

Go through it chronologically, she reminded herself. Richie was a guy who needed a story to be linear. Visual too.

"At eight in the morning, we call in a bomb threat to the police. A single device, deposited in a train station. The police radios will crackle with reassignments, calls to action. Units will rush to the scene, drawing forces from elsewhere. Trains will be canceled. Media will gather."

Richie could see this. He nodded.

"This bomb will be a few sticks of TNT in a backpack, a detonator wired to a disposable mobile. But this bomb isn't there to explode. It's to draw the police. And to establish an aura of terror, first thing in the morning. During the next half-hour, while the police are swarming the train station, we plant a handful of other devices at high-visibility sites. To cap it all off, a man walks into the middle of the museum's courtyard, wearing a suicide vest, which draws every last cop from their normal assignments."

"So, what? You robbin' a bank?" Richie needs to prove how smart he is, which is actually not that smart. "This a heist?"

"One of these normal assignments is to guard the home of an

American CEO who spends time in Europe. This police escort is a privilege he pays for under the table."

This was something Richie could respect. He'd paid for more than his fair share of cops over the years. But sadly there was no buying off feds, at least not American ones. That's what got him exiled.

"The threats will be all over, alerts will be popping up on everyone's phones, coverage will blanket the media, there will be video of this backpack sitting in the station, being approached by a bomb-dismantling robot. Sharing a split-screen with an aerial view of the museum, a suicide bomber standing in the center. Utter terror."

Richie was nodding again.

"So the CEO understands it when his police escort abandons its post. Just minutes later, reinforcements arrive—policemen in one car, an American official in another, a middle-aged guy from the State Department, sent on a crucial mission to protect a prominent American citizen during a moment of extreme peril. Because not only is the city under attack, but a threat has been made against Americans. Specifically against prominent American businessmen. This is a man who always thinks of himself as the smartest guy in the room. So he's proud of figuring out that a person like this bureaucrat, claiming to be from State and showing up in this situation, is lying. And because he's so damn smart, he knows what the lie is."

Richie leaned back, trying himself to be that damn smart too. "CIA."

"Exactly. At the same time that the police escort is called away, the CEO's cell service disappears. Because the trunk of the police car contains a powerful mobile device that jams any and all mobile-phone and data service."

"How do you get the squad car?"

"We don't. We're using an unmarked car. If we need to explain this, it's because all the cruisers have been deployed to the sites of the bombs. Extra personnel have been called in for the emergencies, more bodies than vehicles, et cetera. But we have the siren, a couple of other official-looking accessories."

"What about the CEO's landline?"

"One of the cops heads to the basement to cut the wires, taking out cable and Internet and landline telephone. This complete comms blackout, combined with the citywide attack, makes the CEO very anxious, impatient. Our State-slash-CIA official offers to try to fix the CEO's cell phone, but fails. Sorry, he says, I couldn't help."

"He doesn't really try?"

"He disables everything, including all geo-location services. So as the minutes tick by, the CEO grows increasingly frustrated. He demands a solution."

"The embassy?"

"That's his first request. Not possible, our guy says, embassy in total lockdown. So the CEO demands other options. Our guy hems and haws, doesn't want to offer the thing that everyone knows he can offer. But eventually he relents, says he'll look into finding a situation. After an understandable delay, he does find a secure location that has working telecom."

"A CIA safehouse."

"Exactly right, Richie. Though that's not the phrase our guy uses, because a CIA officer wouldn't. But this CEO, he's a man of the world, he knows what's what. This appeals to his sense of his own importance. Plus to everyone's romance about the Agency. A CIA safehouse! He wants to see this."

"So you're saying that the CEO *demands* his own kidnapping?" He was nodding appreciatively. "Jeez."

"And that, Richie, is how you kidnap a high-value, high-net-worth target who maintains twenty-four-hour, three-sixty-five armed guards, without hurting anyone."

It was beginning to make sense to Richie, but he saw some holes, wanted to poke at them, see how big they'd grow.

"This is a very complicated plan for a kidnapping. Why don't you just kill the guard, snatch your hostage by force?"

"That's a good question, Richie. Why do you think?"

The guy squinted again, mouth hanging open, like the illustrated-dictionary picture of a dunce trying hard to figure out something. "Afraid of drawing attention?"

"Not especially. I think we could discretely effectuate a quiet abduction in a simpler fashion. We'd still have to draw away the police, but we could do that without a terrorist attack against an entire city."

She could see Richie thinking, his eyes darting around. Then they opened wide, and refocused on her. "You don't want anyone to know that he's been kidnapped."

She smiled. "Not even *he* will know he's been kidnapped."

"Then why doesn't he just walk out the door?"

"Remember, this escape to a safehouse, that's his own suggestion. The city is under attack! And he specifically has been targeted. The CIA has received direct orders—from the highest level—to keep this VIP off the streets, safe from abduction, from assassination, from all sorts of terrifying possibilities. Even if the CEO demands his freedom, our guy simply cannot let him go. For his own good."

"But what if he refuses to kidnap himself from the get-go? What if he *doesn't* demand to be taken someplace else?"

"Unlikely. He'll be desperate to resume communications. To explain his disappearance. To be in touch. To run the empire that he believes only he can run."

"Sure. *But.*"

"In that unlikely case, our man will claim to receive new info from the police radio. The situation out in the streets has deteriorated, there are now explicit orders from the DCI to remove the high-value target to a secure location."

"DCI?"

"Director of Central Intelligence."

"And if he still doesn't agree to this?"

"He'll be forced to. For his own good."

"By just this one fake CIA guy?"

"Also the pair of cops. In uniform. Armed."

"Why cops? Why not American army?"

"The local-law look might come in handy if the team ends up interacting with citizens out in the streets. No one is going to challenge a local cop during a terror attack."

"What about the CEO's security? Why doesn't he bring along his muscle?"

"That's one of the benefits of making it the CEO's idea to leave the apartment: his only option is to go to a safehouse, so it's on the CIA's terms. And his guard is local, not an American citizen, so he can't be allowed into any secure Agency facility."

"Is that true?"

"None of these people will know it isn't."

"Once this guy is at this facility, what if he asks to leave?"

"We tell him he can't."

"If he disagrees?"

"We have three armed men on-site. Our holding area—the safe-house—is an unoccupied building; condemned, scheduled for demo-lition."

"If he tries to escape?"

"We'll subdue him."

"If that fails?"

"At the end of the day, Richie, I really don't give a shit what happens to this guy."

"But you're not going to *kill* him?"

"Ideally, no."

Richie had been following along more or less successfully to this point, but now he became lost. "I don't understand."

"What part?"

Richie looked exasperated; his short fuse was burning quickly. "If you kill him, how the fuck are you gonna get a ransom?"

She leaned back, let her hands rest on her protruding belly. She used to be annoyed by all those pregnant women who couldn't stop cradling their bellies, something self-satisfied about it. Now look.

"Who said anything"—she allowed a smile to spread across her lips, she couldn't help it—"about a ransom?"

48

As soon as the elevator doors begin to open, Kate can see that a security team is crossing the courtyard, headed in her direction— She flattens herself against the wall, out of view, and reaches over to hit the door-close button, again, *again*—

Closing . . . closing . . .

Finally.

She presses −2, which is neither the next level down nor the lowest, both too obvious.

This building must have an exit other than the front door, a place for loading bays, service elevators, delivery entrances, fire exits, all accessible from the *sous-sols* levels, the garage, mechanicals, a warren of tunnels, of corridors that connect one wing to another. Kate has been beneath plenty of these old European buildings, and they're all similar in their lack of similarity, their wildly disparate layouts and the incomprehensibility of their floor-plans, no rhyme or reason to what's where, spaces that have been repurposed again and again for centuries.

Kate could easily find a place to hide down here, wait out the security team's search. But there's often no mobile signal in those deep levels; she'd be cut off from Inez, from Dexter, from school, from her kids. She wouldn't be able to access any useful apps, any maps. She wouldn't be able to accomplish anything.

So, no: Kate can't afford to waste time hiding out down here.

She looks right, left. Right would be toward the front of the building. She turns left.

The rough-hewn stone walls are whitewashed, but that doesn't totally disguise the dankness. At the end of the hall Kate turns onto another long stretch, plenty of doors on either side, but none of them marked for exit.

The police aren't going to drop a dragnet on Kate today, but tomorrow might be different. There are the cameras in the elevator, at the security hut, in the waiting room. There will be a surfeit of footage of Kate gaining illicit entry to this building, sneaking through these halls. There's also the beaten-up security guard, the receptionist, Schuyler. They'll all be shown this footage.

Under close scrutiny, the wig will not help, nor the eyeglasses. Not if the investigators are diligent, not if they press these witnesses, not if they use software to remove these eyeglasses, to change this hair, to provide alternative superficialities to help focus on the bone structure, the shape of the face, the jawline, the eyes.

"Yes," Schuyler will say, looking at a picture of Kate Moore. "That's definitely her."

SORTIE.

Kate opens the door gingerly, as if it's an injured limb that she doesn't want to move too quickly, it might hurt. She listens . . . listens . . .

Nothing.

The door closes behind her. She's in an institutional stairwell, cinder-block walls, steel-tube handrails, emergency lights. Empty. Silent.

She drops her bag. Removes her jacket, throws it to the floor. Yanks her blouse over her head, rolls it up into a tight cylinder. She leans over, shoves the blouse—

What's that?

Voices. A tinkle of laughter. Two people, up a few flights. The unmistakable click of a Zippo being opened, the scrape of the flint wheel, the *whuff* of the flame igniting.

"*Merci.*"

The lid clicks closed.

"*De rien.*"

Surreptitious cigarettes. They're going to stand up there for five minutes, smoking.

Kate moves more carefully now, silently. Reaches into her bag, pulls out a different cloth cylinder, rolled up with a rubber band. She pulls this T-shirt over her head, shimmies in, tugs down the bottom.

Now she takes off the blond wig, the bobby pins, the clunky eyeglasses.

She pushes her hands through her real hair, shakes her head. Runs bright lipstick across her mouth.

There: now she's a Frenchwoman. No middle-aged American woman would wear this T-shirt proclaiming VIE DE MERDE, the Shitty Life, which encompasses so much disappointment in so many things, the way young people feel, always have, everywhere. But not well-off middle-aged American #expats; they want to message the opposite of VDM.

Kate tiptoes up to the next landing, another fire door with a narrow vertical panel of safety glass to provide a view out to a hall, a way to check for flames, smoke, assailants.

Nothing.

This door squeaks on its hinges, but there's no one to hear it except Kate and the surreptitious smokers, and they're not going to come investigating—

But damn, here comes another woman, turning at the far end of the corridor.

Kate doesn't slow down. She smiles at this woman, says *"Bonjour"* while making firm eye contact, a preemptive attack of collegiality. Kate is a person who belongs here, who's hiding nothing.

"Good afternoon," the woman responds in English. The lingua franca here isn't franca, it's another place where English has taken over, another domino, one office at a time, city by city, country by country.

This woman doesn't even think of challenging Kate.

Bluffing: it always works. Almost always. And if it hadn't? Kate was ready—maybe eager—to use other means. One of the things Kate has learned over the past couple of years is that being the manager of other ass-kickers is not nearly as satisfying as doing the ass-kicking yourself. Not remotely.

The rear exit leads to a narrow side street lined with cluttered shops whose windows display ribbons and buttons and bolts of fabric, cash registers at the front, worktables in the middle. A specialty commercial strip that's visited by the same people all the time, it's a community that congregates here, coffee and gossip, draping saddle bags onto motorbikes or hopping into those little three-wheeled mini-trucks with a boxful of supplies, headed back to the dry-cleaner's, the seamstress shop. Their day is going on, mostly as normal.

Kate is darting through the thick mid-afternoon crowds on the busy street, dodging businessmen whose eyes are taking in her VDM T-shirt stretched tight across her breasts, a double-distraction.

At one end of this street: police.

Kate heads in the other direction, past salons offering cheap haircuts, Chinese restaurants offering cheap lunches, eight euros for the *menu rapide*. She slows when she notices a trio of soldiers up ahead, olive-drab camouflage fatigues, blue berets. They're scanning faces, body language, looking for something wrong, someone wrong.

But they're not looking for her. It's the Paris police whom the 4Syte receptionist called, not the French army. The army is looking for terrorists, and Kate isn't one, and none of this has anything to do with her.

Though Kate is beginning to suspect that maybe this isn't true.

She'd been blind before. She'd refused to be suspicious back when Dexter moved the family to Europe on short notice for a big new job—big client, big money, a big adventure. She'd been seduced by it all, by the prospect of living a different kind of life, of reinventing herself. As with all seductions, she chose not to see the inconvenient, the insincere, the incredible.

Dexter had no client. There was no job.

The real reason they'd come to Luxembourg was for Dexter to orchestrate a complex cyber-intrusion, to steal a fortune—fifty million euros—that he would split with his partner, an FBI agent who was investigating this massive theft in order to ensure, with absolutely certainty, that the crime would not be solved. That agent had followed Dexter to Luxembourg, where she was calling herself Julia MacLean; her bogus husband was Bill. The MacLeans infiltrated themselves into the Moores' lives—Julia fashioned herself into Kate's best friend; Bill, Dexter's. Dinner dates and tennis matches, dancing in Paris and skiing the Alps, the fast friendship of fellow expats.

All four of them were pretending to be something they weren't, someone they weren't, each lying to everyone else.

Those memories of Luxembourg are dimming. Time is speeding up, the kids are growing so quickly, details are beginning to dissolve—the wallpaper in the Luxembourg hall, the route Kate drove to the international school, her first meal with Julia.

Although some edges of memory have become dull rounded corners, other details are sharper than ever. If only Kate could choose which she would remember, and which she could forget.

A clear picture is forming in her mind, but Kate knows she's painting with a strong bias, a suspicion based on previous events, which may have no objective connection to today. Facts, she tells herself. Focus on facts.

Fact: Hunter Forsyth is not at his office, where he really ought to be.

Fact: nor is he at his apartment, where he might have reason to be.

Fact: an American who claimed to be from the State Department escorted Forsyth somewhere that's supposedly secure.

Fact: Forsyth brought along his assistant, who'd been with him since early morning. They'd had plenty of time for a quickie, if that's what was going on, before Forsyth got down to the business of CEO'ing, preparing for an important press conference at which he's going to announce a huge deal. It didn't even need to be quick. A longie.

Fact: Forsyth has now been out of pocket for nearly five hours, and it looks like no one from his company has any idea what has happened to him, and they are beginning to panic.

So: who could have caused that? And why?

A few suspects come immediately to mind.

One: this assistant-concubine, the last person to see him on this day when his company is being assailed internationally, and the city engulfed in terror.

Two: the purported State official. The more Kate thinks about this, the more it's clearly a lie. But just because the guy's identity is false doesn't point Kate in the direction of any particular truth.

One plus two: it's possible that the State imposter and the assistant are in league.

Three: Forsyth himself. Is his disappearance connected to his press conference? His big deal? Is this a last-minute bargaining tactic? Has he orchestrated his own disappearance? As a response to the terror threats?

There's a fourth suspect too. And a fifth. Both of them connected to each other. Both connected, intimately, to Kate.

❧

She has to consider abandoning him, doesn't she? And doing it right now, before a net can fall. Taking the kids, driving out of Paris into the rolling farmland, the yellow mustard fields and long rows of vineyards, stands of cypress trees along property lines, the monumental wind turbines presiding atop the ridges, the occasional castle clinging to a hillside, its keep crumbling, tumbling down to the red-tile roofs of the village below.

Out of France then, into Luxembourg, no border to cross but clean passports in the glove box anyway, a million euros in getaway cash stashed in the farmhouse. Just a couple hundred miles away, they'd be there by dinnertime, schnitzel and spaetzle at the quiet inn the next town over, she'd light a fire while the old radiators took their time.

Dexter would have to fend for himself. He'd come and join them when he could. If he could. And if he couldn't? That would be because he's guilty, and Kate and the kids will be better off without him.

She feels like a monster for admitting this into her consciousness. It's deplorable. But she'd have no choice, if for no other reason than to protect the children.

Kate knows that Dexter isn't guilty—she *knows* this, doesn't she? He wouldn't get himself involved in anything that would put the family at such risk, not again, not after Luxembourg. Would he?

She needs to get back across the river quickly, get to her husband. And she's beginning to worry about what she's going to find over there.

Favor? she types into her phone.

Inez responds almost instantaneously: *Oui?*

Meet at Palais-Royal?

OK. I am at the office. Dix minutes.

Kate locates the financial app on her phone, way back on the fourth screen; she consults it roughly never. So it takes her a bit longer than it would take most people to find what she's looking for, but hoping not to find.

She does.

❧

It won't be difficult for the police to put it together.

Yes, Schuyler will say, nodding. That's the woman who lied her way into our offices, then brutalized a security guard so she could escape.

Which that woman did just hours after 4Syte's CEO was kidnapped.

Which combined with these international threats in Hong Kong and Mumbai—and this widespread attack across Paris—has caused 4Syte's stock to crash.

Which was precisely the unlikely development on which this woman's husband had wagered a substantial sum of money.

Which this husband just did after decades of a widely known, easily documented grudge against that very same kidnapped CEO.

Which is all an overwhelming volume of evidence.

49

"*Monsieur*, I do not think this is a good idea." Colette stares into his eyes. What is it she's looking for? His resolve?

"I understand," Hunter says, as quietly as possible without whispering; he doesn't want to seem to be plotting anything. "But we have to try before it's too late."

"Too late? For what?"

"To survive."

Colette is taken aback, but not convinced, at least not as immediately and unequivocally as she usually accepts his orders. Because they're not at work, and if they're not at work, then Hunter is not her boss, he's just the guy whose fault it is that she has been kidnapped. He's not necessarily part of the solution. He's part of the problem, is what he is. Not just part of it, he's the whole goddamned problem. Is that what Colette is thinking?

"Are you ready?" he asks. This is his subtle way of opening the door just a crack, enough for her to rush through with her strenuous objections, *No, Monsieur, I am not ready, I am not going to participate in this horrible plan* . . .

But she doesn't, thankfully. She nods.

Hunter walks over to where Simpson sits, too far away to hear, but still observing with well-warranted suspicion.

"Listen, Simpson. My assistant has to go to her kid's school. An important meeting with a teacher."

Colette has a seven-year-old, or maybe it's six, or five, Hunter can't keep track; he doesn't pay attention to any information about any children. Even though he wants to be a father, he can't bring himself to get interested in other people's kids. He doesn't even pretend to try.

Simpson turns to Colette, standing a few meters away. "Son or daughter?"

"*Fille*," Colette answers. "Séverine is nine years old."

Nine? Okay, he was off by a couple of years.

"And you scheduled an appointment for a day that you knew was going to be very busy?"

That's a good point.

"My husband Guy, he is the one who is planning to go. But I fear he will not arrive."

Hunter is impressed with Colette's on-the-feet thinking. As always.

"Why's that?" Simpson asks.

"Guy is returning from Dubai on a flight that will arrive midday. But I believe that all flights will be diverted, *n'est-ce pas*? Certainly all flights from *les pays arabes*. And as you know, I have no way to contact him."

Simpson considers this. "I can't imagine that any schools in Paris will be having normal meetings this afternoon."

"The school is outside of the city, *Monsieur*. We do not live in Paris."

Simpson has no rebuttal to this.

"I cannot simply abandon my child, *Monsieur*!" Colette is growing self-righteous, angry, loud. "It is a very important appointment."

Simpson sees that he's trapped. He has no rational, humane reason to prevent this agitated mother from moving on with her life. Yes, Hunter realizes, this was a good plan; he's proud of himself for thinking of it.

Hunter would be so happy to be wrong, for Simpson to relent, allow Colette to leave. Because if not, this guy will be acknowledging something else, and Hunter and Colette will have to initiate the only plan he has been able to come up with.

"I have sympathy, Madame Benoit. I really do—"

Hunter's heart sinks while his adrenaline spikes. He knows that a minute from now, he might very well be dead.

"—but I'm sure your daughter won't be the only such child, on an extraordinary day like today, plenty of parents will have trouble with transportation. The school will make arrangements."

They are staring at each other, Simpson and Colette, both of them fuming, both of them lying to the other. Colette's husband isn't in Dubai, he isn't flying back to Paris today, there's no school appointment.

"It is necessary for me to leave."

"I'm sorry, but I can't allow it."

Colette glances quickly at Hunter, and he blinks once at her, a long blink. This is their signal. No turning back now.

She takes a deep breath, girding herself, and turns her eyes back to Simpson. "I will," she says.

"No," Simpson says firmly, "you will not."

Colette starts walking toward the door, stomping. Everyone knows full and well that the door is locked, that Simpson holds the key, that she will not be able to open the door. But nevertheless both men watch to see what she's going to do when she reaches the threshold.

Which is: bang with her fists, one, two, three times.

Then she screams, *"À l'aide!"*

Simpson stands, pushes his chair away from the table. It's a heavy wooden desk chair, the type you find in a library, or a bookstore, the seat worn into butt-cheek buckets by generations of occupants sitting down, sliding around.

"Stop it," Simpson says and takes a step toward Colette, his back now completely turned to Hunter.

"S'il vous plaît!!" She bangs again, with both fists.

Simpson takes another long stride, and that's when Hunter makes his move, rushes up to grab the two rear legs of Simpson's sturdy chair, keeping his wrists firm, his forearms flexed, maintaining his balance with all his core muscles engaged, everything straining to stay in control, as Colette continues to bang on the door, and Hunter pushes up from his quads, lifting the chair aloft, holding it above his head now, taking quick steps to catch up behind Simpson, with Colette's racket providing aural cover for his footsteps, and Simpson helping the effort by yelling, "Stop!"

Hunter squeezes his grip even tighter, and raises his arms higher, his muscles burning, everything straining as he begins the swing while he's still hustling up to his target, just one more stride will do it—

The chair-back meets Simpson firmly on the top of his head, and Hunter continues to power through with a full swing, the wood now hitting the guy in his upper back, he's buckling, collapsing to his knees, and Hunter is losing his grip, he doesn't fight it, he lets the heavy piece of furniture fall onto the guy, another insult to the injury, and now all this wood is in the way, so Hunter shoves it aside with his knee, and yanks Simpson by the hair, spinning the guy's face around so Hunter can punch him once, twice, the guy's nose bleeding and his upper lip split—

Colette drops to her knees and reaches inside the guy's jacket and finds the holster and removes the gun and leaps back to her feet, fumbling with the weapon, which almost slips from her hand once, now twice, and she steadies her hands with both fists encircling the grip, aiming the weapon at the man who's lying on the floor, not moving, not at all.

"Okay," Hunter says, breathing heavy. "Good. We're good."

His hands are already hurting, possibly broken bones in both of them. Fuck. This is why you wear boxing gloves.

"Are you okay?"

Colette doesn't answer. She's entirely focused on her white-knuckled death grip of the pistol, hands shaking, eyes wide.

"Okay," he says again. "We're good." Trying to convince himself as much as her.

He finds the keys in Simpson's jacket pocket. "I'll take that gun now." Hunter needs to pry Colette's fingers off the weapon, then fills her empty palm with the keys. "Here. You're going to unlock the door, and turn the knob, and pull open the door while you step away in that direction." He points to the far side of the door. "Understand?"

"*Oui.*"

"I'm going to be over there, lying on the floor, aiming the gun at the opening of the door. If anyone is waiting for us on the far side, I'm going to shoot."

"*Oui.*"

"If no one is there, we will wait one minute in case someone arrives. We will wait in the same position, you there, me there, hidden, unmoving, until I get up. Then we will leave, me in the lead. In front. *D'accord?*"

She nods.

"You did good, Colette." He rubs her upper arm. "You did great."

"*Merci.*"

"Are you ready? We should not wait long." How long has it been since she started banging and screaming? Sixty seconds? Is that enough time for someone downstairs to rush up here?

"*Oui.*"

Hunter crosses the room, and drops to his knees, then stretches himself flat on his stomach. He extends his arms, grips the semiautomatic with both hands, aiming at the edge of the door, up at an imaginary spot that's four feet high: center of mass for a man at the door.

"Okay," Hunter says. "Now."

Colette turns to the door. The first key she tries doesn't fit, nor the second. She looks over at him.

"It's okay," he says, "one of them will work."

The third does. Colette turns the key slowly, trying to minimize the noise. Then she leaves the key in the lock, the whole ring hanging there, and places her hand on the knob. She glances at Hunter again, and he nods.

She turns the knob—

50

"The license plate of the van?"

"Van? What van?"

Ibrahim has been on an extended break. He went to the bathroom, ate a sandwich, called his parents. They know what is going on in Paris, they know that their son is at the scene. They know he cannot talk about it on the phone.

Now he is back in position, along with all these other men who have been up here for four hours.

"The van that delivered the bomber here."

"Ah. That van."

"Its license plate was reported stolen three weeks ago, from a car park in Reims."

"Naturally. If the name painted on the side of the vehicle is a fiction . . ." The speaker trails off, probably shrugs, what do you expect.

"Maybe the bomber was visiting for the harvest."

"Muslims do not tend to be Champagne connoisseurs, you know. They—"

"I was kidding."

"Ah, I see. Very amusing. It was a public car park with a security camera at the entrance. The vehicle whose plate was stolen—a farmer's truck—was parked for forty minutes, during which ninety-two other vehicles were in the building."

"Ninety-two, okay, we can work with that."

"Of those, only seventeen exited while the *camionette* was parked."

"Seventeen? That is a much more manageable number."

"Of those seventeen, two are registered here in Paris."

"Only two?" An appreciative whistle. "We should send teams."

"They are already en route."

Ibrahim can feel the satisfied silence all around him, these men congratulating themselves, in their minds, for the solid, industrious work of their underlings.

"This is how we find them, you know. Every plot has its holes, blind spots that even the author cannot see. One tiny mistake, that could make all the difference."

❧

"Is this Dr. Féraud?"

"Yes."

"My name is a Colonel Étienne Desmarchais. You are on speaker-phone with a number of military, law-enforcement, and political personnel."

"That is unusual."

"You have a patient named Mahmoud Khalid."

Silence on the phone.

"Doctor? Mahmoud Khalid is the name of the man standing in the middle of the Louvre, wearing a suicide vest."

More silence.

"Doctor, did you hear me? Do you understand?"

Finally: "How is it that you think I can help you, Colonel . . . ?"

"Colonel Desmarchais. Please, tell me, what is wrong with Mahmoud Khalil?"

"Well, Colonel, if what you say is true, then what is wrong with Mr. Khalid is that he is standing in the middle of the Louvre, wearing a suicide vest."

"Are you trying to joke with me?"

"Unsuccessfully?"

"Listen, Doctor Fér—"

"I am sorry, but I simply cannot share a patient's confidential records with someone who calls without a proper medical reference. I am sure you understand."

"Reference? No, I certainly do not understand."

"Doctor. This is now the deputy chief of police speaking."

"Hello deputy chief."

"We can get a court order."

"Then I look forward to examining it, and I will respond as quickly as circumstances allow. Now, if you will excuse—"

"This is not finished."

"I do not doubt it. But I am simply following the *law,* which, as a law-enforcement officer, I am sure you can appreciate."

❧

"The back-trace is now complete. Here, look . . ."

"What? What is this? I do not understand what I am looking at."

"This is a map of Paris, sir."

"Am I stupid?"

"Of course not, no sir, I was . . . er . . . Using the surveillance-camera network, we have traced the van's route back to its first movements of the day, at seven this morning."

"Good. This is quite good. And this is it, here, this big red dot in Clignancourt? Okay. We should breach as soon as possible."

"Yes, the teams have already been dispatched. Arrival in five minutes."

"But the driver will not be there now, will he? Have we traced his route?"

"We are still trying. It appears that he entered the parking garage here at this spot, then entered the Métro system here. It is likely that he walked right past a patrolman who was stationed at the entrance."

Ibrahim is beginning to fatigue of holding this position, this level of concentration, this preparedness. Also of listening to these men, and saying nothing.

"It does not really make a difference, does it? The type of cancer. The treatment."

"Well . . ."

"There is obviously a very large difference between Stage I carcinoma and Stage IV lung. In terms of his thought processes. His motivations."

"Yes, obviously, I understand, but does any of that matter to *us*? To our decision-making? Listen. Perhaps Mahmoud Khalil is a very sick man, a dying man, so he has nothing to lose by dying here today, because he may very well die tomorrow."

"Exactly."

"But still, the fact is that he is standing here *today,* ready to die *today,* and perhaps ready to take half the population of Paris with him—"

"Oh, let us not exaggerate—"

"—and create a crater of the Louvre that will be radioactive for a century. Regardless of his own prospects for a tomorrow, this man is a threat to Paris, to all of us, *today.* And I assert that regardless of the severity of his illness, it is time for us to blow his brains out all over the cour Napoléon."

"What a surprise! The police want to shoot a Muslim man. I am shocked."

"Everyone, calm down. Keep this rational. And *civil.* I am talking to you, Yves."

Hrumph.

"What precisely do we have to lose by waiting?"

"*Control.*"

"Control? Are you out of your mind? We already do not have control. We cannot lose what we do not have."

Ibrahim knows that sooner or later everyone will accede, and his long period of inaction will come to an end; that might happen any moment.

"If it *looks* like we have control, Bertrand, then we *do* have control. And at this moment, there is only one way for us to create that perception."

It will be such a small motion, a nearly imperceptible physical exertion, it will last less than a second. Then his role will be finished.

⚜

"*Fils de pute.* The van driver, we lost him. We have him all the way to this Métro platform, there, do you see? But then we lose him in the station. Three of the cameras are broken, which was noticed yesterday, and a work order was created immediately. The repairs are scheduled for Friday."

"*Hmm.* Suspicious. And surface cameras?"

"None seem to have captured him."

"Are there any other exits from the station? Service tunnels? He could have used the unmonitored station to disguise himself."

"Yes, that is possible."

"Then he could have returned to the platform. Or to the platform of the other direction. Or he could have changed platforms to another line. Or he could have fled through the tunnels."

"Yes, those are all possibilities. Where is this station?"

"Odéon."

"Odéon? In St-Germain."

"Obviously."

"That is where one of the cars is registered."

"Cars? What are you talking about?"

"The cars that were in Reims at the same time the license plate that was on the van that delivered this bomber to the Louvre was stolen. Those cars."

❖

"This is bad."

"What?"

"The wife: she was killed during a police action in Belleville."

Belleville. This time, Ibrahim holds his tongue.

"I remember that. It was the roundup after the arrests at Bastille, yes?"

"Yes. But Neela Khalid was completely innocent."

"That is what they all say."

"*They all*? You really are a racist son of—"

"No, truly, she was walking to the station after visiting her colleague, who was just home from hospital."

Ibrahim remembers this. How could he not? Belleville is where he lives.

"Oh yes. This woman was a complete bystander."

"That is right. She was hit by a stray bullet."

"And it was not just any stray bullet, was it?"

"No."

Ibrahim feels a hand on his shoulder. He flinches, almost screams, *Do not fucking touch a man whose finger is on a trigger.*

"Officer, is everything okay?"

"Yes sir," Ibrahim says.

"Good. Can I ask, what is your confidence in this shot?"

"My confidence?"

"Yes. What are the odds of an instantaneous kill?"

When the bullet exits the muzzle, it will be traveling at 900 meters per second. During flight, the bullet will slow due to air friction, but the target is only about 400 meters away, so the speed diminution will be negligible, and will not compromise the trajectory. The wind is practically nonexistent, and there is no sun in Ibrahim's eyes. He is in a comfortable, stable position, not overly fatigued. The sightline is clear. The target is surrounded by nothing distracting, nothing that might move at the last second.

The conditions could not be more perfect.

The flight of the bullet will last a half-second, and it will make contact with the target somewhere inside a zone that is about the size of a mobile phone. A small mobile phone.

"One hundred percent."

51

Colette yanks the handle, and the door flies open.

Nothing.

There's no one on the other side, nothing but the dim quiet space, the dingy dinged-up walls, the chipped-paint floorboards.

Colette is standing behind the open door, flat against the wall. Hunter is still lying on the floor, twenty feet from the door, obscured from view by furniture but not totally hidden, aiming the gun at the now-open doorway, waiting for someone to arrive.

Will he shoot absolutely anyone who appears? He hopes he wouldn't shoot an innocent old lady, a curious little kid. But he's not confident that he'll have the poise to tell the difference.

He's really fucking terrified. And he has only the vaguest idea of how to handle this gun.

Ten seconds have gone by, and no one has appeared.

Twenty seconds.

Hunter once had a shotgun pressed upon him for the purpose of shooting skeet. Making a sport, a casual pastime, out of hurling high-speed bullets at things. Whooping it up with those guys, wearing the ludicrous outfits, the glasses, the padded-shoulder vests, it's always about the accessories, the toys. He abhorred it. He was disappointed in himself for allowing anyone to talk him into it.

He has never before held a handgun. Handguns aren't for sport. Handguns are for only one purpose: killing other humans.

Thirty seconds.

Colette is still behind the open door, trembling.

Hunter shifts his weight slightly, so less of it is pressing down on his right elbow, which is beginning to hurt.

Forty.

New York still won't be open for another hour and a half, if he can get out of here now, get himself to a working phone, make a couple of reassuring calls, let people know he's alive, push back the press conference a few hours . . .

Fifty.

He's relieved that he hasn't yet needed to shoot anyone. But he's also disappointed that he hasn't yet shot anyone, because that means his captors are still out there, unshot. And now he needs to get up, walk out of here, and either get by them or confront them.

Hunter tiptoes toward the door, toward Colette. He nods at her, she nods back. He steps through the doorway first, into the short hall with the stairwell opposite. Just a single light, a bare bulb hanging from a cloth cord. Are there neighbors at home, people who heard this commotion, peering through peepholes, peeking through cracked doors? Is someone going to intervene? Call the police? If the police show up, he doesn't particularly want to be a man creeping around holding a gun. But if they don't, he does.

He creeps to the stairs, which turn back upon themselves in all four directions, a narrow shaft in the middle, he can see all the way down to the bottom, it looks like fifty feet. He tries to carry the gun like guys do in films, which is how we all learn to hold guns: actors, in movies, where the good guys shoot the bad guys. In real life, though, it's almost always the other way around.

Hunter takes one tentative step down. Another. Another and another until the first landing, the first turn, affording a different angle on this stairwell, on the openings to the other floors. Still no sign of anyone.

Colette follows a half-dozen steps behind.

Hunter picks up his pace, descends all the way to the floor below without pausing. Should he peek his head into this hallway? What might he find? Nothing useful. Just a way to get himself shot.

He keeps moving as quietly as possible, but that's not silently, because his leather soles are clicking on the wooden stairs, which is not a loud noise but it's definitely enough to hear, bouncing off all these hard surfaces. He looks up and sees that Colette is carrying her heels, she's padding down the stairs in her stockinged feet, stealthy silent.

Hunter looks down again to the bottom, still no sign of anyone. He's approaching another doorway to another hall. He slows, moving more quietly, the gun aimed at the opening, tiptoeing past . . . one more step to the next stair . . .

Still nothing. He takes a step down onto a loose floorboard that squeals like a pig, an extremely loud noise, an alarming noise, and he spins to see if that has attracted any attention, just in time to—

52

If there's one principle everyone agrees upon, it's this: markets hate uncertainty. When confronted with uncertainty, people are quick to panic about their money. When they panic, they sell whatever it is they can sell. Everyone knows this. It's right up there with buy low, sell high, kill or be killed: panic begets more panic. Panicked selling leads to falling prices, and falling prices leads to more panicked selling, accelerated sell-offs. Panic consumes wealth, wolfing it down, poof, gone.

The uncertainty engendered by the attacks in Paris has been making prices fall broadly all day. Dexter hits UPDATE. The algorithm loads the latest share prices of his various positions, and compares all the current sell prices against his initial buys, and deducts transaction costs and taxes, and calculates his bottom-line aggregate delta, which appears at the very top of the screen instead of at the bottom, so Dexter doesn't have to scan down the page to see, at a quick glance, the so-called bottom line—

Still red.

But because of the falling value of 4Syte's single stock futures, Dexter's overall position is heading steadily toward zero. Today's goal, though, is not merely a mitigation of red numbers, it's a transition well into black.

His attention is suddenly drawn to one of his screens where 4Syte's logo is split with a pair of talking heads. Dexter turns on this broadcast's volume—

". . . in Mum*bai,* where the office building has been com*plete*ly evacuated on the credible threat of a bomb."

The anchorman considers his response for longer than normal. The inclination, on these shows, is to bluster ahead.

"To be sure," he finally says, "it's *far* too early to say for certain that there's a *definitive* connection between these ongoing attacks and 4Syte." He's trying to sound reassuring; he could get in well-deserved trouble for igniting an unwarranted panic, a sell-off, hundreds of millions at stake, billions.

"That's true: so far there is no *proven* correlation among the three cities, other than what very well may be the completely *coincidental* locations of the attacks."

"Indeed."

"And in Paris, as you know, the bomb threats are *not* against the 4Syte offices, which are I believe in *two* locations, one in the center and one in the outlying business district of La Défense. But it *is* in Paris, later today, where 4Syte founder and CEO Hunter Forsyth is meant to give a press conference, in what is expected to be the announcement of a *major* deal."

"And have we received any comment from 4Syte?"

"No, not as of this moment."

No comment? This is a company that's nothing if not PR-friendly, with an international army of polished spokespeople, well-armed with facts, figures, carefully worded press releases. Dexter searches the web for their counternarrative, but finds nothing.

He checks 4Syte PR's social postings, in the US, in France, in Asia. Nothing.

He finds Hunter Forsyth's social feed: the last post was 7:55 this morning, a photo of sunrise over the city, *Good morning Paris! Looking fwd to a great day ahead.* Six hours ago. This is a man who normally posts every few hours, no matter how anodyne. And this silence is on a day when he wants everyone in the world to pay attention to him, closely, constantly.

Dexter checks for 4Syte in other trends. There's no hard information, anywhere, about Hunter Forsyth. Dexter's initial reaction is joy—what could be better, really?

But on second thought?

They met two decades ago, two young tech guys who'd arrived in the Bay Area at what would later prove to be the exact right moment, for some of them.

Hunter had skipped the whole shared-house-in-Mountain-View pupae stage, moved directly from Stanford B-school into full-fledged adulthood in Nob Hill, where he hung his diplomas from Groton, from Yale, lined his built-in bookshelves with tennis trophies, a preppy Wall of Fame, this guy *owned* it. There are people who are born to rule the world, and Hunter Forsyth was one of them.

Dexter is reminded of Jake's misunderstanding, back in Luxembourg, about the palace guards: "Epaulets," the little boy asserted, with the supreme confidence of misinformed little boys, "are so people know you're in charge." Which was not at all true. But epaulets did let everyone know something, that was for sure. Hunter wore his proudly.

Dexter was an early hire in Hunter's first startup. But Dexter didn't have the competitive instinct, didn't have office-politics savvy, didn't understand how to flatter and pander, to dissemble and cajole. He was a hard worker, a great engineer, but that wasn't enough. That wasn't even required.

He eventually left in a huff, burning a bridge with a rising star, not doing himself any favors in the community, which was soon filled with old friends and colleagues who'd been hit by one filthy-rich lightning bolt or another, VC infusion or IPO or corporate buyout, a constant churn of liquidity events generating Gulfstreams, weekend houses in Cabo, Ferraris. Dexter was still driving a Honda.

You get to make only so many bets in a lifetime, and the things you choose not to do may be just as consequential as the things you choose to do. What Dexter chose not to do was stay in Silicon Valley. A college buddy had a spare bedroom in DC, where Dexter met his future wife. Also where he ran into that old friend from college, the one who cooked up the scheme that led to Luxembourg, to Paris, to this career, this moment—

"Holy crap."

The banner running across Dexter's screen announces: *Breaking News! 4Syte announcement postponed.*

"—now have *confirmation*, Robert, that the 4Syte press conference, which was meant to start less than two hours from now, has been postponed."

"Has it been rescheduled?" Re-*shed*-yuled.

Dexter feels himself hunched forward, mouth hanging open, he must look simian. But who cares, he's alone, as usual. Sometimes when not alone, Dexter has to force himself to maintain awareness of that, to chew quietly, keep his pants buttoned. He spends more time with his children than with anyone else, and they're rubbing off. He's modeling the kids' behavior. It's supposed to be the other way around.

"No, Robert, not at this time."

"Has any reason been given?"

"None. But spokesperson Schuyler Franks advises that a statement *will* be released by the end of business today, if not earlier."

Dexter refreshes his screen again, hitting the button compulsively, a new addiction.

"Thank you for that report, Tessa." Robert the anchor turns back to face the camera. "So. Still no *official* word from 4Syte or its CEO, Hunter Forsyth, on the possible threats against 4Syte's international offices, and the ongoing situation in Paris, where the announcement was to be held. Nor any connection these events might have to this *very* surprising postponement of a *major* announcement."

In the past minute alone, 4Syte has lost 2 percent of its value, a rapid acceleration of the slow slide that started this morning.

The top, the bottom, these are not fixed points, they are fluid positions, and there's never any definitive moment when either is completely clear to anyone. It's only in hindsight that you can see if you held too long, or sold too early. Timing is everything.

The situation looks promising. But things often look promising and turn out not to be. That's how he found himself in this predicament in the first place, and how he got himself into his original European fiasco: by choosing to see the things he wanted to see, and ignoring those he didn't.

He knows he shouldn't have left Ben's present to the last minute, *of course* he knows that, he's not a moron. No excuse, it just slipped his mind, again and again.

Like the inhaler. Which was Kate's last straw.

It was a Sunday. The boys spent the entire day at a birthday party in Passy, driven out by the overbearing woman whom Kate calls Hashtag Mom. Dexter stayed behind in St-Germain, read even the soft sections of the newspapers, took a long walk, indulged in a decadent lunch, self-rewards for his grueling weeks of solo-parenting. Kate had been away longer than anticipated, a work trip that kept getting extended, "I'll be home in a couple of days," over and over.

The kids came home just before bedtime. Ben was coughing, pale, short of breath.

"Okay, kiddo, let's get your inhaler." Dexter walked into the bathroom, and collected the little canister. It felt light, and a stab of worry shot through him. He didn't want to test the device in case that test squeeze turned out to be the final dose.

So Ben was the one who squeezed the little pump into his mouth; it was Ben who discovered that the final dose had been inhaled yesterday. The canister was empty.

Sunday nights, nearly all pharmacies are closed. Something would be open somewhere; Dexter was pretty sure there was a twenty-four-hour drugstore over in the fifteenth, perhaps another down in the thirteenth, neither particularly nearby, and both no doubt mobbed with sick people, whimpering children, waiting for hours—

That's exactly when Kate walked in the door, wheeling her luggage full of dirty laundry, looking like she'd just been dragged through something awful.

Dexter was standing there, holding the inhaler. "We just realized it's empty."

Kate barely glanced at her husband before turning to her obviously ill boy, you could see it in one glance. "Let's go, Sweetie," she said, holding out her hand.

"Where, Mommy?"

"To the hospital."

❧

Kate didn't talk to Dexter for the better part of the next week, nothing but monosyllables and hostile glares and cold shoulders; she literally turned her back on her husband, repeatedly. He apologized a hundred times, uncountable times. To his wife, to his son.

"It's okay, Daddy," the boy said. "It wasn't your fault. It was mine. I should have been keeping track of the counter."

Dexter hugged this beautiful boy, so grateful for this kid, so disappointed in himself.

"I'm sorry," Dexter told Kate. He bought her an extravagant watch, a belated anniversary gift. A bribe. And an action figure for Ben. "It won't happen again. I promise."

And he meant it: he would never again neglect the inhaler, the nose spray, any of the boy's meds. Dexter checked these supplies daily, it had become an OCD tic, took up a disproportionate share of his consciousness, so much that there wasn't sufficient space for all the other chores he was supposed to remember. Like this birthday present.

That's what he told himself.

Dexter steps out into the world, in search of Lego and lunch and sanity. He needs to calm the fuck down or he's going to have a stroke.

He can see that people are unsure how to behave today, is it the end of the world or just a single-news-cycle blip, or something in the broad spectrum between. Waiters huddle in conspiratorial clumps, shopkeepers are conferring on sidewalks. Some businesses are shuttered, while the *quincaillerie* is packed with people buying flashlights and batteries, and others are lugging home bottled water, canned beans, jars of cassoulet, full-scale Armageddon panic.

Dexter doesn't know where he falls on this continuum. It's a choice, it's controllable, and he's trying to choose to occupy the less hysterical end. It will all be okay. Perhaps bombs will take some lives today, but that's true every day, somewhere. Today it will not be his life, nor his kids', nor his wife's. They will still host their dinner party, and the TV will remain on during cocktail hour with the volume muted, tracking the latest developments, the investigation, the police will be raiding mosques while expats sit around discussing the events between bites of chicken stew, putting their bread directly on the tablecloth, the French way, though none of them is French.

In the hours before then, Dexter will, hopefully, make a fortune.

And he'll find this Lego. There are two stores within striking distance that are likely to have the thing in stock. He tried calling ahead. At the nearest store, the clerk confirmed their inventory, but she did it quickly, dismissively, like someone who hadn't checked anything. The other store's clerk put Dexter on hold, supposedly to go look for the item, and never returned. Dexter has grown accustomed to this type of customer service, more take-it-or-leave-it than in America, where nothing is worse than losing a sale.

It's cool on the shady side of the street. In Paris, in Luxembourg, in this general part of the world where Dexter has been living, the seasons skew early. By late August it already feels like autumn; early November is full-on winter.

He buttons his jacket, turns up his collar against the wind. Maybe it's time to switch out this navy cotton jacket for the gray wool, suede gloves in the pocket, a cashmere scarf.

Dexter is a creature of habit, he wears a uniform, he eats the same things in the same restaurants and cafés, a salad here and a sandwich there, the Tuesday special fish. He keeps to a regular schedule of tennis matches and gym routines, of morning newspapers and online research, Asian and European trading, late lunch followed by New York's markets.

He has always wanted this life, a life of predictable regimen, the same satisfying thing day in, day out. He takes comfort in the certainty, in the daily consistencies and the predictable variations, school pickup three days per week, cooking dinner on Wednesday nights, sex on Saturdays.

But it's not as consistent as it looks, nor as permanent. Kate travels often. Her trips arise quickly, last an uncertain duration, and end with no warning, with unexpected interruptions while she pops home for a day or two—or ten—before heading out again, to Palermo or Lisbon, Copenhagen or Marseille, or wherever the hell she actually goes when she claims to be in these places.

School holidays intervene. American bank holidays. The weather makes outdoor tennis unpredictable, the kids get sick, dinner parties, birthdays, birthday-present shopping.

Even if Dexter doesn't succeed in finding this Lego, Ben is not going to fall apart, the boy is not that sort of child. It's not the fear of meltdown that's motivating Dexter. It's that the kid would be quietly, sullenly disappointed, and this would break Dexter's heart.

And Kate would be apoplectic. Dexter has used up every one of his free passes. His wife has been awfully mad at him lately, morose, hostile. Her response to his next offense might be cataclysmic.

As he passes the entrance to his garage, it occurs to him that perhaps he should drive. Maybe on a normal day, yes. But today, who knows what traffic will be like, which streets will be open and which closed, which bridges passable.

No, the car would be a mistake. He'd end up caught in a closure, penned in, trapped for hours. He'd have to abandon the Audi somewhere, parking on the street, which he avoids like the plague. Parisians don't think they've parked successfully until they've used both front and rear fenders to expand the dimensions of their space, a push forward here, another push back, forward and back, like bumper cars, which may have made sense in the days when cars had actual bumpers, but they don't anymore.

He resumes walking, faster now, rushing. Glances at his watch—

"*Pardonnez-moi, Monsieur.*"

Dexter turns. It's two cops approaching him. Where did they come from?

"*Oui?*"

"*Un moment, s'il vous plaît.*"

53

Kate races up to the street, then spins around the corner and guides the moped through the bollards into the pedestrian-only sector. Here she putters slowly, not wanting to draw attention, nor the ire of shopkeepers, waiters, customers.

At the next corner she exits the Montorgueil car-free zone, back out to another traffic-clogged street, but Kate doesn't need a lane, she's zooming past buses, weaving between taxis, a dangerous but critical component of her most aggressive surveillance-detection route: make it physically impossible to follow her.

Kate is no longer concerned merely with being tailed by counterespionage, by intelligence, by a curious husband. Now she also has to worry about counterterrorism, about French police, Interpol, anyone, everyone. The stakes have become much higher than the security of her legend, than the secrecy of the Paris Substation. It was just a couple of hours ago when those were her primary concerns.

She pulls to a stop, looks around at all the open space that surrounds la Bourse, a broad hulk of building that opened two centuries ago as the stock exchange, now obsolete, a victim of automation and internationalism, merging with Brussels and Amsterdam and Lisbon, capitals of colonial empires that for centuries had been global trading centers. The *bourse* became fallow, lolling here in the middle of the city, hosting temporary exhibitions, expositions, waiting for a new purpose to present itself. Stocks these days are all traded elsewhere, anywhere, everywhere, men sitting at home wearing sweatpants and T-shirts, in between tennis matches and birthday-present shopping, eating sliced apples and Nutella sandwiches—

That *bastard*.

How is she going to keep him out of the grasp of French authorities? Should she try the US Embassy? Or go directly to the Paris Substation's safehouse? Or would they be better off completely DIY? Kate could take him to that other location, much closer to home, with less of a connection to anyone else, completely unknown to anyone in any intelligence service.

She doesn't want to have to trust anyone. Because it's definitely possible—it's likely—that there's hard evidence against Dexter, beyond the mere circumstantial. His phone records, browsing history, e-mails, who knows what. There could be plenty that makes him look guilty, creating ample incentive for people to turn him in.

But could Dexter actually *be* guilty?

It was much easier to be an intelligence operative when it wasn't her husband in her crosshairs.

❖

Back in Luxembourg, when Kate finally confronted Dexter with her suspicions, he explained the rationale for his conspiracy: he was a vigilante, not a mere thief; he was meting out justice on a global scale, taking a monster's money and his life, making the world a better place; he was avenging the murder of his brother, who'd been an American peacekeeper in the Serbian civil war. The money was beside the point, mostly.

His arguments were not without merit.

Kate's counterargument was simple, moral: even if it was true that the man Dexter robbed was a horrible person—an arms dealer, a murderer—and even if this man did deserve the harshest possible sentence, Dexter himself did not deserve to benefit from it. Certainly not with a stolen twenty-five million euros. That wasn't justice, that was opportunism; it was illegal, and unethical. Dexter couldn't keep this blood money, not if he wanted to keep his wife.

He didn't put up a fight.

And, Kate added, one other thing: he had to give up his partner, the person who'd lured him into the whole plot, who'd used him, who'd ruthlessly put Dexter and Kate and their kids—their lives—at mortal risk.

She realized that she was lashing out in anger, but she did it anyway. Kate was the one who made the immunity deal, who set up the CIA sting. Kate was the one who lured the woman called Julia MacLean to collect the account number for her share of the heist, with the Agency van wait-ing around the corner, ready to take her into custody. It was all set up.

But at the last moment, in an unexpected burst of sympathy, Kate had a change of heart. She allowed Julia to go free, to escape the clutches of prosecution, to avoid the worst consequences of her crimes.

Not, though, with her twenty-five million euros. Just with her hus-band and her freedom, or some semblance of it.

A framed map of Europe hangs in Kate's office, and behind the map is a safe mounted in the wall. This is where Kate keeps a few thousand in cash—walking-around money for bribes, payouts, secret salaries. Also an expensive wristwatch that she ended up possessing after a series of boneheaded missteps on the part of an asset; Kate didn't know what else to do with this tacky piece of jewelry.

If anyone ever has the temerity to break into the office, to crack the safe, they will be excited—hey, look what we found, it's the secret stash.

It isn't.

In the kitchenette, the small microwave's back panel can be removed in less than thirty seconds with a Phillips-head screwdriver. That's where Kate stores another hundred thousand euros, plus a few passports with her picture but different names and nationalities. She also used to keep an untraceable SIG Sauer in there, but she brought it along for Peter, and hasn't gotten around to replacing it. It's been a few years since Kate has needed a gun.

She keeps hoping that her days of shooting people are behind her. After Oaxaca, she'd told herself that it had been a fluke, an extraordinary confluence of circumstances, something she'd never need to repeat. But then she did, and not just once. Oaxaca was nearly two decades ago.

She never imagined that she'd kill a person, that she'd be a cold-blooded killer—of course she wasn't, that was so obvious, wasn't it? Look at her, with her station wagon, her coq au vin, her little-kid birthday-party favors. This isn't what cold-blooded killers look like.

Kate descends the stairs from the rue des Petits Champs, and walks through the *passage* out into the airy gardens of Palais-Royal, one of

Kate's favorite places in Paris, where the Moores attend a semi-regular weeknight picnic with other families, chilled rosé and good pâté, kids inventing games while adults play progressively more vigorous rounds of pétanque, surrounded by other people everywhere, packed into the cafés in the colonnades, reclined in the green metal chairs, strollers and loners and smitten lovers.

Kate hopes she doesn't have to leave Paris, now. Not like this.

Inez arrives, kisses her on one cheek. "*Ça va?*" she asks, and kisses the other. Just like any other pair of friends.

How's it going? Terrible, that's how. "Inez, I'm in a bad situation. Dangerous. I can't get to my weapon, and I think I might need one."

Inez nods, understanding. She reaches her right hand inside her jacket while leaning forward, all the way into Kate, and brings her left hand up to Kate's shoulder, around it, a close embrace. Inez gives a squeeze, as if in support—it's so good to see you after so long, I'm so sorry about your mother, your job, your problems—then leans away. "*Bonne chance,*" she says.

Somewhere in the middle of that, Kate felt the handgun fall into her pocket.

✤

One ring.

No answer.

Two rings.

Her unanswered call isn't going straight to voice-mail, which means the device isn't powered off, isn't out of range. The phone is ringing. Just not being answered.

Three.

And then that's it, voice-mail: *Bonjour, it's Dexter, please leave a message.*

"Hi," she says, "it's me." As a rule Kate doesn't leave messages, just ends the call; Dexter knows to ring back. That's how life works now.

She doesn't want to say anything too specific. In fact she hasn't wanted to make this call at all, she's almost certain that his phone is compromised, not just the meta-data but probably the actual content of the communications too, the location, everything. But she needs him to get out of their apartment, and get rid of his phone.

"Call as soon as you can, okay? It's important."

Kate still remembers her parents' first answering machine, a Sony the size of a dictionary, it sat on the kitchen counter next to the phone books, white pages stacked under the more frequently consulted yellows, life used to be easily divided, social contacts here and commercial there, dog-eared corners and circled numbers for mechanics and doctors, plumbers and pizza, take-out menus tucked inside, bills of service too, business cards. Phone books served as filing cabinets, booster seats, leaf presses, paperweights, weapons. She hasn't seen a phone book in years.

Why is he not calling her back? Dexter isn't a husband who doesn't answer, not one of those guys who's always in meetings, on conference calls, at business lunches, you know how it is, crazy-busy, I can barely come up for air. Dexter is a reliably available person. Even in the midst of his big trades, he always has thirty seconds to talk to his wife.

What Dexter is also—inconveniently, at this moment—is a guy who refuses to enable location services on his smartphone, a guy who's a zealot for maintaining the most private settings on his device, who refuses to install apps that could track him, apps whose systems could be hacked. Dexter is ultra-paranoid about electronic intrusions, about hacks. Because Dexter is a hacker.

There are plenty of good reasons why he wouldn't answer his phone. He could be on the Métro, in one of the tunnels with no cellular service, on his way to buy Lego. He could be in the middle of a complex trade, can't distract himself. He could be standing on the street, talking to a neighbor, doesn't want to be rude. He could be watching extremely compelling porn, concentrating hard.

Maybe she'd believe any of those reasons, on any other day.

Her phone buzzes, another intercept of Schuyler's line.

"*Hi, sorry to bother you so early? My name is Schuyler Franks, I'm calling from the Paris office?*"

"It's . . . what time is . . . Jesus. Why are you calling me at home at five A.M.? Who are you?"

"We have a, um, situation here? Can you gather the board of directors for a conference call as soon as possible?"

❧

It was an immense favor that Kate did, allowing Julia and Bill to escape the clutches of the CIA, of arrest, humiliation, prosecution, prison. Julia deserved so much worse.

That was one point of view.

As that final encounter faded into the past, Kate began to accept that there was another possible point of view: that she'd deprived Julia of a fortune the woman had spent the entirety of her adult life pursuing, money stolen from a despicable criminal who didn't in any way deserve it, money that was now sitting in a numbered account, unrecoverable, forever. Kate had sentenced someone who'd once been her closest friend to a life on the run, a life of aliases and temporary homes, of fleeting friendships using fictional identities. Half a life, at best.

Perhaps Kate had been too punitive, like the Allied powers in the aftermath of World War I, engendering fascism from their own vindictiveness.

From this point of view, Kate's final encounter with Julia in that café may not turn out to be final. And gratitude was not what Kate should expect. Not at all.

Revenge was. Another world war.

PART IV

NOTRE-DAME

54

"Would you prefer English?"

"Yes," Dexter says, "thanks."

"You are a tourist, *Monsieur*?"

"No, I live near here."

"*Ah oui?*" Eyebrows raised.

One policeman is doing the talking, while the other lags behind, silent, waiting.

"I see that you look into this parking. Could I ask, *Monsieur*, why?"

"I keep a car there."

"*Une voiture? Ici?*" The cop purses his lips to expel a burst of air, a French gesture that can connote a wide breadth of emotions—exasperation, surprise, disappointment, frustration. Dexter understands what it means here, coming from this policeman: you must be plenty wealthy, *Monsieur*, to house a car here in the middle of St-Germain-des-Prés.

"I was thinking of using the car. To run an errand."

"Errant?"

Errand. How do you say this? "*Je dois faire une course.*"

The cop looks confused. Dexter doesn't know if he got the vocabulary wrong, or the grammar, or just the pronunciation. There are a lot of ways to be wrong.

"But I decided against it."

"No? Why?"

"With what's going on at the *gare*, and the Louvre, I thought traffic would be bad. Streets closed. Bridges."

"You are correct, *Monsieur*. It is not a good day to drive a car in Paris. You keep the car here all the days?"

"Yes." Dexter glances at his watch. He really has to get moving. "Is there something I can help you with?"

"If you please, yes: could I ask you to admit us to *le parking*? There is no attendant. And no person answers the telephone."

Dexter doesn't respond immediately; he doesn't want to get involved in whatever this is.

"Are you in a rush? I do not want to ... er ... *detain*? Is this the correct word?"

"Yes," Dexter says, but he isn't so sure. *Detain* has a couple of different meanings, especially in the context of police.

"*Bon, merci,* I do not want to detain you."

"I am, actually, in a hurry."

"Oh yes? Why?"

"I have to buy a toy. A birthday present."

The cop smiles indulgently. Or maybe ironically. Toy shopping during a terrorist attack.

"This will not take long, *Monsieur.* If you please."

"*D'accord.*" Dexter starts walking, it's just a few steps back to the garage entrance, the ubiquitous keypad that confronts Parisians at every door, a code to punch, then the overhead light begins to flash red, the door starts to rise, slowly, loudly.

"When you want to exit, press this button." Dexter points to the big SORTIE, realizing too late that this is a completely unnecessary instruction. Insulting.

"*Oui.* Could I ask, what car do you drive?"

Why the hell is he asking? This cop is starting to make Dexter nervous.

He feels his phone buzz a half-second before the ringing commences. He reaches into his pocket—

It's Kate again. He hits IGNORE.

"Is it necessary for you to answer?"

"No."

"You are sure?"

"Yes, it's fine."

"Thank you. *Donc,* your car?"

"It is an old car, a *break.*" French for station wagon. "Good for the family."

"Family? You have children?"

"Yes. Two boys."

"*Ah, c'est bon.* They are at school now?"

"Yes." Why the fuck is this cop asking him all these questions? "Officer, if you don't mind, I really must . . . I have to . . ."

"Yes, I understand, just one more moment." The cop reaches into his pocket, takes out his notepad, continues to rummage around in there. "It is necessary . . . for our records, do you understand? Ah!" He has found what he was looking for, a pen. "Your name, if you please? And your address? Phone number?" He extends the pad, the pen too.

Dexter doesn't want to provide this information. But nor does he want to refuse, to get into an antagonistic relationship with this cop. He has that immigrant's innate fear of law enforcement, you don't know what they can do to you. Keep your head down, do what you're told.

He's getting a queasy feeling about everything here. A fake name, fake address, fake phone number: these are what he's going to give the cop.

Dexter reaches for the pad, eager to get this over with, and his nerves about the cop, plus the general anxiety of today's make-or-break trade, not to mention the terrorist siege of the city, all this is enough to make Dexter jittery enough to fumble the handoff, and he drops the pen to the pavement with a tinny little clatter, and stumbles slightly as he bends to collect it, and mutters an apology, and comes up flustered and a little lightheaded.

The policeman stares at him.

Dexter starts to write, and can't help but notice that his hand is trembling.

55

Hunter's vision is blurry, but nevertheless yes, he can tell that it's the same place. He's now sitting in a chair, and he can't move his arms, nor his legs. He is tied up. And gagged.

"Ah, you're conscious." Simpson is applying ice to his own skull. "Good."

Hunter can't respond.

"That wasn't very smart of you, Mr. Forsyth. I'm disappointed and frankly surprised. I would've thought, a man like you, a business genius, a master of the universe. But don't you remember how that ended?"

Hunter furrows his brow.

"*Bonfire of the Vanities*? Tom Wolfe? Never read it? But surely you saw the movie, Forsyth. No?"

Colette is on the other side of the room, also tied up. By the ankles and wrists only, and she's sitting on the couch. She's not the one being punished.

"If I were as stupid as you, Mr. Forsyth, I'd be punching you in the face right now, getting revenge, *pow pow pow*. But I'm not. Because I have foresight. Foresight!" The guy laughs. "Ironic, isn't it? But I don't want it to look like you were *recreationally* beaten. If you end up dead, that's one thing. Honestly that's an outcome I wouldn't mind. But tortured? Very different implications."

Simpson looks over at Colette, then back at Hunter.

"Speaking of: you probably need water. But listen, Forsyth: if you start making a racket, annoying me? I'm going to beat the living shit out of you, and—full disclosure—I'm going to enjoy it. It's true that I'd rather it not look like you were tortured, but that's just a slight preference, not a requirement. You understand me?"

Hunter nods, and Simpson retrieves one of the water bottles that had been delivered earlier, along with ham sandwiches, back when hunger was relevant, when Hunter's biggest problem was lack of a cell signal.

The guy yanks out the gag. Tips water into Hunter's mouth, waits for a swallow, tips again.

"You all right?"

"Yes," Hunter says, a raspy sound. He coughs. "You've *kidnapped* me?"

"*Kidnapped?* I don't know about that. You came voluntarily, in fact it was your idea. And we're not seeking ransom. So I think *false imprisonment* would be more accurate."

"No ransom? Then what the hell do you want?"

"Merely the pleasure of your company, Mr. Forsyth."

"Oh come on."

"Believe it, don't believe it, I don't give a rat's ass." The guy shrugs. "Actually, to clarify: the *pleasure* part, that's a lie. Your company is not enjoyable. You're a prick. You know that, right? I can't be the first person to have told you."

"How much?"

Simpson raises his eyebrows, says nothing.

"What would my freedom cost?"

The guy still doesn't respond. His face is hard to read, with the big beard and tinted glasses and wavy hair draped across his forehead. Which must be the purpose of the whole getup: disguise.

"A million dollars?" Hunter starts, leaving plenty of room.

He'd flirted briefly with the prepper culture in the Valley, guys like him who were buying tracts of land in New Zealand, hardened bunkers in Nebraska, helicopters and motorcycles and private islands, stockpiling canned foods, water, fuel, ammunition. Like other guys with their hunting, their fishing: excuses to drink beer and talk gear.

Hunter himself wasn't going to build any bomb shelter, he didn't go in for that level of alarmism; he was too confident in the durability of the world order, and his place in it. But this burgeoning panic did have an effect, along with less apocalypse-themed horror stories of people who'd confronted problematic situations with prostitutes, with drugs, with cops, with legitimate mistakes of their own doing as well as setups, entrapments, frame-ups. And then to exacerbate matters there'd been the election of that unqualified unprepared irresponsible lunatic as president, a man who's capable of Lord knows what irrational behavior that could produce life-threatening conditions at any given moment, anywhere in the world.

Hunter sent Colette out to find a gold dealer on the rue Vivienne to buy the Krugerrands, then a leather-craftsman to retrofit his wallet with special slits that are snug enough so the coins won't slip out without requiring a bulky snap or zipper, but loose enough that the gold can be removed without destroying the wallet. Hunter never travels without this gold—anonymous, untraceable, universal liquidity, the sort of thing you can slip to a police officer, a prison guard, an immigrations official. "Look," Hunter could say to anyone, anywhere in the world. "Google it."

He is always prepared to purchase his safety, to negotiate for his release. Everyone has a price, and Hunter is willing to pay it. But the Krugerrands are not the right order of magnitude for this situation.

"Two million," he counteroffers himself.

"You think you can buy your way out of this?"

"Why not? This is about money, isn't it? Everything is."

"Okay, that's valid. But if you're really trying to buy your freedom, stop fucking around."

"Two million dollars is fucking around?"

"We both know, Forsyth, that it is."

"So this is a negotiation?"

"Not really. But maybe you'll blow me away. Shift my paradigm, as they say. So go ahead, Forsyth: your very best number."

What should Hunter say? Should he offer everything he could possibly get his hands on? There's no such definitive number, not without a timeframe. "How long do I have?"

The guy thinks about it. "Forty-eight hours."

One of Hunter's takeaways from those prepper dudes was that he needed to assess how much cash he could raise on short notice. Turned out it was only a couple hundred thousand, which wasn't going to get him very far, not in a bona fide cataclysm. So he began shifting things around until he could reasonably expect to be able to walk out of a bank branch with a million cash on any given day. If he has a few days' warning, a lot more; on the weekend, much less. He hopes the apocalypse doesn't begin on a Friday night.

"Okay: four million."

"Really? You're telling me that's your best number?"

"Five?"

"You disappoint me, Fors—"

Pounding at the door startles both men. Colette too, who has been completely silent, sitting in the corner, bound but not gagged, her big eyes moving from one man to the other, both of them probably looking to her a lot like different varieties of enemies.

Simpson undoes the locks and admits one of the French cops, with whom he confers at close range, low voices, then turns back to Hunter. "Listen: I need to run out for a few minutes. We'll pick this up when I return. Meantime, if you make any trouble, Claude is fully empowered to pinch-hit for me. *C'est vrai,* Claude?"

Just the pleasure of your company—what can that mean? It must have some meaning, it's not a random lie, it has a ring of truth, or partial truth, or—

Yes.

Hunter gets it all at once, the whole thing bum-rushes his brain—the early-morning terror attacks to draw away his police guard, to divert all police, and the telecom outage, the timing of it, and naturally there'd be no ransom, no interaction with the company or the family, with the police, with any authorities, with anyone at all, much safer without any communications, just remove Hunter from the office, from the press conference, from the multibillion-dollar merger, which will thus appear to be collapsing, speculation that the whole company is imploding, so inevitably the share price—

Fuck.

There is no transfer of any practical level of ransom that could possibly compare, no amount of cash inducement that Hunter could offer. Three million, five, ten: drops in the bucket. If his captors have access to real investment money—and they obviously do—they could make hundreds of millions today. Just like Hunter was going to.

Yes, he can see the whole ploy now.

Except one component. One not-at-all-minor detail that he can't see clearly, perhaps because he really does not want to: how does it all end for him?

56

Wyatt walks quickly. The street is quiet but not completely un-occupied, with most but not all of the shutters closed. Some-one might be observing him from any one of those apartment windows above, or from the stores below, the cleaning ladies who are mopping the bar's floor, the café waiters cleaning up after lunch service, the attentive owner of the cramped little *tabac*.

About a hundred meters up ahead, another pedestrian is walking away. Farther along, a lone man stands in a doorway, wearing a baseball cap, a bulky hoodie, sunglasses, though it isn't sunny on this close stretch of street.

Wyatt rubs his hand through his brand-new buzz-cut, self-administered fifteen minutes ago in the tiny bathroom of a brasserie that faced off against a *bar-tabac* on the far side of the intersection, the Métro station in between. The same setup everywhere. Wyatt is sick of Paris.

Remember the money.

He flushed his hair down the toilet, dropped the electric shaver in the trash. He took one final look in the dingy scratched-up mirror, nodded in appreciation: if anyone did a police sketch of the driver of the van, that sketch would not match the dude in the mirror. That driver doesn't exist anymore, that guy who'd scouted sites all over Paris, taking notes on the number and location of police and military, on the positions of security cameras and anti-ramming bollards and steel-toothed wedge barriers.

"Shouldn't I be worried about being noticed?" he'd asked. "While I'm taking all these notes?"

"No." The bearded guy was not concerned at all. "These are busy places, tens of thousands of people pass through every day, everyone typ-

THE PARIS DIVERSION | 263

ing into phones, taking pictures. No one will think you're doing anything unusual. Taking pictures of Notre-Dame? Please."

"But afterward? There are surveillance cameras."

"That's why you'll be wearing the eyeglasses, this hairstyle, these clothes."

It had been the same outfit on every recon mission, the same as this morning, this daily uniform. Except the few times when he'd been told to wear the athletic clothes with the cap, to carry the same canvas bag as he'd done this morning, that fucking bag.

"After you change your clothes and cut your hair and throw away the glasses, everything about the surveillance footage will look like someone who's not you."

As part of his interview process for this job, he'd needed to provide documentation that included a photo of himself. Which didn't seem odd at the time.

"Someone in particular?"

"No. Just not you."

"But facial recognition soft—"

"You're an *American*. That's not where they're going to look. No one looks at white American men as terrorism suspects. Not even in America, where practically all terrorism is perpetrated by white American men. Plus it's not as if you're going to be staring into the cameras, smiling for headshots."

Wyatt hadn't been convinced.

"Seriously," the guy said, "I know what I'm talking about here."

"Isn't that what everyone says who doesn't know what the fuck they're talking about? What makes you different?"

The man nodded, respecting the question, the challenge. Then he leaned forward, elbows on the table, eyes boring into Wyatt. "Because," he finally said, "I spent two decades working for the FBI."

Wyatt turns into the *passage,* which is divided into two lanes. One lane is a narrow street, one of those ridiculously long Parisian blocks that can really piss you off if you discover yourself at the wrong end of it. The other lane is a tall, slim tunnel carved out of the ground floor of a concrete-clad hulk of a building, spray-painted graffiti and glued-on concert posters, chunks missing from the exterior to reveal the cinder block underneath and the brick under that, with cauterized electrical wires and a capped-off plumbing pipe, piles of dogshit and a chained-up bicycle that has been stripped of most of its parts, one flat tire resting in a pool of what smells like urine. Somebody pissed on this poor abandoned bicycle.

This tunnel had once been the drive-through loading area for the building when it was a small factory, or a warehouse. The loading bays are now covered in plywood, the ground in trash: empty beer bottles, cigarette butts, a few hypodermics, condom wrappers, the full assortment.

There's no light in there.

Wyatt doesn't spook easily, he even relishes extracurricular violent encounters, muggers, panhandlers, junkies, he's more than happy to kick anyone's ass who even remotely merits an ass-kicking, plus plenty of people who don't.

Even for him, this is one scary-ass tunnel.

Wyatt won't be surprised if someday he ends up getting murdered. Hopefully he won't see it coming, won't feel a thing. One minute he'll be minding his own business, and the next someone will have shot him in the back of the head. That would probably happen in a place like this. This is where he himself would kill a guy like him.

He's glad he still has the weapon. He'll have to get rid of it soon, a firearm is not something he can take to the airport, and he probably shouldn't even bring it to the train station. Maybe after the transaction he'll leave it here in this tunnel.

Wyatt is also glad he'd arranged for backup. A side deal that the boss wouldn't know a damn thing about.

"I don't trust this dude," Wyatt had said to Blake, in that nearly empty bar in the eleventh. They knew each other from Afghanistan, then both had migrated into similar private-sector arrangements. "I need someone to watch my back."

"No doubt," Blake said sagely, then took a sip of beer. "You got it, brah."

"You'll need a gun."

"Already have one."

"Don't hesitate to use it."

"Dude."

They had a good laugh at that, both pretending it was funnier than it was, exaggerating their own heartlessness, their recklessness. In their line of work, it was worth actual money, this reputation, it was a bankable asset, like a hundred-mile-per-hour fastball, or a close friendship with a Trump. Things that could be relied upon to get you paid.

Wyatt stands in the tunnel entrance, peers into the darkness. Then he glances up the street, where the man in the hoodie has started walking in this direction, closing the distance. But there's no sign of anyone in the dark tunnel. Wyatt takes out his phone, composes another short text: *Here.* His finger hovers above the SEND button for a few seconds while he looks around, then his fingertip meets the touch screen—

The flash of light is almost immediate, preceding the sound by a split-second, the unmistakable ding of an incoming message, just twenty meters ahead, the device's light dimmed by a pillar but its sound amplified, bouncing off all the hard surfaces here, not quite an echo but something like it, an elongation, the psychological effect of sound in darkness.

The bearded American is already here.

Wyatt slides the phone back into his pocket, and replaces his grip around the handle of his pistol. He takes another step forward, deeper into the dark.

Remember the money.

57

K ate accelerates, weaving through traffic once again, cars are stopped everywhere, complete impasses at major intersections, police re-directing this way and that. She wends a path between cars, up on sidewalks, through a pedestrian plaza, the police aren't going to bother with some woman puttering around on a scooter, pleading about retriev-ing her children from school.

Kate alights on the Left Bank where the Gare d'Austerlitz borders the Jardin des Plantes. The first time the family visited Paris from Luxem-bourg, they drove up to this very stretch of street, and Ben exclaimed from the backseat, "Mommy, look! There's an ostrick over there!"

"An ostrich?"

"Yah! Right there!"

She didn't see anything except trees. "I don't see it, Sweetie. Are you sure?"

"Yah. But it went away."

She didn't believe him; there weren't ostriches roaming the streets of Paris. But Ben was four, alternative facts were still excusable, an un-derstandably hazy line between real-life and make-believe. A year later, when they finally made a visit over to the *ménagerie,* there it was, an os-trich enclosure, right here abutting the quay.

"You were right," she said to Ben. She felt terrible for not having be-lieved him in the first place. "There *are* ostriches here."

"Yah," he said. "I know. Let's go back to the baboons."

Kate tried harder here. She became more patient, more present, more competent than she'd been in Luxembourg. Most days she could convince herself that it was fine—no, more: it was good, maybe great, yes, this was definitely what she should be doing with her life. Late at night, though?

Yes, she had learned how to be an expat, friendly with strangers in cafés, in bookstores, at school, accepting every invitation, open to new people, to new experiences, the default position was yes. But what she had not mastered was how to be a full-time stay-at-home mom. Even on the days when she found it satisfying—and there were more of them as the children grew more manageable, and her existence more comfortable— she was also aware that this stage was so finite. In the blink of an eye, the kids would be grown. Then what would she do? And when would she do it?

When she figured out what had really gone on in Luxembourg, she was able to come up with at least one of the answers: now. She would go back to work. Start fresh, wiser this time, better equipped to handle the problems, to attain the balance. This time, it would all work out.

Now she understands that she was wrong. That she'd allowed herself to be deceived by selfishness, by vanity, by the delusional charade that she could have everything, that maybe she even deserves everything— the husband and kids and career and money.

No.

There are two distinct possibilities, and Kate can't quite decide which is worse.

One: Dexter is part of—the architect behind?—an international con-spiracy to kidnap 4Syte's CEO while manufacturing terror threats at the company's global offices and general terror in Paris to obscure the spe-cifics while causing a widespread dip in securities valuation throughout the world's markets and in particular an extreme loss of value in 4Syte's stock, ensuring immense profitability for his 4Syte short-sell.

Two: Dexter is being framed for all that. And there's only one person in the world who'd be doing the framing.

Kate is almost home, taking a corner at high speed, when the Peugeot in front of her slams on the brakes, and she's forced to slow down. She cranes her neck to peer up ahead, where a police car is parked partially on the curb, half-obstructing the traffic lane. The Peugeot overreacted, prematurely: the obstruction is still a couple hundred meters ahead.

"*Connard!*" Kate curses, loudly.

The profanities that Kate mutters to herself, that she sputters at strangers, these are mostly in French, like the numbers of the access code to her office building. This isn't purposeful; it's evolutionary. She can't even say the word *coffee* anymore, it sounds ridiculous to her.

She re-angles the scooter, trying to get a better view of what the cops are doing, why they're blocking the street. There, she can see a pair of them at the entrance to a garage, it's her own garage actually, and—

Oh God no.

Her stomach falls away.

What the hell can she do about this?

The simplest solution is impossible: she can't just walk up to a pair of Parisian cops and shoot them. Not here in broad daylight. There's a pedestrian halfway between the corner and the garage, a witness—

Christ, did she really just formulate that thought? That she's not going to shoot policemen because she's *afraid of getting caught*?

No, she needs to divert them, and she sees how immediately. She spins the Vespa back onto the cross street, just out of the police's sight, then around again, ready to return. She has no time to waste; it could be too late already.

Earlier this morning, Kate worried that at some point today, any given second might end up counting. This wasn't what she was envisaging.

She draws Inez's gun out of her pocket. Kate glances around, there are a few people walking on these sidewalks, but no one is paying attention to her. Afterward they will. And then . . . ?

And then: fuck the consequences.

She releases the safety, aims, and squeezes the trigger, twice, *pop-pop.*

A pedestrian is screaming as Kate tears around the corner as fast as possible, trying to look like a woman fleeing in sheer terror who pretends to notice the police and comes to a screeching, swerving stop.

"*S'il vous plaît!*" she yells at the cops, pointing back up the street. "*Un homme—*"

She doesn't want to say more than necessary, doesn't want her accent to betray her. She's wearing a VDM shirt and riding a Vespa, she might very well be French, nothing whatsoever to do with any American man the police are questioning here.

"*Restez ici*," one of the cops says to the civilian, who answers immediately, "*Bien sûr.*"

Both police jump in the car, and the driver starts reversing before the passenger has closed his door, backs up violently to the end of the block. The car fishtails to a stop, then shifts, and speeds through the intersection—

"Get on," Kate says to her husband. Saving him, yet again, from his own stupidity. "Let's go."

It was such a complex web of dishonesties and betrayals in which Dexter had gotten caught, long-term entanglements with savage criminals and international law enforcement, with stolen Russian fighter jets and ruthless African warlords, cutting-edge electronic intrusions and high-class hookers, bank break-ins and heartless torture, a townhouse in Belgravia and a farmhouse in the Ardennes and fifty million stolen euros divided in half, in two separate numbered accounts for two separate people, both planning to never work again, to never want for anything.

This was a plot that doesn't come to a definitive finish, not until everyone involved is dead. Maybe not even then.

Kate has never stopped looking over her shoulder, never stopped watching, waiting, planning. Never stopped expecting that one day, it would catch up to Dexter. To her too.

58

Chris steps from behind the pillar, makes himself visible. His hands hang at his side, empty. He doesn't want to look threatening, he wants to put Wyatt at ease, and the guy is obviously in a state of high anxiety, you can see it at a glance, even from a distance: a dangerous armed man with adrenaline coursing through him. It wouldn't take much to push him over the edge.

"Hello?" Wyatt takes another step into the tunnel, straining to see through the darkness. Chris can't see Wyatt's gun, but he can tell by the guy's stance.

"Yeah. I'm back here."

Wyatt takes another slow step, looking around side to side.

"Everything okay? Any problems?"

Wyatt continues to approach, but doesn't answer. Chris instinctively shifts his weight to his right, toward the safety of the concrete pillar.

"Affirmative," Wyatt says. He takes another couple of steps, stops. "There actually was a problem. A pretty fucking big one."

"And that was?"

"When I abandoned the van, there were two people . . ."

Wyatt looks around again, nervous about . . . what?

"They saw you? These people?"

"Affirmative."

"And?"

"Well . . . You know."

"No, I don't. It's just me here, Wyatt. No one's listening, I'm not recording. So tell me what happened."

"I took care of it."

"Okay, that's good. But I need to be one hundred percent sure I understand what it is we're talking about."

"I. Took. Care. Of. It."

"You mean you killed them? Two people in the garage?"

Wyatt nods. He seems to be avoiding saying anything specific aloud, maybe worried about creating recorded evidence. That's a surprising level of paranoia to adopt at this stage of the game, considering what they've already discussed aloud, in circumstances in which a recording would've been far easier.

But that was all before the fact. Plotting is not the same as executing. Plotting can always fail to coalesce, plotting can fall apart, plotting is just words, plotting can turn out to be bullshit.

In this general type of situation, Wyatt is probably right: paranoia is an asset, a survival mechanism. But in this particular situation, he happens to be paranoid about the wrong thing.

"Does that, um, event present any further threat to you? To the op?"

"Negative."

"Okay. Any other issues?"

Wyatt shakes his head.

"So everything else went as planned?"

"Affirmative."

"You went to the Odéon station to change clothes, swap bags? No problems?"

"None."

"You changed trains and ditched the bag on the Métro? Which line did you end up on?"

"Does it matter?"

It doesn't. Maybe he shouldn't push too much, should leave well enough alone, end this interaction before anything goes awry.

Then again: no. He can't show any weakness. He can't give Wyatt any idea that he's a man who can be taken advantage of. Even though this is the final time these two will meet, it's important to maintain the balance of power. Wyatt needs to understand that he can't simply decide unilaterally to turn this final encounter into something more adversarial, more profitable. He needs to remember who's boss, and why. And if he doesn't remember, he needs to be reminded.

Which is why Chris says, "It matters because I'm asking." Quietly, but firmly. "So tell me, what fucking Métro did you leave the bag on?"

Wyatt seems to wince at this quiet tirade, but it's hard to tell. "The 8."

"Thank you." The two men stare at each other across the divide of darkness, of wariness. They'd needed to trust each other until today, but now that Wyatt's job is finished, everything has changed. "Anything else I need to know?"

"No sir." Unmistakable hostility in that *sir*. Ironic obedience, like a petulant teenager addressing a gym teacher.

"Now I'm going to put my hand into my breast pocket. Get your envelope."

"Slowly. If you don't mind."

"You're the one with the gun." Chris had been halfway expecting Wyatt to pat him down, had planned for that.

"Thank you. You've done good work."

"Uh-huh." Wyatt takes the envelope, glances inside. A chunk of cash, an RER ticket to Charles de Gaulle, a boarding pass to Miami.

"So are you gonna tell me now what any of this has been about?"

"Sorry, that's not how this works." He knows Wyatt doesn't care, at least not much. Doesn't care whom he killed directly, whom he might kill indirectly, whom he killed in the past. Wyatt is willing to kill anyone for a price, and it's not even that high of a price.

Which makes this so much easier.

The guy actually boasted, in his interview. At least eighteen confirmed kills. In Afghanistan on behalf of the government, that was defensible, though the glee in it was not. But then in Sudan, Kenya, Syria. Not just a mercenary, a murderer; also a human trafficker.

The world is going to be a better place.

He does feel bad about the guy's sick kid. When he first heard Wyatt's story, he thought it was horseshit, exactly the kind of sad-sack fiction that an unimaginative asshole would invent to make himself appear sympathetic, to cloak the selfishness of his motivations. Parental love of a sick child: who can argue with that?

So Chris checked out the story, and was surprised to discover it was true. That's one of the reasons you check out stories, even the unlikely ones.

He was sympathetic. Chris too had his own familial responsibilities to consider, as a husband, as a father. Also as a son, that whole fucked-up fiasco with his mother. He was completely surprised by it; he'd ignored the signs. He's forever surprised by people's ability to surprise him.

"Okay then." Wyatt nods once more, this time a final goodbye. He turns away.

Chris won't waste a second now. He raises his right hand, back behind the concrete pillar, where his fingers immediately find the pair of bolts that he himself drilled into this wall at waist height. Similar to what some guys have in their garages with pegboards, to hold tools, except this is just the one tool, which he now swings in front of his body, the thing longer and heavier because of the bulky sound suppressor attached to the end.

He steadies his arm, taking careful aim through the darkness at the silhouette's center, now five yards away.

Chris has practiced this countless times, but that was decades ago, back in training. The physical motion is easier than tying your shoe, turning a doorknob. Mentally, though?

He has spent so much of his life pretending to be hard as nails, but he isn't, not at all. He has never even meted out a serious beat-down, much less killed anyone. But from an early age he learned to act, as many boys do, then as he grew older he took the acting more seriously—acting for football, for law enforcement, for high-stakes international crime.

The disguise helps. Looking like a different sort of man while behaving that way, fake it till you make it. Till you become a guy who can do this.

It's possible that at the very last instant Wyatt hesitates, slows his step, something of a syncopated beat of a stutter step, maybe suspecting what's going on, maybe considering his options—should he break into a run, should he fall to the ground, should he leap to the side, should he draw his own weapon while dropping to a knee and spinning, the things you can do to make it harder for someone to shoot you—but in the end he doesn't have time to do any of those things, or even to come to a decision, before the first bullet hits him square in the middle of his back, an immediate blinding wave of pain, and perhaps he's aware that he's beginning to sink to his knees, but he's unable to will his body into any other movement, any evasion, and it's just a half-second at most before that thought is obliterated, along with any other thoughts, as the second bullet explodes through the back of his head.

This is not exactly how Wyatt imagined it would happen. But it's pretty damn close.

⚜

Chris stands over the inert body, gives a kick, an abundance of caution. The dead man's arm moves against the shoe, but nothing in the lump of flesh responds.

He drops the bulky gun into his pocket, adjusts the angle so the grip isn't sticking out. He kneels, reaches into Wyatt's jacket, extracts the cash and travel paperwork.

What about Wyatt's gun? Chris had been planning on leaving the weapon with the dead man. But now this gun has become a ballistics match to a double-murder, bodies with the toxic van in a parking garage, and that's not something that should be associated with this corpse. He should take it, dispose of it. Which will entail first walking around with it. A gun in each pocket, double-fisted, like the psychopath villain in an action-adventure movie.

The smell of gunpowder hangs in the air. He glances around, sees nothing. He listens, hears nothing.

He takes one final look at Wyatt. Ex-Wyatt. A man who long ago seceded from the brotherhood of man, and now has finally been erased as a further threat to humanity.

Chris starts to walk away, his mind moving onto what's next, when, where—

⚜

"Not so fast."

He freezes, staring ahead at a man who has appeared in the tunnel's entrance, a silhouette backlit by daylight, wearing a hoodie and a baseball cap, holding something in front of him. Chris can't confirm with absolutely certainty what it is, but he certainly has his goddamned suspicions.

59

"Tell me what the hard parts will be," Mahmoud said.

"For one, you would have to send your children away in advance. Back to Egypt. Your kids cannot be here when you do this job."

"That sounds ominous."

"Yes." The bearded American looked grave. "It is."

"I will never see my children again?"

The man did not answer.

"Because I will not be able to leave France?" Mahmoud realized that he sounded irrationally hopeful.

"No, that is not it."

"My children, they will be okay?"

"Yes."

"I see." Mahmoud realized that he had known, even before this meeting. "I will not." This was the obvious explanation for all the solemnity. But it was not until this moment that he allowed himself to articulate it. "My job will be to die."

"Yes."

"How?"

"Painlessly."

Mahmoud let out a short snort of mirthless laughter. "One hopes. What does that mean, in effect?"

"Are you sure you want to know?"

"Yes." Though was that true? "I think so."

"It is your choice."

Mahmoud gave it a few seconds' thought. Wild, disorganized thought, ideas shooting off in every direction. *Thought* was perhaps not the activity that was going on in his brain.

He nodded.

"Okay. It will be—" The man cut himself off. "Are you sure?"

"Please."

"Okay. One possibility is that you will be shot by the French police, or army, using a high-powered sniper's rifle."

"That is horrible."

"It will be painless."

"And what is the other way?"

"You will be wearing a vest packed with explosives. That vest will detonate."

"A suicide vest?"

"Either way, the end of your life will be instantaneous."

"How will I know which?"

"Does it matter?"

Did it?

"You will not know. *I* will not know. There will be no warning. No alarm bell will tell you that you have one minute left, or ten seconds, nothing like that. One moment you will be standing on this earth, and the next you will be in paradise."

A better world for him, that is the promise. And a better life here in this world, for those he leaves behind. For his children. That was the only conceivable motivation, and that was exactly what was being offered.

He had not thought it was possible, that a moment could be worse than receiving your death sentence, with the doctor's hand on his shoulder.

"There is nothing to be done?"

The doctor shook his head, looking very sympathetic. It must be horrible, telling people they are going to die, there is no hope, you have twelve months, you have four, one.

"Surgery?"

"It is too widespread."

Mahmoud was about to ask about chemotherapy, radiation; he had been educating himself. But when the moment came, he did not want to make this conversation worse for Dr. Féraud, who was a very nice man. This was not an argument Mahmoud could win by trying harder.

He nodded his acceptance to the doctor, to himself. I am going to die very soon.

That had been the worst moment of his life. Until this one: kneeling in the airport, with his children gathered in his arms. The awfulness of it grew and grew, expanding outward like an explosion, a nuclear detonation.

"I love you," he said to the boy.

The infinite awfulness of it, of knowing that he was seeing his son and daughter for the very last time. He tried desperately not to cry—he did not want to make the children cry, he did not want to alarm them—but he failed, it was so far beyond his control.

"And I love you," to the girl. "You are in the heart of my heart." He pressed both fists to his chest. "Here."

He had told all of them—his children, his in-laws—that he wanted to save as much money as possible, that he would forward it to them in Egypt, that he would rejoin them soon. He would be working all the time, he said, he would not be able to care for the children properly, he did not want their education to suffer, he did not want to neglect small children who needed attention. It would be only a few months. He would save so much money that when they did reunite, they would live well.

Today is when his wife's parents will discover the truth. But hopefully his children will never know every detail. Hopefully the money will help, if they do.

Mahmoud had already accessed the numbered account. He had changed the password, he had verified that the first payment had been transferred; it was so much money. He had sent the necessary details to his in-laws. He had done everything there was for him to do.

"I wish I could tell you something different." Dr. Féraud took Mahmoud's hands. "But you will be dead within the year. There is no question about it."

"You can leave your children poor, Mr. Khalil."

Mahmoud wishes he could control it, pull the trigger himself, put

278 | CHRIS PAVONE

himself out of today's version of misery, after many months of living with a different misery, and a year with another. More than his share.

"Or you can leave them rich."

He had not wanted to ask the final question, because he knew he did not want the answer. But it was unacceptable to leave it unasked. He had to know.

"None," the man answered.

Mahmoud was confused. "Excuse me?"

"You will not kill anyone."

How was this possible?

"Only one person will die."

Perhaps this strange American man was lying to him. Mahmoud accepted that he might never know the truth. Not in this life.

"You."

60

"Don't move," the guy says.

This new arrival must be some confederate of Wyatt's, backup, a bodyguard against the possibility that Chris would turn out to be a double-crosser. Which he was. So as a bodyguard, this guy has been a profound failure, what with the dead body he was tasked to guard lying right there. Maybe he was supposed to be a bodyguard, but decided to play it different. More lucratively.

Chris should've seen something like this coming. What would he have done different?

"I don't wanna hurt you." The drawl is Deep South. Alabama, maybe. Mississippi.

"I appreciate that," Chris says. "I don't want to get hurt."

He can see that this guy is gripping his weapon firmly with both hands, sighting just below eye level, arms extended rigidly in front, with one leg slightly ahead of the other, his torso half-turned to the side. A trained pose. This is no mugger.

"You're gonna lie on the ground." Of course—the accent is Louisiana. Just like Wyatt. "Facedown, legs spread, hands behind your head."

Chris looks down at the disgusting filth. "Come on, man, is that necessary? Let's—"

"Do *not* move. Not a fuckin' muscle."

"Okay, let's stay calm."

"I'm plenty calm, don't you worry about my level of calm. You worry about your level of obedience."

"Okay."

"When you're lyin' down, I'm gonna walk over to you, reach into your pockets. Relieve you of your weapon. Your cash. Then I'm gonna walk away. You're gonna remain lyin' on that ground for a count-a hundred. You understand?"

"Sure do."

"If you, um, *deviate* from these instructions, you know what's gonna happen?"

It's apparently not a rhetorical question, so Chris nods.

"I'm glad we understand one another."

Chris doesn't give a damn about this cash, he'll be making so much money today that this couple hundred grand will amount to a rounding error. But the money isn't the only thing this guy is planning to take. This is not a guy who simply showed up here, noticed an opportunity, and seized it. This is not a crime of opportunity. And this guy is not going to let any witnesses walk out of here.

This whole thing was a horrible plan. A greedy plan. An *insane* plan. Chris shouldn't have agreed to this, he has known it all along. And now his child will grow up without a father, his wife without a husband. Although knowing Susanna, she may solve that problem quickly.

He has always just gone along with other people's schemes. Sometimes midstream he'd try to take ownership of a plan—a frat prank, a ski trip, a sting operation—by being confident and competent, by being a leader, he was all those things. But he was never the one with the ideas. He worries that this means he's stupid, a self-awareness that's arriving—among others—with the onset of middle age. And, as self-realizations tend to be, after their utility.

"You waitin' for somethin' in particular?"

"I guess not."

He wishes he'd had the chance to remove the various components of his disguise. Shaved off the ludicrous beard, cut away the long wavy hair, peeled off the cosmetic facial scar and the fake forearm tattoos, removed the colored contact lenses. If he's going to die here, he wants his corpse to be identified as himself, an innocent American. Not as the mastermind behind today's citywide terror siege and kidnapping.

The primary witnesses, the most important actors, will be dead: Wyatt is dead already, and maybe even Mahmoud too. But there are also the bit players, the people who deposited the bomb-filled bags around town, and the ersatz cops waiting for him back in the condemned building, and

Forsyth and his assistant, and the stray freelancers whose jobs had been to construct alternate narratives, starting conversations on street corners, planting physical evidence in residential courtyards.

It was more than one narrative that they constructed: one to implicate their target, another to exonerate him.

Any of these piecework freelancers will be able to identify the black-eyed heavily bearded American with the cheek scar and the tattoo sleeve, if this incarnation of him is what they're shown by police.

"Go ahead, then. On your knees."

Chris knows he's out of time. He takes a deep breath, getting ready. "Okay."

He begins to kneel, but instead flings his body to the side, falling, meeting the ground with his right shoulder, rolling toward the dark wall—

The unmuffled gunshots sound like sonic booms in this tunnel, once, twice, the explosions echoing off the hard surfaces. A third shot strikes something metal, a loud ping, a ricochet.

Chris has been hit, he knows this instantaneously, but he can't yet assess the severity, can't tell if he has absorbed a bullet into a fleshy part of his arm or if an artery has been severed, a vital organ punctured, his life slipping away in the next minutes or even seconds.

He continues another rotation of roll, and as he comes to a stop he reaches into his pocket to grasp his own weapon, yanks it out with a tear of cloth—

Another shot explodes from the other man's muzzle—

The source of the pain is somewhere on the upper left of his thorax, the chest or the shoulder, it's a deep burning, it could be very bad, but he can't afford to dwell on that as he lies in a puddle of urine, with the angle of his prone body presenting the smallest possible target, the only thing that could be shot now is his face, he has no time to spare, he squeezes the trigger once and shifts his aim and squeezes again and shifts again and squeezes again and once more, a cluster in the other man's direction.

He can't hear the body hit the pavement. But Chris does see the man fall, completely limp. Is it possible that he's playing possum? No, why would he do that, he had the drop, the upper hand, every advantage. And he has the most to lose by drawing out the duration of this exchange.

No, this isn't a ruse. The guy is down. Definitely. Permanently.

The pain is now flooding through Chris, radiating from his shoulder in pulsating waves.

His breaths are quick and shallow and extremely painful. Oh this hurts.

Okay, what now, what now, what now . . . ?

He can hear voices beyond the tunnel's entrance, in the street. This is a grubby neighborhood but not a violent slum, people here aren't going to ignore gunfire, pretend they saw nothing, heard nothing. No sane person is going to come into this darkness to investigate an ongoing gunfight, but someone will call the police, very soon. Maybe already has.

Would that be terrible? At least he'd get medical attention, have a chance to survive this gunshot, which is definitely not an incidental flesh wound.

Then what? How could he explain this shootout? He's in possession of all this cash, what can his story be? The passport in his pocket is fake, but his real identity will be confirmed quickly. Then what?

Jail, that's what. In France. Or America. Or worse: a black site in the mountains of Romania, in eastern Poland. No lawyer, no trial. No exit.

Is he thinking clearly? He can't tell. Can you tell when you're not? Or is part of not thinking clearly not knowing that you're not thinking clearly?

Jesus, it hurts so much. But he needs to get up. And he needs to do it right now, or he never will again.

61

"Come on." Kate hops off the scooter. She looks across the small spit of river that separates the Île de la Cité from the Left Bank, at the flashing lights of police cars surrounding Notre-Dame, an army truck as well. This is such a big production, today's terror threats.

"What happened back there?" Dexter is hustling to catch up.

"I fired into the air. To divert the police."

There's a good-size crowd in the small plaza here, as usual, mostly American tourists—loud bachelorettes in matching berets asking strangers to take group photos, middle-aged American men wearing golf-brand caps, teenagers in flip-flops staring at phones, Chinese-character tattoos on characters who aren't Chinese.

The attached café is packed, mostly coffee drinkers but also a few glasses of wine have appeared. Paris may be besieged by terror threats, but the afternoon is creeping along without any detonations, without any fatalities, and *l'apéro* hour is approaching.

"Why do I need to be gotten away from the police?"

Kate glares at Dexter, but doesn't say anything.

"What are we doing here?" he asks.

English speakers come to this bookshop from all over the city to buy current magazines, or the latest bestsellers from New York and London, or the Lost Generation classics, paperbacks of *The Little Prince*. Or just to hear English, to interact in their native tongue with other college students, other expats. All Americans seem to find their way here, which means no one would remark upon another one or two showing up on a late afternoon, walking past the register and through the warren of low ceilings and uneven floors, books jammed onto every surface, shelves above your head when you pass through one room after another all the way to the very back, where they find the proprietor bent over a counter, peering at paperwork, presenting to the world a violent explosion of blond curls that emanate every which way, like a small-town Fourth of July fireworks display, the grand finale, streamers shooting willy-nilly, the point not art but just light and noise and—if everyone is being honest—more than a little bit of danger.

"*Bonjour*," Kate says. "I'm wondering if you can help me?"

The woman looks up at Kate and smiles, then notices Dexter. "Delighted to." She's a younger woman than you'd imagine would own an old shop like this.

"I'm looking for a gift. Could I ask you to show me some first editions?"

Big smile. This is something booksellers love to hear. "Please, follow me."

Dexter leans toward his wife's ear. "What the hell are we doing?"

Kate still doesn't answer. They follow the owner back the way they came, out the shop's front entrance, and through an adjoining door, propped open by a workman's pile of bricks. These stairs are rickety, uneven, and men are working on an elevator shaft, which is shored up with wood planks. They climb, and climb, then come to a stop. The woman flips through a big key ring, finds what she's looking for. Turns a couple of locks.

This is another book-lined room, with a dining table and chairs, a table with a printer and office supplies, a window that looks out onto the Petit Pont, the Seine, Notre-Dame.

"This way." Through the narrow kitchen, boxes of biscuits, tea, mismatched plates, old dishrags. Up a couple of steps into a utility room, washing machine, bathroom sink, linen cabinets. She unlocks another door, and they all step into a bedroom, blue walls, vintage posters, more bookshelves packed with old hardbacks, a small desk with a bright red typewriter. This window faces onto nothing, just another window whose curtains are drawn.

Kate shuts the door behind them. "Thanks so much," she says. "This is Dexter."

The two shake hands.

"I'm sorry but I don't have much time," the woman says, turning to an armoire. "Look." She pulls the armoire's door open, there are a few things hanging, a rain slicker, a windbreaker, a cable-knit cardigan. She pushes the hangers to the side, revealing the furniture's back panel.

"You put your hand here, like this. And push."

There's a soft click as she presses into a section of wood, and the panel releases on a hinge. It's a small door, two feet wide and four tall, carved out of the wall behind the armoire.

"There's no light switch back here, so you'll have to use your phone. There, you can see now. Come, have a look. We built this hatch during the Occupation."

Dexter peers in. It's the landing of another staircase, not the one they ascended.

"You follow this down to a short hall that leads to the backdoor, which lets out onto the other street. There's an old bicycle hanging on the wall next to the door, if you need it."

Now she fumbles again with the keys, removes a couple. "Here." She presses the keys into Dexter's palm. "There's a toilet across the hall, a shower round the corner, I'm sure a bit to eat in the kitchen."

She scans a bookshelf, yanks down a clothbound volume, opens to the endpapers, and scrawls a price with a pencil that she yanked from the hidden depths of her hair. "When you leave, pay at the front." She thrusts the book at Kate. "I hope one day you'll explain all this to me. Good luck Dexter." She kisses Kate on both cheeks. "Kate, you too."

"What the hell is going on?" Dexter asks.

Kate watches her husband closely as she says, "Hunter Forsyth is missing." It certainly looks like genuine surprise on his face. But then again, he'd be prepared for this.

"Missing? I guess that's why the press conference was canceled. You think he was kidnapped?"

"I'm almost positive of it. Listen, Dex: how much money have you made today?"

His eyes cut away. "I don't kn—"

"*Dexter.*"

He winces at her tone. She's pissed, and wants him to know it.

"Last I checked, it was about two hundred K."

A lot more than she would've thought possible. "That's just from shorting two-fifty worth of 4Syte?"

He cuts his eyes away again.

"Jesus, Dexter. What else?"

He doesn't answer. She's fed up, and without really thinking about it she punches her husband in the arm.

"Hey. What the fuck?"

"Tell me right now, goddamn it."

"Okay, I also used funds from a Swiss account. Another two-fifty."

She shakes her head. "I can't even . . ."

He'd lied to her, again. But at the moment that's not what's important. Which is that Dexter invested a total of five hundred, and so far has made a profit of two hundred. And although that's certainly a profitable one-day return, it's not anywhere near a sufficient order of magnitude to justify today's conspiracy. Dexter is a man who once stole fifty million euros; he wouldn't do something like this for two hundred thousand.

Which means that Dexter can't be one of the conspirators; he must be innocent, relatively. That's a relief. But there's still a conspiracy, and he's in the middle of it.

"Dexter, did anyone see you this morning, between say eight and nine-thirty? This is when I think Forsyth was being kidnapped."

"You're asking for my alibi? Jesus, Kate."

She glares at him.

"Okay: Luc, as you know."

His friend, tennis partner, and guy who served as the conduit for the insider-trading information to begin with. Luc is not an alibi. He'll look like an accomplice. He'll be arrested too, if he hasn't been already. Maybe that's what he deserves.

"How exactly did you meet Luc?"

"Message board."

"Were you identifiable as you?"

"Um, not really. I guess."

"No? Or not really?"

"No, I don't think so."

"What's your handle?"

"LuxDayTrader."

"Really? A Luxembourg day trader who now lives in Paris? You don't think that's identifiable as you? Are you an idiot?"

So that's a possibility: Luc was a plant, used to lure Dexter. In which case Luc would definitely not be an alibi. He would no longer even be findable.

"Okay, anyone else?"

"Julien." Their everyday waiter. A guy who'd probably be willing to lie for a high-tipping regular customer; another non-airtight alibi.

"What about people you don't know? Did you stop somewhere to buy water? Wave to a baker?"

"Yes, there was an old man waiting at a street corner with me—just *Bonjour, comment ça va,* chitchat while we waited for the light. And a woman too."

"At the same light?" That would be an awfully friendly corner.

"No, she was right after tennis ended at nine. I kind of crashed into her, at the park. Spilled her groceries everywhere. I helped her pick up, and I apologized, but . . ."

"What?"

"I got the sense that I'd seen her before."

He'd seen her before. "She attractive, Dexter?"

He looks like he's about to say no, but changes his mind. "Yes."

What does this mean? Two alibis, at either end of the hour when he played tennis in the Luxembourg Gardens? That's not a coincidence. But there's no way to find these alibis, they're just strangers on streets, no connection to anything. They're useless.

"Why are you asking about this?"

"Because you're being framed, Dexter."

"Framed for what?"

"What the hell do you think?"

"But there's no way . . . how could . . . ?" He shakes his head. "Why would I kidnap someone I'm well known to hate? No one would believe I'd be that stupid."

It's true. Not at a trial, with lawyers, a jury, judge. But at first glance, he looks too guilty not to investigate, and the investigation wouldn't even need to get anywhere near trial to ruin their lives. That, Kate now realizes, is exactly the point: not jail, just ruin. An eye for an eye.

"Who's framing me?"

Kate turns back to her husband. "You know damn well."

"*Bonjour?*"

"Hi, it's Kate."

"Kate! We're *so* looking forward to tonight."

"Yeah. About that."

"Oh dear. Is something wrong?"

"I'm afraid so."

Kate promises herself this: you will never, ever again use that nickname, not even in your head. If this woman does this enormous favor for you, forevermore you must call her by her real name, even in—especially in—your mind.

This will be hard.

For a split-second it escapes Kate, she uses it so infrequently, but then she remembers Hashtag Mom's real name: "Hailie, could I ask for a *huge* favor?"

Kate looks around this small room, exactly how a place like this should look, a refuge for visiting writers above a Left Bank bookshop. How long will Dexter hide out in here? Where will he go next? And will Kate—will the kids—go with him?

"I'm going to leave you," she says.

Dexter's jaw drops open, devastated. Misunderstanding.

"Not permanently," Kate clarifies. "But I have to go."

She arranged for Hailie to pick up the kids, and to call around to the other families to cancel dinner.

"So, what?" Dexter asks. "I'm just supposed to hide here? Above a bookstore?"

"We can't risk you being seen by any police. We'll need to get you new clothes, a shave, a haircut, a new everything. Did you give the cops your name?"

"Fake name, address, phone number. But they do know that I keep a car in the garage."

It won't be hard for the police to find Dexter, if they try. Will they?

That depends on what else the investigators find in the coming hours, and what clues or evidence or anonymous tips are provided to help them. But if the police are hunting for an American in connection to terrorism, this bookstore refuge will last only so long. Dexter would be in custody within a day, and he might never be released. Who knows what would happen to a man like him, in a French jail, facing the sorts of charges that could be trumped up against him.

Kate will need help getting the police called off, intervention from a legitimate authority. That will have to come from America; that will have to be part of the cleanup. Tomorrow. The day after.

But maybe that won't be necessary. Maybe there's another solution, one built into the problem itself. Kate thinks she knows what it is, but not how to find it. And she's running out of time.

62

He pushes himself up from his right side, his uninjured side, but it's not as if the right is unconnected to the left, and the pain is immense, it's overwhelming, and his arm buckles, and the pavement rushes up—

❧

How long was he unconscious? It couldn't have been for more than a few seconds, a minute, the light seems the same, the noise beyond the entrance to the tunnel, everything. No one has yet joined him here in the darkness. He's still alone. Still shot. Still bleeding.

He has to get up, get out of here. He braces himself for the pain, he knows it's going to be horrible, he doesn't want to be caught by surprise again, that was his mistake the first time.

Use your lower body, he tells himself. He twists onto his stomach, and pain explodes from his shoulder. He pushes his weight into his knees and from there into the ground, and rolls onto his toes, and with every movement the pain continues to mount, it's getting worse, and worse—

Don't pass out . . . *Don't* . . .

He pushes, and pushes, and—

He's standing. He did it. He's dizzy, he's out of breath. He can feel the blood trickling down his chest and stomach, warm and sticky, his shirt is already soaked, cool against his skin.

He starts to walk. Stumbles past Wyatt's corpse, it seems like a lifetime ago when he shot the guy.

The gun slips from his grasp, clatters to the pavement. Damn. He starts to bend but realizes that's a mistake, blood will rush into his wound and to his head, he'll lose his balance, he'll pitch over, crack his head—

Instead he squats. Reaches for his weapon, manages to retrieve it without losing consciousness.

He can hear the voices gathering out on the street, he can't go out there, a crowd will be amassing. He walks in the other direction, toward the far end of the tunnel where it merges with the parallel street.

The voices behind him grow louder. He walks faster.

Open daylight, blinding bright. He raises his hand to shield his eyes, surveys this very long block, maybe a quarter-mile to the next intersection. There are a couple of people near the far end walking in his way, but they don't seem to be in any rush, they're not investigating gunshots, they're not coming for him.

A car turns the distant corner, also heading his way.

He takes a quick glance down at his shoulder. It's pretty clear there's a bullet hole in his jacket, but there's no blood visible, or at least very little blood, it's hard to say because the whole front of his clothing is soaking wet from lying in that pool of urine, and now that he's giving himself the once-over he sees that he's a complete fucking mess. He can't stumble around the streets looking like this.

The car is fifty yards away, decelerating as it approaches the split with the tunnel. As it approaches him.

He sidesteps off the sidewalk, into the gutter, and takes another step and another, he's in the middle of the roadway, it's a narrow street with no room for parking on either side, no room for this car to swerve around him.

Through the windshield he can see that the driver looks confused, then angry, then worried as he gets near enough to clearly see the state of this man who's blocking the street. The driver seems to debate his options, whether to get out and help, or to roll down the window and inquire, or to throw the thing in reverse and get the hell out of there.

Chris staggers sideways toward the car, keeping his right side shielded from the driver's view, the uninjured side of his body, the side whose pocket holds the gun, which he slowly draws until he arrives at the window, places the muzzle directly against the glass, just inches from the guy's face—

"*Sortez!*" Chris screams. "Get the fuck out! *Maintenant!*"

The guy's hands are raised, as if he's being held up, eager to show that he isn't armed, please take my wallet, there's no reason to shoot. He slowly lowers his left hand to the door handle.

Chris takes a half-step backward, away from the door, in case the driver grows bold and tries to fling it open as an attack. The car is a beat-up old Renault the color of rust, like it came from the factory pre-shitty. The owner of a car like this shouldn't take heroic measures to prevent its theft. Better off with the insurance settlement. But you never know, maybe there's a bag of cash in the trunk.

The door opens. One foot emerges, a running shoe, planted on the pavement. Then the other. The driver hoists himself up, then returns his hands to the *please-don't-shoot* pose.

Chris uses the gun to motion the guy away from his car, to the sidewalk. *"Asseyez-vous!"*

The man obeys, sits at the curb.

Chris tumbles into the seat. He realizes, a split-second too late, that it's going to hurt like a motherfucker when he attempts to close the door with his left hand, and he screams out in pain, squeezes his eyes shut, shakes his head back and forth . . .

The driver looks worried. *"Monsieur? Si vous voulez . . ."* He mimes pushing. Is this guy actually volunteering to help someone steal his car? Maybe what's in the trunk is a dead body.

Chris nods, then warns, *"Attention."*

"Bien sûr." The driver approaches tentatively, shuts the door gently, backs away.

"Merci." Chris shifts into gear—it's an automatic, thank God—and executes a jagged six-point U-turn while the driver watches, getting a better and better look at him, this guy will be able to help the police draw a sketch, he'll be able to identify a photo, he'll be able to provide a positive ID if he's confronted with something to compare . . .

But who he'll be able to identify is an American with a mountain-man beard and unruly hair and eyeglasses and a long scar on the side of his face. A version of a person that has only ever existed here, in this city, over the last few months. There is no long-term past tense of this person, no match to be made.

Unfortunately, this wound suggests there won't be a future tense either.

Chris wishes it were true that he's too young to die, that he doesn't deserve it. But he knows that neither is true.

Excruciating pain shoots through him, and he barely manages to extend his arm to the machine, to pull the ticket out of the slot. The parking garage's barrier raises, and he rolls the car slowly down the ramp, finds an empty space in a quiet corner. He's panting, shaking, his vision blurry.

He needs to think. And he needs to attend to his wound. He needs to think about attending to his wound.

The trunk. Maybe there's a first-aid kit in the trunk.

No such luck. What does he find back there? A neon nylon emergency vest, a warning triangle, the things you're legally required to keep in the trunk to pass safety inspection. Also a soccer ball and a pair of cleats, a plastic jug of motor oil, a half-full bottle of cheap vodka, an old sweatshirt, a roll of duct tape.

A plan forms.

With no small amount of effort and pain, he removes his shirt. He uses a window as a mirror to examine his wound: the bullet passed through. That's the good news. The bad news is that these gunshot holes are seeping a lot of blood, and have been exposed to a surfeit of bacteria. He needs to disinfect.

This is definitely going to hurt something fierce, maybe too much to stay conscious. He doesn't want to soak the driver's seat in vodka, in case he needs to drive again, so he walks to the passenger side, opens the door.

He rips a few long strips of musty fleece from the sweatshirt. Tears lengths of duct tape, hangs them from the car's roof.

He sits. If he passes out, he wants to already be in a sitting position, no way to fall and crack his skull open.

Okay, now there's nothing left to do but to do it.

Okay.

He really doesn't want to do this. But he has to. Now.

Now.

Now—

He splashes vodka on his front entry wound, and it hurts so immediately and so much that his vision goes dark, and his whole body seizes.

He feels a fresh wound appear on his lower lip, where his top teeth have dug into his flesh.

The pain recedes, barely, from the brink of unbearable. He sits there, panting.

That was bad. But he made it.

The back will be worse, but fuck it, this time he doesn't delay, doesn't indulge in any pep talk, just throws a splash over his shoulder, which lands in the wrong spot—no pain—so he does it again, and then again, alcohol streaming down his back until—oh, God—there it is, and this time it's the same sensations as with the front wound but doubled, trebled, it's too much, it's—

He comes to with a start.

The vodka bottle has fallen from his hand. The glass remained intact, but most of the liquid spilled out.

He wraps a few strips of sweatshirt around his shoulder, looping under his armpit, then secures the cloth with duct tape. He adds more strips at a different angle, more duct tape . . .

Is this going to make any difference? Is this going to keep him alive? Maybe not. But it's all he can do right now.

He and his wife had discussed a wide variety of foreseeable problems, including this one. He knows what he's supposed to do next.

If only she'd listened to him—if he could've convinced her—then he wouldn't be sitting here in this stolen Renault, shot, dying. He'd tried. But there was never any convincing her of anything.

It had taken him a while to come around to the big-picture viability of the scheme. At first it seemed so utterly outlandish, so completely unfeasible. Then she explained one element at a time, gambit after gambit, how the whole thing would coalesce. At the end, there was only one facet he still wasn't sold on: framing Dexter.

"It's an unnecessary level of complexity," he said. "It'll make it that much harder to pull off, it adds challenges to every other component. We'll need to choose our primary operative based on his looks, which is obviously not the best determinant for finding talent. We'll need to re-search Dexter's wardrobe, eyeglasses, sunglasses, everything, then we'll need to buy all that, which will leave a trail—"

"Not if we're careful."

"*Yes,* even if we're careful. The trail may be faint, but it will be there. And we'll need to steal that ridiculous hat? Then replace it?"

"The hat is the nail in the coffin."

"We'll need to disable the security camera in the Métro station so our asset can change wardrobes. We'll need to run the risks of the guy actu-ally doing that."

"Please, it doesn't even matter if someone—"

"Yes, I know, I know: you can dismiss any one of these as quibbles. But as a whole, framing Dexter will add a lot of unnecessary risks to what's already a very long list of necessary ones. You can't deny it."

She didn't, so he pressed his advantage. "Plus it's an irrational choice. You *know* this, Susanna: the scheme is not stronger by framing Dexter. It's weaker."

She shook her head, closed her eyes, trying to be patient. "If we don't frame Dexter, we can't get the fifty million."

"*So what?* So we make only five million euros? Ten?"

She snorted, as if ten million were chump change, not worth getting out of bed.

"It's a good scheme," he continued. "No: it's brilliant. We can get rich *and* play it safe. *If* we leave Kate and Dexter out of it."

She shook her head again.

"For fuck's sake, why not?"

"Because they're *the whole reason.* Don't you see that, Chris?"

They hadn't used their real names in years. Back when they were living in Luxembourg, they'd played characters called Bill and Julia MacLean. When they were forced by Kate to run, to hide, they adopted new names, variations on the names given to them by their parents: Craig Malloy and Susan Pognowski. He became Chris; she, Susanna. These were the only names they'd used for the past two years. That's how new identities become real.

"I worked *so* hard," she said. "I planned for *so* long. Then she made a fool of me."

"A fool? No, that's not what happened."

"They sat around, the two of them, and discussed how to screw me out of my fortune. I was going to be rich! And now look."

"Yes, exactly, *now look*: is this really so bad?"

"That's not the point."

"No? Then what *is* the point?"

"That she *took* it all from me."

"But she didn't. All she took was the money."

"Don't give me that shit." Gritted teeth. "You know it wasn't only the money."

Susanna was right. Kate Moore had taken much more than the money.

"Just because we managed to get some things back, that doesn't mean she didn't take everything. Plus, we won't be hurting anyone who doesn't deserve to be hurt."

"Deserve to be hurt? What does that mean?"

"You know exactly what that means. Our primary investor is a life-long criminal, a rat, an informer. Our driver is a psychopathic murderer. A random douchebag amoral trader-bro in Hong—"

"Is this really what you want?" he asked. "To put *Dexter* in jail? He didn't do anything to you. Not really."

She snorted. "Dexter will never go anywhere near jail."

"Then why the hell do you want to do all this?"

"Because I want her to fear for her freedom, for her life, her home, her precious kids. It's that terror I want Kate to feel. To live with."

This wasn't surprising. His wife was charming; she was intelligent; she was clever, witty, sexy; she was beautiful. But she was not nice.

"She didn't *need* to ruin my life, Chris. She *chose* to do that."

He'd known this all along, well before they became a couple, he'd known this back when they were casual colleagues at the Bureau, sitting in the same meetings in the same conference rooms, everyone was impressed with her, but also at least a little bit scared.

"So now I'm going to make her pay. Force her to make a horrible choice."

His eyes had been wide open, no one else to blame. Life is compromises.

"Give me the fifty million euros, or I'll ruin her fucking life."

❧

He has to put distance between himself and this car, which the police could be tracking this instant, surrounding the block, weapons drawn.

Chris staggers up the ramp.

He can't type this out in a text-message, or an e-mail. It needs to be a conversation. And it needs to happen right now, before he gets caught. Or dies.

She answers after one ring. "Hi."

"Hi." He's approaching the street, nervous about exiting, what could be out there. He stops, peeks around a wall: looks normal. He continues walking, and talking. "Things have . . . um . . . deteriorated."

She doesn't respond.

"I'm injured." This type of voice communication—it's not exactly a phone call—is supposed to be secure, but who knows anymore. "It's bad."

Pause. "I'm very sorry to hear that."

"I can't travel the way I planned. Not sure I can travel at all." The pain is making him dizzy. "I need medical attention."

He wants her to say: do whatever you need, get to a hospital, save yourself, don't worry about me. But that's not what he expects, nor what he gets.

"You're prepared for that, right?"

This is one of the contingencies they'd discussed: avoiding hospitals, their records, the police that can often be found in emergency rooms.

He swallows back the nausea that accompanies his intense pain and dizziness. He has already thrown up, which hurt so much that he almost passed out again. "Yuh."

"Is there something I can do for you?"

There isn't, is there? "Don't think so."

"Okay then." She pauses. "Good luck."

He's pretty sure this is the last conversation they'll ever have, which makes this the last thing he'll ever say to her: "I love you."

He hopes his wife makes the same choice. He waits, and waits, and wonders if the connection has been dropped.

Then he hears: "I love you too." And the line goes dead.

63

Kate rides past her building without slowing, searching for signs of surveillance, men sitting in cars, leaning in doorways, loitering in the lobby of the hotel at the end of the street.

No one.

She doubles back and parks the Vespa. Inside, she takes the stairs, creeping up, peeking down each hall, her hand in her pocket, resting on Inez's gun. It's a long climb to the top.

Still no one.

Her apartment door appears to be undisturbed. These are hard locks to pick, but not impossible. She opens the door slowly, just halfway, until right before the point in the arc where it squeaks.

A few months ago, Dexter said, "I'll fix that now. Just needs some oil."

"No, leave it."

He looked at her with furrowed brow.

"It's a good alarm." Which she doesn't want to trip now, in case someone is waiting inside. She tiptoes through the hall, skirting the creaky floorboard near the boys' bedroom, down to the end, the office. She looks around carefully. No one has been here.

She sets to work quickly, removing the screws from Dexter's CPU, setting aside the panel. Then her phone rings.

"Gunshots are reported," Inez says by way of hello. "Witnesses say that the men who are shooting, they speak English. Two are dead. Another is injured, and he stole a car."

Kate isn't sure exactly what this means, but it's definitely not nothing. "Where?"

"*Le onzième.*"

"Exactly where?"

"I will send the position to you."

During Kate's first months working for Hayden's new Paris Substation, it slowly dawned on her that her manager wasn't really monitoring almost anything she did, and neither was anyone else. She was, in effect, completely unsupervised.

Maybe, she thought, this was a test. Of her dedication. Of her responsibility. Of her maturity. Doing what you're supposed to do, even when no one could know if you're not.

Sometimes Kate believed that Hayden's hands-off management style was because he liked to give his subordinates the freedom to make their own decisions, to succeed or fail based on their own actions and the ensuing consequences, enough rope. But in darker moments it occurred to her that Hayden's scarcity reflected a more nefarious motivation: a deliberate attempt to maintain his own plausible deniability.

Little by little, she began to act on the presumption of complete autonomy. She recruited assets that had nothing whatsoever to do with any of her active operations, nor any reasonable expectation of future ops. She pursued her own private interests, cautiously, always ready to get caught, to get called out—what the hell do you think you're doing?

It never happened.

Her personal agenda was modest. It wasn't as if Kate was trying to overthrow a democratically elected president. All she wanted was a single discrete piece of information.

Kate's search was both broad and narrow. Broad, because she could be looking almost anywhere in the world. Narrow, because she was looking for something very specific.

And although in the abstract her target could be anywhere on the planet, Kate was confident that the effective search range could be much smaller. There were language considerations; Romance countries were most likely. And the quality of life, the rule of law, the general level of medical care, these were not irrelevant. There had also been a previous lifetime of living in the pampered plush of the United States, and now there would be a child too. A certain standard of living.

These factors made Kate feel safe ruling out large swaths of the planet.

Europe was by far the most likely, especially the Mediterranean. France, though, was unlikely. Luxembourg completely out of the question.

Kate added one piece at a time. She recruited a functionary in the Turkish border control, a federal bureaucrat in Madrid, another in Switzerland. A Portuguese diplomat living in Brussels, a German police chief, a Greek mayor, an Italian minister's assistant. She gained access to real-estate transfers, visa applications, immigration rosters, birth records. She hired a freelancer named Henri to sort through all of it. He came in one day per week, like the cleaning lady.

It used to be easy to disappear; the main challenge was resisting the temptation to make contact with your old life. But the digital age shrunk the world exponentially, with every new database, every app, every electronic intrusion to which we voluntarily submit ourselves in exchange for the promise of a more convenient life, while in the meantime dragging everyone else into a global surveillance state.

It's impossible to completely hide. Not if you want to live any version of modern life, with a family, with the Internet, with bank accounts and airline tickets and healthcare records. There are cameras everywhere, digital footprints, satellite images, centrally collected phone records, all searchable and sortable. There are informants, hackers, leaks, spies. Any data can be bought, or stolen, every interaction that anyone has, every purchase, every e-mail, every phone—

Yes. That's the solution.

Kate calls Inez again. "Can you access mobile meta-data?"

"*Oui, c'est possible.*"

"Sometime right after the gunfight, a telephone call was placed from that vicinity. Or soon will be."

"I am sure many."

"Can you get records of all of them?"

Kate can hear Inez take a drag on a cigarette. Kate has never been a smoker, but she has always envied this thing smokers have, this tension release, this dramatic pause, this purchase of small bits of time, this thing to do after orgasm, when there's otherwise nothing left to do.

"*Mais oui.* You are looking for something specific?"

"Yes. A call from that immediate area to one particular city."

⚜

Kate continues to destroy evidence—disassembling Dexter's computers, removing hard drives—with her phone on speaker. She can hear Inez barking commands, rapid-fire instructions—*maintenant, vite,* the voices of a couple of men responding.

"*Alors,*" Inez says. "There has been none."

That doesn't make sense. "She must be using more than one phone."

Kate can hear fresh commands being issued, gruff voices responding, *non, désolée.*

"I am sorry," Inez says. "We find nothing. But the records, they are not, how do you say, instantaneous? It is taking ten, twenty, maybe thirty minutes to appear in the database."

❖

Kate's phone dings with a new text stream, an update. She responds quickly: *Grazie. I will wire payment immediately.*

She dumps Dexter's hard drives into her bag. She opens the bottom desk drawer, the combination-locked strongbox, and begins to transfer the contents to her bag: an extra burner, and all eight passports—the four real ones and the corresponding fakes—and small bundles of various currencies.

Her phone rings again.

"It happened."

"The call?"

"*Oui.* And then the phone in Paris, it is immediately dead. Powered down."

Who turns off a mobile on a day like today? Only someone trying to be invisible.

"Do you have the last location of the Paris phone?"

"I send it to you. Also, bad news. The police, I believe they are looking for you."

"For me?"

"A woman of your description, who is riding a black Vespa, last seen in St-Germain-des-Prés, who is firing a gun."

The last item Kate retrieves from the strongbox is her own handgun. Now she has two.

"This is you, *n'est-ce pas?*"

64

S o. This is not the outcome for which she'd been hoping. Obviously. But it is one for which she'd planned.

She stares at the phone, now a useless piece of garbage. No: worse than useless, this cheap electronic device has become a piece of damning physical evidence. She pops out the SIM card, cuts it in half. Opens a desk drawer and removes the ball-peen hammer, which she uses to pummel the phone into shards. She opens the window and tosses this shattered plastic into the narrow canal forty feet below.

Don't cry, she tells herself. You have things to do.

She turns back to the computer, all those red numbers, all those downward-facing arrows. And in particular 4Syte, whose rate of decrease is continuing to accelerate. Perhaps trading will be suspended, any minute now.

Goddamn it: Do. Not. Cry.

This moment may not be perfect, but it's more than good enough. An injured Chris could be taken into custody any second now, and you never know what someone is going to do when hurt and desperate. She doesn't actually expect him to throw her under the bus, but she needs to be prepared for the worst case.

She's continuing to tell herself not to cry, like a mantra running in the background of her brain. But it's futile, it's counterproductive—

Okay, she tells herself: go ahead, cry.

For ten seconds.

Then get your fucking money back.

⚜

"But . . . I don't understand . . ."

Richie looked at her like she was an idiot, or insane, how could she not understand what he doesn't understand, the whole point of this whole endeavor, of every endeavor: "If there's no ransom, how do we make any money?"

That's the question, isn't it. That's everyone's question, what we all do, the paths we take, the decisions we make, the choices: what will I do, and who will I be, and how much will people pay me?

She doesn't know what level of deliberateness other people bring to bear while making their lives' most important choices. For example, Richie Benedetti: did he sit in his childhood room, assess his skills and predilections, weigh his options, and come to the rational conclusion that, yes, I will become a professional hoodlum? Or did he stumble into a life of crime one half-assed ill-considered decision at a time?

Not Susanna. Her choices were not a series of spur-of-the-moment schemes, not some opportunistic lark. She had a carefully considered, meticulously constructed life plan.

At first she didn't know exactly which exit she'd end up taking, but she did decide that the road to her destination would be the FBI. After a couple of years working at the Bureau, poking into one corner and another, it became clear that she should specialize in something with a very high barrier to entry, a niche that could endow her with an impenetrable cloak of specialized technical knowledge: cyber-crime.

How long would the whole thing take? Five years, ten, thirty? She wouldn't rush it. This was the work of a career, and as with any career she took the necessary steps—to pay her dues, to establish her reputation, to prove her work ethic, to develop her expertise, to rise to a position of authority, of independence, of unassailable integrity.

She recruited a wide network of experts to help her identify money-laundering operations, illegal transfers to offshore entities, the kind of financial activities that have practically no legal justification, the proceeds of exactly the sorts of crimes, perpetrated by exactly the sorts of criminals, that she eventually intended to use: drug cartels, arms dealers, human traffickers, merchants of one type of death or another.

Someday, she knew, the perfect situation would present itself, the culmination of this career-within-a-career. Her own version of partnership, corner office, golden parachute: she would get immensely rich by robbing a criminal kingpin.

This was admittedly not exactly what the FBI was invented to do, but when it comes right down to it, it's not that different.

She'd probably have only one shot, but she was confident that she'd need only one.

She was wrong.

❧

It's time to tie off the loose ends.

She opens the messaging app on another mobile, finds the contact, types the short message.

After this, she'll walk out the door, lock it, leave the keys in the stairway's light fixture. She'll drop this phone into the water from the back of Lorenzo's speedboat as they bump across the lagoon, on the first leg of her journey to a new life.

She hits SEND.

Events will now unfold quickly, and will mostly be out of her control. So far, she has been the one orchestrating the action, but as of this moment she'll become just another private citizen, responsible for only herself and her baby.

She bundles up Matteo again, straps him to her chest.

Before the kid was born, she couldn't have fathomed the extent to which parenting meant ceding control. For a long while, especially when you're a child yourself, it looks like the opposite: parenthood *is* control. Untrue. So much of a parent's life is determined by the biological imperatives and whims of this tiny inchoate animal. Trying to control it is an exercise in frustration.

It's one thing to learn this, another to live with it, to accept it. In general, Susanna has trouble accepting lack of control. She knows this makes her a difficult person to live with, and for a long time she didn't give a damn. Then she realized that she wanted this man to be her husband; then she realized that if she wanted to keep this husband, she had to make some accommodations. More than none. That's what it means to be married.

She stands at the desk, leans over the keyboard to execute the trades, first one, another, another, dozens of them, small transactions and big ones and a number of midsize, nothing unusual, nothing noteworthy, using brokerage accounts connected to banks all over Europe, with untraceable aliases and shielded identities, LLCs and SARLs.

As she waits for the confirmations to arrive, she rocks from one foot to the other, trying to keep the baby in his soothed state. There is no excuse for disturbing a contented baby.

Secure messages begin to arrive to her in-boxes, confirmation numbers, amounts in US dollars, in euros, in British pounds, transferring funds from all these disparate sources into a single account at a Swiss bank whose originating branch is just over the Alps, a few hours' drive.

This whole process takes ten minutes.

Almost finished.

Finally she double-clicks the large black *X* icon on the bottom of her screen. The program launches, a dialog box opens, and she initiates a three-stage protocol that requires three different passwords, until at last:

Are you sure you want to destroy this device?

Her finger pauses for a second. The default answer—the button you'd hit by mistake—is NO.

She clicks YES.

Nothing happens. Her heart sinks, she can feel anxiety welling up, what if this doesn't—

The screen goes blank.

Then she hears a soft fizzing noise, like a fresh soda bottle being opened, slowly. A wisp of smoke appears from the side of the CPU, another from the bottom.

The smell is acrid.

The blank screen flashes, then goes dark again. Then darker.

A loud pop, and it's done.

⚜

The bulk of their belongings have already been packed, picked up by a moving company, sitting in a warehouse outside of Treviso, awaiting delivery instructions, which she will provide tomorrow. The ultimate destination depends on what else happens today and tonight.

She'd picked out two different locations, in two different countries.

The preferred scenario is that she'll head east to a busy tourist town on the Croatian coast, just across the Gulf of Venice, a few hours away in Lorenzo's speedboat, if the weather cooperates. Croatia is the option if everything has gone okay in Paris, and her husband escapes unscathed, hops a TGV to Nice tonight, then tomorrow morning a short flight to Zagreb.

Happily ever after.

The other option is to fly west to Spain, to a White Village in the sparsely populated Sierra de Grazalema Mountains of Andalusia, where she made a week-long reservation in a modest hotel in an area where vacation properties abound, month-long stays, year-long leases, she won't have a problem finding a comfortable place to live. Her Italian will help her learn Spanish, and she will have an immense amount of money to help with everything else.

What she won't have in Spain is a husband. She'll be a single mother of a young child. Life will be challenging, but people will have sympathy.

Her husband doesn't know anything about the Andalusian option. The White Village is in case of his capture, or his compromise, or his demise; it's the option if she needs to cut connections. She has a pretty clear set of guidelines in her head, different scenarios, different levels of risk she's willing to tolerate. If he's detained by the police. If he's questioned, but let go. If he's identified, being hunted. If he's dead.

And if he's seriously injured. She can't be weighed down by that, can't subject herself and Matteo to the risks attendant with traveling with someone who has wounds to treat, someone seeking medical attention, undergoing surgeries, removing bullets whose ballistics might be traced, administrative records that are fed into centralized databases, blood types, fingerprints, dental records.

If he's seriously injured, she knows what she needs to do.

❖

"Okay." Richie picked an imaginary piece of lint off the hammy thigh of his tight pants, then turned back to face her. "I've got some concerns."

She had just finished explaining what needed explanation, but that left ample room for questions, of which anyone in their right mind would ask plenty. Richie may not have been the sharpest tool in the shed, but he wasn't crazy.

"First, obviously: how do we not get caught?"

"To begin with, you don't need to worry about yourself. You're completely in the clear. No one knows we're here, we barely even exist."

Richie understood.

"Most important, Richie: no Internet for any communications, ever. We need to use the Internet for research, but we do everything that's necessary using a single computer set to a masked IP address, at a physical location that will not be traceable to us. Before the day itself we destroy the computer and scrub the apartment."

"How do we communicate?"

"Burner phones, using code. Nothing complicated, just enough to avoid key-word recognition."

"How many people are involved?"

"A couple of handfuls."

"Tell me about them."

"Okay. Chronologically, it's *one,* a woman posing as a scientific researcher at the cancer ward, to buffer the recruitment process of *two,* the suicide bomber. *Three,* the driver who delivers a couple of the bombs and the bomber. For the kidnapping, a pair of fake cops, that's *four* and *five.* Plus *six* and *seven,* a couple of freelancers to deposit additional bombs. *Eight* and *nine,* incidentals doing small piecework, completely firewalled from the rest."

"Piecework?"

"Just some advance intel." She doesn't want to explain this legwork, which veers into territory that she intends to keep from Richie, for the benefit of everyone.

"What about the State-slash-CIA guy?"

She pointed at Chris.

Richie turned to examine him. "Interesting."

"To generate the other international panics, two people—number *ten* in one country, *eleven* in another."

"How much you paying all these people?"

"Wildly varying compensation, for very different responsibilities and risk levels. Only two will be large. Most will be small, not enough for anyone to think they're doing anything serious. A few hundred euros, leave this backpack over there, that kind of thing. By the time any of these people realize what's really going on, they'll have no way of changing their minds, no way of contacting us, no way of ID'ing anyone."

"So what's the grand total?"

"In sum the freelancers will cost about four hundred thousand."

Richie mugged an exaggerated frown, wise-guy for *not bad*. "Other expenses?"

"Another two hundred K for flights and apartments, hotel rooms and meals and wardrobe and living expenses, plus the van, other supplies. And another couple hundred for the bomb materials." She'd budgeted every single item, line by line. The nuclear waste had been particularly expensive. "Overall, it's just over three-quarters of a million of non-recoupable expenses."

A drop in the bucket, considering the upside. But that upside will be worthwhile only if they raise copious quantities of additional investments. With a couple of million, they'll break even. One or two high-net-worth investors, that's all they need.

"So who's managing all this on the ground? I'm assuming not you." He indicated Susanna's swollen stomach. By the time everything had come together sufficiently to seek investors, she was visibly pregnant. She'd been pregnant a few times before in the past couple of years, but this was the only one that had advanced to viability, to visibility. Every day that she didn't miscarry felt like a miracle.

"I am."

Richie turned to Chris. "You know what you're doin', huh?"

"I'm not incompetent."

"Oh no? What sorta jobs you work?"

"I have the same professional background as my wife."

"That right?" This tickled Richie. "You two meet on the job?"

Neither answered. Richie didn't press it. "So, you gonna tell me who this CEO is who you're gonna kidnap? And where this is all gonna happen?"

"Eventually."

"What exactly are you waiting for?"

"For you to commit."

"Why this particular guy? You have something against him?"

"Probably."

"The fuck does that mean?"

"It means that although I don't personally know the CEO, every indicator suggests that he's a jackass. But his jackassery is beside the point."

"Which is?"

"Pure opportunity, Richie. This scenario would work with any number of targets. This particular individual is simply the one who's most available."

This was the first significant lie she'd told Richie. She didn't want to loop him into that component of the plan, the real reason that the target needed to be Hunter Forsyth. Because that would smack of revenge-driven motivation, which everyone, even Richie Benedetti, knows is bad for business.

⚜

"Here's something I don't understand."

"Shoot."

"If there are never any negotiations, never any demands, how is this gonna make sense to the cops? How will they believe they've solved the mystery, stop looking for us?"

"They'll find a duffel bag on the subway containing burner phones that connect to the bombs. They'll understand that something went very wrong with the attack, and that's why the bombs were never detonated, communications never established, a negotiation never initiated. The police will think that the duffel and its owner got separated somehow. Or he got cold feet, he got arrested, he got killed by a double-crossing confederate. They will have many theories."

"Won't they look for him?"

"Of course they will. It will be an extremely bad day to be a Muslim man in this city."

"But they won't find anyone?"

"Oh, they'll find someone. Someone who looks very guilty."

"And what's to prevent that guy from talking?"

"What do you think?"

Richie got it. In his line of business, there are always bodies. "And this is a guy who'll look like the brains behind the operation?"

"No, this is a guy who'll look like a mercenary bagman. It will literally be his bag that the police find. With his change of clothes, his fingerprints, hairs, everything."

"Won't law enforcement be able to back-trace his steps?"

"Yes they will. Which will lead to an empty apartment. To a stolen van with stolen plates and no connection to us. To electronic communications with someone who doesn't exist."

Richie looked skeptical.

"Listen, Richie." She leaned forward. "We have a huge amount of experience in things like this. We know what investigators look for, obviously. We know what they find, how they find it. We have a combined half-century of experience here."

Richie didn't seem completely satisfied, but he was willing to move past it, at least temporarily. "When does this go down?"

Ah, good: he was thinking about the practicalities from his own point of view. First schedule. Then he'll have another, larger question.

"Two to four months from now. After we have all the pieces in place, and the right moment presents itself."

He nodded, then leveled his gaze at her. Here it comes.

"So."

"Yes, Richie?"

"What's your ask?"

She met his eye. "This is for winners only. Like everything else in life, right? You get to make a lot of money if you have a lot to begin with."

"But you don't, do you? That's why you're here."

"Exactly. That's why I'm here, giving you this chance to exploit me."

"Yeah, exploit you. To what tune?"

Don't blink, she told herself. "It's a ten-million-dollar buy-in."

Richie whistled. He had a good whistle, a clean sound, the whistle of a guy who'd spent his whole life whistling.

"What if something goes wrong?"

"I'd be surprised if a variety of things didn't go wrong. That's why this plan is replete with redundancies. Verifiable threats in the company's international locations, a handful in the city. Global terrorism on global TV. Is there any way whatsoever that this doesn't trigger a generalized sell-off?"

He made an *I'm-reluctantly-satisfied* face.

"And if you want to hedge your bets, by all means spread your short positions around to various sectors. That's definitely the safe move, and that's what I'd do if I were you. A couple diversified million will be enough to guarantee profit. Everything is going to be down three, five percent intraday. Except maybe defense-industry companies."

She leaned forward.

"But the guaranteed big money, Richie? That comes from shorting the CEO's company."

"Sure. And what if its trading is suspended?"

"Why would it be? Because some exec is on a bender? Or run off with his secretary? There's no reason to suspect anything more nefarious, no reason to suspend trade. That's why we're not manufacturing any events in London or New York: to keep the markets open. And that's why the abduction is secret: to keep trading open."

She could see that Richie got it, he had dollar signs in his eyes, he understood how an investor like him could clean up. It's all about privileged access to actionable information.

But that wasn't how Chris and Susanna were going to make their fortune. Which would not be dependent on the markets. And would be much more lucrative than Richie's five or ten or fifteen million euros in profit.

"It's time for a decision, Richie. You in?"

"I'm definitely intrigued. I need some time."

"I definitely understand. You've got five minutes."

"Fuck you."

She didn't respond.

He didn't flinch.

They stared at each other for ten seconds. Twenty. Thirty—

"Okay," he said. "Sure. I'm in."

"Thanks. I'm glad. But that, in and of itself, is not quite good enough."

"The fuck you want from me?"

"A gesture of good faith, Richie."

"Oh yeah? How good?"

She took a sip of her water—the relentless hydration of pregnancy—then put down her glass deliberately. She wiped her lips with the small napkin, placed the linen back on the mirror-topped table. Then she looked back up at him.

PART V

TOUR EIFFEL

65

Kate is climbing off her moped when her phone buzzes again. What did people do before smartphones? She can barely remember. It seems like historical fiction, in her memory.

It's another message from her Italian source, an alphanumeric string—tail numbers—and an originating airport code. But no destination.

Grazie, she replies.

Prego.

Kate barges into a shop, inexpensive clothing targeted at teens, blaring the English-language pop that harasses you everywhere across the Continent. Like bad pizza, and Zara.

In the changing room, she puts on her wig again; better to look like the intruder at 4Syte than the woman who discharged a gun in the street and then abducted a person-of-interest from a police interview. She buys a lightweight motorcycle jacket, rips off the tags, zips it closed to cover her shirt. She retrieves a handful of magnetic bumper stickers from the Vespa's helmet case, slaps them onto the metal.

A different person, yet again, riding what now looks like a different moped.

The last-known location of the mobile phone is a half-mile away from the shooting, which is unfortunately nowhere near here. Then the phone was powered down. Anyone who's careful enough to power down a phone is also going to be careful enough to move afterward.

Kate isn't confident that she's going to find the person she's looking for. But you do what you can do, use what you have. Sometimes things work out, just because you tried.

During Kate's long-term global search, what made her task appreciably easier was that she wasn't asking her sources for much. She wasn't

looking for missile blueprints or troop movements or the aliases of double agents, she wasn't looking for classified information, she wasn't looking for anything that was going to get anyone fired, or jailed, or killed. In
fact, the thing she was looking for wasn't a state secret—it wasn't even a
secret—and no one had any special interest in preventing her from getting the information.

It didn't take very long.

"*Madame?*" Henri said one day, standing in her doorway, big smile on
his face. "I found her."

This did not completely solve the problem, but now it could be managed. Monitored. Contained. At least that's what Kate had thought.

Before she gets on her moped, she phones Inez again. "Another favor,
I'm afraid. Are you in your office?"

"*Oui.*"

"Can you access international flight plans?"

Kate parks a hundred yards past the address, and across the street. She
needs to be extra-careful here.

She takes in her surroundings, the pedestrians, the parked cars, the
idling taxi whose driver is talking on the phone, the store selling African
clothing wholesale, front door wide open. Not a particularly busy stretch
of street, nor quiet.

Kate scans the building. He's probably gone. But he could also still
be in there, or maybe in the buildings to either side; GPS coordinates for
mobiles are not always reliable. The only thing remarkable about the five-
story structure is that its ground floor is a public garage entrance.

Yes, that must be it. He wouldn't want to drive long distances in a stolen vehicle, he'd want to get that car off the streets asap, perhaps trade it
for another, one for which the police aren't already searching.

Yes, he's in this garage. Or was.

Her pulse races.

Kate descends the ramp slowly. She fights the urge to retrieve Inez's
gun; she shouldn't be walking around with a gun drawn.

It's a clean, well-lit garage. There are, no doubt, surveillance cameras.

Kate sees it immediately, the rust-colored Renault, parked along the far side. She approaches slowly, obliquely, her feet falling almost silently, while her heart hammers loudly in her ears.

Twenty meters away from the car, she stops. She's shielded by a tall SUV, whose windshield she peers around.

The Renault appears to be empty.

Kate continues to creep toward the passenger side. She reaches her hand into her pocket, grasps the gun, but doesn't draw it out. Not yet.

Another step.

Now she's separated from the Renault by just a single car, alongside which she crouches, still shielded from the most direct view, but not completely hidden. If there's someone in the stolen car, and he's paying attention, he'll be able to see her now.

But he doesn't, because he's not there.

The Renault is empty.

Kate catches a strong whiff of alcohol. There's a big jug of vodka lying on the ground near the passenger door; some liquid remains in the bottle. Also what appears to be a strip of cloth and a roll of duct tape.

She comes closer. She sees blood splatters on the floor, fresh ones, still wet, still red, not yet oxidized—

Kate spins, her eyes scanning everywhere quickly. It has been a matter of minutes, at most. She kneels, peering under all the cars, looking for someone lying there, hiding, or maybe dying.

He's injured; she knew that already. He dressed his wound here, he tried to sanitize it with alcohol, he used cloth and duct tape as a bandage. Then he put distance between himself and the car he stole.

It's a lot of blood on the ground. Now she sees blood smeared along the door too, the trunk. He's hurt badly. What would he do now?

What would she do?

66

He tries to tell himself that he's lucky, shot in the shoulder. At least he's able to walk. If he had the same wound but in the leg, he never would've gotten out of that alley.

Chris climbs the steps between the streets, up the hill, the old streetlamps, the wrought-iron banisters, people taking pictures, walking dogs, schoolchildren headed home, mothers carrying grocery bags with baguettes poking out. Normal life continues to swirl around him. He continues to bleed.

The suit jacket does a nearly acceptable job of hiding his wound, but not entirely. At least one person has noticed, probably more. He has to get off the street. He has to get treatment.

The doctor's office is at the top of these stairs, around the corner. He pauses, leans against the banister. Looks back down the hill, Paris spread out there, the domes, the spires, the Juliet balconies and mansard roofs and dormer windows, the sinking sun, the late-afternoon golden light. It's a beautiful world.

Now is not the time to quit. Quitting now is quitting forever.

He turns back up the hill, and keeps climbing.

The *cabinet médical* is just off the lobby, mere steps from the front door. But this door is locked. He rings the buzzer.

Please answer.

Please be open.

Please let me in.

Nothing.

He rings again, then hears—

Bzzzzzz . . .

He pushes the buzzing door open. There's one person sitting in the small waiting area, an old man, dozing, plus the doctor who's standing behind a desk; there's no receptionist. The doctor looks at Chris with obvious concern.

He turns away from her, toward the door that he pulls closed behind him. He locks it.

"*Monsieur?*" she asks.

He turns back, and her eyes go wide.

"*On y va,*" he says, walking toward her and the old man, gun in hand.

The doctor pauses, considering her options, then nods. She takes the drowsy old man by the elbow, helps him stand, leads him to the examining room.

"*Parlez-vous anglais?*"

"Yes," she answers. She plants the old man in an upright chair—he doesn't seem to mind this change of routine—then turns back to the armed invader, who's trying to take off his jacket, but failing. He can't move his shoulder.

"I can do it," she says, and slides it off, very gently, but still the pain is excruciating.

"*Mon Dieu,*" she says. "Gunshot?"

"Yes."

He can see that she understands his predicament. He's here to get whatever level of medical treatment he can, then get the hell out, as quickly as possible. This is not going to be a permanent solution to his serious injury, but it will buy time, and time will buy distance, and distance will buy safety.

He notices a framed photo on the wall, the doctor is in the middle of the image, standing between a young girl who looks like her and an old woman who also looks like her, all of them wearing surgical scrubs.

"This," the doctor says, holding up a pair of scissors, "is going to hurt."

67

Insistent banging. The Parisian cop strides to the door, unlocks it, pulls it open. He leans in to listen as the other policeman whispers, urgently. Hunter thinks one of them says, "So what the fuck do *you* think we should do?" and the two have what looks like a heated debate. Then they appear to come to an agreement, nodding.

"Okay," the talkative cop says, turning quickly back to Hunter and Colette. He yanks a knife—a big one—from his back pocket.

"Hey, what are—"

"Oh shut up." The guy stands in front of Hunter, brandishes the knife. "Don't be foolish."

"Never," Hunter says.

The cop glares at him, then drops to one knee and saws the knife quickly through the rope that binds Hunter's ankles, then again at his thighs. He walks around to the back of the chair, and Hunter can hear the soft whoosh as the knife releases his arms too.

Hunter shakes out his numb hands.

"Get up."

Hunter suspects that he shouldn't obey. Maybe it's because it wasn't that long ago when he heard the sound of gunfire nearby. He imagined it was Simpson out there, shooting someone. Perhaps shooting someone who'd come to rescue Hunter and Colette, and failed. Then Simpson hadn't returned.

"Come. The two of you." This cop looks like he's on the edge of panic. Something is wrong. Something new, beyond the plenty of things that were already very wrong.

"Why?"

"We're leaving."

Is this good? Or is this very, very bad?

"Why?"

The cop returns the knife to his back pocket, and withdraws his gun again. "Why do you think?"

Well that's exactly the problem, isn't it? Hunter glances at Colette, who also seems uncertain, scared. This man's suddenness, his brusqueness, the debate between the two cops; none of it seems right.

"Now. We don't have time."

Why not? Hunter is too scared to ask any questions; he's afraid of the answers. He knows he'll be lied to, and he'll recognize the lies for what they obviously are, and he'll no longer be able to deny what's really about to happen to him.

He struggles up from the chair, legs trembling. He glances at the cop's hand, at the gun resting there, almost like a cell phone, the way some people are always holding their phones, absentmindedly, permanently planted in their palms. People like Hunter.

He glances down at the floor, sure enough, it's his own necktie that had bound his wrists. Now it's a piece of two-hundred-dollar silk garbage.

The four of them walk out the door; Hunter notices that no one locks up. They hustle down the tall flights of steps, one cop in the lead, the other sweeping up the rear, both holding their weapons, neither brooking any further nonsense from their captives.

"Get in the car. Same as before."

Is this the time to object? To scream? To flee? To fight?

Hunter glances around. He doesn't see any signs of life in this court-yard. He doesn't see any way of getting out, other than the big door through which the car is going to drive. This is not where Hunter is going to make his escape, not where he's going to prevail in any confrontation. This is not the time to take his stand. He can only hope that another chance will present itself.

The car comes to a stop, and the driver shifts into PARK. This was a quick trip. How long was the ride out this morning? Hunter can barely remember it. When was that? Six hours ago? Seven? That had been a much longer drive.

"Get up."

The tarp is yanked off again, the darkness is replaced with light, with Colette's face just inches from his. He tries to give her a small reassuring smile, which, after an uncertain pause, she returns.

He hoists himself off the floor, looks out the window. It's an outdoor parking lot they're in. But no, that's not it, there's something wrong with all these cars, missing wheels, broken windows, flat tires.

"Get out."

He doesn't want to get out here. "Why?"

This is a mechanic's yard. A junkyard.

"Out." The talkative cop turns around, brandishing his gun. "Now."

This is the sort of place you bring people to kill them.

68

"*Maintenant, c'est fini.*"

"Now? What do you mean?"

"Now is when we end this."

Ibrahim has been listening to the men behind him all day, having their debates, making their arguments, covering their asses. He knows where this has been leading, it was just a matter of time, and the time appears to be now.

"I have received the order."

"From?"

"Directly from the chief. And he received *his* order directly from *le Président de la République.*"

The last time Ibrahim looked, there were a dozen men arrayed on the roof. All of these men are, for a moment, silent.

"It is final."

Ibrahim feels a presence at his back. He turns slightly, just enough to confirm who it is.

"Officer Abid?"

"Yes sir."

"There are many officials here, but only one who is your commanding officer," the man says. "That is completely clear to you, correct?"

"Yes sir."

"So if I give you an order, you are obligated to follow it. Everything else . . ." He indicates the other people here, taking in their uniforms, their communications, their chains of command. "Everything else is not your concern."

Ibrahim does not answer; it was not a question. But it is ludicrous. Not his concern?

What will happen after he squeezes the trigger? Yes, the *préfecture* will try to keep his name private, or at least they will claim to try. But will they succeed? Even if they do, will Ibrahim himself be able to keep this secret? Not a word, even to his parents?

Perhaps he will. Then what? Will he drive himself crazy with doubt, with guilt, with self-loathing?

Or will he admit his role to his parents, in quiet confidence? Maybe to his brother? Will these relatives of his remain completely silent? Or will one confide in a friend at the café, a colleague at the store, a schoolmate, the greengrocer, a cousin? How long will it take for this information to spread around the neighborhood? Will the community shun him? Will people hiss at him, spit on him? Will some fanatic exact misguided retribution for the wrong crime? Sneak up behind Ibrahim on a dark sidewalk?

Not his concern?

No, perhaps he is not the one who will face internal criticism, a disciplinary hearing, a formal reprimand on his record, maybe even be forced out of the police force, spend a few months on extended holiday in Corsica before settling into a new job, something more lucrative in private security.

None of that is what will happen to him. Instead he will be shot in the back of the head. Payback in kind.

⚜

Who *is* this man about to be put down like a rabid dog? This hardware-store clerk whose wife was murdered by the police? This widower with the two small children and terminal cancer? What exactly is this man doing, and why?

Perhaps he is just another man being used for someone else's agenda. By French nationalists, manufacturing an excuse. By American spies, manipulating public opinion. A cheap life, easily expended. By Ibrahim.

"With all respect, sir, that is simply not true."

"Excuse me? What is not true?"

"That the concern is not mine."

The commander takes a few seconds to consider his response. All these other powerful men around, a story that will be told many times, up and down the corridors of power, in well-appointed offices and exclusive clubs, in casual cafés and formal-dress soirees, whispered among other powerful men while their elegant women stand by, *It was a tense moment,* they will confide, *and then the lieutenant calmly said—*

"I understand that this is difficult. I do." He places his hand on Ibrahim's shoulder. "But it is a difficult act, not a difficult decision. You do not have a decision here."

This is true, Ibrahim knows it. All he could hope for is to change this man's mind. But he has heard what he has heard, and he knows this is not possible.

"Now is the time, Officer Abid."

Ibrahim's face has been turned halfway between his captain and his target, looking at neither, but instead facing the direction of the Tuileries Gardens and Concorde and, beyond, the Arc de Triomphe, the Eiffel Tower. It is a spectacular vista from up here; he should have appreciated it more. In a minute he will be escorted away to begin the debriefing. Then he will be ordered to take a few days off. Then he will be reassigned. This is Ibrahim's last moment up on this roof.

"Yes sir."

He settles over his weapon. His finger finds the trigger.

"You are making a big mistake, Marcel. I urge you to reconsider." This is just for the record, for the stories he will be able to tell. Everyone here knows that Marcel is not going to reconsider.

The suicide-vested man has not moved, nor has Ibrahim's weapon moved, so the target is still in the middle of his sight. Center of mass in the center of crosshairs.

Then Ibrahim hears, "It is necessary, you understand, for it to be the head."

His breath catches.

"You know this, yes? That vest, it is an impediment."

The head.

"A single thorax shot might not be lethal. At least not immediately. There is the vest, its contents. We cannot have him writhing on the ground. Yelling, bleeding. Dying slowly."

Yes, Ibrahim can see this image clearly, a film playing in his imagination. It would constitute torture. Inhumane.

"We do not want you to need to take multiple shots."

The head is a smaller target, a less certain shot. And a much more awful thing to do in this context. A more awful thing to be videotaped, to be broadcast around the world. It will not be a body slumping over, suddenly dead, a dark pool spreading beneath, smooth red streams in the little grout canals between the paving stones. Instead a head will explode, there will be blood and bones and brains expelled from a gory crater on the far side of the skull, pink mist sprayed into the air, gray matter everywhere.

It will be horrific.

People at the periphery of the courtyard will scream, the sound will bounce around the stone surfaces even as the rifle's report is still echoing. People in their homes will gasp when they see it on their televisions, on their smartphones, they will be screaming in the streets of Paris, they will be screaming in London and Brussels, in Istanbul and Beirut, in Tehran and Baghdad and Damascus and Riyadh, in Rabat and Tripoli and Khartoum and Addis Ababa, in Kabul and Islamabad and Karachi and Jakarta. A billion and a half Muslims, a quarter of the world's population.

"Also, hitting the vest might risk detonation."

And the other three-quarters, they will see it too.

Ibrahim does not argue. There is nothing for him to say except "Yes sir." Then he returns his eye to the sight. Adjusts his aim. It is just the tiniest movement on his end, four hundred meters away from the target.

The head.

"Fire when ready."

When ready! How will he ever be ready?

It is his job to always be ready, more so than it is to actually make the shot. His job is to be prepared to take a life, every time he arrives to work. But he has never before done it, not while wearing this police uniform. Not in Paris.

Ibrahim takes a deep breath in, exhales slowly.

Another breath, another exhale.

Now—

69

As soon as she stepped out of the garage, Kate sent another text to Inez: *Flight plan?*

While she waited for an answer, she searched for nearby doctors. The closest was two blocks away, but that was a pediatrician's; not a first choice. Another quarter-mile farther afield was a general practitioner, with a name that suggested it might be a father-and-son operation. That's where Kate would go—more than one doctor, more chance of more supplies, more expertise, pain medications, perhaps surgical experience, maybe even familiarity with gunshot wounds.

Or maybe it was a mother and daughter. Two sisters.

Inez replied: *Still waiting.*

Kate drove away from the garage, from the surrounding commercial clutter, headed up the Montmartre hill, Sacré-Cœur looming off to the side, high up on its commanding perch, surveying the city below.

The doctor's office should have been right around the next corner.

It wasn't.

According to her map it was *right here* damn it, but somehow this was not the correct spot, the real-life street did not match the virtual one on her screen, she was supposed to be on an adjoining street, one farther up the hill, separated from this one by—what? Here it was: a long staircase.

She couldn't drive the moped up that.

This is the problem with GPS-powered maps: they make you believe that they're showing everything, that they're infallible. But their fallibility is the same one that maps have always had: limited to two dimensions.

The street dead-ended. This was taking too long. She was running out of time, she could feel it.

She spun the bike around, tried another route, a curving street with a switchback on the confusing mess of a hill, where adjoining streets can be inaccessible to each other, necessitating long journeys like the one she was on now, wasting precious time, zigzagging up the *butte,* not dissimilar to the plateau of Luxembourg surrounded by deep gorges, another place where Kate used to chase people, and get chased.

In fact, these very same people.

Kate comes to another stop, this time on a steep street next to a tall retaining wall that prevents a lush garden from spilling onto the sidewalk. The houses here look almost suburban: driveways, yards, fences with gate latches. Hard to believe this is the same city.

She looks at her watch, that present from Dexter. Kate thought she knew what he'd been apologizing for with the exorbitant gift, but now she's less sure.

The gunfire was more than two hours ago, a long time with a gunshot wound. More than time enough to go into shock, to bleed out, to die. Also more than time enough to find a doctor, to treat the wound, to bandage up, to escape.

Kate may get only one chance here. If she barges into the wrong doctor's office, the police will be called, and a unit might be anywhere, just around the corner, one minute from responding, on-edge from the day's events, ready to fire first and ask questions later.

If she barges into the right office? She might get shot that way too.

And if she does neither? Then she will have no leverage, nothing to bargain for Dexter's freedom.

Nothing except twenty-five million euros.

Kate reminds herself, yet again, that it's not her money. It's not even her government's money. It's no one's money, and it's sitting untouched in that numbered account, accruing minuscule interest, which is exactly how it will remain for eternity, unless someone transfers it out, reintroduces it to the economy, to the pockets of chambermaids and grocers and restaurateurs and the devious woman who tricked Dexter into stealing it. Would the world be any worse off?

The street is paved in cobblestone, bordered by an exceptionally narrow sidewalk even by Paris standards, barely wide enough for one person to walk. Kate peers down at the pavement directly in front of the building, examining every discoloration, chewing gum, dog poop—

There.

She kneels, and dabs her finger into the ovoid splat. Nearly dry, but not quite. Blood.

The front door is recessed in a shallow alcove. The doctor's buzzer is at the very top, number 1, it must be the ground floor, front of the building.

Kate steps backward, into the street, trying to get an angle to see through the windows. But the shades are all drawn, she can't even tell if lights are on.

She checks her phone: still no message from Inez. No flight plan. No further information.

Kate senses movement, it's the door opening, someone is exiting, and she returns to the alcove just in time to catch the door before it closes—

The lobby is very small. The door to the doctor's office just steps from the front.

Kate has known a good number of policemen. American cops, Mexican, Colombian, Italian, German. All of them somehow able to subsume the completely rational fear of dying, to subjugate that fear to the will of their professional responsibilities, enabling themselves to do this supremely terrifying thing: go through the door.

It has never really been Kate's job to burst through doors, but she has nevertheless done it a handful of times. And even in this very finite sample size, she has managed to confront, more than once, the thing that no one wants to confront, ever: an enemy with a gun.

She draws her own. Puts her other hand on the doorknob, and exerts just the tiniest pressure, testing to see if the door is unlocked, if the knob turns—

It does.

"Your phone, please."

"What? Why?"

"You ask that question way too fucking much." The police officer extends his hand, the one that's not holding an automatic weapon. "Just give me your goddamn phone."

Hunter complies.

"Yours too," the guy says to Colette. He no longer seems to have a French accent. How long has that been going on?

"Please," Hunter pleads. He's not sure exactly what he's pleading for, but he doesn't like the look of this junkyard. "What are you going to do to us?" He knows he sounds like he's about to cry, it's definitely not an attractive sound, but he's finished trying to be attractive. Now his focus is staying alive.

"The State Department will deny any involvement," the man continues. It's now clear that he's neither French nor a cop. "The CIA too will decline to comment one way or the other. No one will answer any questions posed by anyone, including you. So it would be better if you didn't bother asking."

"Why?"

"There you go again, with that fucking question. Can't you just accept anything?"

Hunter obviously doesn't want to argue with this guy, who's pointedly holding a gun.

"You'll look like a self-important, delusional, conspiracy-theory lunatic. And you see how easy we got to you today? We can do it again tomorrow. Keep your fucking mouth shut."

"Understood."

"So what are you waiting for? Go."

"What? Where?"

"There's a Métro station five minutes in that direction."

"And?"

"And? And you'll probably want to get on it."

"I mean: and that's the end of it?"

"Of what?"

"Of . . ." Of what? That's a damn good question.

"You should just be grateful that you're alive. There were other possible outcomes, you know?"

Hunter nods.

"In fact"—the guy raises the gun—"there still are."

The whole transfer could not have been easier—apartment to speedboat to airport to private jet, gangplank raised and wheels up, all in less than a half-hour. It's amazing, the conveniences that can be bought with immense amounts of money. The appeal of this whole operation. One of the appeals.

Susanna can't decide what she's looking forward to most: the riches or the revenge.

Kate Moore had taken their liberty. Kate Moore had taken their identities, their families, friends, homes. Kate Moore had taken their twenty-five million euros.

In the end, Kate in her ostentatious largesse had allowed them to avoid arrest, had let them loose to flee Paris, a sinuous trip of local trains that lurched from one station to the next, snack-bar fast food, increasingly disgusting bathrooms, saggy beds in the sorts of hotels that don't maintain records, and finally a third-class ferry across the Mediterranean on their way to erasing their trail in the undocumented anarchy of North Africa, a grueling twenty-hour crossing in rough weather.

That's where it happened: on the ferry. In an iron-walled windowless bathroom off the main lounge, three toilet stalls, only one of whose doors had a fully functioning lock.

She was barely showing. Almost no one knew. There were few people to tell; she didn't have many friends, not that much of a life, her career had come to an abrupt end. All she had was this new husband and this new human growing in her, and the promise of a large fortune on the immediate horizon.

When that fortune was yanked away at the last minute, she fell into a tailspin of anxiety and furor, exacerbated by frantic uncomfortable travel, and finally that rolling, groaning ferry.

She banged into that middle stall clutching her spasming stomach, bent over double, one hand bracing herself against the door while she fumbled with the lock.

That middle stall. That was where she lost her baby.

⚜

Just a few minutes after the plane levels off, Richie mutters, "Jesus."

She looks up. Richie is sitting across from her in a quartet of big soft leather seats that are the exact same color and visual texture of tiramisu. He's staring at the computer in his lap. "It happened."

"*Che?*" asks Gianna, who clearly serves double-duty as girl Friday and concubine. She also adores Matteo. It seems to be universal, the way Italian women love babies. That might be useful later. Soon.

Richie doesn't answer Gianna. He leans forward, extends the laptop to Susanna.

Even though she knew this was coming, still she recoils when it happens. The sequence ends, and she can't help herself, she hits REPLAY.

What does she see? The footage is blurry, grainy. A man is standing in a vast courtyard, all alone. He shifts his weight. She imagines that his feet are aching, his lower back too. Maybe he's thirsty. He needs to pee, or he already has, relieving himself inside the rubber liner he's wearing for this exact purpose. He has been standing in this position for nine hours. You can see the fatigue in his posture.

With no warning there's a sharp crack, and a spray explodes from the side of his head, and he slumps to the ground.

The camera angle changes slightly, and the image blurs while the lens refocuses on the body—the corpse—in this new prone position.

A sizable portion of his head is, simply, gone. Blood is gushing from the crater. The image is horrifying, the undeniable reality of a life ended violently.

The vest: intact, undetonated.

The silver briefcase: just sitting there.

And everyone in Paris wondering: what happens next?

⚜

This was built into the plan, it was preordained, to be followed inevitably by outrage, protests, unrest, reprisals. Markets will continue to stagnate and suffer for days, for weeks, stocks will be falling everywhere, short positions will be immensely lucrative.

"What if they never decide to shoot him? What if they take him into custody?"

"He'll resist. Then he'll be shot."

"Why will he resist?"

"Because that's what we're paying him to do."

"You're actually paying a guy to get killed? That's sorta fucked-up."

"Is it?"

"Isn't it?" Richie seemed amazed that she was willing to be so brazenly inhumane. This was at their follow-up meeting, she was providing some of the details that she'd withheld at first. Now she had Richie's money.

"Not necessarily. Listen, Richie, this is the same principle as a high-value assassination. All it takes is one person willing to sacrifice his life, and you can kill any other person in the world. That has always been the case, and probably always will be."

"The trick is still the same: finding the one person willing to die."

"Exactly. But everybody dies. In ten years, or twenty, sixty. It's hard to find a willing participant if he thinks he has sixty great years ahead. But what if he knows for certain that he doesn't?"

Richie nodded, then moved on. "So what's the big secret in that scary briefcase?"

"It will appear to be a dirty bomb. Probably nuclear."

"*What?* Are you out of your fuckin' mind? You're gonna detonate a nuke? In Paris?"

"Please. I'm not even going to procure one. But that's what it'll look like."

"What, just because it's a metal briefcase? Won't the police or army—whoever—won't they have a, whatchamacallit, one of those things that measures radiation?"

"The police will call military experts, scientists. They will procure a device that can measure ionization-induced fluorescence—"

"The what?"

"—and they will indeed detect alpha-particle radiation—"

"The fuck is an alpha particle?"

"—but the device will not be a *bomb,* Richie. Just a piece of hard luggage with some radioactive material packed in, surrounded by explosives. But the triggering mechanism will not work. Literally impossible to detonate."

"And where in the name of Christ Almighty will you get radioactive waste?"

"Asia." As if that explained it all. It ended up being a strange transaction, a surprisingly modest sum of cash.

"You understand that this can't be used for a weapon, yes?" the man asked. He didn't want her coming back, demanding a refund.

"I do."

He glanced down at her pregnant stomach. "It's just really *bad* for you."

"Yup." She had done her research, as always. "Got it."

"The nuclear bomb is a hoax, Richie. With the very specific goal of preventing the military or police from acting too aggressively, too early. They wouldn't risk an escalation to a nuclear detonation, or a conventional explosion that releases lethal agents."

"Lethal agents, huh?"

"Although the case's contents won't be known for certain, the possibilities are too terrifying, especially at the Louvre."

"You're fuckin' crazy, you know that?"

"Richie," she said, "I'm going to take that as a compliment."

Ten minutes later, Susanna and Chris were back out on the *calle,* walking away from the hotel with a bagful of cash.

"How can you trust that guy?" her husband asked. "He's complete slime. He's not only a career criminal, but also a snitch. He's not even an honorable crook."

"You're completely right. I don't trust him, and I don't like him. Those are two of the main reasons why I want to use him."

"I don't understand."

"Don't you? For the same reason we're using that sociopath to drive the van in Paris."

Chris continued to not understand.

For a long time, she'd hoped that one day her husband would eventually prove himself to be smarter than all previous experience had suggested. But he kept disappointing her, again and again. Luckily, he had other useful qualities.

"We're going to need to destroy the evidence, every last shred. Every link to us."

That's when he finally figured it out; she could see the recognition cross his face. "Who?" he asked. "*Me?*"

"No, you'll be taking care of that piece of shit in Paris. Me, I'll handle Benedetti. I've been waiting a long time for it."

Susanna looks down at the Alps, bathed in the last of the rosy late-afternoon light. She can see the Matterhorn, its shape easily distinguishable even from up here. Some things are unmistakable, no way to be wrong no matter how you look at them.

They must be flying above Switzerland.

Huh.

It hadn't occurred to her until this moment that the pilot would need to file an international flight plan, but of course he did. All rules may not apply when flying private, but some do.

This is a nice plane, less opulent than she expected from Richie, but then again he bought it used from a distressed seller, so he didn't get to make any choices about the décor. The pilot is polite, the hostess obsequious. There was no waiting to take off, there will be no long taxi at the other end; the travel time is minimal.

There are many undeniable benefits to flying private, but for this flight the most operative one to her is this: no one cares if you bring a gun.

72

he door bangs open, Kate pushed it too hard, not calmly, not in control, expecting that on the far side will be a gun pointed at her—

There isn't.

What's in the waiting room is a doctor wearing a white coat, her sleeves dabbed with blood and a large stain on the front. Beside her is an old man, naked from the waist up, next to a messy pile of clothes exuding the stench of vodka.

"You are here for an American with a gunshot wound?" the doctor asks, in English. She seems completely unsurprised by the appearance of a woman with a gun. "He left. Two minutes ago? Perhaps three. He too has a gun. I should tell you that I have already called the police."

Kate glances at the old man, who looks furious, his mouth working up to something, eyes burning into her.

"That man," he finally sputters. "He stole my clothes!"

Kate can feel the Vespa's tires on the verge of slipping as she tears around the corner, onto a broader street with at least ten pedestrians in her sightline, but none is a man wearing a tweed jacket or a pink shirt.

She continues to accelerate, then has to slow to turn another corner onto an even busier street, a commercial thoroughfare, there are dozens of people visible, near and far, and her eye is drawn down the hill, where a gaggle is gathered under the glass *édicule* of a Métro entrance, a large group emerging from the subway, trying to get their bearings—which way is the Moulin Rouge, Picasso's studio, Sacré-Cœur—and dispersing just in time for Kate to see a grayish jacket, and just the sliver of pink collar, disappear down the stairs.

She lunges for the elevator doors—

Too late.

Stairs, then. This platform is the deepest in Paris, more than a hundred feet underground, signs tell you how many more steps before the top, encouraging you, pep talks. The two hundred stairs are divided into sets of ten, to make the climb up seem more manageable.

But Kate is going down, down, racing around the circular stairwell, the murals whizzing by.

She bounds onto the platform. A train is already in the station, and all the disembarked passengers are moving away, others are now boarding, she doesn't see the gray jacket anywhere, and she's sprinting toward the train, sprinting, the doors are beginning to close, she has just a few more steps but she can see that she's not going to make it, but she keeps trying anyway, another step, another—

Fuck.

She doesn't make it. The doors are closed.

"Mademoiselle?"

She is grateful for two things. One is that a man is holding open the next set of doors for her. Two is that he's a good-looking young man who just mistook her for a *mademoiselle.*

She can't waste time. If he's even on this train, he might exit at the next station, he might change directions, he might depart the system.

She pushes her way through the crowd. It's rush hour now, the subway is packed. Luckily there are no doors between the cars, no barriers of any sort, so she can see a long distance.

He's relatively tall, the man she's looking for. She suspects that his face won't be recognizable, not from afar. Maybe he's wearing facial hair, or eyeglasses, or he has an unusual hairstyle, or he's cue-ball bald. She knows what he looked like a couple of years ago; she spent no small amount of time examining his face.

She can still remember his frank open stare, his unabashed invitation to adultery, propositioning her right there on the Grand Rue. She wishes her memory is that she never even considered it, but that's not what happened.

He wouldn't look the same now, not here, doing what he's doing. He'd be disguised. As she is, but more so. Much more.

The train is already slowing for the next station and she's only halfway through, and hasn't seen him yet.

Kate's phone dings an incoming text: *Destination Le Bourget.* Paris's general-aviation airport. That woman is on a private plane en route to Paris.

Of course.

There's a pair of very tall, very skinny African men standing in her path, and Kate can't see much beyond them. "*Excusez-moi,*" she says, and when they part she can see all the way to the rear of the train, she can see everything clearly.

73

The Métro is nearly empty when they board. They take seats in a corner, ride in uneasy silence. The train sits for long stretches, delays that are explained by PA announcements that neither listens to. Colette and Hunter are not concerned with service delays, not after what they have been through.

They disembark in a big station where three lines meet. Colette will transfer here to get home, and Monsieur Forsyth can find his own way to wherever he wants to go—home, office, embassy, police, the bar at the Meurice, she does not care anymore.

"À *demain*," she says. Now that home is within grasp, she is growing extra-impatient to get back to her husband and daughter, away from her boss, his problems.

"Colette, wait."

She stops, but does not immediately turn back.

"We should discuss this," he says. "What we will tell people."

With her slight pause, she hopes to make her boss understand that she has had enough of today, does not want to discuss this, cannot. Tomorrow, that will be another day, she is planning to go to the office, they can talk then. Not now. Tomorrow.

That would be the smart thing to do, the rational and sensible thing: go to work tomorrow. She will be able to tell the story to her colleagues, the whole ordeal, the guns, the fight, the flight, the life-or-death confrontations. People will stand around with their mouths hanging open, gasping, *Mon Dieu,* clutching her arm.

Her narrative will help everyone understand, later, when she resigns. It was too traumatizing, she will say. She could not get over her fears, her flashbacks, she could not sleep, she was having panic attacks, yes she had seen a therapist, she was taking anti-anxiety medication, but the drugs left her feeling stupid, dull, tired, unable to enjoy eating, drinking, fucking.

She has no choice, she will say. It is for her own health, and also for her role as wife, as mother. She simply cannot function this way.

"Are you okay?"

He takes both her hands in both of his, and she forces herself not to recoil.

"Oui Monsieur."

Colette has faced many indignities in her life, an attractive woman in the business world, working in tech, every office populated almost exclusively by men. Come-ons of every type, double-entendres, sexual innuendo, lewd jokes, overt propositions. She has been massaged, she has been caressed, cornered, kissed, squeezed, groped, all manner of sexual assault short of the traditional legal definitions of rape.

But perhaps the greatest indignity has been the ignominy of pretending to enjoy the company of this man, this sexist elitist anti-intellectual lout. His eyes always on her, his lust oozing off him, enveloping her in its suffocating stench.

On second thought, maybe she will not go to the office tomorrow. That too will make sense to everyone. After all, it was just minutes ago when she was climbing out of that car, thinking she was about to be shot, stuffed into a rusted-out automobile, and set afire.

Everyone will understand if she needs to take a day or two.

She had not known exactly what would happen, or when, but she had definitely not imagined that she would end up dragged into today's events. That was M. Forsyth's fault—he was the one who insisted she accompany him. If he had not, she would have been left behind with Didier the bodyguard. She would have gone to the office. She would have stood around with everyone else, speculating, wringing their hands, making reports, taking ineffective action.

"At least let me get a car to take you home," he says.

"Merci bien, Monsieur." She shakes her head. "But the train will be faster."

Colette had also not expected that anyone would be in any physical danger. Certainly not herself. She had been well assured of the contrary. And she had continued to believe that this was the truth, right until the moment when it was not.

But it had all turned out okay, just as the handsome bearded American had promised. No one had been hurt, at least not seriously. The two Americans had gotten the worst of it, wounds inflicted on each other, by each other.

"All I want is to be home with my family."

It was just a few small pieces of information that she provided. Details about M. Forsyth's morning routine, his bodyguards and police escort, the security code to his building, the location of the telecommunications boxes, the model and operating system of his mobile.

The entire meeting had taken an hour, at a working-class *bar-tabac* out in La Villette, someplace where Hunter Forsyth would never deign to visit. Colette left that café with a thick envelope bound in a rubber band.

"Je suis épuisée, Monsieur."

Then this morning she had been slipped another large sum, this time tucked inside the oversize sunglasses case that is right now sitting in the zippered compartment of the leather bag hanging from her shoulder. Twenty thousand euros cash, nontaxable.

"I will see you tomorrow," she says.

She will tell her husband that this money was part of 4Syte's settlement, alongside the actual settlement they end up paying. It will not be insignificant. She has been through a lot.

"Okay," M. Forsyth says, with a smile. "Good night, Colette."

Then she smiles back at him, it is for once a genuine smile that she gives Hunter Forsyth, because she just decided that she will not see him tomorrow, nor ever again.

74

He eases back into consciousness, a fade-in, the lights coming on slowly, images resolving themselves, awareness resuming . . .

He's on the Métro. He's been riding for—how long?—who knows. He has changed trains, trudged through those tunnels, rush-hour crowds, delays, more crowds.

And now he remembers: he has been shot.

He fingers the lapel of the sport jacket that he commandeered from the old man in the doctor's office, and peeks inside. The bandage has leaked, and there's a fist-size blot of blood near the shoulder of the old man's pink shirt.

The pain medication is fading.

The subway crowd has dwindled, and the few remaining passengers are giving him a wide berth. He thinks he may stink—yes, he rolled through a pool of urine in a dark alleyway, right after he was shot. His pants are filthy, his shirt and jacket don't fit, he's wearing facial hair that could be mistaken for a homeless man's beard, and a large fake scar on his cheek, and crazy-person hair. He has been fading in and out of consciousness.

He'd stay the fuck away from him too.

He wonders what his wife decided to do. She could have stuck with Plan A, and is already in Croatia, settling into the top-floor flat with a view of the sea, feeding the baby, unpacking the bag, waiting for her husband.

Thankfully the police have left him alone. The cops have priorities far more urgent than sweeping bums off the subway.

He is almost positive he's not going to make it to Croatia by morning. He's not going to make it to Croatia ever. He's not going to make it at all.

He feels this definitively in the pain in his shoulder, in the coldness that has enveloped his body, in his inconstant consciousness, in the echoes of the doctor's warning, "It is necessary for you to have surgery."

He nodded, trying to climb into the old man's clothes, failing. She helped him.

"This wound will not repair itself. You will bleed, and bleed, until you die."

"How long?"

"Impossible to say."

"How about a guess?"

She said *Pfft*.

"Please."

"At very most, twenty-four hours." She shrugged at the unlikelihood of this. "Probably much less."

Maybe his wife didn't go to Croatia. Maybe—hopefully—she opted for Plan B, or some secret Plan C. But he doubts he'll ever know.

Kate is growing impatient, riding this Métro, watching this man, wondering if this is futile. But he's her only leverage. And he must be on his way somewhere relevant.

He suddenly stands, exits the train, staggers down the platform.

Kate lags behind to take off her jacket, to change her first-glance appearance, even though this is probably an unnecessary precaution. The man she's following isn't aware of other people, he's not using any countersurveillance tactics, not making any evasive maneuvers. This man's situational awareness isn't heightened; it's nonexistent. He must be in intense pain, or on intense pain relievers, or both. He has been easy to monitor—moving slowly, falling asleep on a Métro seat. She thought, briefly, that he'd died.

She follows him into the *correspondance* tunnel, continues round a bend, up some stairs. Then she confronts a fork in the tunnel. Which direction would he take? She has no inputs to help her choose, it's a coin toss. She walks left.

This transfer tunnel deposits her onto the middle of the platform, rather than at the end. From just inside the tunnel, she can't see any of the other people waiting on the platform she's about to enter. But she can see across the tracks, to the far side of the station, to the platform for trains heading the other way.

That's where he's sitting, eyes staring straight in front of him. Straight at her.

⚜

No. He cannot recognize her, there's no way. It has been years, and she's disguised. She's wearing a wig and glasses that cover half her face, she's fifty yards away, the light is not great, there's no way he's prepared for Kate Moore to possibly appear on the opposite Métro platform.

She glances at the arrivals board. The train on her side is due to arrive in one minute. The other one in two.

Yes, that will work.

She turns to face the direction from which the train will arrive, presenting her profile to the man she once knew as Bill MacLean. Profiles are much harder to recognize.

Kate waits.

She can see the train arriving, it should be here in seconds. At that point she'll be shielded from his view, and she'll spin on her heels and dash through the station to his platform, and he'll think that this woman had simply boarded the—

But what's this? The train for her platform has stopped, just short of entering the station.

Across the way, she can see that the other train is due to arrive in one minute, while the train on Kate's side is now just sitting there, waiting for something, for the love of God what? She can hear the opposite one getting near.

Damn.

She can't continue to wait. She retreats into the tunnel.

Behind her, she can feel the rumble of the other train arriving, and she turns a curve into the corridor, and now breaks into a full sprint, up a flight of stairs, another turn, a dead sprint on a straightaway—

Kate can hear it down there, the doors are open, people are exiting.

Down the stairs three at a time, each jump a chance to miss, to twist her ankle, to lose balance and go tumbling down facefirst, breaking her nose, her jaw, splitting her forehead open on the sharp edge of a riser—

She lands at the bottom, and it's just another few steps around the corner.

This is one of those Métro stations whose platform entrances and exits don't use the same corridors. People who are arriving don't need to face off against people trying to depart, no trench warfare of shoving, shuffling, bags bumping, elbows flying . . .

So no one impedes Kate as she bursts onto the platform, and through the train's open doors, and into the very same car where he is already sitting, watching her board.

She doesn't make eye contact. She turns and walks away, grabbing seat backs for balance, passing empty rows. Anyone observing her closely would realize that she's putting distance between herself and someone else, who must be that disheveled wild-eyed man.

Does he himself realize? Did he notice that she's the same woman who was on the opposite platform? And on his previous train? Not to mention the same woman who deprived him of twenty-five million euros? The same woman whose husband he has come to Paris to frame for kidnapping, conspiracy, insider trading, maybe even murder?

Kate takes a seat, one that faces his side, so she can watch him unobserved but he'd have to turn to see her, it would be obvious.

Her adrenaline is spiked. She takes deep breaths, focusing on the PA, the recorded woman's voice announcing the next station, they always say each station name twice, the first as a matter of fact—perhaps a gentle suggestion, maybe a bit tentative—but the second with a completely different inflection, as if this woman has had enough of your shit, she's putting an end to the whole debate, severe stress on the final syllable—Chatelet—and now shut the fuck up. This is a woman who has ample experience disciplining small children, firmly, the way French mothers do. Kate has respect for this woman.

The train is pulling into the station when Kate's phone rings.

She knows, from just the single syllable: "Kate." According to her screen it's no one, no area code, no country, no way to ID, to locate.

Kate doesn't respond.

"It's been a long time."

It's been two years.

This subway is relatively empty, there are no conversations going on. When mobile signals were introduced to the system, Kate worried that the Métro would become unbearable, like commuting in a customer-service call center. But surprisingly few people choose to have conversations here. If Kate starts speaking in English, it will be noticeable. She remains silent.

"Do you have any idea how much evidence there is, Kate? The police are going to solve this so quickly."

Kate stands, and walks farther away from him.

"The first thing that's going to happen is that a Métro worker finds a duffel bag that contains a wardrobe change. Clothes that are the exact same outfit that your husband wears basically every day. Displaying the same lack of imagination today that was apparent even two decades ago, back in college. People don't change, do they, Kate?"

Not much.

"This bag also has lots of visible residue from a tennis-court surface, which will be easily ID'd as from the Luxembourg Gardens. This bag, it's obvious, is your husband's tennis bag."

That's all explainable, Kate thinks. All could have been fabricated. But she knows there's more to come, and it will be worse. She knows how this woman tells stories, little to big.

"But what makes this bag *really* suspicious—what provokes an emergency call to the police—is that it also contains disposable phones. Burners that were purchased on the boulevard St-Germain, just a few minutes from your apartment. The American who made this memorable purchase—he's six feet even, tortoiseshell eyeglasses—was also wearing a unique article of clothing. You know what that was, Kate?"

Kate's mind hops around for a second before she alights on the answer. But still she says nothing.

"A white hat with a ludicrous logo. How many American men in Paris could possibly own such a cap?"

One.

"The police are right now examining surveillance footage of the landmarks that were targeted today. They will notice that one person appears again and again, standing around in the place Vendôme, at the Gare de Lyon, Notre-Dame. Often wearing this navy jacket and white shirt and blue jeans and brown shoes. Sometimes wearing that ridiculous cap. And always—*always*—looking around, taking notes. As if what, Kate?"

This is far worse than Kate had imagined.

"As if casing the joint."

She'd thought it was going to be a few clusters of circumstantial evidence, digital footprints that could be explained away, or obliterated.

"But wait, Kate, there's more. Your husband also received calls on a regular basis, for weeks, from a phone that will be discovered on a dead body. Do you know what body?"

Of course she knows: the suicide bomber at the Louvre. Those were Dexter's daily robo-calls. Not from an insurance salesman.

"So then, to summarize: *means,* yes; *opportunity,* yes; and what about *motive?*" She chuckles. "In addition to your husband's compulsive research into 4Syte Inc., his browser history also features an obsession with the personal life of Hunter Forsyth that, frankly, looks a lot like stalking."

How much of this browsing history will still be retrievable, now that Kate has thrown Dexter's hard drives into the Seine? That depends on how careful he had been.

"A disturbing pattern. But an easy narrative to understand, isn't it? An ex-friend, ex-employee, afflicted with debilitating jealousy of Forsyth's gigantic success. The tech boom passed Dexter by, didn't it? While everyone around him got filthy rich, especially this guy he hates *so much.* It's almost impossible to *not* believe that Dexter would plot revenge. He is, after all, a master plotter of extremely complicated crimes."

This is mind-bogglingly thorough. Psychopathic, is what this is.

"But don't worry, Kate. Because although there's plenty of evidence that implicates Dexter—though, no, it's more than *implicates,* isn't it? There's ample slam-dunk evidence. But there's also evidence that exonerates him."

Yes, Kate knows: there must be, because he's innocent. But she can't think of a single shred of it.

"There are a few witnesses who saw him at strategic times this morning. People who can prove that there was no way for Dexter to be kidnapping Forsyth, or dropping off any bombs, because he was somewhere else at the time."

Now she understands the old man at the intersection, the attractive woman at the Luxembourg Gardens: setups, planted in Dexter's path, for this purpose.

"And the incriminating electronic trail, that too can be disguised. Dexter already installed the sequence to do that, unwittingly, when he opened an e-mail from the so-called inside source, forwarded to him via his tennis pal. You know what source I'm talking about, right? The one who supposedly leaked the negative intel about this merger?"

What forethought, planning, legwork. Investment of money too. The payoff must be commensurate.

"The malware is just waiting for my—"

"Enough," Kate says, firmly but perhaps too quietly.

"Excuse me?"

"That's *enough*." A few decibels louder. "What do you want?"

"Are you kidding? You know exactly what I want."

She does. "And what do I get in exchange?"

"Certain tips will not be called into the police. Instead, evidence will be destroyed. And other evidence provided, constructing a different, equally credible narrative. Pointing to a different suspect."

Kate is not in any position to bargain; this isn't a negotiation. She has been outplayed. The patrolmen have already interacted with Dexter, and unless the cops start searching somewhere else, they're going to track him down and look at him ever more closely. It won't take long.

She has to capitulate, or flee. At this moment, Kate still has the choice. "How do I know you'll keep your end?"

"The normal way."

"How's that?"

"Half now."

Half?

"The other half after the second suspect is ID'd, exonerating Dexter."

Half doesn't make sense. What this woman wants from Kate—what Kate can provide—is a bank account number to go with the password that the woman already possesses. This account number is stored on Kate's phone, in her notes app, on a page that seems to be filled with details about the kids' teachers, and a few school administrators, and the kids' American social security numbers and passport IDs, and Ben's doctors' names and specialties and addresses. This page is a one-stop resource for all this parental data, the items that Kate used to have to hunt for every single time the need arose, which was always in situations that were unpleasant to begin with.

It had taken Kate a few years to realize that there was a simple solution to this recurring problem, if she'd only recognize that it wasn't a one-time problem that just happened to repeat itself, unexpectedly, again and again. It was an expected, ongoing state of affairs. And the only person who could mitigate it was herself.

The long string of digits is labeled SCHOOL ID. No one who glanced at this page could have any idea what that could mean. There's no such thing as a school ID number.

The code is a simple one. If you knew you were looking at a code, and you knew anything about cracking codes, you could do it in minutes. But even if you succeeded in decoding the number, you'd still have only half of the puzzle, with no way to obtain the other half. Not unless you were the sole person in the world who already knew it.

If Kate provides this number, the woman she once knew as Julia MacLean will have access to a bank account containing twenty-five million euros. You either have access to the account, and everything in it, or you don't. There's no possible half about it.

"Half? What are you talking about?" But even as she's asking it, Kate realizes with a sinking heart what the only possible explanation is.

"Are you fucking kidding me? You know exactly what I'm talking about."

"We don't have—"

"I'm assuming you spent—how much? That's a nice apartment of yours, fancy vacations, et cetera. But you're not profligate, I know that about you. Maybe you've spent two million? Three?"

It has been only one. Not even spent; just set aside.

"So, tell you what, Kate: for that second payment, I'll take just twenty."

"Are you out of your mind? We don't have *any* of that money anymore."

"Then find it. Twenty-five million right now, twenty by the end of tomorrow. Forty-five million euros, or Dexter goes to jail."

"I don't . . . I can't . . ."

"I guess you have to ask yourself, Kate: what's your husband worth?"

76

Hunter is hailed as a hero by the staff who still remain, the vice-presidents and lawyers who have spent the afternoon fighting the fire of his disappearance, plus the handful of assistant-levels who understood that they should not leave the office until their bosses do, all these people gathered in the conference room, everyone except the young guy with the spotty beard and eyebrow ring and tattoos—the full complement of millennial self-adornments—whom Hunter sent to the apartment to pick up a clean suit and shirt and tie.

"I'll explain everything later," he says to the assembled. "But our first priority is to reverse the stock slide." The stock did not slide so much as fell off a fucking cliff, but Hunter is in spin mode now.

"Let's do everything we can, as quickly as we can, to reassure share-holders, investors, the international financial community, our business partners, our employees. Let's get a teaser out that I'll be making an announcement"—he checks his watch—"at eight-thirty local."

"That's too late for legacy press."

"Of course. So we'll need to do this live on 4syte.com, and feed the video to all digital and social. Georges and, um, Ninon, you two collaborate on the asset. Élodie, put together distribution lists for text-messages."

"*Oui Mons—*"

"Something like this: due to terrorist attacks and personal safety concerns and inconvenient luck, CEO was forced to take precautionary measures that unfortunately rendered him unreachable for some hours, a situation that was one hundred percent unrelated to 4Syte business or its major announcement, which has been rescheduled to, um"—he pauses, recalculates—"let's make it eight P.M. Central European. Not eight-thirty."

"That's too long for Twitter."

"Fix it, split it, do what you need to do. Get me language within five minutes. Then start working on a revise of the release, a new top graph with apologies." He looks around the room. "Everyone help everyone, we'll get through this, and you can all go home at a reasonable hour."

The stock slide will halt within minutes. Maybe even begin to climb again, baby steps first, then a giant leap after the announcement.

"Someone order some food," he says. Leave it to them to figure it out.

Hunter reminds himself that he has not yet lost any actual wealth today. He still has time to turn this day completely around, and fall asleep an enormously rich man.

"Let's go," he urges, and for good measure claps his hands, the quarterback breaking up the huddle, and winces from the pain in his swollen knuckles. "Time is—literally—money."

What's that noise? Dexter holds his breath, listening, seized by fear. He approaches the door, puts his ear to the wood—

It's people. Women, talking. The plunk as a cork is pulled, the glurp of wine pouring.

He walks down the hall. Three young women are sitting around the table, a baguette, a pile of pink ham, a wedge of pale-yellow cheese, an open bottle of red. Dexter is hungry.

"Evening," says one of the young women. She has a laptop open in front of her.

"Is there any news?" Dexter doesn't know what's happening out there, and he can't go see for himself. "My phone is out of juice."

"Not really, no."

The window faces the Seine, the cathedral of Notre-Dame. A tourist barge floats by. Things must be getting back to some level of normal. "Mind if I take a look?"

"Be my guest."

He leans over the laptop, types in a search, looking for—

Shit.

"Sorry, could I use this for a few minutes? I really need to take care of something."

"Sure," she says.

Dexter logs onto his account, fingers flying, desperate to get to the transaction window, to confirm, to unload his position before it's too late. The share price has been inching up, but it hasn't gotten very far. Not yet.

He executes the first trade, doesn't waste any time figuring out his profit, he has no time for that now, he logs onto the other account, he can see the share price has already ticked up again, but—what?—*Access denied.*

Fuck. He clears all the fields, and starts afresh, typing slower, precisely. Whew.

He looks up. The young women are all pretending they weren't staring at him.

"Thanks." He closes the window, quits the browser. "That was really helpful."

Now he allows himself to calculate, quickly. Then a second time, carefully. Both times, the result is the same.

"You want a glass of wine? You seem like you need a drink."

He smiles at this small kindness, at these young people just starting out, embarking on this adventure, they haven't yet made any major mistakes, even if they think they've faced disasters—that year wasted on the wrong major, or the wrong boyfriend—they don't realize how eminently overcome-able it all is, even while in the middle of overcoming it.

"Thanks," he says. Dexter's mistakes have been much bigger, much harder to overcome. But with a couple of clicks, he just did.

Harder, but not impossible.

Paris is on the same latitude as Vancouver; north of basically everywhere in the United States that's not Alaska. Seasonal daylight swings are extreme. In spring, in early summer, dusk seems to last forever, the sun just hanging there, reluctant to dip below the horizon, the last drunk guest to leave a raucous party. Then after sunset, the sky continues to clutch onto last light, and it doesn't get fully dark till ten at night, after all the blue has slowly drained away.

But in autumn and winter, the opposite: nightfall jumps out of nowhere, a predatory mugger lurking in a doorway, attacking with quick furtive movements before anyone has time to react. That's what happened while Kate was on the Métro: night fell.

"Okay," she said as the train sped under the city. Kate had weighed her options, and realized she had none. The only thing she could do was surrender—or pretend to—and buy herself time. "But I don't have the number with me."

"You have thirty minutes."

Then the line went dead.

Kate's eyes were fixed fifty yards down the train, at the man slumped in the seat. Was it possible that Julia just offered to throw him under the bus? Her own husband? Is he the other suspect? Or is there no other suspect? Is she bluffing?

But of course there must be another suspect, because Dexter is not guilty, and someone obviously is. That guilty someone must be Julia's husband. So who else could she offer . . . ?

There *must* be another man whom Julia set up to look guilty, a man with Dexter's build who wore Dexter's clothes, his cap, and bought a bunch of mobiles on the boulevard, and loitered around landmarks, and delivered bombs. That's the man who will look guilty. That's the man who already does, if only people will search for—

Kate's mouth fell open; she actually muttered "Oh" to herself. She realized that she doesn't need to find this alternative suspect. He's not going anywhere. He's already dead, killed in that gunfight in the *onzième*. His opponent is right here, wounded.

For much of her life, Kate had been reluctant to ask for help, she'd seen it as a sign of weakness, a fatal flaw for a woman in her career, working for her organization, all the men would say, *That's exactly what we thought, women can't hack it, always need help.*

It took her a long time before she was able to stop worrying about what all the men thought. That's when she realized that asking for help wasn't a weakness.

She sent Inez another message: *One more favor?*

He staggers into the park. Kate follows at a safe distance.

She realizes that her children are not far from here, this is Hailie's neighborhood off the Champ-de-Mars, the rue St-Dominique is Hailie's hashtag high street, with her daily bakeries and *boucheries,* the same expat-housewife life as Kate's. Almost.

Kate checks her watch. There has been more than enough time to arrive at Le Bourget and then drive into the center of Paris. That woman could be right here, now. She could be waiting up ahead, or following from behind—

But no, she isn't going to preemptively kill Kate. She can't get what she wants from a dead Kate. After she gets her money, though? That'll be different.

Kate feels the weight of the two guns, one in each pocket.

She still thinks of the woman's name as Julia MacLean, though for years now Kate has known that Julia is not her real name. That real name is Susan Pognowski, an ex-FBI agent who has recently been living in Italy as Susanna Petrocelli with identity documents procured in Sicily. Her husband is now called Cristoforo. Their newborn son is Matteo.

Julia MacLean had been nothing more than a character, a role this woman played in Luxembourg. Julia MacLean had been Kate's friend, her best friend, briefly. Her BFB, her frenemy, then her arch enemy. A relationship that was always on its way somewhere, though Kate never knew exactly where, until now. Here.

It ends tonight.

❧

Kate sends another ping of her location. It won't be hard to triangulate the path she's on.

The queues to ascend the Eiffel Tower are staggeringly long; there's no way that's his destination. Kate had briefly imagined this was where he was heading, tricked by a lifetime of movie-watching experience to expect that real life might look that way.

He passes the tower, and exits the park. Across the street, the small carousel is packed, the concessions mobbed, everyone wants ice cream. Kate pauses, watches him turn, make the descent to the riverbank. She looks left, looks right, and here it comes, the lime-green Vespa, puttering near the curb, pulling to a stop.

"He went down to the quay," Kate says.

"*Oui.*"

"Are you sure you want to do this?"

Inez gives a *what-are-you-kidding* smirk. Kate recognizes the attitude: obviously I'm willing to do this, more than willing, this is what I do. Kate too.

"*Merci,*" Kate says. She reaches into her pocket, where she retrieves Inez's gun, wrapped in a silk scarf. "I got my own."

❧

Down on the riverside, there are more long queues for the *bateaux-mouches,* hundreds of people waiting to board the barges for nighttime cruises under the bridges, past the islands, the grand monuments, the splendid museums, the elegant apartment buildings, the busy boulevards, everything lit up in full glory. It was Baron Georges-Eugène Haussmann who ordered more than fifty thousand gaslights installed as part of his ambitious plan to transform a dirty diseased agglomeration of villages into the world's metropolis—mapping a new street plan, erecting train stations, parks, boulevards, row upon row of apartment buildings, a central market, everything. This one man Haussmann created this City of Light.

Kate unlocks another bicycle, and pedals along the street, high above the riverside quay. Beyond the barge docks, the crowds dwindle quickly, just a few couples strolling hand-in-hand, sitting along the embankment, drinking, kissing, until finally it's just the one lone man, walking slowly.

There's limited egress down there, ramps or steps every few hundred meters. He has nowhere to go but straight along the riverside. To where? Why is he down there?

He walks past a houseboat, seemingly unoccupied. And another. Is he going to a houseboat?

A bridge is looming. A lot of bridges cross the Seine, and their undersides tend to be well lit, well maintained, for obvious safety reasons. But the lights under this particular bridge seem to be out, it's dark under there, though not completely, Kate can still see vague forms, the line of the embankment, a supporting pillar, and—

Damn.

She pedals furiously to the bridge, abandons the bike at the top of the stairs, and scampers down, spins around a landing, down again to the bottom.

This is a wide, low bridge, with a big dark space underneath. Plenty of room to shelter from the elements, to hide from people, to wait unobtrusively. To rendezvous in a prearranged fallback position. To tie up a motorboat, like the one right there.

Kate can see someone standing in the bow, a man holding a gun.

Shapes resolve themselves, backlit by the indirect ambient light of a big city. A person is bent double at the waist, reaching down to the paving stones. It's her—Julia, Susanna, Susan. She's trying to pull up someone, it must be her husband, he has apparently collapsed.

They are just steps from the boat, mere seconds from escape.

Kate raises her weapon, and creeps forward in the darkness that clings to the embankment. She can barely hear Julia's voice. "Come on, you can do it," she implores. "Get up."

Julia can't hoist him all by herself, not the dead weight of a full-grown man.

"I . . . can't."

"Richie?"

"Yeah?"

"Help me."

The man in the bow tucks his gun into his waistband, and gingerly steps up onto the gunwale, careful to keep his balance, this guy doesn't want to stumble, to tumble into the Seine, he's preoccupied at this moment, and so is Julia—

Now is Kate's chance.

She charges forward, gun sighted in front of her. "Stop!" she yells. "Don't move!"

Everyone freezes. A long second passes before Julia asks, "What is it you think you're going to do here?" She lets go of Bill's arm, stands.

The three people in front of Kate form a dimly backlit tableau vivant. On the street above, the traffic light changes, and now there's the noise of engines, the thrumming of wheels.

"Lie down on the ground," Kate orders, continuing to advance.

Julia doesn't obey. "This doesn't change anything, Kate. I still own Dexter's freedom. And your livelihood."

The traffic noise grows more insistent, the buzzing of an engine.

"Unless you're going to kill us all? In cold blood?" Julia doesn't seem to be worried about that possibility, not at all. "Is that what you're going to do, Kate?"

This engine buzz is different, on a different aural plane. Kate realizes what it is.

"*Murder* us all?"

"You!" Kate yells at the guy called Richie, who has moved a few steps away from the boat. "Very, *very* carefully, toss your gun into the water."

She can see him pretending to consider his options. Maybe he's the type of guy who's never willing to admit defeat, not without making a show of something.

"Understand that I will not hesitate to shoot," Kate says. "And there is absolutely no chance I'll miss."

He begins to comply, reaches into his waistband, then Kate senses movement on the boat, she cuts her eyes over there but keeps the gun trained on the man, and—damn, yes—it's definitely another person—

"*No!*"

—and Kate hears Julia's scream but doesn't know who her scream is directed at, or why, and she rotates her arms in a rapid arc toward the boat, to find this new target, to neutralize—

Shit.

It's a young woman. She's holding a baby to her chest. Another unexpected young woman. Another unexpected baby.

Shots begin to explode.

brahim Abid exited the *préfecture* headquarters through the public doors on the place Louis Lépine, around the corner from where the media was camped, waiting for formal comment, which would be edited down into a seven-second sound bite and spliced into a ninety-second package, leading the hour before moving on to whatever is the latest crisis in the Middle East, and the worst of today's sub-equatorial natural disasters, and the inevitable Johnny Hallyday retrospective.

What they would have loved, these reporters, was to talk to him. The shooter.

They would never imagine it, this dark-skinned man wearing baggy jeans and a hoodie. The media were more likely to imagine that such a man was a relative of the bomber, or a friend from madrassa, just now being released after an hour of questioning, cell phone confiscated, ordered not to leave town.

Ibrahim's debrief had taken an hour. There will be more tomorrow, plus psychological evaluations, and trauma specialists, and solicitous meetings with upper echelons, pats on the back, firm handshakes. Sooner or later, someone will present him with a medal, a private ceremony. But no press release. No public acknowledgment.

He bypassed the Métro entrance. Without making a purposeful decision not to take the subway, he started to walk in the direction of home. Through the flower market, where on Sundays street vendors sell birds, which makes the place seem more like Africa, or Asia. He took the pont Notre-Dame, walked past the Hôtel de Ville, from whose roof someone was at that moment looking down on him, another sniper up there, wondering who was that man, what did he want. Ibrahim did not look up. Past

Beaubourg, all that self-referential intellectual-architecture exoskeleton; he does not go to museums, not since primary-school class trips.

Ibrahim took a zigzag through the Marais, the sidewalk cafés full of men, tight jeans and tight tees and tightly cropped facial hair. Then the Jewish street, which had become a shopping street plus falafel, hundreds of people standing in queues for sandwiches, dozens more simply standing, taking pictures of their overstuffed pitas, shopping bags at their feet.

Up through Oberkampf, young people spilling out of loud bars, tattoos, cigarettes. Graffiti here and there, dilettante stuff, token resistance. Like the tattoos.

One Paris after another, none his own.

Little by little, the grandeur gave way to concrete apartment blocks with laundry hanging from twine lines, radar dishes, pinned-up bedsheets as curtains. Jackhammering, a torn-up street, a crumbling building behind rusted-out fences, covered with graffiti that was more political, more convincing.

As Ibrahim climbed the hill, store signs began to appear in Eastern alphabets. The languages he heard were no longer English and German and Japanese; what was not French was Arabic, Chinese, Farsi. There were Turc kebabs, Moyen-Orient grocers, the *traiteur chinois,* the smell of five-spice everywhere.

He was exhausted. He had awoken before dawn, was at the museum by eight, worked a full and horrible day, and now had walked for an hour into the night.

After taxes, his net salary today was 120 euros. Some days, his job is an easy way to earn that money, enough for a new pair of shoes, or a few days' meals for the family; his household responsibility is the midweek *supermarché* run, bags of rice and dried beans and the dark-meat parts of chickens, the sinewy segments of lamb, the less expensive everything.

Today was definitely not one of the easy days.

Some people earned a lot of money today, sitting around, pushing buttons on a keyboard. Not Ibrahim. He worked hard, for not much.

His feet are sore, his body aches from the tension of the day, his brain is tired, he is not thinking clearly. So when he sees the police lights flashing, it does not occur to him that he should turn the other way.

❧

It is dark here, the nearest streetlight is not functioning, but even in the darkness and from a distance of hundred meters, Ibrahim can see that it is Samir who is being hassled, frisked. A handful of people are watching with passive interest, but no one is surprised, Samir is a small-time neighborhood operator, no stranger to the police. But Ibrahim has known Samir since crèche; this guy is no terrorist.

The two patrolmen do not look familiar to Ibrahim. But it is dark. Maybe when he gets closer, he will recognize them.

Samir says something that must be really inadvisable, because one of the *flics* kicks Samir's legs out from under him, and Ibrahim's childhood friend face-plants into the concrete, starts screaming in pain.

It all happens so fast.

Samir spins on the ground and lashes out, kicking upward in anger, catching the arm of one of the *flics,* who responds with his nightstick, one quick shot to the ribs, one to the face. It is a disproportionate reaction, brutal.

"Hey!" Ibrahim yells. He takes a couple of quick steps, then yells "Hey!" again, this time louder, and breaks into a jog. "You are hurting him!"

The *flic* who is not beating on Samir spins, his gun already drawn.

Fifty meters away.

It is so obvious, to Ibrahim, that he himself is one of the good guys.

"I am police!" he yells, continuing to jog toward the confrontation. Today of all days, it does not occur to him that he could look like anything else. But it is dark, he is wearing civilian clothes, a beard, it is a tense scene, he understands that misunderstandings are possible, of course he does, so he knows he needs to clear things up, which is why he reaches his right hand into his sweatshirt's pocket, for his badge.

Crack.

He hears the sound, but he does not understand where it came from, who is shooting at whom, another overreaction, he certainly hopes no one is taking potshots at cops, the whole neighborhood could end up in flames.

Then he feels it, and understands.

He stops running.

Most people see it coming from a distance, from the clear vantage of hours or days, from months or even years or decades, they can see the rapid organ failure or the slow general decline, the inexorable march, the inevitable end.

But other people do not, especially young people, people who are on the cusp of the prime of their lives, people who have never given any real thought to it, nothing more than a few fleeting seconds, now and then, in a completely abstract way, nothing like this:

Ibrahim Abid staggers, and stumbles, and falls to one knee, then the other, and is kneeling there in the middle of the street, holding his badge in his palm, never even realizing that he is already dead.

80

K ate drops to the ground, her ears ringing from the booming reports bouncing off all the surfaces under this bridge, the stone, the
iron, the water.

She might have been shot, but she can't feel it yet, she doesn't seem
able to feel anything, she's rolling to free her right arm, her shooting
hand, bringing the weapon up, sweeping left, and right—

Where the hell is Julia?

It's all very dark, then suddenly it's not: the moped's headlight ignites,
and now she can see Bill lying there, unmoving, and the man who threw
a shot at her, he's kneeling near the wall, and Kate is about to squeeze
the trigger when another shot explodes in bright fiery light, and the man
crumples. Hit by Inez.

But where the hell is Julia?

This has been Kate's main question for years, her primary mission,
the target of her professional resources. Kate recruited policemen, she recruited hospital administrators, shopkeepers, she eventually had dozens
on her payroll, in Sicily and then in Venice, to track this woman who
never went anywhere recently except a couple of nights alone at a hotel in
the Lido, but otherwise stayed put in Santa Croce with her baby, it must
be the same baby who's in the boat right now, but Kate can't see—

No.

That's not possible. Is it? No. It's impossible that she shot a baby.

No, no, NO, she did *not* shoot the woman holding the baby, she did
not shoot *anyone.*

Did she?

How long has it been? One second? Five? Fifty? She can't tell. Shouldn't the baby be crying? Why would a baby not be crying from all this noise, this yelling, this gunfire? *Why?*

Kate feels like she's falling, down, down through the paving stones, the packed-earth of the embankment, the bedrock beneath, down through the earth's crust to its core, to the molten burning pit of a hell that until this moment she didn't believe in.

⚜

What is the very worst thing you can do? What if you do it? How do you live with yourself?

She just did it.

Kate lies in the dark, frozen with fear, with horror, with self-loathing. She just killed a baby.

Kate should show herself, that's what she should do. She should stand up, present herself in the harsh light of judgment. She should leave her gun lying on the ground, she should leave her hands at her sides, she should wait for her penance, her punishment.

Yes. That's what she deserves. She shifts her weight, pulls in her arm, starts to—

Another startling burst of light, this one in the distance, it's the Eiffel Tower's light show commencing, and—*there!*—there's a backlit Julia, who in turn sees Kate in this sudden illumination, and raises her arm—

⚜

So this is it, Kate thinks. This is how I die.

Time stands still.

I did all right, I guess. The children I made are wonderful, they will go out into the world and be good people, lead fantastic lives. What else does any of us leave behind? Kate Moore is not Baron Haussmann, she is not fashioning a world capital out of her imagination, not creating lasting art, curing disease, leading nations, peace among men. Whatever second act Kate may have conjured would have been smaller, not larger, than her modest first. She has led one insignificant life, and it will have continued to shrink until she became nothing but an unremarkable ex-spook, hoping her children phone on Sunday night.

What had she wanted? It's hard to remember, exactly. She'd tried to do no harm, but she did plenty of it, didn't she? That's disappointing. And it's a failure if you can't tell your husband, your children, what it is you've done with your life, if you have to be ashamed. That's obvious.

What should she have done instead? Should she have had more fun? More sex with her husband? With someone else? Torrid affairs, scuba diving, hang gliding, Antarctica? Should she have played more, kissed more, tried more? Done more?

You don't get any medal, at the end. There's no ceremony, congratulations, you've been a paragon of goodness, we are pleased to present you with this fine gold watch. And she already has the gold watch anyway. Her husband gave it to her.

She watches Julia, flickering in the tower's light show, turning toward Kate, toward Kate's end, both arms up, swinging in her direction.

This is it.

With all this light, all this sound, all these bullets and adrenaline and fear, Kate has not realized that when Inez fired her gun just a few feet from Kate's right side, the loud close explosion deafened Kate's right ear, the same ear that's facing the river, facing the boat, and this deafness is what's preventing Kate from hearing the loud noise that's emanating from the boat: the sound of a terrified baby crying at the top of his lungs.

Nothing happens.

Then: still, nothing happens.

Then Kate begins to hear something, a high-pitched sound, yes, it's the baby, and Kate opens her eyes, and what she sees is that Julia's arm is raised, and what she's holding is not her gun, it's her baby.

Bill is dead.

The other man too, whoever he is.

The woman who'd been holding the baby has run into the night, sobbing.

Inez has also fled, and advised Kate to do the same. The police will be here very soon, and there will be a lot of them.

Julia, unarmed, is holding her baby, staring at Kate, who is holding her gun.

In that final instant before death, this is what Kate realized was the thing she'd done wrong with her life: she should have been better. She should have been nicer, more frequently, to more people.

That's what she regretted. That's what had led her to tonight's mortal crisis: she'd chosen to be mean.

That's what she will do differently. Beginning right now.

"Here," she says, and thrusts something into the other woman's hand.

Julia looks down, confused. It's Kate's business card—phone number, e-mail address, affiliation with an ersatz consulting enterprise. Kate turns over the card to where she has just written a long string of digits.

Julia turns her eyes back up to Kate. "Why?"

Kate doesn't have the time to explain everything, all the people she has wronged, and killed, all the lives she has ruined, all the times she has deceived her husband, screamed at her children, all the things she has done that she absolutely knew were wrong.

She can see police lights flashing, the cars are coming over another bridge, they'll be here in a minute.

"Because I'm sorry. And I want this to end." Kate pulls off her wig, tosses her gun into the Seine. "But if you ever come near me or my family again?"

Julia nods, she understands.

"Please try," Kate says, "to do something good."

Then she turns away. Her bag is still slung over her shoulder, but a few items spilled out when she dropped to the ground. The case for her reading glasses, that unofficial credential of middle age, like a badge you have to carry everywhere, all the time, if you hope to be able to do anything. The old hardcover from the bookshop, Graham Greene's *The End of the Affair*. And the box of Lego, a bit crushed, trampled upon, but all the contents are still inside. Not perfect, but it'll do.

A moment will come when the boys are finished with Lego, it will happen without warning and sooner than expected, and it will be months later before anyone notices that the Lego has gone untouched, the kids don't play with it anymore, they've moved on to video games, to board games, to sports, to girls, to alcohol, and from that future vantage Lego will look so innocent, Kate will long for the past, for that period in life when she did this tedious thing every single day, this top-line job description: she bends over to pick up Lego.

Then she sprints up the stairs. At the landing she can see that Julia is pulling the boat away from the riverbank, throttle in one hand and baby in the other, speeding away from the police.

Kate never did pull her trigger tonight. It wasn't Kate who shot anyone on the quay. And she never will again.

Her bicycle is lying on the sidewalk. She looks over her shoulder, sees the police closing in. She pedals away with all the energy that her exhausted middle-aged body can muster, which as it happens is not inconsiderable; she can still be mistaken for a *mademoiselle,* after all. She bikes at breakneck speed back toward the park, back toward the twinkling tower, back toward her kids. Back to her life.

After weeks of rain and gray and increasingly hostile chill, today was an autumnal jewel, a reprieve that everyone knows will be brief, and the warm weather has drawn out not only throngs of tourists but also flocks of locals, it looks like everyone in Paris has arrived in a good mood at a surprise party, Kate cycles by young and old and everyone between, the cafés are all full, people packed onto the terraces, making conversation with strangers and neighbors, making out in corners, holding hands across tables filled with glasses of wine and bottles of beer, bowls of peanuts and ashtrays overflowing and half-eaten slices of tarte tatin, it's still early enough that children are everywhere, playing on sidewalks and in the park, running and jumping and joyous noise, chasing balls and dogs and that final bit of fun before the unseen clock expires, and suddenly you're called to come here, to go home, to go to bed, kids know this better than anyone, that you have to do it all right now, everything, because this can always happen without any warning whatsoever: you're out of time.

ACKNOWLEDGMENTS

"This book would not exist without" is a phrase that has a very loud ring of inauthenticity. For this book, it's demonstrably true:

The Paris Diversion is my fourth published novel, but I've also written bits and parts and entireties of others that are lying around, as if in long-term care, awaiting a new drug or a revolutionary surgery that will breathe fresh life into them. As we're reminded every day, life is short. I haven't yet gotten around to removing some metal ornaments that we found screwed to our garage when we bought an old house, back when the kids were infants; they're now in high school. I won't have the time to pursue every single book idea.

I've spent all of my forties—a decade when we're supposed to know important things about ourselves—writing novels, but I still don't have a solid answer to this fundamental question: how do I choose which books to write, which not?

A few years ago, I was happily writing a completely different fourth novel. Midsummer arrived, and my wife took the kids to remote Ontario for an annual week-long vacation that as a rule I choose to skip. This Canada trip coincides roughly with my birthday, and Madeline's gift was sending me by myself to Paris, where as soon as I arrived an entirely new book idea intruded on my consciousness, urgently, merging an old idea—an apparent terrorist attack that turns out to be something else—with my long-simmering desire to write a sequel to *The Expats,* and a new impulse to set a novel in Paris.

I started immediately, with a laptop in a café in St-Germain-des-Prés every morning, then setting out for the afternoon. I didn't have any responsibilities. I didn't need to worry about anything, not the kids, the dog, the house, bills, taxes, inexplicable sinkholes in the driveway. I could free my mind completely, and immerse myself in these characters, in this story, trudging mile after mile, stopping on street corners to scribble notes. Over the course of a few days, the entirety of *The Paris Diversion* resolved itself—every plot twist, all the characters, the most important scenes and reveals and red herrings. It all became clearer and clearer to me, more and more exciting. Each night after dinner, I'd open the computer and write some more.

This was my most productive week of work ever, and it was a gift to me from my wife, who has always allowed me ample space to pursue this second career that I'd chosen to hurl myself into in midlife, when I could no longer countenance the idea of going to an office every day. This was an irresponsible, indulgent, irrational choice that I'd made, but she supported me without hesitation or criticism or the barest hint of doubt.

Thank you, Madeline McIntosh.

In the middle of that Paris week, I went to have a drink with Sylvia Whitman at Shakespeare & Co., and I ended up staying for five hours, talking to regulars who came and went, and Sylvie's husband and son and dog, seeing this whole expat life laid out, in this remarkable bookshop that hosted events in the *place* facing Notre-Dame, and the stream of visiting authors, and the tumbleweed kids reshelving books, the whole terrific operation guided by this wonderful principle: be open to new people, be welcoming to strangers. It seems so obvious as a decent, deliberate way to go about life. But it's not usually a business plan.

I was struck with a newfound sense of the enormous importance of deliberateness, about everything. I spent the rest of the week focused on how *The Paris Diversion* should relate to *The Expats*, and what the themes of the new book would be, and whether it should really be the next thing I wrote, and why the book should exist in the world.

Productivity isn't just moving forward; it's also figuring out which direction to move in.

Thank you, Sylvia Whitman.

After I'd turned that week's frantic scribbling into a hundred pages of readable manuscript, I sent it to my literary agent, David Gernert, who was already in possession of a hundred pages of that other novel I'd been working on.

The business of book publishing revolves around the judgment of individual people; almost everything is subjective, matters of taste. I think one of the hardest choices for everyone is figuring out whom to trust, about what, and this is especially true for authors: whom we trust can make all the difference.

I first met David more than a quarter-century ago, when he was editor in chief of Doubleday and I was a junior copy editor. He was the supreme authority, the person in charge. I'm now (alarmingly) a lot older than David was back then, but for me he's still the authority, and there's no one I trust more about editorial matters or publishing ones, and possibly everything else too.

So I asked David: which of the two different 100 pages do you prefer? His answer was the book I was calling *Diversion* (he didn't think the title was quite right), and that's why you're holding this one.

Thank you, David Gernert.

And now, the more traditional acknowledgments:

These people provided invaluable feedback on early drafts: Ned Baldwin, Layla Demay, Jack Gernert, Kathryn Lundstrum, Libby Marshall, Libby McGuire, Alex McIntosh, Hannah Marie Seidl, and my editors Lindsay Sagnette at Crown in New York and Angus Cargill at Faber & Faber in London. Sincere thanks to all of them, and also to everyone who helped turn the manuscript into a book: Chris Brand, Caspian Dennis, Rose Fox, Rebecca Gardner, Elina Nudelman, Mary Anne Stewart, and Heather Williamson.

My novels have all been published simultaneously by Crown and Faber, and I'm immensely grateful for the years of support—expertise, enthusiasm, and energy—from everyone at both houses, and especially the essential handful who've been working with me since the very beginning: Sarah Breivogel, Terry Deal, David Drake, Maya Mavjee, Stephen Page, and Molly Stern.

Finally, a note about facts:

There is no International School of St-Germain; the Louvre's real-life security measures do not exactly match those depicted herein; I'm unaware of any bookstore that features an escape hatch built during the Occupation; it's not so easy to short-sell stocks anonymously; et cetera. These are purposeful deviations for legal, ethical, and dramatic reasons. I didn't try to write a guidebook to Paris, nor a manual for perpetrating a terror attack or manipulating securities. This is just a novel.